SMASHING BOOK 5

Real-Life
**Responsive
Web Design**

Lars Beck, Runeinboots, Alecsandru Grigoriu, Sonali Agrawal, Kamela Kondili, Arevik, Thomas Mathew, Vladimir Stolyarov, Prashant Sani, Jared Vorkavich, Arevik Harutyunyan, Pavel Pomerantsev, Art Blanc, Tuukka Uskali, Michał Leśniowski, Vanessa Schmidt, Valerio Francescangeli, Mathieu, José R. Quevedo, Melanie Witzmann, Eimantas Likas, Víctor Rodríguez Lledó, Mervyn Van Goethem, Alex Mccullie, David Lemesle, André Spencer, Jean Dat, David Roessli, Aaron Vanston, Gabriel Constantin, Sebastian Zimmermann, Jason Bailey, Redfox Media, Sven Hermesdorf, Michael Raffaele, Lance Redgrave, Adrian Robb, Franz Thüs, Lasse Laube, Joanna 'senthe' Falkowska, Carl Smith, Mike Buchan, Alexey Alexeyev, Justinbasile, Dennis Heibült, Johannes Rubenz, Bradley Palmer, Lukas Guschlbauer, Kevin Forbes, Mr.lozchka, Jordy Van Raaij, Kiwi Casey, Hapiuc Robert, Jan-claas Dirks, Linus Metzler, Sammy Sadati, Simon Busborg, Özgür Ersil, Jovstern, Leonard Eshuis, Teo Dragović, Kraig Walker, Alex "hi Mum!" Moyler, Carolina Bettencourt, Pixelpulli, Aidan Threadgold, Cédric Aellen, Jessika Rosemeyer, Pol Escolar Soler, Marcel Maurice Naef, Nino Naumov, Marius Schulz, Kevin Lozandier, Matthew Vandenbossche, Chris Brandrick, Shiki Ryu, Kaspars Milbergs, Michiel Renty, Magdalena Kacicka, Matthias Harreither, Steffen Weber, Christy Kiltz, Design By Kiltz, Aaron Parker, Bri Piccari, Gabor Lipa, Stefan Judis, Paulo Coelho Alves, Maciek, Winfried Van Loon, Onur Degerli, Matt Penko, Tobias Sommer, Tomi Toikka, Manuel Hanel, Antonis Pavlidis, Maciek Kaszubowski, Poloni, Dominika Pawluś, Bryan Colle, Mladen Bićanić, Oliver Breuer, David Yarde, Norman Wehrle, Jeremias Dombrowsky, Astrid Descelles, Çınar Düzen, Dayjo, Vinod Patil, Alex Crooks, Đurica Bogosavljev, Mark Howells-mead, Mihail Stoychev, Marc Hinse, Arnold De Guzman, Jonáš Krutil, Yann Kozon, Pete Casson, Fardeem Munir, Abinti Carol, Jonathan Kelly Elly, Tomasz Florkiewicz, Martin Parsons, Emily Sw Liu , Jef Aerts, Tania Bolio, Rakhat Jabagin, Jeff De Wit, Serge Savranchuk, Alex Hunt, Mirko Poloni, Tobias Althoff, Ross Hammond, Marcel Weber, Ulf Walter-laufs, Mark Swaffer, Marie Guillaumet, Krishan Taylor, Refael Mimran, Taykey, Petar Toskovich, Dominik Steinmann, Clemens Pfister, Helen Burgess, Nick Plekhanov, Sarah Croughwell, Lee Wood, James Webb, Mike Timmerman, Tom Valorsa, Blai Pratdesaba, Lucas Da Silva, Boban Radeski, Joyce C.m. Herben, Michael Price, Yann Skargovskii, Erwin Romkes, Chen Hui Jing, Robson Junior, Adam Bunke, Dejan Hadziomerovic, Loïc Goyet, Zach Young, Ryan Scott, Nick Van Dyck, Drazen Mokic, Diego Acuña, Jonas Jappe, Diogo Silva, Wilburlikesmith, Julien Winant, Matt Northam, James Bavington, Michael Irigoyen, Fabian Pammer, Andrea Glauser, Christoph Friedl, Hugo Giraudel, René Stalder, Alain Hornair, Andrej Talajić, Kristoffer Forsgren, Arnopaul Roskam, Enoch Appathurai, Piemel Peters, Wilson Ngo, Sascha Moeser, Martin Rademacher, Greg Barnes, Wolf Baker, Juana M. García, Bogdan Prigorie, Bjarke Rønnow, Jonathan Kutnowski, Mantas Kaveckas, Samuray, Giovanni Micocci, David Moulton, Yaprak Ayazoglu, Jeffrey De Graaf, Markus Knecht, Douglas Hensel, Tim Wright, Heath Loden, Cristiana Raquel Pinto Santos, Jodie Doubleday, Johan Huyser, Brandon Dely, Maxime Richard, Pepijn Fens, Ahmad Shadeed, Maurica Loden, Rian Triharyana, Marc Stalfoort, J. Edgar Montes, Thomas De Barochez, Sinead Baldacchino (gibraltar), Matthijs Molhoek, Ilia Draznin, Jeff Minor, Hendrick Lange, George Parks Davie, Andrea Melzi, Brent Porter, Gustav Ernberg, Stepan Rysavy, Hans Mugge, Fenil Patel, Claude Wild, Jae Barclay, Damien Chatry, Michał Gołębiowski, Paul Lambert, Aleksandar Ackovski, Steven Aerts, Martin Knorr, Birger, Matthew Hager, Devon Crosby, Joeri Goedegebuur, Richard Reddy, Lukas Gächter, Kristina Gottli, Patrik Jarl, , Koen Karsten, Flodar, Heisa Media, Benny Jien, Ian Mcdonald, Jessica J. Hernandez, John Gibby, Sebastián Tello, Stef Van Wienendaele, Samo Tepeš, Duaa Hattab, Paul Vance, Marco Bertoni, Christopher Abate, Jeff White, Asna Farid, Mary-katherine Mckenzie, Machteld Vlietstra, Ross Drakes, Douglas Clark Design, Frank Gjertsen, Scott Whitehead, Joe Booth, Ihor Khudo, Jonas Calvo, Michelle J. Flynn, Fuyuko Gratton, Hasse Ramlev Hansen, Colin Brady, Job Kuipers, Arjan Van Deelen, Piotr Nalepa - Sunpietro, Elementare Teilchen, Cem Sever, Kurt Franz, Mike Watkins, Shay Hurley, Matt Malone, George Tsimenis, Kevin Pennekamp, Edwin Duinkerken, Antoine Minoux, Morgan Estes, Phil Sinatra, Erwin Liemburg, Marco Korradi, Steven Six, Marlin Jackson, Yevgeniya Kobrina, Rob Le Boutillier, Dejan Veljanoski, Giulia Casadio, (david G. Smith :-), Izzy Grosinger, Richard Jurinovics, Boris Milosevic, Dan Atrill, Hajós Bálint, Ronnie Kroon, Remi Grumeau, Dion Van Rijswijk, Michal Jedrzejczyk, Alex Boros, Łukasz Krebok, Abinash Mishra, Michael Labschütz, Loïs Saublet, Mario Meyer, Stanisław Olszak, Isabel Heylen, Jonathan Werner, Sara H., Emma Hughes, Sallay Arnold, Brett Jones, Deryck Oñate Espinel, John Enderby, Elliott William Evans, Brian Mcgrath, Sander Van De Vondervoort, Leo Dillon, Robert Boedigheimer, Jason Stephens, Yogev Ahuvia, Emiel Nawijn, Mark Bucknell, Arjen Van Dieren, Tyler Lesperance!, Victor Tsen, Robert Krieg, Brendan Harriff, Kevin Nagurski, Andrew Jd Hudson, Pati Montero, Yavus Kus, Christophe Roncalli, Clément Oriol, Lionel Lonkap Tsamba , Edson Simão Jr., Christian Bowie, Sarah Preston, Lu Amado, Mark Jones, Urbansoul Design, Luka G, 2am Webworks, Will Harvey, Mcslayer, Dug Clark, Radimir Bitsov, Anil Kumar Krishnashetty, Peter Swiek, Deborah Foerst, Alessio Cavone, Luke Cooper, Chris Adams, Daniel Holpfer, Cahit Okten, Jorge Girao, Pavel Podkopajev, Guy Amiel, Céline Coelho, Jan Kohlhof, Saxony Betts, Klaus Thenmayer, Scott Mcewen, Jan Skovgaard, Mischa Helfenstein, Stephen Kao, Dorijan Čovran, Patrick "lippe" Lipinski, Peter Müller, David Mann, Cathy Clarke, Tim Kimberl, Kevin Kuhl, Febby Gunawan, Steffen Krummel, Chidambara Kumar K, Andrew Walker, Mediavrog, Marc Klis, Ákos Molnár, Mann Made Media Ltd (uk), Bill Payne, John C. Dailey, Ph.d., Nicholas Szyngiel, Anne Thomas, Art Duszynski, Laura Jolly, Andreas Næsager, Mark Rabey, Nathalie Christmann-cooper, Martin Garnett, Robert Scully, Jason Foo, Jeffrey D Olson, Homiera Emam, Sir Dale Inverarity, Stefan Dourado, Raoul De Best, Bjarne Dahlin, Klaus Ruediger Peters, Paul Rose, Marielle Lorentz, Nicole Lane, Brian Downey, Rowdy Rabouw, Kieran Eves, Martin Ortiz, Tania Kelvin, Ludwig Königsberger, Rachel R. Vasquez, Ben Callahan, Ioannis Belegrinis, Giorgos Theodorakis, Panayiotis Velisarakos, Richa Sehgal, Igor Vrdoljak, Zane Sensenig, Tom Hare, Iulian Costin Nitulescu, Adrian Boiciuc, Brian Artka, Brian Tobias Amick, Martin Lenngren, Suzy Jones, Vompiris Hlias, Nelson Correia, Petar Bikic, Tomasz Olędzki, Tomasz Bednarek, Paweł Charasimiuk, Ciprian Tepes, Hans Christian Feßl, Bonnie Palmer, Laurie Nicholas, Fabio Lino, Usman Daud, Attilio Zorahrel, Tiberiu Wagner, Rachel Baker, Anthony Firka, Patrick Zuidema, Simone Viani, Stuart Giles, Todd Reeves, Rui Freitas, Jeroen Kuijpers, Alex Wright, Sean Frederick, Marc Rinderknecht, Thomas Lindbjer, Sergey Yanovitsky, Alan Every , Jonathan Seligsohn, Kevin Herman, Stefan Baumgartner, Nir Oz, Dan Bovey, Romain Deltour, Sheff, Chris Burnell, Paul Drummond, Jens Wildner, Jimmy Le Pannenkoek, Dominique Wiels, Carsten Henkelmann, Stefan Janik, Bastien Leprince, Florian Herrmann, Scott De Jonge, Theresa Mcmurdo, Dason Johnson, Emma Patricios, Brandon Bruno, Mike Wheeler, Charles Hall, Simon Goodwin, , Thibault Fagu, Robin Witteman, Richie Kastl, Christian Steininger, Jeff Cooperrider, Erika Jarvi, Laurent Emile, Matt Crandell, Ivan Denisov, Tyler Bailey, Tom Erik Nielsen, Eduardo Bouças, Febby Gunawan, Lars Kreuzmann, Don Nelson, Collin White, Anthony 'wainsworld' Ainsworth, Adrian Furtuna, Mike Houben, Nathan Edwards, Pat Lam, Nick Phillipps, Evan Wieland, Riaz Budree, Tobias Henze, Mickaël Mao, Christopher Siegel, Dan Rose, Lorelai Jackson, Meghan Cannizzaro , Wes Brooks, Schepp, Peter Schmolze, Davide (Dex) Espertini, Arun Kumar, Matteo Cavucci, Jan-mikael Uusikylä, Jacob Bøtter, Jon Kyte, Dave Redfern, Bartłomiej Wojcieszek, Sonny Prince, Ryan Bell, Marco De Luca, Julien Mulac, Albert Antiquera, Alexey Taranik, Alex Stroh, Sebastian Lenton, Joacim Gunnarsson, Michael Palmer, Chris Houlding, Samuel Thompson, Scott Whitebread, Raj Khera, Mike Rudolph, Mark Hatch, Soireesoftware.com, Juha Lakaniemi, Ben Travis, Greg Price, Jason Green, Andullah Alhaqbani, Philip Jacobsson, Pavol Salgari, Jack Crawford, Tomasz Kowalski, Cliff Nowicki, Ricky Odin Matthews, Joshua Bock, Bilal K, Hermann Dettmann, Daniel Gusenbauer, Jeff Bridgforth, Erik Runyon, Izabela Kowalska, Carlos Alexandre Fuechter, Daniel Mate, Jan Hesselvig Krogh, Xandro Castañeda, Kelly Andrews, Jon Izquierdo, Wojciech Wiedeński, Jonathan Markevich, Lars Lauridsen, Eric Colantropo, Debra Niedermiller Chaffins, Ghalib Ali, Rod. Mckendrick, Sergii Tkachenko, Fabien Kupferschmid, Gabriel Tomescu, Codeepic, Photosjob, Alex Goetz, Eric Duval, Benjamin Ulstein, , Liz Kucharska, Jacob Frederiksen , Girish B, Saschlong, Jodie Watson, John Grayson, Patrick Heneise, Freek Van Gorkum, Jorge Diaz Gutierrez, Gabriel Alcalde, Karen Uppal, Eric Steuten, Ross Wintle, Juraj Kiss, Benjamin Favre, Kelly Dip, Ken Perry, Ole Petter Talgø, Jasper Versteege, Emil Forsmann, Elena, Kelvin Travers, Michaël Knauer, Timo Rinta-aho, Dariusz Franczak, Imanuel Benny, Lucie Gaunt, Jeff Dempsey, Simon Gaffke, Phil Deaton, Jon Shaffer, Robert Heckels, Logothetis Valasakis, Cædman "cads" Oakley, Denis Valcke, Youngjang, Christopher Murphy, Nicole Blais, Emma Rosenberg, Maria Inês Pires , Richard Mclain, Cesidio Dibenedetto, L. Blake Mcleod, Miesjel De Lange, Toni Trivkovic, Dawn Hanson, Sean Hester, Antoine Derrien, Sebastien Pencreach, Katrine Falck, Chris Jurthe, David Mcelroy, Formpartner Ab, Dessy Wijaya, Dan Sullivan, Jens Loleit, Phong Huynh, Dionne Aiken, Kenny Tran, Torsten Stelling, Rick-ktips, Catalin Vasile, Jan Willem Henckel, Luis Trindade, Petya, Albena Lobutova, Stephanie Petersen, Alejandro Pinto, Sean Mcemerson, Magnum80, Mehdi Brillaud, Terence Lucas Yap, Dustin Tauer, Erick Jones, Steve Paduchowski, Nathan Rivera, Sunil Bhatia, Marcos Alfonso, Eric Josue, Jens Grochtdreis, Julia Rechkunova, Lucija Kordic, Timo, Kori Ashton, Peter Loveland, Mathieu Cailleaud, Coderaiser, Vivien Lemoine, M. Phani Sasank, Adam M. Hofbauer, Chris Couture, André Romão, Paul Mohr, Chris Homan, Pavel Gerega, Julien Vitte, Akshat Goel, Rok, Peggy Lee Oster, Melissa L. Johnson, Moritz Weber (clesma), Radhika Dutt , Danielle Dunker, Marco Biedermann, Luis Pozo, Jan Grage, Björn Staaff, Ratkat, Peter Anglea, Patrik Dvořák, Rob Widdick, Fabian Irsara, Taylor Kirk, Tino Hußlack, Robin Welsh, Kent Kadim, Travis Ricks, Cole Smith, Damir Podbojec, Sande Wetmore, Peter Chau, Cord Media Company, Jeremy Zauder, Debasish Panda, Stefano Peloso, David Henrich, Bob Poliachik, Gauthier Eloy, Alvin Ourrad, Webatelier.be, Grant Vinson, Bruno Felício, Christine Toh, Katrina Carpenter, Nathaniel Hoyt, Jake Pang, Harris W., Charles Cousins, Adrian Bentley, Valeriu Tihai, John Slater, Zach Wheat, Shanti Hadioetomo, Jeff Daze, Imran Khan, Peter Doolaard, Spencer Bywater, Ben!, Jodi Parker, Nicktivity, Keith Hollis, Pablo Contreras, Jugal Manjeshwar, Niklas Oberwoerder, Jerich Calderon, Brian Hough, Carlos Viloria, Romanos Tsouroplis, Mandy Michael, Christine Kowalski, Niels Müller Larsen, Ariana Escobar Casares, Mark 'mol' Smith, Joseph Calvo, Rasika Jangle, Paweł Grzybek, Guillaume Bourdages, Marie Azcueta, Tim Dawson, Kimmi Gan, André Hedberg, Ilnar Nizamutdinov, Johnathan Tan Tze Chiang, James Holdren, Dalaney Vartenisian, Eugenia Sergueeva, Hiran Perera, Muhammad Bilal, Sasha Endoh, Michael Gorman, Peter Fitzearl, Victor Aganoke, Pipe Salom, Craig Harrington, Damian Samolej, Kevin Danielson, Karen Lewis, Carlos Silva, Katie Purdy, Nancy Wu, Nicklas Mundbjerg Jakobsen, Lee Fuller, Drew Buchter, Mathieu Spillebeen, Duane Adam, Brandon Knapp , Floris Van Der Haar, Andrew Boyd, Marc Aubé, Dominick Washburn, Mee Cha, Lim Tzyy Shyong, Dario Rigon, Tom Offringa, Eric Yang, Ahmed El Safty, Benjamin Milde, Philip Serefoglou, Chris Rickels, Lindsay Hardy, Adam Dugdale, Komfushee, Quentin Cole, Jules Martingrove, Vasanth Krishnamoorthy , Kyle Cearley, Lukas Klusis, S. Carter, Yoke Trisanti, Kenneth Chen, Pei Cheng, Betterweather Llc, Marco Maisel, Marigold Bollozos, Irina Glotova, Bram Derudder, Collin Brady, Timhecker, Haitham Al-beik, Harmen De Vries, Tala Ghazaleh, Jesse I Cooper, Nicole Corbin, Wolfram Twelker, Milinda Verage, Cheng Shuyun, David Jensen, Amy Dannwolf, Katie Russo, Bryson Caldwell, Alan Howshall, José Ángel Herrera Marfileño, Todd Bromley, Ryan Yurkanin, Dominic Colaso, Joel Burris, Roger Rodriguez, Katherine Kenny, Christian Bardin, Dave Curry, Jure Tufekcic , Alisha Trigatti, Daniel Niemann, Nicholas Fiorentini, Tomas Miskerik, Emily Berry, Mario Megela, Bimal Tailor, Daniel Knowlton, Markus Hübner, Tan Boon Tatt, Lynn Mueller (minsun Oh), Jordan Mogck, Saumitra Dey, Oliver Blaum, David A. Becker, Marcos Peebles, Aleks Hudochenkov, Moishy Lew, Ricardo Javier Rodriguez, Andrew Homsher, Braco Collins, Marie-josee Paquet, Justin Branon, Thorsten Born, Nick Downs, Ardalan Naghshineh, Alexander Kazachkov, Josalm, Shirley Allaway, Emma Roos, Kesha Antonov, Stuart Mccoy, Kiyoung Bang, Gina Bolano, Koen Knol, Manfred Oeding, Jenni

Kirkruff, Jason T. Featheringham, Jonathan Decoster, Igor Antoshevski, Dirk Höntzsch, Dj Far, Lance Charlton, Iulian Costin Nitulescu, Heather Daggett, Darryl Young, Peter Bösenberg, Prasad Chavan, Didier De Vos, Kenneth Zarecki, John Ellison, Abdullah Norozi Iranzad, Ivelin Belchev, Devin Rajaram, Devin Rajaram, Ricardo Vazquez, Michael Staudenmann, Max Elman, Olivier B. Deland, John Bohls, Ian Cameron, Florian Nagel, Andrea Zilibotti, Elina Kim, Jeff Mears, Jean-marie Lafon, Joe Galicia, Akhilesh Sabharwal, Kelly Personius, Michal Králik, Ihab Shoully, Ken Corless, Rodrigo Hahn, Carol Ratcliff, Nikko Bautista, Stephanie Stimac, Brandon Thomas, James Nock, Julian Van Der Giesen, Guillermo Basombrio, William Ukoh, R Guru, Dan Gramada, Ragnhild Krogh, Priit Karu, Julian Scaff, Hetal Thakkar, Mark Wouda, Nathan Doyle, André L, Heather Migliorisi , Olga Smirnova, Tommy Olovsson, Clayton K. Lose, Rastko Pivar, Daniel Fuchs, Ian Lucas, The Kewl Kitteh, Michiel Looman, Samuel Hilarus, Tom Bennet, Chris Manciero, Andrew Delman, Johan Svanstrom, Darren Swan, Trevor Barnes, Henning Orth, Zachary Morgan, Patrick Champoux, Maude Lavoie, Hillary Watts, Jefferson Steel, Vanessa Roy, Jan Van Hee, Jimmy Hsu, Larry Schooner, Moriah Ellig, Kyle Mchatton, Arturo Tadeo, Sigfried Seldeslachts, Iona Sangster, Jonathan T. Manas, Vico Van Den Eventuin, Greetje Jongen, Cristian Mateiciuc, Kristien Melaerts, Mieke Kemme, Alan Currie, Elke Steegmans, James Cocker, Abdelhadi Cherif , Abdelhadi Cherif, Mathias Szanto, Seth Hardy, Lars Kloster Silkjær, Jeff Sebasovich, Tj Fogarty, Aaron Fisher, Pez Pengelly, Dave Thackeray, Matthew Lynch, Pierre-luc Babin, Kaitlyn Noone, Pedro Thomaz, Avaz Bokiev, Paul Wilde, Lennart Friederichs, Filipe Pinto, Luuk Arens, Stephan Cass, Thomas Harrer, Dominik Ogilvie, Kendra Orr, Heather Shadix, Joshua Romero, Björn Steinborn, Mark Castell, Ben Arledge, Stian Martinsen, Webrocker, Anneke Sinnema, Gustav Jorlöv, Oleg Kislitsyn, Rubem Mota, Patrick Schriner, Calvin Szeto, Mark Spijkers, Robert Ster, Paul Bacon, Elif Bayrasli, Dominique Bosselmann, Ruben Oliveira, Gregory Kendall, Dylan Companjen, Rémy Saint Cricq, Ana Neagu, Vicker, Fabian Eichenberger, Peter Donker, Malin Antonsson, Metin Uçar, Milan Vogels, Ari Venguer, Cavell L. Blood, Morten Lines, Peter Van Der Hulst, Michael Dippold, Christophe Guilcher, Tom Millard, Nagy Viktor Gusztáv, Scott Beckman, Michel Bozgounov, John Fischer, Jeff Ballweg, Jorge Medrano, Richard Moger, Benjamin Denhartog, Ben Van Treur, Andrea Downey, John Fischer, Jordyn Nehmsmann, Christian Hellmuth, Jess Pritchard, David Simon, Rafał Borowski, John Franks, Evie Milo, Megan Franks, Andreas Prietzel, Annie Ngo, Neil Anderson, Blake Nafzinger, Anthony Devine, Quelu, Kim Lee, Brett Mason, Kimmicca, Clement Vial, Maria-rosa Lonetto, Grokabo Tetepipe, Lars Gyrup Brink Nielsen, John M. Wargo, Cam Macduff, Rok Bevc, Felix Osina, Sander Muru, Sajit Mehdi, Vanessa Rusu, Nick Van Der Sangen, Martin Weber, Rachell Underhill, Justin Torres, Alex Shenia, Robert Haritonov, Johannes Busch , Katarzyna Jasik, Daniel Kleiner, Łukasz Szadkowski, Jason J. Anderson, Diederick De Geest, Filipe Roque, Manuel Quero, Sam Lau, Lacy Alexander, Valerio Di Fonzo, Nicole Pribicevic , Michael Braithwaite, Douglas Lambert, Ian Heggaton, Morgan Schwertfeger, Nelly Harvey, Jo Craddock, Timothy Dang, Matthew Anderson, Abhishek Sachan, Nicholas Ruggeri, Santosh Kumar Molugu, Pervez Choudhury, German Pichardo Beer, Tim Watkinson, Rolf Ahlborn, Chameleon Logic, Yoram Blumenberg, Iris Diakoumi, Janette Noel , Spyros Charmanis, Christian Zumbrunnen, Fabian Liehret, Erin Tocalino, Mohamed Medhat, Manon Michel, Nikki Bryan Enriquez, Diane Domingo, Ramón Torres, Pete Barr, Hoogesh Dawoodarry, Lionel Barnabas Low, Robin Cajulis, G. Brad Hopkins, Annalyn Aguilar, Bettina Schwarz, Moe Louanjli, Super-fucking-man, Miguel A. Estrada, Rihnna Fe Macasaeat Jakosalem, Thomas Houk, Saman Majrouh, Jaime León, Tomas Petrašiūnas, Jessica Kelley, Victor Tolosa, Henry "henza" Zados, Ninja Multimedia, Oliver Kucharzewski, Richard Huf, Matt Shull, Vivian Tianyun Chen, Sompop Suksawat, Stephen Seng, Kimee, Matheus Baumgart, Honorico Carpeso, Lewis Hankinson, Glen Rosie, Iugo Pty Ltd, Adelaide Australia, Carlos Escalante Delgado , Rick Kaminski, Hugh, Andi Saleh, Cesar Leon, Edward Chung, Indah Ibrahim, Irfan, Marina Boaventura, Angelo Albiero Neto, Steve Beck, Cloudowl Inc., Jose Rojitas, Greg Vissing, Aaron Rutley, Bayu Hendra Winata, Christin Carolina, Stephen Saw, Rafal Pekacki, Keith J Sweeney, Chew Chit Siang, Melanie Sumner, Kinro Syo, Morgan (kristen), Gansukh, Logan Franklin, Damon Carter, Corey Bruyere, Melissa Hodge, Walter The Mak, Parth Umrani, J. Michael Frank, Kate Newbown, David Vogler, Heather Bryant, Mohammad Nadim Attari, Greg Culley, Ramzi Kanazi, Sam Blanaba, Sam Blanaba, Jesse Graupmann, Corinne Roosen, Simon Willcock, Leonardo De La Fuente, Viraj Sirimanna, Kevin Klein, Chad Schulz, Asam Munir, Niedhui, Dinh Hong, Nerijus, Si Keane , Bruce Moerdjiman, Craig Myles, Dave Dirt , Benoist Lawniczak, David Devdavido, Marco Hagemann, Antony Tanuputra, Ondrej Vertat, Stanislav Halai, George Antonakos, Branson Werner, Jonathan De Jong, Douwe De Haan, Dawn Marie Manlapaz, Chesca De Jesus, Ley Lee, Myoung-hee Jeong, Fokkejan Meijer, Unnikrishna Menon Damodaran (umd), Andrew Holmes, Dirk Eckert, Alina Karpelceva, Gytautas Pilkauskas, Ben Van Looy, Joachim Wasteels, Faizan Sheikh, Jurgen De Bruijn, Barbara & Stefan, Danny Koelewijn, Emiel Kwakkel, Tamas Palecian, Randall Lozano, Mustafa Alic, Julien Rondeau, Dennis Schaa, Adarsh Prabhu, Heinrich Ferreira, Matt Lawless, Ahmed Magdi Elnifily, Martin Chaov, Jan Brinkmann, Herri Wanglai, Jeremiah Bousquet, Milestone Systems, Edward Kosasih, Ivar Johansson, Daniel Mensing, Artem Kobyakov, Abdus Salam, Tohbbe From Sala, Vitali Kukyan, Julian Schoemaker, Aliona Tsiatsera, Radu Luchian, Alberto García, Cillian Bracken-conway, Rolf Meyer, Will_richards, Grégory Ponthus, Jacek Kawiak, Rowena Leung, Anders Johnard, Johan Rosenson, Mathijs Rutgers, Tomáš Běloch, Anythingoes, Jordan Warren, Michael Pallister, Jamie Buckell, Thomas Krajewski, Ruud Timmermans, Sebastian Christiansson, Corinne Massacry, Izabela Furdzik, Schnitzl, Daryl Oeben, Avinash Kumar, Shoaib Khan, Canute Amirthanayagam, Kristijan Novakovic, Tony Watters, Dimitrios Kalaitzidis, Frederik R. R. Toft, Umberto Di Lorenzo, Sadiq Hussain, Chris Cieślik, Robert Fahy, Frank De Wit, Mohamed Bahaeddine Chakroun, Chris Brown, Daniel Humphrey, Stephanus Budiwijaya, Zhongde Liu, Lailson Bandeira, Igor Gotal-lukša, Tom Blaymire, Martin Pruss, Robin John, Theodore Vorillas, Celinedesign, Nikesh Patel, Kineticuk, Alex Synge, Igor Ćirić, Andy Wilke, Andrea Vaghi, Mikhail Bryukhovets, Gerhard Dinhof, Zsolt Revay G., Mihai Ciobanu, Jake Kronika, Magnus Olsson, Jonathan Devine, Courtney Myers, Luis Pedro Lopes, Steve Weineck, Bram Zijp, Kodify, Kodify, Fdf, Jin Ah Chon, Amanda Brown, Jay Ocean, Rich Blyth, Robert Rafiński, Louise White, George Goeschel, Bram De Haan, Samer Kamel, Michał Czajkowski, Radek Drwęcki, Albert Tsang, Piotr Rafiński, Anne Franco, Max Maier, Jono Goldsack, Tom Nijns, Katrina Roaix, Ricardo Lynch, Mathias Lauble, Kaelig, Lorenzo Di Rienzo, Ian Trembirth, Sandeep Parkhande, Tomi Carr, Karachalios Panagiotis, Steven Leek, Heeyeon Cheryl Lee, Kay Kazemi , Ashish Gupta, Giuseppe Rodriguez, Florian Niebuhr, Alla Gringaus, Darius Sveikauskas, Sarah Huny Young, Michael Inguillo, Maud Rodin, Johdi Ananmalay, Robert Spatz, Victor Castrejon, Stavrev Krasimir, Zlatina Petrova, Sachendra Yadav , Andrés Laplace Kellogg, Paulina Valdés, Benjamin Minnich, Nigel Nighthawk, Webslingerm, Tom Munz, Kyle Garcia, Anita Chang, Sarah Trafford, Jeffery Bennett, Anita Chang, Christine Q. Rader, Martin Smti, Jacob Beltran, Bo Reurekas, Cris Elias, Venkata Sukumar G , Nick Irion, David Aimi, Rachel Cunliffe, Strahinja Krstić, Lion Timmers, Mattias Miezans, Richard Holland, Julian Oczkowski, Gerd Wippich, Isabela Nastasa , Paul Lapkin, Ilya Sitnikov, Nicola Elvin, David A. Hoffman, Daniel Mace, Alicia J Olivares, Sergey Arustamov, Marko Danailov, Beau Davis, Stephen Piana, Frank Henselmans, John Goode, Maxwell Rice, Carlos Maldonado Berra, Brigitte Cheng, Shardool Singh, Julio Braña, Omotayo Ishola, Emily Serven, Matt Kay, Bruno Calou Alves, Yassir Yahya, Johanna Ruiz, Matthew Andrade, Michael Gutierrez, Rosemary Armocida, Hamad Al Zadjali, Ronald, Reinhard Weidl, Rachel Loh Sook Yee, Rob Busio, Florian Wenzel, Vinodchelmeda, Karol Górecki, Julian Scheele, Akmal Adnan, Yitzhak C, Roland Kedde, Kai Brueckers, Marco Terzo, Damjan Gataric, Deepa Anand, Julien Jourdain, Saroj Shahi, Philip Elliott, Jack Roscoe, Paul Verbeek, Robert Mills, Michael Kühnel, , Wakkos, Chris Seaton, Andrea Palermo, Olivier Lebon, Nicolas Mahler, Dave Rojas, Matthew Passmore, Daniel Stein, Gavin Elliott, Mermelada De Sesos, Marco Mascia, Mirko Friedrich, Brian Wangila, Robin Björklund, Estelle Chevallier, Matt Alley, Zayd Media, Aleksandar Macanović, Martin Bean, Peter Carless, Tom Unonius, Patrick Stadler, Jeremias Dombrowsky, Ansh Deb, Alexander Pütz, Christian Althoff, Stian Kristiansen, Pelle Lagermann Jensen, Gunther Groenewege, Ashwin Van Dijk, Philipp Bauer, Mathias Kastrup , Pourikas Emmanouil, Martijn Gorree, Neal Mattox, Yeongju Jo, Ben Winters, Jonathan Colyar Meyer, Szymon Grzybek, Szabolcs Légrádi, Halcom D., Bernardo Baquero Stand, Gaurav Gandhi, Kyle Baldry, Alessandro Petrelli, Ignas Butenas, Marcello Palmitessa, Jerome Zeck, Sue Mara Akong, Paul C. Wampler , Cas Cornelissen, Juraj Macejko, Rebecca Nyman, Indah Ibrahim, Simon Gustafsson, Teodor Bitca, Tim Luigjes, Gita Adi Ramdhani, Luke Barber, Michal Zigo, Serg Nesterov, Kevin Constantine A. Codamon, Maze , Marco Lesch, Rink Pijpker , Christoph Sippel, Mark Skeet, Terence Williams , Andy Gongea, Martin Wyatt, Kris Olszewski, Mateusz Cygan, Jesse Kelsey, Alena Sarakapud, Kishor Sonawane, Alvin Lee, Giuseppe Scappaticcio, Marcelo Soto De La Fuente, Ajay Prasannan, Studyportals, Deji Ogundairo, Máté Tóth, Josejavier Velasco, Brandosaurus, David Wollschlegel, Susan Jang, Boris Agatić, Tim Duffey, Max Mai, Juanjo Melgar, Morgan Lindsay, Taru Muhonen, Nicolas Martel, Polietilena, Dana Norwood, Adrian Martinez, Casey Morris, Ciro Urdaneta, Aaron Brako, Mario Serrette, Numa Quevedo, Sebastian Brieschenk, Christophe Coutzoukis, David W. Desjardins, Sylvain Puccini, Dave Hauser, Michele Foley, Victor Ariel D'agata, Julie R. Smith, Rod Sampera, Mariano Arrien-gomez, Janosch Oltmanns,

Our Web Design Community Is Responsive, Too.

These pages are dedicated to our lovely community, to everybody who has been supporting us over the years. Without you, this book wouldn't be possible. We appreciate your trust. You are Smashing, and you should know that.

Mike Bishop, Denis St-michel, Martin Heindl, Cody Hamway, Ion Popa, Danielle Vautier, Lars Dol, Daniel Schoone, Doodool Tala, Gideon Caspi, Kurt Stremel, Tomas Peniasko, Simon Michel, Chrissy Collins, Goroguedesigns, Hudson-peralta, Russell Ahlstrom, Birnou Sébarte, Tracy Locke Castro, Chauncey Garrett, Jana Siegle, Ryan Valle, Charles Ratkie, Mauricio Ibarra, Maria Mayskaya, Lochlan Bunn, Srinivas, Aboudou Ali, Ricardo Gimenes, Ram Lakshman, Boon Gee Wai, Efim Solovyev, Chathura Asanga Kulasinghe, Juha Lehtonen, Jussi Virtanen, Tim Van Daatselaar, Romualdas Daskevicius, Michael Seibt, Kishan Sanghani, Tan Tat Woei, Luciano Jesus Lima, David Watson, Nikolay Shevchenko, Chris Alexander, Darko Stanimirov, Paweł Łuczak, Melissa Harris, Interactivechris, Gauthier Geerolf, Joshua Theissen, Aj Hemaratne, Shannon Hicks, Manuel Medel Jr, Smokie Lee, Ryan Raplee, Jem Bijoux, Siarhei Fedarovich, Belinda K Lane, Branislav Maksin, Ricardo Sanchez, Corby Simpson, Francisco Torres, Benjamin Mintz, Alessandro Fuoco, Gray Ang, Marcin Zieliński, Laurel Webster, Bernhard Weiler, Jon Dinero A. Delos Reyes, Divy Tolia, Boghaert Pieter, Oscar Adolfo Monzón, Marcie Folsom, Joel Rdz, Anja, Martín Del R3o, Riccardo Flemming, Ahmet B., Brad Bartell, Mark Gervickas, Marc Dittrich, Trevor D. Thurlow, Amy Torgunrud, Stephen Oates, Luke Underwood, John Rice, Jenny Veens, Hansel Tanuyaputra, Bruno Fraga, Dan Abrey, Håvard Brynjulfsen, Pipsqueak Productions, Llc, Lloyd Saulpaugh, Tau Ming, Saulo Venâncio , Mohammad Faizan Atiq, Labed Khaireddine, Aftab Alam, Serhii Demydko, Ilithya, Dilip Gupta, Stefan Meisinger, Yow-long Lee, Naresh Babu Baleswaran, Tania Abanina, Leah Garber, Michael Huss, Epebinu Oluwafemi, Abhijit Shirsath, Jachimike Njimogu, Mohammad Reza Akbari, Warren Croce, Jenny Lu, Nikolai Villarin, Jasper Zonneveld, Nicolai Knecht, Arthur Sousa, Jessica Prater, Jona Wetter, Cristiano Sarmento, Chris Hore, Michael Morales, Design Scribe, Rodrigo Galleguillos, Sebastian Cruz, Danny Valle, John Larwood, Daniel P. Chen, Woud Hobbelink, Florian Bielsky, Juan Carlos Villar, Marek Gebka, Andoni.

Published 2015 by Smashing Magazine GmbH, Freiburg, Germany.
Printed in the EU. ISBN: 978-3-945749-21-0

Cover Design by Jessica Hische.
Cover Illustrations by Guillaume Kurkdjian.
Layout and Typesetting by Markus Seyfferth.
Editing and Quality Control by Vitaly Friedman.
Copyediting and Proofreading by Owen Gregory.
eBook Production by Cosima Mielke.
Typefaces used: Elena and Ideal Sans.

The book has been written and reviewed by Andrew Clarke, Ben Callahan,
Bram Stein, Chris Coyier, Dan Mall, Dmitry Baranovskiy, Eileen Webb, Emily
Gray, Fabio Carneiro, Jake Archibald, James Williamson, John Allsopp, Lisa
Maria Martin, Marko Dugonjić, Matt Gaunt, Patrick Hamann, Sara Soueidan,
Tom Maslen, Viljami Salminen, Vitaly Friedman, Yoav Weiss, Zach Leather-
man and Zoe Mickley Gillenwater.

TABLE OF CONTENTS

FOREWORD · BY VITALY FRIEDMAN

A RESPONSIVE WAY FORWARD

R ESPONSIVE DESIGN HASN'T MADE THINGS EASIER, has it? The flourishing diversity of web landscape — from form factors to connection
types to input modes to browsers — has only amplified the unpredictability of user experiences on the web. This unpredictability is remarkably
difficult to tackle unless you embrace the inherent fluidity of the web as a
guiding principle in your work. In many cases, going responsive seems like the
most reasonable strategy for covering the entire spectrum of user experiences,
ranging from tiny viewports to ultra-wide HD screens, with a wonderfully convenient, and often deceptively sneaky *one-codebase-for-everything* approach.

We've learned by now that responsive design is much more than that.
Responsive design affects *everything* and *everybody* in the design process, and
in practice, a few media queries, fluid grids and flexible images aren't enough.
Screen considerations alone aren't enough either. We have to entirely rethink
and relearn our design practices, tools and processes; we have to adapt new
technologies and break down complexity of UI components; we also have to
deal with performance issues and hostile rendering environments and apply
content choreography to keep priorities and structure intact.

As a result, the craft of designing and building websites has become complex and elaborate, often difficult to estimate, test and support; and it seems that everybody is still trying to figure out just the right techniques within just the right design workflow to create fast, scalable and flexible design systems. Responsive design ain't easy, but it doesn't mean that it has to be difficult — if you have a good process in place, with a knowledgeable team, and a versatile set of reliable design patterns.

When we set out to create this book, we wanted to explore just that: design workflows, front-end techniques, UX strategies and design patterns that would help web designers and developers get better results, faster. The result lies in your hands now: a compendium of techniques, strategies and patterns that work well in real-life responsive designs — written by well-respected designers and developers spending every day crafting and maintaining responsive websites on both small and large scale. Think of it as a handbook with practical guidelines and precise pointers that will help you tackle any level of complexity in responsive design, intelligently and efficiently.

As you can see, the book isn't particularly small, and we hope that you'll discover quite a few useful gems in here. All links mentioned in the book are also collected on www.smashing-links.com. We hope that by the time you flip over the last page, you'll feel empowered to craft accessible, fast and flexible responsive websites that will stand the test of time and unpredictability — whatever devices come next. Happy reading!

Vitaly, editor-in-chief of Smashing Magazine

THE MODERN RESPONSIVE DESIGNER'S WORKFLOW

DAN MALL

THE MODERN RESPONSIVE
DESIGNER'S WORKFLOW

IN OUR INDUSTRY, WE ARE OFTEN SUBJECT TO THREE THINGS: titles, tools and output. We sort ourselves into buckets based on our *job titles*: designers, developers, content strategists, information architects, and others. It's often cleaner that way.

We sort ourselves by *tools* as well. Designers use things like Photoshop and Sketch, and developers use things like Sublime and CodePen. If you walk by somebody's desk, and they're using Omnigraffle, it's likely they're an information architect.

We're also categorized by *output*: designers are expected to produce comps; developers are expected to write code. Our deliverables and output are severely outdated, limiting the squishy, giddy, icky, amazing, multi-device world that we live in.

We're good at placing ourselves within these specific buckets, but what often goes wrong in projects happens within gaps between the job descriptions and deliverables lists.

When I started my design collaborative called *SuperFriendly*, I was determined to find a new set of tools and outputs to better suit the people who hire us and to better serve their customers. I had a few specific goals in mind that I wanted to achieve, goals that would make my workflow more productive and more efficient.

- First, I wanted to figure out how to achieve the highest fidelity in the shortest amount of time.

- The second goal was to remove abstractions wherever possible, so I could clearly see what I was designing and building.

- The third goal was to ensure that during the process, all deliverables would come with conversation.

To this end, I found that I often prioritized frameworks over processes. As an industry, we talk a lot about processes, but I find it more useful to think about what frameworks I want to put in place.

Consider this example. A Newton's cradle is a *process*. It's a repeatable system that's optimized for efficiency, not innovation. It always starts the same way: You lift a sphere on one of the ends, release it, it hits the one next to it, and it continues in that system. It doesn't deviate from that system. There's nothing surprising about it; there's nothing unexpected about it. That's what it's good for.

By contrast, a football field is a *framework*. Every game is the same length; it's played on the same type of field; it follows the same rules. Everyone knows where out-of-bounds is, and everyone knows where the goals are. Yet what happens within the ninety minutes is a surprise every time.

I wasn't looking for a process for my agency — I was in search of a new framework, one that would work well with my workflow. After a lot of experimentation, failing and trying again, I found what works very well within general project constraints, at least for me. This is exactly what this chapter is about: a couple of things that I found in my responsive design workflow, with a few techniques and ideas that have proved useful in my own work.

Plan

The first piece of that framework might sound remarkably unremarkable: de-signers should be more involved in planning. Conducting interviews are a great way to start planning.

Recently, I was working on a project for a magazine with a primarily female readership. Before we did anything — before we did any comps or any informa-tion architecture — we just spent some time interviewing.

We talked to readers of both the print magazine and the current website, and found things we couldn't have assumed otherwise. When we went to the kick-off meeting with the client, we brought a deck of observations we gleaned from the interviews. We weren't making any recommendations at that point; we were just saying, "Here are some things we found interesting, and we'd like to have a conversation about it." We found that:

- Most readers are obsessed with Pinterest. While that might have been a safe assumption, we heard specifically from actual readers that they often have Pinterest open at the same time they're reading the magazine.

- An unexpectedly high number of these readers mentioned something they called "emotional context" while they were reading. That seemed to be a striking phrase that was common among interviews.

- They didn't use the navigation very much. They often just browsed along with the content and used search as a last resort, but often skipped the navigation.

- Surprisingly, readers expected commercial offerings as a service of the website. Many of the readers we talked to said, "I would love this magazi-ne to tell me what products to buy." That was a huge advertising oppor-tunity, and something the client had never done before because they just assumed that readers might think it was pushy advertising and skip over it. But the readers trusted this brand so much that they wanted recommendations for products to buy. They were leaving millions of dollars on the table simply because they hadn't even talked to people about it and had dismissed it.

Interviewing is a very valuable skill in a designer's toolkit. It's a simple technique that can empower you to make the right decisions and smart design choices for your clients. We should use it more meaningfully and more often.

On that project, I worked with Jennifer Brook, a great user experience designer and researcher. Jennifer always asks me to *hypothesize*. When we work together, she usually prompts me with questions and thoughts like this:

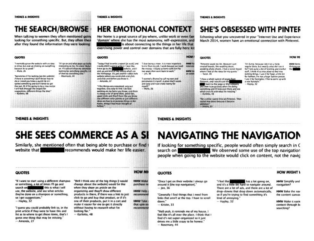

By conducting interviews, you can learn a lot about the product and what it lacks. These insights can then be grouped, ranked and presented as a deck.

> 66 *As an experienced professional, what do you think should be on the site? Tell me your vision for the site, and I'll go find research that supports it. But, if I instead find research that refutes it, I'll come back to you with that research and we can adjust the hypothesis together."*

We don't hypothesize enough as an industry. We should be guessing more. Let's validate our hunches with research, but don't be afraid to take some guesses.

WRITING-FIRST DESIGN

Before I start designing anything, I write. When I have trouble designing, rather than trying to force my way through Photoshop and design tools, I put the tools aside and jump into a text editor instead. I write manifestos for myself (I've also heard them called *creative briefs*, *strategic briefs*, or *communication briefs*).

Basecamp's designers have been following a similar approach for years. Instead of jumping into a visual tooling environment, they prefer *"writing-first design"*[1], whereby interfaces and interactions are sketched out in a text editor as plain text first, and are enhanced and refined with visual assets later.

One tool I've found useful for this is *Ommwriter*[2]. What I love about it is that it forces me to go fullscreen, and it will give me either a handful of subtle backgrounds or a blank one; Ommwriter also provides the option to play ambient background music. It compels you to focus and prevents distractions. I love this *isolationist* version of writing, where you're perfectly alone with your thoughts and a blank canvas.

I also tend to use *Notational Velocity*[3] a lot, and particularly a fork of Notational Velocity called *nvALT*[4], which supports Markdown. It's pretty much on every machine I use for work, and it's on my phones, too. What makes nvALT so useful is that it's easy to sync notes back and forth, so you always have your notes synced without having to put them into Dropbox or email yourself. Having a tool like that is handy because I always have my thoughts accessible to me no matter where I am. In fact, this little tool has been one of the greatest design tools for me — a virtual, digital notepad wherever I go.

So, how exactly does a manifesto help in the design workflow?

---

1 https://signalvnoise.com/posts/3801-writing-first-design
2 http://www.ommwriter.com/
3 http://notational.net
4 http://brettterpstra.com/projects/nvalt/

A good manifesto has to contain creative direction, a point of view, a perspective. Without strong creative direction, everything feels a bit too vanilla. I love vanilla as much as the next person, but sometimes I want salted caramel. To create something memorable and unique, you need a very distinctive idea, a different angle: that's what creative direction is. Flat design isn't a point of view. CSS transitions are not a point of view either. A good manifesto should go beyond that, saying what you're going to do and, more importantly, what you're *not* going to do.

Let's make this clearer by looking at one example with a strong creative direction and another without. What you see below is an architecture of a website. Could you guess what site it is?

Explore | Albums | Songs | News | Store

Perhaps you could narrow it down to being the website of a band? But which band? It's hard to tell which one. The reason for that is that the architecture here is *vanilla*. While it works for a lot of bands, it doesn't work for a specific one because it's so generic. It doesn't provide any help for you to identify precisely which band because there's no unique perspective that relates to a particular group.

Let's look at another example:

Songs | John, Paul, George & Ringo | From Liverpool to the Hall of Fame | News | Store

That's right: this site structure makes the band much easier to spot. This is the architecture for the Beatles website. This has a point of view, a perspective. What kind of manifesto could lead to an architecture like this? I imagine it could look something like this:

The Beatles are the greatest band of all time. Their songs and history are deep and dramatic tales; few institutions have been loved the world over for so long. The range of music they performed spanned many genres.

Their music became much more than entertainment; it evolved into an embod-iment of ideals that well-represented its era. Their website should reflect that richness from every angle.

Admittedly, that's pretty assertive, but notice how much of a point of view it has. This is something that can't be mistaken for another organization. A vision like this can't be mistaken for another band. This type of bold approach is severely lacking on the web today. If the web had stronger creative direction, it would be much easier to identify brands (and bands), what they stand for, and whether or not you wanted to be associated with them.

If you're interested in what manifestos or creative briefs contain, there's a very good article by Jared Spool called the "The Magical Short-Form Creative Brief"[5]. It offers some very helpful tips on what a good manifesto or creative brief should have in it, including the project objective, the key personas, the key scenarios and the key principles.

If you look at the planning tools I've outlined in the chapter so far and the output they provide, it looks quite different from a designer's usual output. Thinking differently about your skills and tools opens up more opportunities for the types of activity that you could be doing to add value for your teams and co-workers and clients.

Inventory

We could spend a lot of time planning what we are about to design and build, but to do it efficiently we need to have a clear understanding of the guts and inner workings of the interfaces in a project. That's why the second part of my framework is Inventory. There are many different kinds, but the first type that I tend to use a lot is an *interface inventory*.

---

5   http://www.uie.com/articles/short_form_creative_brief/

Interface inventories help us to regain consistency and sense of control in the design process. Source: http://bradfrost.com/blog/post/interface-inventory/

In the example above, front-end designer Brad Frost conducted a thorough inventory of all of the buttons on his bank's website. The sheer amount of buttons used throughout the website was a clear sign of inconsistency deeply

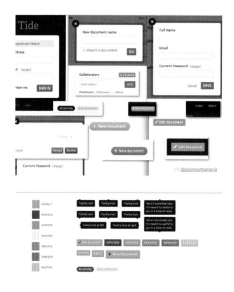

embedded in the design. It's one single brand, but there are so many different colors and typefaces and sizes and proportions that it might be hard to believe that all these interface elements co-existed on one website.

Drawing up inventories can be immensely helpful. Whenever you're lost, disappointed or disillusioned somewhere in the middle of your project, conduct an interface inventory; it will help you stay on track and regain confidence. Sometimes projects start to slowly drift away from you, gradually becoming inconsistent and fragmented, and there's no easy way to notice that until it's too late. Interface inventories help you prevent this from happening. They help you notice what disparate elements you might have, so you win back a feeling of control in which you are building a scalable design system instead of a loose set of components or common layouts.

Designer Jason Santa Maria used exactly this approach when he was designing the app *Editorially*. He conducted an inventory of all the different interface elements that he had created and noticed just how much disparity there was across them. He decided to consolidate some of those elements: some were similar enough that they could be combined into one, while others needed to be refined. The interface inventory also revealed the gaps that existed, and Jason was able to create a few more components to cater for scenarios he hadn't considered previously. The inventory alone helped him set up a sound foundation for a style guide. That style guide was then able to transition to front-end development and helped everybody involved in the project.

Interface inventory conducted by Jason Santa Maria when working on Editorially.

Apparently there are a number of ways to design a link to an article. Grouping and prioritizing options helps establish consistency and hierarchy in a design

When I was designing the new O'Reilly site[6], I did an interface inventory in the middle of the project. I realized I had designed 22 different ways to link to an article: everything from a title with an image to a title with a deck; a title with a

6 https://beta.oreilly.com/

deck and a byline; and a title with an image, a deck and a byline. It was just way too much. We didn't need that many elements. By designing one piece at a time, we reached a state where there were too many different states for our own good.

We decided to consolidate. We created categories called "Definites" and "Maybes" and ended up with three definites and two maybes. Going from 22 to 5 allowed us to work with a much tighter set, which was ultimately better for our working team, the client, and the users of the site.

PERFORMANCE BUDGET

Visual components aren't the only area that can benefit from inventories. *Performance budgets* are another helpful type of inventory.

Recently I worked on a project for Radio Free Europe/Radio Liberty, an organization that reports news in countries where the free press is banned by the government or not fully established. Their work can be dangerous: people have been incarcerated or even hanged for accessing the content. We heard stories about places like Uzbekistan, where people were crossing borders illegally just to read the content on the website; that's how important this content is to their readers.

Performance was an extremely important consideration for this project — it could literally be a matter of life and death. Radio Free Europe was already working intensely to achieve good performance, doing smart things both on the server and the client with progressive enhancement to ensure that core content was loaded as quickly as possible on even the slowest connections. They serve hundreds of millions of page views every month, powering 150 sites in over 60 countries. Their readers face very hostile environments; many of their readers access the content exclusively on mobile devices where 3G is the fastest possible speed.

Because we were talking about performance, we started to use new tools. One of those tools was WebPagetest.org[7], where you can to plug in the URL and see how well it performs under different connection types. WebPagetest grades sites using a few specific metrics such as first byte time, start render time, speed

---

7 http://www.webpagetest.org

index, and how well the images are compressed. It gives you recommendations to improve those metrics and consequently improve the performance of your site.

Based on this data, we decided to create a performance budget to ensure that performance was prioritized from the very start of the project. The site should be fast, but just *how* fast is fast enough? We ran the current Radio Free Europe site—specifically their mobile site, which was their fastest digital property—through WebPagetest. As we ran it through, the tool returned a set of numbers: 4.193 seconds for "Start Render"; 5.565 seconds for "Visually Complete"; and 7.93 seconds for "Fully Loaded".

Once we had our data for those metrics, the next thing we could do was gather the data from our main "competitors," just to make sure that we were at least on a par with them. Radio Free Europe is a news site, so they don't have competitors in the traditional sense, so we inventoried sites Radio Free Europe admired. We gathered data from sites like National Public Radio (NPR), the Guardian, Al Jazeera, and the BBC. Surprisingly, the Radio Free Europe was the fastest of the bunch.

Site	Start Render	Visually Complete	Fully Loaded	80% Start Render	80% Visually Complete	80% Fully Loaded
rferl.mobi	4.193	5.658	7.930	3.354	4.526	6.344
npr.org	5.175	13.542	26.377			
theguardian.com	20.87	18.82	22.177			
m.bbc.com/news	8.392	15.875	18.067			
america.aljazeera.com	6.272	8.022	63.756			

Performance budgets don't look fancy: they're just a spreadsheet with metrics and performance goals. In this case, our goal was to be at least 20% faster.

We could have stopped there, but we didn't think that was good enough. Tim Kadlec, my developer on the project, wrote a post a few months before this project called "Fast Enough"[8]. In the post, he highlights some fieldwork in researcher Steven Seow's book *Designing and Engineering Time*[9] that suggests people perceive tasks as faster or slower when there's at least a 20% time difference. We didn't just want to beat the other sites in terms of speed; we wanted regular readers of Radio Free Europe to notice an improvement in loading time for the new site.

8 http://timkadlec.com/2014/01/fast-enough/
9 http://www.engineeringtime.com

We looked into those initial timings — "Start Render", "Visually Complete" and "Fully Loaded" — and calculated what we should aim for, shaving 20% off the fastest results we discovered. Instead of starting to render in 4.19 seconds, we wanted the site to start in 3.35 seconds. We wanted the site to be "Visually Complete" in 4.46 seconds, not 5.57. This simple calculation provided us with times to target.

But that wasn't enough, because we really need page weight to make this actionable in a design process. All of these times we were using WebPagetest's suboptimal mobile 3G speed, which is 768 kilobits per second with a 300 milliseconds round-trip time. We measure page weights in bytes, not bits, so we have to do some conversion. 8 bits is equal to 1 byte, so...

768kbps ÷ 8 bits/byte= 96 kilobytes/second.

We can use that number to create some handy conversions. Here's our handy formula:

Target time (in seconds) × 96 kb/s = Target weight (in kb)

If we want the site to start rendering in 3.354 seconds, we do:

3.354s × 96 kb/s = 322kb

That's the maximum page weight we can have in order to get the site to start rendering in 3.354 seconds or less on a 3G connection.

We can use that number as a ballpark figure for the assets we need on the site. Those assets usually come in these five categories:

- HTML
- CSS
- JavaScript
- Images
- Web Fonts

Using HTTP Archive[10], we can find some average weights:

- The average HTML page weighs about 60kb,
- The average CSS file weighs about 58kb,
- The average JavaScript file weighs about 295kb.

When we add those up and measure it against our target kilobyte weight, we get 413kb (*60kb of HTML + 58kb of CSS + 295kb of JS*), which is already 91kb over our 322kb Start Render budget. If we followed the average usage of all those assets, we wouldn't even have any images or web fonts on the new site!

Now that we know what to expect from the average size of a page, we can do some budgeting. Perhaps we talk to our developer and ask if there's any way we can get that JavaScript number down. She might say, "I've been meaning to try a project without jQuery and just do plain old JavaScript." If we strip the 266kb jQuery out of our 295kb JavaScript file, that gets us to 29kb, which leaves 175kb left in our budget. We could split that between images and web fonts, giving us about 87kb for images and 87kb for web fonts: perhaps four 20kb images, and six 15kb web fonts on a page. Here's what that complete budget would look like:

- HTML – 60kb
- CSS – 58kb
- JS – 29kb
- Images – 87kb
- Web fonts – 87kb
- Total – 321kb

We can even optimize a bit further. You now have a budget for six web fonts, but you might not need all six; perhaps you can get away with just four. If we reallocate some of that weight, we could move 2 web fonts worth (~30kb) over to images, giving us a new 117kb budget for images (roughly 5 images at 20kb each) That budget would look like this:

---

10   http://httparchive.org/

- HTML – 60kb
- CSS – 58kb
- JavaScript – 29kb
- Images – 117kb
- Web fonts – 57kb
- Total – 321kb

For designers, this kind of information is incredibly liberating to have before starting a design. Knowing that I can use six images and four web fonts before jumping into Photoshop means that I'm using performance as an ingredient in the design process, rather than trying to squeeze it in afterwards. We do our best work under constraints, and knowing this constraint up front is invaluable.

VISUAL INVENTORY

American philosopher Eric Hoffer once wrote, "Language was invented to ask questions. Answers may be given in grunts and gestures, but questions must be spoken. Humanness came of age when man asked the first question."[11]

When I start a design, I have many questions. What colors and typefaces should I use? Should there be an underlying metaphor or concept to this design? Is showing the application on a shiny laptop the best way to sell it? Can the brand pull off a minimalist design approach? Should the copy be more playful?

Our industry's typical response is to craft three comps representing three different directions: one comp to explore and answer each major question individually. While a comp is one of the highest-fidelity types of deliverables, they're a major time commitment to create, especially when we end up throwing away the majority of that work once a client picks one of three directions. In my experience, we lose far too much time in the process by crafting comps — it's doable and sometimes necessary but extremely time-consuming. There has to be a better, smarter way to do this.

---

11 *Reflections on the Human Condition*, 1973

Crafting comps takes time. What about exploring the visual atmosphere and direction by showing examples in a Keynote presentation?

Rather than starting my design process in Photoshop or Sketch or Illustrator, I tend to use Keynote. When a client asks for a "playful" design, I could create an original "playful" comp for them, but that may take a few days. Instead, I'll create a default Keynote document and paste in a screenshot of a "playful" website like the *GoGo squeeZ*[12] site. I write a little blurb next to it, like, "How playful and whimsical should the new site be? For instance, the GoGo squeeZ site is full of smiles and catchy illustrations that make you grin as you explore the site." I'll also Photoshop the client's logo into the screenshot as a simple way for them to see themselves in a different way. I'll compile 10-20 of these to send over, which I call a *visual inventory*.

Remember "*the highest fidelity in the shortest amount of time*" from the start of this chapter? How do we achieve that? Obviously, a comp has very high fidelity, and it's the most realistic version that you can achieve (or almost, short of building the actual site), but it always takes a lot of time to get there. On the other hand, a visual inventory achieves a high fidelity that is close to a comp in terms of its actual look and feel. Photoshopping the logo takes a short amount of time. Highest fidelity, shortest amount of time.

12   http://www.gogosqueez.com/

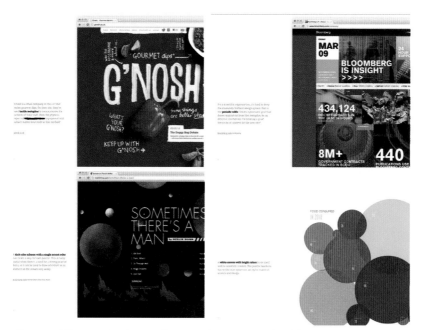

Showing different styles alone is often enough to start up a fruitful conversation on the art direction of a site.

Feedback on a visual inventory can give you a checklist of things the client responds well to. For example, they might think flat design isn't a good fit for their brand, but highly saturated design is; or that software as lifestyle is not a concept that's going to work for them, but a case study-driven site would work better; or that the tone might need to be more professional than playful.

We can start receiving precise, helpful answers to all those questions within a much shorter amount of time. Unlike mock-ups or comps which take a few days or weeks in Photoshop to produce, a visual inventory can be put together within a few hours. It's a helpful shortcut that allows you to avoid spending too much time and effort on things that won't make it in the end. Instead of making random guesses, you're working with tangible, concrete material that will find its way into the final result.

I published a little article[13] about the visual inventory technique and have Keynote and PowerPoint templates if you want to get started with one.

As designers undertake more inventory, we'll more often use tools like WebPagetest, Excel and Keynote to make assets like visual and interface inventories, and performance budgets. Again, that's very different from what we've been used to. In my experience, these are the most valuable tools that modern designers need to know and use — and use well — in order to adapt to the complexity of the multi-device world we have.

Sketch

Planning first, inventorying second: what's next? The third piece of my framework is *sketching*. I don't necessarily mean sketching with pencil and paper, although that's certainly useful as well. By sketching, I mean being able to generate and refine ideas quickly.

ELEMENT COLLAGES

Two years ago, I worked on a project with an organization called Reading Is Fundamental[14] (RIF). They have one simple mission: to give books to kids who had never had books. RIF found a significant correlation between communities with low literacy and low-income levels, high crime rates, and high welfare payments. By increasing literacy, crime rates fall, incomes and graduation rates rise and the government pays less welfare in the affected areas.

During our kickoff meeting, our team spent a lot of time listening, asking questions and sketching. The photo below is a shot of my notebook sketches from that meeting. I always try to pay attention to important keywords and recurring themes that arise in the conversations. The RIF team repeatedly mentioned particular words and phrases that were important to them. For example, they kept saying "electric" when referring to their brand.

---

13 http://danielmall.com/articles/visual-inventory/
14 http://readingisfundamental.org/

Listening at the first meeting. These keywords will be used later as visual hooks to transform ideas into an actual design element.

They also repeated the words "shape," "book," "heart," and "bubble". They kept saying "visual book lists," "pages themed in books," and "turn the page for step two." Those words alone brought rich imagery and metaphors to my mind.

We weren't scheduled to start the design phase for another couple of weeks; we were going to do some content work first and understand the structure of the site a little bit more. When I got home, however, I couldn't help but hear their words in my head. I opened Photoshop and created an empty canvas. I just wanted to illustrate, to do some sketches of what these concepts could look like.

Obviously, at this point I had no idea what the art direction would be. I didn't know whether the color was right or the typeface appropriate. But it didn't really matter at that point. I just wanted to get a few ideas out of my head and into pixels.

What does "turn the page for step two" look like? Maybe it's a button that flips over like a page turn when you roll over it. That led me to think about what could be displayed on the other side. A color change? Suggested donation amounts?

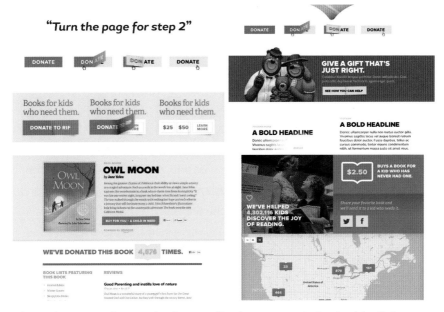

As you design more elements, the element collage becomes more refined and detailed.

   The same goes for "visual book lists": what would that look like? An interface that allowed kids and parents to browse the site visually, and find books they like — what would be a good representation look like? "Pages themed in books"? How could I play on affection and nostalgia for stories like Harry Potter or Goldilocks and the Three Bears and get people to donate or take action based on that?

   I'm no copywriter, but I had a lot of fun writing copy for those elements. One of my favorite parts of designing an element collage is that it gives me a chance to design the things I'm excited about without worrying about the rest. When you create a comp, you might not have an idea for the footer of a site, but you can't just skip it; without the footer, your comp is incomplete. With an element collage, however, you can really just focus on the things you're most passionate about.

   The other nice thing about an element collage is that it gives you the opportunity to show your clients how well you listen. Clients often have ideas that they've been refining in their head for a long time; an element may be your first opportunity to help them visualize it.

One of my favorite parts of every project is helping turn clients' powerful phrases into visual hooks. Clients will tell you what's important to them — sometimes we just don't listen for it. If you listen hard enough, they'll tell you exactly what they want to see.

After I had all the different elements for RIF placed on a Photoshop canvas, I created a new document and placed all these elements down the center as if it was a long scrolling webpage. That page included a variety of elements, from carousel states to typographic explorations, donation ideas, book reviews, and more. Frankly, I didn't know if we were even going to have book reviews on the site at that point, but this visual exploration helped me discover a direction for the site that influenced every phase of the project.

Getting these ideas out of my head led me to helpful conversations that influenced the information architecture. A typical waterfall process for web design tends to start with information architecture leading into graphic design and then development, but a framework that allows every piece to influence the others is an incredibly powerful opportunity. The element collage I did for RIF allowed our team to sort out some information architecture decisions. In a new responsive framework, all of those things can be rearranged to great benefit: you could have IA influencing design, but also design influencing IA. You strike a nice balance, a nice back-and-forth between all the disciplines involved in the design workflow.

When I showed the element collage to the clients they said, "Obviously this isn't a website, but I see how it could be one"—a great client's perfect response to a modern design deliverable. At every stage of the web design process, we ask our clients to imagine the next one. We explain ideas and expect them to imagine what the site will look like. We show wireframes and expect them to imagine what they will look like after we've applied typography, color and layout. We show a layout and expect them to imagine how the rollover states will work. When a client tells you they can easily imagine, you're in a great place. The most successful projects are the ones where we've successfully asked our clients to imagine, and they can. The feedback I've received from clients tells me that it's possible and that this approach is helpful in achieving that.

To approach the complexity of today's web, we need to be strategic in how we craft websites. We need to build scalable, flexible design systems. By deconstructing the design into simpler components and elements, we build a solid foundation for responsive design — but most importantly, we can create this foundation quickly without spending too much time polishing comps.

Showing an element collage to a client instead of a comp might sound like a scary proposition. But the main problem with a comp is that it's a moment in time, one that may never exist for a particular user. When you make a deliverable like an element collage, you're intentionally removing the context of a specific moment in time and instead replacing it with a collection of moments. You're helping your clients understand the overall narrative and asking them to imagine the chapters. Rather than showing them every screen at multiple sizes, you're teaching them how to imagine it on their own. That's a much more valuable offering that you can deliver.

An element collage for TechCrunch, containing type treatments, social media buttons and more.

A useful detail that helps clients understand the idea behind element collages is displaying interaction states, like rollovers or animation states. Since we aren't showing a webpage, those kinds of "visual tricks" are a very good way to make it clear to clients that what they're looking at isn't an actual webpage. This reduces confusion and helps avoid conversations like, "What page of the site is this?"

Once I started using element collages, I began to discover more and more situations and responsive projects where they made sense — and significantly sped up the design workflow. For the next project I worked on, the TechCrunch redesign[15], we also created an element collage. Because TechCrunch is a technology news site, we spent a lot of time exploring typography and type combinations to make sure that the type was beautiful yet also very functional. TechCrunch publishes 80 to 100 articles a day, so we knew that typography and the reading experience were critical.

It wasn't enough to rely on tools like Photoshop, Illustrator or Sketch. We needed to set type in the browser and have access to a huge catalog of typefaces. We used Typecast[16], a tool that increased our access to typefaces we didn't have. I love buying typefaces, but there are only so many I can buy without going broke.

With Typecast we knew that whenever we applied a typeface, the result was literally what it would look like at the final stage. Showing the typeface in the environment where it would be read was a huge benefit. Working within the medium helped us avoid wrong decisions and notice the smallest inconsistencies right away in its native environment. I was able to design some components in Photoshop, set typography online in Typecast, take screenshots and then bring them into Photoshop and work with them there. Going back and forth between browser and Photoshop worked really well.

For TechCrunch, we looked specifically at things like sharing clusters and breaking news elements. Through this process, we were able to refine a typographic hierarchy even before we did anything with the layout of the site. We spent a lot of time on typography, nailing down the nuances of what articles,

---

15 http://danielmall.com/articles/techcrunch-responsive-redesign/
16 https://typecast.com/

headlines, body copy, and all the typographic elements would look like — and eventually putting everything into a growing element collage.

Horizontal Element Collages

More designers and agencies are starting to use element collages these days, including UK design agency Clearleft. In one project, the Clearleft team sent an element collage to a client, only for the client to believe they were looking at a half-finished webpage. To fix this, Jon Aizlewood at Clearleft adopted a wide horizontal canvas instead and increased the size of some elements, "so that the discussion revolves around the overall visual aesthetic, rather than the pixel precision and font sizing of certain components."[17]

This change helped the clients move away from the webpage paradigm towards a clearer canvas view, with a distinct connected system of components that will comprise a page later in the process. This early stage is an exploration of compound units of a design, and it shouldn't be confused with an actual output.

I loved that horizontal approach, so I decided to try it out in my next project. When we worked with *Entertainment Weekly*[18] on the

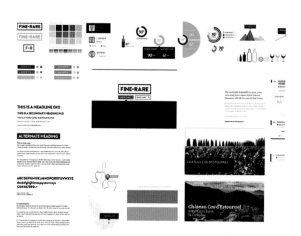

An horizontal of a vertical element collage.

A horizontal element collage for Entertainment Weekly.

17 http://clearleft.com/thinks/visualdesignexplorations/
18 http://www.ew.com/

design of their mobile site[19], we decided to produce a horizontal element collage, which worked well for everyone involved. We had very productive conversations about the elements, and we never once had to explain the purpose or goal of the canvas. First, we had the right conversations with the client, so when we showed them the collage it felt like a natural part of the process — it was pretty much what they expected and didn't cause any confusion. The client had no difficulty understanding those elements as building blocks of an upcoming page. If you want to make it very clear that what you're designing isn't anything close to an actual webpage, horizontal element collages are a great choice.

ON DESIGNING IN THE BROWSER

Not every designer (and not every client) will feel comfortable with designing element collages instead of webpages — at least at first. I spoke with Paul Lloyd, one of the designers at Clearleft at the time, about this process as well. When I talked to him about what he liked about element collages, he said:

> 66 *You know when you're in Photoshop, and right before you send something to a client, you turn off a bunch of the layers, because they're the ones that you don't want them to see? Element collages are like giving your client a peek at all those hidden layers. You're showing them all the different variations of things; you're not just showing them the final thing that you've decided to reveal. You're making them part of the process."*

You might be thinking, "Well, element collages are really good, but why bother with that stuff and design it all in the browser instead?" Well, I've got a couple of qualms about designing in the browser.

When people talk about designing in the browser, they often mean just skipping the design phase entirely and jumping straight into building something. Construction workers need blueprints. CGI artists rely on sketches, previs, and small-scale models.

---

19 http://danielmall.com/articles/responsive-mobile-entertainment-weekly/

Design isn't just theming or skinning components in the browser — it's about honing a concept, and that's difficult to do in the browser. Most importantly, sites designed in the browser often look like no one considered the visual treatment, or the art direction, colors and typography. You can't just color a wireframe and call it "good design".

To be fair, I don't think that's anybody's fault; it's the fault of our tools. We don't have the right tools to allow us to design in the browser in the way that we could. Consider for a minute the way that we code. We open up a code editor and we type. We don't see what we're doing. We save, and we switch to a browser and refresh — and it's always a surprising jack-in-the-box moment.

Sometimes we see something we like, but more often we see something else, perhaps due to a bug, so we go back to the code and revise it and then — Jack-in-the-box again. That's a problem with the way we use our tools; it's a problem with the way we code.

In a presentation called "Inventing on Principle"[20] given in January 2012, Bret Victor talks through a code editor prototype he built that shows changes in realtime. He shows a particular tool that gives him an accidental idea about the functionality and experience of the game he's building. "How would I ever have discovered that [animation idea] if I had to compile and run each and every change? So much of creation is discovery, and you can't discover anything if you can't see what you're doing."

Perhaps rather than designing in the browser, we could be *deciding* in the browser. We often regard Photoshop as the primary tool where all design decisions are finalized, but I think we should treat Photoshop and similar tools as the place where ideas can be *initiated*, and the browser as the place where those ideas can be finessed.

We could think of our tools as lying across a *spectrum*, not simply as a binary choice. The earlier in the process, the more useful an expressive tool like Photoshop; later on, the more useful a production tool like Sublime Text or the web inspector.

---

20 https://vimeo.com/36579366

PROTOTYPING

Here's how I think designing in the browser should really work. I worked on a project with my friend Jamie Kosoy[21], and Jamie has a unique way of writing code. He refers to himself as a developer, but I think he's very much a designer— he just uses code to do it. What I love about working with Jamie is that he's not one of those developers who waits for the design to be done and then just codes what's been delivered in the comp. When we work together, I start my work on day one and he starts his work on day one, too.

How does it work? Jamie has very specific guidelines for sketching in code:

1. **Each prototype must take less than one hour to make.**
   If a prototype takes longer than an hour to create, it's not a prototype anymore — you're building something, and that's not the point of sketching, whether in code or not.

2. **The first prototype should be something that anybody can build.**
   The second prototype gets increasingly more complex, as does the third and the fourth and so on. More on this in a minute.

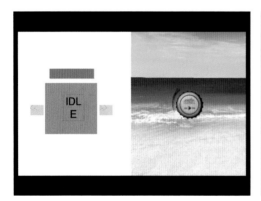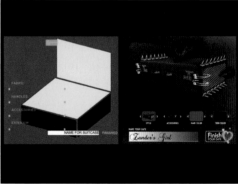

Crude sketching in code.

---

21 https://twitter.com/jkosoy

3. **Build ugly**.

   If you take a look at the screenshot opposite, what you see on the right-hand side is the comp, and what you see on the left-hand side is a fully functioning, ugly prototype.

When most people build prototypes, they end up being so similar to a finished product that it's actually "good enough." No one ever goes back to put the final polish on "good enough." You've got bigger fish to fry, and, hey, it's "good enough" after all.

If you build ugly though, you have to go back. You cannot launch an audio player that's a bunch of lime green boxes and Comic Sans text, even if it's fully functional. You're forced to go back and finish it. That's the value of building ugly.

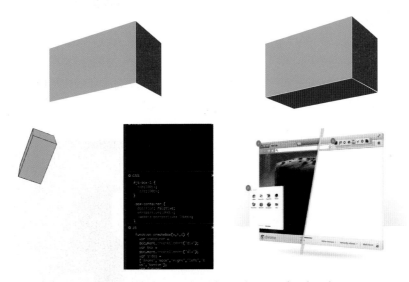

An evolution of a sketch: from a crude early mockup to refined working prototypes.

Two years ago, Jamie and I worked on a project for a big technology company that rhymes with *Moogal* (you probably have never heard of them.) As we do, we brainstormed together before doing anything else and ended up with the idea that you should be able to see the product "from all angles." We didn't specify whether that meant physically or literally.

From there, we both started exploring different options and routes we could take in our own ways. I went off and designed the sketch displayed on the previous page. I didn't have any navigation; I didn't even know if that was the right copy. It was just a starting point. If you look at the image above, on the left you see my sketch and on the right is Jamie's crude prototype.

Jamie started with this sketch. Remember *guideline #2*: something that anyone can do. It was a green `<div>` that had a width and a height. That's prototype number one, and it's finished.

- Once he had this first prototype, Jamie moved on.
- Second prototype: skewing it with CSS transforms. Something that anyone can do, but with a little bit more knowledge.
- Third prototype: adding another face.
- Fourth prototype: adding a third face to create a 3-D box. This is something that most people who write HTML and CSS can do, but it's a little bit more advanced than just putting a `<div>` on the screen. Every single prototype was another step taken, another decision made.

If Jamie ever has to bring another developer into the project and they don't know how to do what Jamie's doing, they can figure it out by tracing the steps in his prototypes. Normally, that's just lost in the Git history. By seeing all the prototypes, you can go through the history and get a better idea of what's happening behind the scenes. Every prototype has a unique URL, so you can go to 001 and 002 and 003 and 004 and see all of the prototypes right there. Each prototype is designed to solve one and only one problem, and once it's solved, Jamie moves on to the next one.

After working this way for a few days or a few weeks, Jamie will have hundreds of prototypes that do one thing and one thing only. Prototype #76 will have solved using the History API. Prototype #25 works out a unique navigation interaction. Prototype #98 is a demo of the animation in the footer. Once you have everything worked out individually, you can start to put them together. Combine prototypes #11 and #52. Combine #29, #41, and #6.

Finally, once you combine enough prototypes, you realize you actually built an entire site. That leads us to our last piece of the framework: assembly.

Assemble

The hard work in building a great, modern responsive site is in figuring out what you want to make. You figure that out through smart planning, exploratory inventorying, and uninhibited sketching. That stuff takes the most mental and physical effort. Then you put it together, which is the easiest and least time-consuming part—if you've done it right.

In cooking, there's a principle called *mis en place*, which translates literally to "putting in place." Ask any good chef, and they'll stress the importance of good prep. You don't start chopping the onions when the chicken's already in the pan. You do all your preparation long before service. You chop your onions and slice your cheese; you put your peas in a bowl and strain your soup. When you're ready to cook the dish, you pick up the ingredient you need, throw it into the pan or sprinkle it on afterwards and the meal is finished — much quicker.

We can apply this principle to the way we think about our work. If we've prepared everything well — the planning, inventorying and sketching — then all we need to do is assemble the pieces.

Libraries in Photoshop allows you to store particular components and then drag them in when you are building a website.

One of the greatest new tools I use is a new Adobe Creative Cloud feature called *Libraries*[22]. It allows you to store and share elements, so you can simply drag them in from a panel when creating a screen.

---

22 http://blogs.adobe.com/jkost/2014/10/the-libraries-panel-in-photoshop-cc.html

When I'm putting together an element collage or a style guide, I design all the pieces — comment threads, headers, footers and so on — and I store them in the library. Then I can just drag them in as I'm designing, say, small-screen comps, and within a matter of seconds I've created a comp. I might have to change an asset here or there, but that's not difficult once I've got all the parts — I can just assemble it. That's a fantastic way to work, because I've spent all the time planning and figuring out the components earlier on; now I just test how they work together. I'm building pages in minutes, as opposed to days or weeks.

Atomic design[23] is an approach to building design systems, rather than a loose set of pages. The design process starts with designing and building components, and as you combine components, you start building parts of the website. At some point you have enough components, so you can start building a page. The page isn't something we start with, but rather a result of what we are building.

If you prefer code, *Pattern Lab* is a great tool that replicates this idea. Front-end designer Brad Frost created it while we were working on the Tech-Crunch and Entertainment Weekly projects together. The main idea behind Pattern Lab is very similar to the process I outlined above, except that it's done in code. You identify the smallest building blocks — *atoms* — and you combine atoms together to form molecules. You combine molecules into organisms, and then templates and, eventually, pages. On the technical side, it can be done with any templating language; for example, a series of `includes` in PHP.

When I worked with Radio Free Europe, our team was surprised how receptive the client was to the entire idea behind atomic design. Throughout the project, we worked through an assembly list at a spreadsheet level, listing all the atoms we were going to have on the site, and combining them into molecules, and then organisms. Instead of talking about comps or pages, we had discussions about each organism, each molecule, within the spreadsheet itself.

---

23 http://bradfrost.com/blog/post/atomic-web-design/

It allowed us to reach actual results way, *way* faster. We did our planning in the knowledge of what we were going to assemble at the end.

Remember "highest fidelity, shortest amount of time"? We asked ourselves what was the deliverable that we could have the conversation about that wouldn't require us to spend two or three or eight weeks working on. We listed all the patterns and atoms and molecules and organisms, and we wrote a little explanation for each, explaining what it did and how it was helpful.

Then, for every molecule, we wrote down the atoms required, and all the atoms and molecules required within each organism; this established the relationship between the different components of the site — the very nature of a bulletproof design system.

We started to map the site this way. Although not right for every client, Radio Free Europe was a great client to have this conversation with. This framework gives us the ability to have discussions about elements before we get into Pattern Lab before we have to revise code, even before we start coding.

We just had a couple of slides with comments, where the client started to annotate the spreadsheet and ask questions like "Do we need

Atomic design principles for Radio Free Europe with PatternLab in place, discussed using basic spreadsheets.

this organism? Isn't this organism the same as that one? What about these molecules: could we integrate them here?"

The critical point here is that we started having this discussion about development *before* starting development, which significantly sped up the entire workflow. For us, doing a very quick two-hour inventory rather than taking a day to set up Pattern Lab, allowed us to have a conversation that would profoundly influence our work a lot sooner. It was an incredibly robust and quick process, and it saved us a lot of time and a lot of headaches.

Our assembling tools, then, include Creative Cloud libraries and Pattern Lab, mechanisms to help us bring together elements under the *mise en place* concept. Each element should be in its place so that when the time comes to serve it, all we need to do is put them properly together, spice them up a little bit and assemble them in the way that works best for the clients and their users.

A Workflow Before and After

It's been a long journey, but let's take a closer look at the design process before and after. Before, our output as designers was just comps — that's pretty much all we were responsible for. With responsive design and mobile, designing comps is becoming far too slow and time-consuming. But if you take out the only thing we had, what else do we do?

The evolution I've outlined provides great opportunities. If you look at the deliverables that we might create, like manifestos, libraries and visual inventories, you can see that they greatly expand our output and get us thinking more holistically about how we can build websites better, and be more useful to our co-workers and our clients.

All our previous tools were layout tools. But if we start combining tools like Typecast, Notational Velocity, Illustrator, HTML5, and Excel, we can find a different way to create more value for our clients and co-workers.

You don't have to be a master of all of these things. If you're a designer, you don't have to become an information architect or a developer. But appreciation and understanding of what other people do and the tools they use can certainly make you better at your work.

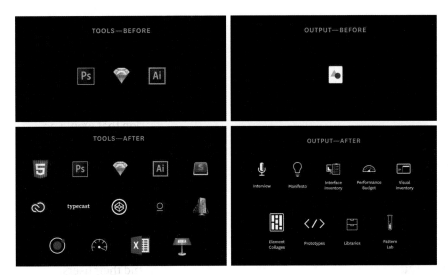

Not only our tools, but also the output of our creative work has changed. Our workflow and our design process have to adapt, too.

Michael Jackson was considered the king of pop, but he didn't play any instrument. Yet he's still considered one of the greatest musicians out there because he *understood* all those instruments intrinsically. There's a great demo clip of Michael Jackson writing the arrangement for *Beat It*.[24] He sings every part: the lead vocal, background vocals, bass line, and minor percussion.

What's so striking is that it's not perfect; it's a sketch of a song. There are times he goes flat when he hits the tonic, but it doesn't matter. He's demonstrating *empathy*. He understands what every contributor to the song is doing, what they need to do, and how he can make them better.

I'm not suggesting that we need to reinvent our roles. What I'm talking about is a natural evolution for a designer. We live in a very different world than we did only a decade ago. People access the Internet from devices that fit in the palms of their hands all the way to giant billboards in Times Square and everything in between.

My challenge to you: expand your tools and expand your output. Now you know what to make.

24   http://smashed.by/beat-it

ABOUT THE AUTHOR

Dan Mall is a creative director and advisor from Philadelphia. He coaches agencies and design teams to help whip them into shape. Dan is the founder of *SuperFriendly*, a design collaborative that brings exquisite creative direction and design to the world's most interesting and important organizations. Prior to opening SuperFriendly, Dan was Design Director at Big Spaceship and Interactive Director at Happy Cog. He co-founded Typedia (an encyclopedia for typefaces) and Businessology (a podcast and workshop series teaching designers how to run better businesses). Dan is enthralled with his wife and two daughters. He writes irregularly at danielmall.com and tweets often as @danielmall. *Image credit: Mark Likosky*

RESPONSIVE DESIGN PATTERNS AND COMPONENTS

VITALY FRIEDMAN

CHAPTER TWO · BY VITALY FRIEDMAN

RESPONSIVE DESIGN
PATTERNS AND COMPONENTS

W E'VE ALL BEEN THERE: RESPONSIVE DESIGN IS MANAGEABLE, but it isn't straightforward; its premise shines through once it's designed and built, but throughout the process it poses hidden challenges and stumbling blocks. Consequently, the workflow often feels remarkably slow and painful. In fact, responsive design prompts us to reshape our mindset and refine our practices, but also to explore new interaction patterns across a wide variety of screens, input modes and connection types. However, we don't have to reinvent the wheel every single time we stumble on a design problem. That's what good ol' *design patterns* — essentially common techniques for tackling common issues — are pretty useful for.

Yet just as design patterns can be helpful and convenient, they can also be misleading, driving us to generic and soulless designs, mostly because we often lack context when applying them. More often than not, we don't know the rationale or the objectives, the failures, usability tests, the impact on conversion rates and all the decisions made along the way, so we have to make our decisions merely trusting other decisions in other, possibly unrelated contexts.

Now, obviously, every project is different. Every project poses unique challenges, with different audiences, goals, requirements, constraints and objectives. So it shouldn't be surprising that sometimes applying design patterns directly will work just fine, while other times it will fail miserably when validated in the face of reality. That's a risky undertaking indeed; with design patterns thorough testing isn't just important, but crucial for getting things right.

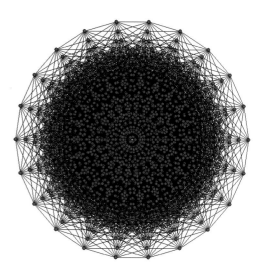

When crafting responsive experiences, we have to consider a number of dimensions at once: not only design constraints such as typography, navigation or performance, but also strategic decisions such as hostile browsers, narrow screens, touch input or maintenance. To tackle this complexity, we have to shift our focus towards designing resilient and reliable design systems.

We've all learned from our own experiences that responsive design isn't just a set of media queries used to patch broken layouts. It's much more difficult than that: in our work we see it as a complex multi-dimensional graph with dimensions ranging from typography to performance. As designers, we have to put just the right dots at just the right spots across these dimensions to ensure that we create a scalable and maintainable multi-device system. Usually it's not simple nor straightforward.

In fact, while design is often seen as a continuous process, going from start to finish in a series of smooth, successive iterations, I find that more often it's a meticulous series of sprints — finding solutions, refining them in iterations, hitting dead ends, and starting over again and again — until you find a solution that works well within the context of a design, which eventually brings you to your next design problem. The main issue is that those dead ends are really expensive. This is when you lose most time, and when recovery can be very difficult and frustrating. Design patterns help you recover from hitting these dead ends; they can reroute your decision-making process efficiently. They can also allow room for creativity as long as you don't follow them blindly.

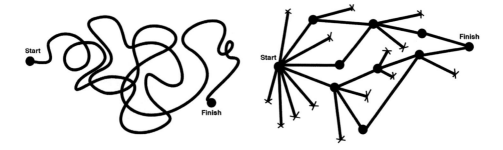

Design process is tricky and unpredictable. It's not a continuous process with successive iterations, but rather hitting and overcoming dead ends over and over again. Image credit: Julie Zhuo.[1]

Over the last few years, I've been spending quite some time in small and large companies, solving responsive design problems, primarily related to UX and front-end performance. I've seen a number of design solutions emerging, evolving and flourishing, and others getting shot down in merciless user interviews or performance audits. I rarely found unique and obscure solutions suddenly coming out of thin air, though; more often they were built on top of already existing (and seemingly established) design patterns, supported and informed by trial and error, and fine-tuned by permanent, ongoing design iterations. Ideas don't come out of nowhere, they are built on top of others; I believe this holds true for design patterns as well.

What does this mean for a design process? Well, I'd argue that it's perfectly fine to choose design patterns wisely and build your own on top of them. When coming into a company to work on a project, our team can't afford losing time because we have just a week or two to produce meaningful results, mostly functional prototypes. We can't spend too much time on high fidelity mock-ups or on complex custom cross-browser components which might take weeks of development. To stay efficient, we can't spend a lot of time on high fidelity in the prototyping stage. In most cases, we have to be pragmatic, efficient and selective; to achieve that, we explore design patterns and test them against reality with actual users — early, quickly and often. Rinse, iterate, repeat.

---

1   https://medium.com/the-year-of-the-looking-glass/junior-designers-vs-senior-designers-fbe483d3b51e

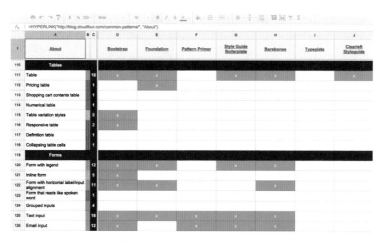

A reference spreadsheet containing components and popular frameworks or pattern libraries in a handy overview.

During prototyping, we often use CloudFour's elements spreadsheet[2] that lists a number of components against frameworks and large pattern libraries. If we need a very specific component, we might find it in there and build a prototype very quickly. It doesn't mean that this is just the right solution for our problem, though, and it doesn't mean that we are going to use this piece of code in production either. But for prototyping, it can be extremely useful.

In these situations, patterns (among other things) prove to be extremely handy time-savers — again, not because they always work everywhere but because they give you a sturdy foundation, and as you keep working on the design they often help you converge toward the final solution much quicker than if you started from scratch. Of course, sometimes you have to start from scratch after all, but knowing solutions that worked (or failed) in real-life projects helps you better shape and guide your decision-making, and limits your options, which I find extremely powerful and liberating in the design process.

---

2 http://smashed.by/elements

That's exactly what this chapter is about: clever design solutions, obscure techniques and smart strategies that I've seen working or failing in actual projects, and which could be applied to your projects, too. You might not be able to use all of them, but hopefully you'll get a good enough idea of just what kinds of solution might work well in common situations when designing or building responsive websites. Let's start. Fasten your seat belts. It's going to be quite a journey.

Navigation Patterns

Surprisingly, making navigation work well across a large variety of devices often proves to be one of the most challenging and involved undertakings in responsive design. And it's often not just a matter of organizing all existing content but rather reducing existing complexity and setting priorities well.

PRIORITY LISTS FOR CONTENT AND FUNCTIONALITY

Priorities are often tough to agree on, though. While asking clients what is and is not important rarely yields meaningful results, listing important pages in a spreadsheet and asking clients to assign priorities to them often does the trick. As one of the first steps in the content audit, we prompt the client to assess and state priorities by marking pages (or features) which are of primary, secondary or tertiary importance. This classification helps group items accordingly and shifts the focus of the experience toward more crucial tasks or content, or at least prioritizes them in the navigation later.

You can actually suggest priorities ("user" view) in a spreadsheet as well, and if they aren't quite right you will surely be corrected by the client. The client's assessment is likely to reflect business objectives ("client" view) which then have to be weighed up and balanced with the user needs you indicated. Even if you don't get a clear overview of what content or features matter most this way, you still introduce the notion of priorities into the conversation which can be helpful to drive the design process in the right direction — towards focused multiscreen experiences, with the focus on content and how it's organized, of course.

THE CONTENT IS FOR EVERYONE: CONTENT PARITY

Having clear priorities is useful, but it doesn't justify removing or dismissing any piece of content or functionality altogether for any screen — just because users expect everything to be available everywhere. That's why, over the years, *content parity* has become an established paradigm for delivering content to users. Obviously, content parity doesn't mean that every experience is going to be identical for every user (it can't be), but all pieces of content should always remain available, whatever settings and input modes the user uses.[3]

In other words, you don't have to show all content or navigation options at once, but they should remain *accessible* on every device, perhaps appearing on a tap in an accordion or via click-through in the navigation drawer.

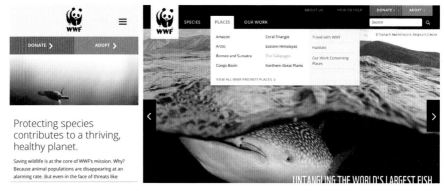

In a narrow view, WWF reduces the entire navigation to three critical items: two calls to action and a navigation icon, leading to primary navigation.

WorldWildLife.org is a good example for this pattern: in a large view, we see a series of drop-downs (actually, every single navigation item is a drop-down), which get reduced to two main call-to-action buttons and a navigation icon (the infamous hamburger icon) in smaller views. Once you click or tap on the navigation icon in a smaller view, you don't see all the navigation levels at once, but only primary navigation items. These links take you to a page containing further navigation options, unlike the links in a drop-down or multilevel accordion, which are all presented at once. In fact, sometimes you don't need to show all

---

3   http://www.lukew.com/ff/entry.asp?1684 and Scott Jehl in "Responsive and Responsible."

options at once; for mobile, prioritization is both crucial and necessary to avoid a cluttered and inefficient interface.

A multilevel accordion could be a useful solution in some contexts, but it's worth testing to see if your visitors actually access a fifth-level navigation item via an accordion or just use search instead. Obviously, it depends on the task, too, but polluting HTML with five levels of navigation or sending AJAX requests to fetch more navigation might be unnecessary.

In some situations, it might be worth deviating from this principle by showing context-sensitive content, based on assumptions derived from screen width, touch support and geolocation. For example, if you provide online banking and your application isn't responsive just yet, you might want to show a link to the mobile banking login, as well as opening hours and the closest branch nearby, like KiwiBank[4] does. The information should be available in the other views as well, but it could be presented differently.

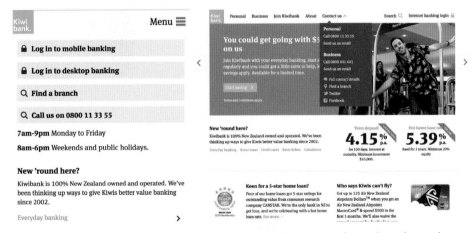

On KiwiBank, all content is consistently available everywhere, but priorities change depending on the viewport. That's a risky undertaking, but it could be worth testing at times.

---

4   http://www.kiwibank.co.nz/

A restaurant could show directions, distance from your current geographical position and expected arrival time, as well as reservation options taking that timing into account — e.g. on tap, in an accordion. Obviously you could argue that these pieces of content would be equally important for desktop experiences, too, but perhaps you'd need to display them differently. Priorities matter: and thinking about them up front can often go quite a long way to help establish a consistent, good user experience.

FANCY HAMBURGERS, OBSCURE CANVASES AND SNEAKY WORDINGS

When it comes to priorities, actual content always deserves special attention. Since the focus of the user experience should always lie on content, everything else has to get out of the way, and this holds true for navigation, too. That's where the infamous off-canvas pattern with the at least equally infamous hamburger icon comes into play.

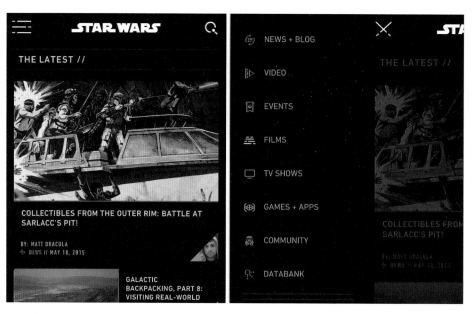

StarWars.com probably has the most unusual "hamburger" navigation, with three horizontal lines turning into lightsaber on click — and a navigation drawer sliding in from the left side.

You know how it works: in a narrow view, users might see a few main navigation options (such as Search, Cart or Menu buttons), but they don't see all available navigation options right away. These options are revealed via a navigation drawer on click or tap on Menu, sliding in from the left, the right, the top or sometimes sliding in between the logo and the main content area. What sounds like a pretty much established and widely accepted paradigm doesn't necessarily work flawlessly in every context. We noticed that navigation items hidden behind an icon almost certainly result in a (much) lower engagement ratio when compared with links displayed on the page — and consequently produce fewer clicks. Besides, if critical items of your interface (such as a shopping cart or login) are hidden off-canvas, users can get impatient and frustrated. Such navigation items would be better off displayed on the page, perhaps with a noticeable icon, in a tab, as a button or as a simple link.

It's not just about engagement, though. We've also noticed that when using the off-canvas pattern we always ended up with an uncomfortable viewport range between the standalone hamburger icon on very narrow views and a fully fledged navigation menu on larger views. The problem: when exactly do you start *displaying* full navigation? Or, the other way around, when exactly do you start *hiding* full navigation behind an icon? And what exactly should happen on screens which are neither narrow nor particularly wide? Well, usually it's dismissed as an edge case, so navigation items are displayed only if they fit entirely on one line, although we might have enough space to show something usable. That's suboptimal at best.

And then, of course, the issue of internationalization comes along: what if, on top of the existing uncomfortable viewport range, you need to accommodate navigation for a dozen languages? To keep your codebase maintainable in the long term, you can't keep creating media queries based on every supported language (e.g. by adding classes on the <body> element); you'd have to create a mess of additional classes, or even style sheets that would need to be revisited once the navigation changes dramatically.

You could use a little JavaScript snippet to measure dynamically how much space you have and either turn a search box into a search icon, or turn navigation items into a menu icon when there is no space left for the container to be fully displayed within the current viewport width. Libraries like makeFit[5] do just that by observing the `resize` event and adjusting the layout accordingly. We tend to use JavaScript as a method of last resort though.

The uncomfortable range. All navigation items could potentially be displayed on narrow views, but instead, they are hiding behind the infamous icon.

Of course, you could solve some of these issues with iconography, but icons aren't always universally understood and often it's just not an option: what icon would you choose to display "Our philosophy" or "Delivery times"? Not surprising, then, that in many scenarios the off-canvas pattern seems like the simplest and safest strategy to keep navigation options out of the way, yet still accessible and unobtrusive, so the navigation won't break or pollute an existing layout, independent of the languages you choose to support in the future.

Another thing we noticed is that, when implemented without a thorough content inventory, the off-canvas drawer might end up containing many unnecessary secondary items and many nested levels of navigation. Sometimes it's

5   https://github.com/aaronbarker/makefit

required and expected, but more often it isn't. Therefore, when we start working on a project, we always look into options of focusing on primary navigation alone. If search is provided, we explore what happens if we remove secondary navigation altogether, both on desktop and on mobile, and how user experience deteriorates as a result. If the result is suboptimal, we add one level of navigation and measure again. If we still notice a UX problem, we keep repeating the process. And if there is *a lot* of content to organize, sometimes we look into providing something like a step-by-step guide from general to specific navigation items, very much like the GOV.UK homepage. When required, different nested levels in mega drop-downs could be accommodated via accordions, although they might not be absolutely necessary if search provides autocomplete or uses the type-ahead pattern.

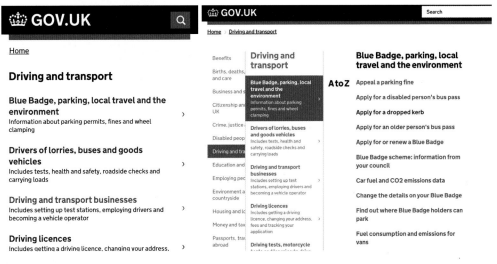

On gov.uk, different levels of navigation are displayed as layers, so all sections are available right away, with one click.

So what are we going to do with these hamburgers and canvases? Off-canvas is a good option, but it's not a golden bullet. In fact, there are other ways to keep navigation out of the way yet still accessible and user-friendly; meet the first one, the shiny Priority+ pattern.

SHOW WHEN YOU CAN AND HIDE WHEN YOU CAN'T

With the *Priority+ pattern*, instead of hiding important navigation items in smaller views, we use all available space to show as many items as possible, prioritized from left to right in LTR interfaces, and from right to left in RTL interfaces. At the end of the navigation list, you then provide an interface element to toggle the view of all navigation options, via accordion, an expandable area, or a discrete modal window. Obviously, the "More" link or full navigation icon would need to be aligned right in LTR interfaces and left in RTL interfaces. As Brad Frost rightfully states[6],

> 66 *This ability to scan these labels left-to-right and feed right into the overflow 'more' link feels like a more natural discovery flow compared to everything hiding beneath an ambiguous icon."*

You could even go as far as displaying navigation options next to the logo, not using any additional vertical space for navigation at all. In that case, making your logo responsive — delivering different logo variants to different views — would be helpful as well, either via an SVG sprite or media queries *within* SVG to adjust some elements in the design. Obviously, it depends on the complexity of the logo, but using responsive iconography to save precious vertical space on the screen for content could be worth considering for icons with a high level of detail.

The Guardian and Google Docs are good examples of the pattern in action. In every view, users see *something*: a few navigation items which hopefully are sorted according to their usage and priority. Because you prioritize important items, critical actions will always be reachable and visible, potentially driving more direct traffic to those important sections or features of the site. This could be particularly useful for cases with a large amount of heavily used navigation sections, such as an online shop which accommodates a mega drop-down in large views.

6   http://bradfrost.com/blog/post/revisiting-the-priority-pattern/

The Guardian shows as many items as possible in a horizontal bar, prioritized based on what's most popular, and the rest is accessible in the "all" menu.

However, it's not always clear what navigation icon to choose for a given scenario. In a few projects targeting elderly users, we found that the hamburger icon wasn't widely understood and sometimes led to confusion. You could argue that it's just a matter of time until the hamburger icon becomes accepted, but it's a safe bet to avoid any iconography altogether and use a clear label ("Menu") with a clear affordance as a button just like Luke Wroblewski recommends[7].

Historically, we used to place the icon in the upper corners of the screen, but larger screens made it difficult (if not impossible) to reach those interface controls with a thumb alone, which is a preferred mode of use by a large majority of users; it might be a good idea to place them as tabs at the bottom of the screen instead, or as a floating navigation icon in the bottom-right corner.

The transparency of the icon could increase as the user keeps scrolling down the page, making it noticeable but unobtrusive, and still providing options on tap. Obviously, you wouldn't want to embark on a hideous journey of `position:fixed` bug fixing, but there are some workarounds, e.g. `position:sticky` polyfill[8].

7   https://twitter.com/lukew/status/443440251042676737
8   https://github.com/filamentgroup/fixed-sticky

If we do use the off-canvas pattern, we always tend to cover *three critical use cases*. First, when users tap on an icon or button to open the navigation drawer, they shouldn't have to move their mouse or finger to close it again; the interface should display the button to close the navigation in exactly the same spot where it initially displayed the menu button. We found out that just as visitors use navigation to jump to the specific content they need, sometimes they want to explore available options without jumping deep into specific areas of the site.

If you have a lot of navigation, as Al Jazeera does, off-canvas is often a bulletproof solution. For less navigation, something as simple as content sliding in might be a better option, as shown on IsraelHayom.co.il.

Second, we tend to bring in a more detailed navigation drawer sliding from the left or right, while we slide more focused or shorter navigation between the logo and the content.

Third, we tend to maximize the amount of content displayed on the screen, so we remove as much secondary content as possible including navigation, logo and any supplemental items. The content deserves room to breathe and the closer we can get to *all* of the space being reserved for content, the better the experience will be. It often means that the logo gets smaller in narrow viewports and the navigation button either disappears or floats with scrolling, while fixed headers, footers or pop-ups are avoided at all costs. Medium[9], for example,

---

9   https://medium.com/

removes the entire navigation when a user starts to scroll down and reveals it again once a user scrolls back up. This technique might work for overviews of products as well as long reads, although we've never had a chance to test it in an actual project.

YOUR CONTENT SHOULD LIVE IN A PERFECT RECTANGLE

We spend a lot of time adding horizontal media queries to adjust layouts, but I'd argue that in many cases vertical media queries would be well suited for any layout adjustments as well. Since users prefer to use mobile devices in portrait mode (90%) and their screen height is usually smaller than a desktop's screen height,[10] you could take into account the viewport area and try to ensure that users always see *enough* content, so the font size would depend on both width *and* height. In fact, you could easily automate the font size adjustment by embedding vh and vw units in your size calculation; for instance, `article { font-size: calc(2em + 0.7vw - 0.3vh); }` could work well for a single-column layout, but might break a multicolumn layout, so choose a value for vw and vh units with caution.

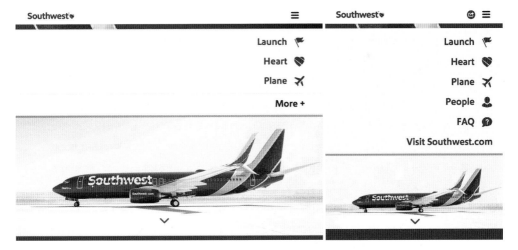

If you have many navigation options, you could use vertical media queries to show fewer items if there isn't enough space to show them all.

---

10   http://www.uxmatters.com/mt/archives/2013/02/how-do-users-really-hold-mobile-devices.php

A good example for vertical media queries would be a layout in which open navigation options cover a significant portion of the content. In such cases, you could reduce the number of displayed items (again, very much like the Priority+ pattern suggests, vertically) and add a toggle to switch to the remaining items if there isn't enough vertical space to show them all at once (see Southwest Airlines example above). Another use case would be a vertical full-height navigation where you might want to adjust the blocks of content to fit the entire content on the screen. Also, paddings, margins, font sizes and icons could be adjusted to tame the content within the screen. If you have a drop-down which appears in the middle of the page, you could review the amount of space available in the browser window under the drop-down, and potentially display navigation options above the drop-down when there isn't enough space beneath it.

You could also detect device orientation and adjust interface controls to better match more comfortable hit areas, pulling them to the left and right in the landscape view, and to the bottom of the screen in the portrait mode. This way, interacting with the UI might be a bit more convenient.

You could even go so far as transforming a content-heavy page, which could feel almost endless on a narrow screen, into an accordion-like table of contents with progressive disclosure, so that users can toggle sections of the page and jump quickly to the content they care about, very much like Wikipedia's[11] pages do.

In fact, in a large variety of scenarios, exactly this pattern — *progressive disclosure with a toggle or accordion* — proves to be a remarkably useful technique to tackle most content-related issues. If you have to break down the complexity of an interface component into something more manageable, or just simplify a seemingly crowded article page, you'll be able to achieve good results quickly, as long as you group content logically and consistently. Whenever you don't know what to do next, think of progressive disclosure as a workhorse at your disposal — it will do the trick more often than you think.

---

11   http://www.wikipedia.org/

BREAKING DOWN THE WALLS WITH ENCAPSULATED VIEWS

Breaking down complexity is probably the most common undertaking when implementing responsive navigation, yet the main mistake we often make is showing all options at once on all screens, basically carrying over a vast amount of navigation overhead from the desktop to mobile experiences (or from mobile to desktop experiences when building mobile first). The problem becomes apparent when the navigation isn't compact and straightforward.

What happens if you are running an e-commerce site with a number of filters for selecting size, color and shape, and you want your users to be able to quickly switch to categories and perhaps compare products? Furthermore, to avoid unnecessary interactions, you'd like to update content automatically in the background when a user selects a filter, without them having to click on the "Submit" button every now and again. If you choose to show all filters at once, users might not see any content at all, so it will be loading in the background but users will have to scroll all the way down to see the content. You could reveal the filters by tapping on an icon in the uper-right corner, but once users have selected a filter and scrolled down to see the content, they will have to scroll back up again to adjust the filters. Both scenarios aren't particularly user-friendly. So, what do you do?

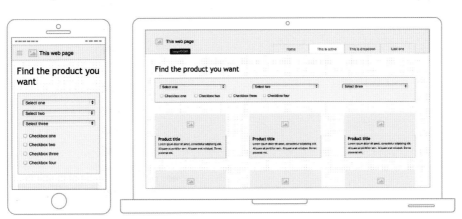

A wireframe of an e-commerce page with a few filters. In a narrow view, users would see exactly zero content, even with selected filters. Image credit: Daniel Wiklund, https://medium.com/@danielwi/view-mode-approach-to-responsive-web-design-914c7d3795fb

The simplest strategy would be to break down the single, large filters section into multiple detached, smaller sections. We then could show them at the bottom of the screen as three to four separate tabs instead of just one large block in the header of the page. Each of the tabs would need to have a clear label (e.g. "Color", "Size", "Price range"), and once tapped or clicked, reveal appropriate filters. Another option would be to have the filters float on the side as users explore the products they have filtered. A slightly more interesting option would be to hide the filters behind an icon in the upper-right corner and display them on tap or click as a persistent layer. This layer would cover a part of the screen (on narrow views, obviously, the less screen it covers, the better), while the content would appear in a semitransparent layer *beneath* the filters layer. So if users have relatively wide screens, they'll see both the filters and the content.

That's also the reason why the layer is persistent: if users choose to close the filters section, they must have made up their minds, so (almost) the entire screen will be dedicated to the content and not filters; otherwise they might need to repeatedly open and close the filter drawer.

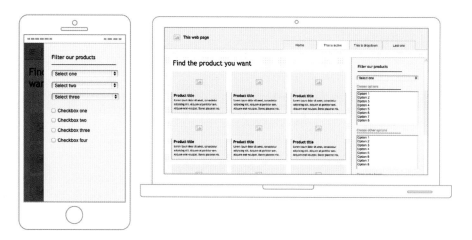

With encapsulated views, we can show both the content and the navigation — as far as possible. In narrow views, we could use a persistent layer covering a part of the screen on the right, and on larger views, the filters could appear on the right side as well, for consistency. Image credit: Daniel Wiklund, https://medium.com/@danielwi/view-mode-approach-to-responsive-web-design-914c7d3795fb

This pattern is called the *view mode* pattern because the features and content of a website are divided into individual, encapsulated views (or cards, or layers) and connected within your interface. This way, you can recoup space even in smaller viewports while gaining the ability to update and process user input (which would need to happen asynchronously, causing a bit of performance overhead). This resembles the off-canvas pattern but could be used for more than just displaying naviga-

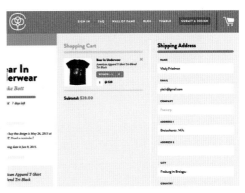

On CottonBureau.com, the checkout experience is designed with the "view mode" pattern in mind. Each step in the checkout is sliding off-canvas from the right, showing both the content and the checkout as far as the space allows for it.

tion. For instance, you could provide autocomplete search functionality in this way, or even design your entire checkout with each step sliding in from the side, showing the actual product being purchased during the entire checkout.

The pattern can be remarkably helpful for complex components, and it could be further improved by allowing users to easily switch between multiple layers by just tapping on them. This technique is used by the Danish Cancer Society[12] to enable users to both browse through the different levels of navigation (on the

---

12 http://www.cancer.dk

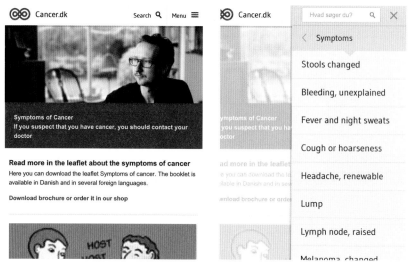

View mode pattern used on Cancer.dk to reveal navigation options *while* showing content on the left side. When users browse through navigation options, the content area is updated automatically.

right) and see the content of the selected section (on the left) at the same time. In fact, the pattern passed usability studies with flying colors, and it's still being used now almost a year later.

THE ALMIGHTY FOLD AND NASTY CAROUSELS

Almost every single meeting I find myself sitting in involves an uncomfortable, toxic ingredient with a lingering and irritating bitter aftertaste. Yes, somebody sparks an endlessly painful conversation about the almighty fold, or more specifically, important interface elements that should stay above the fold. These conversations are remarkably misleading and counter-productive, and usually lack any user research data to prove... well, pretty much anything. When somebody raises a question about the fold and call-to-action buttons, it's usually a warning sign that things are about to go south. Whenever it happens, (rather than freaking out and leaving the room) you could question the validity of their arguments and request actual data.

As it happens, quite often above the fold isn't as important as below the fold. As Luke Wroblewski stated in one of his talks, "The hardest thing on mobile is figuring out the right time and place to display an action" ("Conversions@ Google 2014")[13] — displaying a call-to-action button very early at the top of the page is often neither the right time nor place to encourage that action.

Crazy Egg's[14] recent redesign showed that short, concise landing pages don't necessarily result in higher conversion rates when compared with longer pages. In the redesign, the challenger design was 20 times longer than the control but caused a 30% increase in conversion[15], simply because the design team added testimonials and feature highlights that made a convincing argument at the right time and the right place. Again, to quote Luke from the same talk, *"the issue wasn't whether the call to action was visible, but rather whether the call to action was visible at the point when someone has become convinced to take action."*

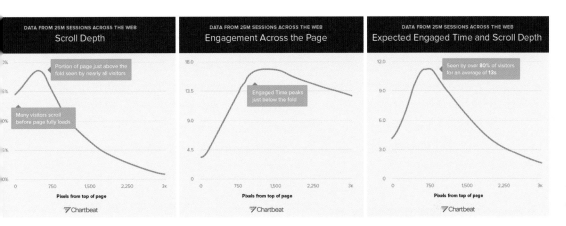

Perhaps "above the fold" isn't the most lucrative area anymore — just above and just below the fold are.

But how do you identify this point? Well, you rely on research. According to a recent Chartbeat study, *"Scroll behavior across the web[16]"* by Josh Schwartz, the very first thing many people do when they encounter a website is scroll down. This is primarily because they can often find the logo, navigation, search field and ads at the very top of the page, occasionally accompanied by a window encouraging

13 "Conversions@Google 2014", Luke Wroblewski, https://youtu.be/Y-FMTPsgy_Y

14 http://www.crazyegg.com

15 http://www.conversion-rate-experts.com/crazy-egg-case-study/

16 http://blog.chartbeat.com/2013/08/12/scroll-behavior-across-the-web/

users to download an app — often there is just no useful content at the top of the page. In fact, some users start to scroll down a page before it finishes loading.

The most viewed area of the page is just above the fold, at about 550px, with just over 80% viewership. The area between 750px and 1,500px is viewed nearly three times as long as the top portion of the page, with the peak at 750px seen by over 80% of visitors for an average of 13 seconds. This is where most people spend most of their time and where a call-to-action button would be best placed, provided that the work of convincing the user has already been done.

Another myth surrounding many conversations in the war room (also called "the meeting room") are the benefits of carousels. Clients love them, but the verdict of the design community is pretty clear: carousels don't convert. The images aren't seen nearly as often as they should be, not to mention performance issues; hence, they should be avoided at all costs.

To be honest, it's not surprising most carousels aren't efficient — all too often they are poorly designed. They are nothing more than an oversized image, with a few hardly noticeable dots (supposed progress indicators) and, if you are lucky, arrows on the side; or, if you are unlucky, automatically rotated images. However, carousels rarely give users any incentive to navigate to the next item, and once they choose to do so, the controls prove to be very difficult to use.

Carousels aren't necessarily dead. Poorly designed carousels are highly inefficient. Well-designed carousels could be efficient: there must be a clear incentive for users to flip it through. Belavia.by and Amazon.de in comparison.

Carousels can be designed better, though. Recently, Amazon adjusted its carousels by adding a vertical bar on the right-hand side to better highlight all items within the carousel using small thumbnails of the products and a descriptive caption of the offers, in effect creating a tabbed widget that is easy to tap and click. Still, the images in the carousel rotate automatically, but the experience isn't obtrusive at all, providing helpful hints for valuable deals that users might indeed find helpful, without obscure dots or navigation arrows. When users click on one of the thumbnails, they know what to expect and they have a good reason to engage with the carousel. Amazon didn't share any numbers publicly, but after initial testing it has been rolling out the new design on every category page, so the results are likely not to be disappointing.

OPTIMIZING FOR LARGER SCREENS

Looking back at the last few years, most of the projects we spent a lot of time on turned out to be redesigns; designing and building a responsive website often boils down to somehow adapting the desktop experience to the mobile space. Consequently, if a component *can* be resized and squeezed into a narrow viewport then it's usually the first option that is considered. However, mobile often requires an entirely different approach; optimizing for narrow views is a matter not just of scaling down, but also rethinking the user interaction and coming up with an entirely different, better suited interface pattern for that interaction.

And just as we have to rethink for narrow views, we have to rethink for larger screens as well. Quite often responsive websites appear to be designed with a maximal screen width in mind, so while they work well from views up to approximately 1,750px, the design feels lost on larger screens, with content stuck either in the middle of the viewport or aligned to one side of the screen.

If you have a robust visual design, you could enlarge the width of the container and increase the font size of its elements for larger views while adjusting the background image or background color of the site. This way, you create an illusion of filled space, like the Institut Choiseul[17] does.

17   http://choiseul.info/

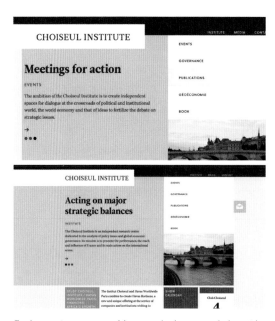

For larger views, you could center the layout and play with the background color to create an illusion of filled space.

If you don't have a strong visual design in place, you could either display different pieces of content separately and prominently in multiple columns, perhaps as overlaying content areas; or shift one of the content areas to the left or to the right. An interesting example for that would be a search page; when users with large viewports click on one of the items in your search, the content could appear on the right with the search results still present on the left, and on narrow screens only the requested page could be displayed. That's what the Kremlin website[18] does, always accommodating the available space intelligently.

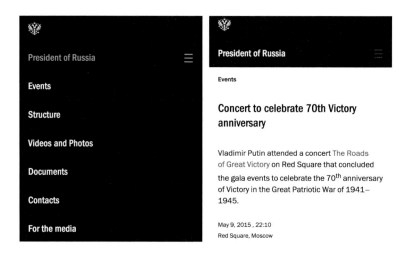

On narrow viewports, the Kremlin site shows either the content *or* the navigation.

---

18 http://kremlin.ru/

If there is enough screen to fit multiple pieces of content at the same time (e.g. both the search results page and the actual search result), you could show both at the same time.

This pattern could be applied in other scenarios as well; for example, if you have a gallery in your article or product page, in larger views the images could float to the right, next to the article; or slide into designated areas in narrow views. The same goes for comments, surveys, and any other supporting content.

TABLES ARE TOO USEFUL TO DIE

There are a few well-established navigation patterns that could be tweaked for specific contexts, but what about more rigid interface components, such as tables? While navigation menus are often merely lists of anchors, pieces of content residing within tables often have firm relationships, manifested by their position and their column and row headings. When it comes to displaying tables, we should not only present the content but also respect these relationships. This causes a few headaches when designing for narrow views simply because tabular data requires some space to be fully displayed.

If we display a table as it comes, the content will likely be hard to scan and read; tables are regularly rendered either too small for comfortable reading, or too large for comfortable navigation. What do we do, then? The few reliable options we have depend on changing the orientation of the table from horizontal to vertical, or displaying tabular data and relationships in fragments.

The first option isn't difficult to achieve: we could either flip the headings to the left or right, or just turn all table cells into block elements and show them in a single column with corresponding table headings serving as labels. This works

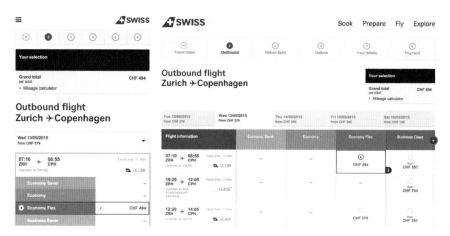

SwissAir.ch provides many interesting subtle examples of a smart responsive design. One of them is a flight selection table, changing orientation from horizontal to vertical between large and narrow views.

well for small tables, but becomes unwieldy for more complex tables, creating long, potentially annoying pages which are difficult to scan. We already know what works well in most scenarios, though: accordions! To keep the `<datalist>` shorter and more compact, you could turn single blocks of content into a series of accordions and reveal content on tap or on click.

Certain tables call for specific and sometimes creative solutions. For instance, if you're designing a table to allow users to select a flight, with outgoing flight options lined up horizontally, and return flight options lined up vertically, you might end up with a table in which every cell contains a radio button. While

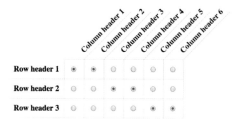

Sometimes you might want to tilt headings a little bit to regain horizontal space by sacrificing some vertical space. It really depends on the nature of the table. Credit: http://codepen.io/anon/pen/WbzbbQ

radio buttons often require a very predictable amount of space to be clickable or tappable, headings in such scenarios would usually occupy more horizontal space, making the table unnecessarily wide. In this case, you could tilt column headings a little (perhaps 45–65 degrees) to regain some of the horizontal space at the expense of some vertical space.

A table shouldn't always remain a table, though. When dealing with a sports tournament table, such as the NFL Playoff coverage archive, for example, a multilevel tabular view might be appropriate for wider views but wouldn't work well in narrow views. You could adjust the spacing, font size and level of detail, but it might not do the trick. Instead, you could altogether reimagine the entire experience, and show the Super Bowl game in the middle within a slider, and allow readers to explore the AFC and NFC leagues by moving to the left or right, perhaps with convenient toggle buttons or swipe action.

A tournament table isn't easy to design: SBNation.com went for turning a table into a slider, although a set of accordions with a more condensed view might work just as well.

Think about the specific properties and structure of a table before settling on a solution. You might discover similar table issues when designing any kind of survey, or selecting tickets for a performance (with dates presented as columns, shows presented as rows), or any other experiences where multiple selection is in place.

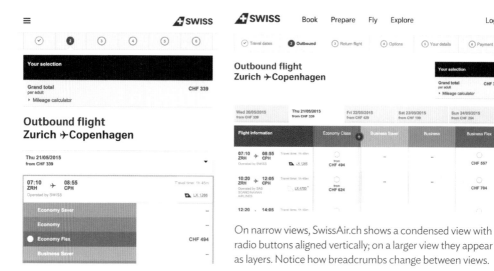

On narrow views, SwissAir.ch shows a condensed view with radio buttons aligned vertically; on a larger view they appear as layers. Notice how breadcrumbs change between views.

Another option would be, again, to display some columns as cropped encapsulated views or layers, as mentioned earlier. That's exactly what SwissAir's website[19] does. If one of the table columns is particularly important, you could also keep it fixed while making the other columns scrollable, so when users start reading the table, they always have a clear association between the content that they read and the row where it belongs.

If the data in your table is mostly numerical, you could visualize it as a graph or chart in both narrow and desktop views, and provide a link to a full table view for users who wish to see the tabular data instead (as well as a "graph" view for users wishing to see a chart on desktop views).

These solutions work well but they aren't always applicable. Content can be incoherent, data relationships could be strict and the table might not have any consistent structure. In these cases, displaying tabular data in fragments — again, reducing the complexity of the component — can work remarkably well. The idea is simple: since we can't make any assumptions about the columns or rows that users would or would not like to see, we could allow them to select columns of interest while at the same time providing an option to show all columns as well.

19 http://www.swissair.com/

The way you could design this experience would be by adding a few buttons above the table: perhaps a "Display all" button that, once activated, shows the entire table at once; and a "Display" drop-down, with all columns listed as checkboxes. If users are interested in specific columns, they can select them and dismiss the others, thereby reducing the amount of content to

We can't make assumptions, and often it's perfectly fine to just ask users what they'd like to see. Perhaps with a "focus" view to highlight data relationships. Source: http://gergeo.se/RWD-Table-Patterns/

display and potentially fitting it well in both narrow and wide views. You'd need to choose the columns to displayed by default and this selection might change depending on the available viewport width (or height).

Such a design pattern is quite manageable; but what happens when the user is interested in seeing all the columns at once? We're back to square one, with a poor initial experience: zoom in, zoom out, add a dash of horizontal scrolling. That's simply not acceptable. In usability tests we noticed that users often feel lost in such complex tables, especially when data is mainly numerical. Users aren't quite sure whether the value they are looking at actually corresponds to the column and row headings that they were interested in at first. To tackle this problem, tapping or clicking could visually highlight either a column or a row or both, and establish a clear relationship between the fragment of data the user is reading and the column and row it belongs to.

Another option is to show the first few columns first, and display a stepper control to enable users to move easily between sets of displayed columns. When a viewport accommodates four columns of a ten-column table whose first column comprises table headings, you could keep the headings column fixed and show the next three columns first, revealing subsequent columns on click or tap, and so on. For a narrower viewport, you could reveal two columns in each step, with the headings column remaining static. Additionally, an indicator could present how many items are currently in view, very much like we do in carousels.

> FilamentGroup has released Tablesaw[20], a comprehensive group of small JavaScript libraries for managing tables. Among other things, it covers many use cases highlighted in this chapter.

These last solutions often seem more appropriate for tables than just turning tabular data into a `<datalist>`, unless the nature of the table requires all columns to be present at all times. In an overview of pricing options, insurance plans or a car comparison, different columns and rows might have different weight for users, so allowing them to select columns or rows of interest could work well. But when it comes to flight selection, seat selection in a theater or checkout in an online shop, the integrity of a table is vital. There, a `<datalist>` (potentially with an integrated accordion if there is a lot of data to show) might be a more appropriate solution.

PULL CONTENT OUT, BREAK IT DOWN, PUT IT BACK AGAIN

While these approaches work well for tables and data grids, they won't necessarily work for calendars: with days of the week lined up horizontally, for example, and time of day lined up vertically. We *could* decide to drop all Fridays as well as a specific time range (such as 12pm–2pm for lunch breaks) but it would pretty much ruin the purpose of a calendar. It might be even more difficult if we decide to lay out days of the month against days of the week. A `<datalist>` option would, again, potentially end up with an annoyingly tall page or an overwhelming number of accordions all at once; and what if a user wants to see a cross-column/row selection after all (for example, all Friday evenings in a given month)? Retrieving this information would require them to open four accordions, for every Friday in a month. That's not user-friendly.

---

20 https://github.com/filamentgroup/tablesaw

In this and similar scenarios, we should take a step back and look into options of reducing the fidelity and complexity of the initially displayed content. Do we need all icons in the calendar? Do we provide any meta information that could be displayed separately? Can we use ellipses to shorten the amount of text? What else can we remove to keep the calendar focused and retain its integrity on narrow views as well?

That's the exercise we run through as a team every time we encounter not only calendars, but pretty much any complex component that can't be modified easily without compromising user experience. By simplifying content fragments *within* the component, we can always break down its complexity and focus on the core content it contains.

Ultimately, there is always the option of pulling the content out of the component, identifying and grouping content fragments logically, and presenting them as separate encapsulated views within a few subsequent sections on a page. For a calendar, you could choose to pull highlighted items and present them in a smaller, focused tabular view in narrow viewports, while all the other items could be displayed in a `<datalist>` underneath the table. If you need to design a city map with numbered markers

Swipe Table with Mini Map

MOVIE TITLE	RANK	YEAR	RATING
Avatar	1	2009	83%
Titanic	2	1997	88%
The Avengers	3	2012	92%
Harry Potter and the De…	4	2011	96%
Frozen	5	2013	89%
Iron Man 3	6	2013	78%
Transformers: Dark of th…	7	2011	36%
The Lord of the Rings: T…	8	2003	95%
Skyfall	9	2012	92%
Transformers: Age of Ex…	10	2014	18%

You could also integrate a mini map and combine it with a selection of columns the user wants to see. https://github.com/filamentgroup/tablesaw

within the map and detailed hints about specific locations displayed on tap or hover, you could reduce the fidelity of a map in narrow views, and pull out the content beneath the map as a `<datalist>`.

What if you are designing a platform for selling tickets to any kinds of event, be they concerts, baseball games or cinema screenings? You'd like venue owners to submit a seating map for their venue to you, along with an overview of the

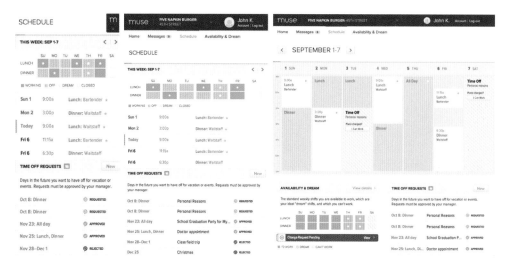

A calendar doesn't have to look like a calendar across all screens. You could use the content from a calendar and display it in two separate views on narrow screens, like Muse (http://objectivelogistics.com) does.

most expensive and most affordable areas, so buyers can visit your site and purchase a ticket to the show. Visitors should be able to select an area where they want to sit, but beyond that they should be able to zoom in to the area of interest and select both the row and, once zoomed in again, the actual seat they'd like. Obviously, the entire interface should be fully responsive, too.

One way of solving this would be to introduce what is known as the *assistant pattern* — complexity is reduced by asking users to set some preferences first (the pricing range or the seating area, for example) to lower the level of detail required on the map and remove markers that aren't useful. We then get a more manageable map, perhaps with slightly larger dots to comfortably accommodate 44×44px hit areas. Underneath the map we could provide an overview of options listed either by seating area or price — adjustable by users. When users choose to explore an option, they are zoomed in to the area of interest and receive further details about the seating in the information area beneath the map. Moving back through the list of options would zoom out the map view. Alternatively, you could also use a slider to enable visitors to define precisely the level of detail they'd like to see.

This experience could translate to both narrow and wide views, and we could take advantage of available space to display a more detailed map in larger views. Again, the strategy of breaking down complexity and creating a few smaller and more manageable content fragments could go a long way in pretty much every responsive design issue you'll encounter.

ADJUSTING MICRO-COMPONENTS

Breaking down complexity isn't always necessary. Components can be relatively simple with pretty straightforward ways to make them work for the whole range of screens — if you have the right idea of how to adjust their design and behavior.

Progress Steps

For example, think about the progress steps or breadcrumbs in a checkout. If a checkout takes four or five steps in total to complete, displaying the entire user path through these steps would require way too much vertical space in narrow viewports. Instead, we could use the content property with a pseudo-class in CSS to display the

Hrvatski Telekom (https://hrvatskitelekom.hr) shows a fully fledged breadcrumbs navigation in large views and turns them into plain text in narrow views. Image credit: Marko Dugonjić.

current step as plain text, with arrows pointing to the previous and next steps (see Hrvatski Telekom screenshot for comparison). A very simple adjustment that doesn't require a lot of work, but produces a perfectly sensible result.

Timelines

For timelines — either horizontal or vertical — marking important milestones or dates on either side, an almost natural solution would be to flip the timeline to a vertical view and perhaps display the content for each milestone via a toggle.

A timeline: horizontal orientation in a large view, vertical orientation in a narrow view. Nothing spectacular, really.

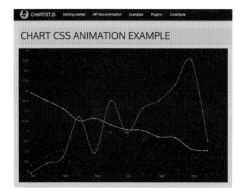

Responsive graphs aren't easy to manage, as long as you create them with SVG, and not as static images. For example, with Chartist.

Graphs and Charts

When it comes to graphs and charts, you could create highly sophisticated, and perhaps even animated, responsive charts with SVG and CSS using Chartist.js[21]; you might need to reduce the fidelity of the chart and tweak the appearance and position of labels to keep them readable in narrow views (also, see the responsive data charts at Informed Design[22]).

21 https://gionkunz.github.io/chartist-js/
22 http://www.informed-design.com/responsive/chart/

Maps

If your chart accompanies a map and you use polygons on the map for user input, sometimes the map's fidelity can't be reduced without making interaction inconvenient for users. For example, an SVG map of the United States, every state a polygon, could allow users to click or tap on polygons to select a state (perhaps as a filter for specific items related to that state); but the further the map is scaled down, the more difficult it becomes to select a state. A bulletproof solution would be to use a simple drop-down in a narrow view, with progressive enhancements up to a fully interactive map when the space allows for it.

The solution isn't as straightforward, though, when you need to display a large preview of the entire map and not only a cropped region of it. First of all, we could use Thierry Koblentz's *padding-bottom hack*[23] to create a fluid map that preserves aspect ratio[24] to keep the focal point of the map centered[25].

In usability studies, we noticed that embedding Google Maps or any kind of iframe often leads to confusion: when users decide to scroll down a page, they get dragged into the map and find themselves scrolling the iframe instead. The only way out is to tap an area outside the iframe and keep scrolling there; but if the iframe could take up a lot of vertical space, and so getting out of it can be painfully difficult.

Travois uses progressive enhancement to turn a simple, accessible drop-down into an interactive SVG map for larger views. http://travois.com/projects/

---

23 http://alistapart.com/article/creating-intrinsic-ratios-for-video
24 http://daverupert.com/2012/04/uncle-daves-ol-padded-box/
25 http://codepen.io/bradfrost/pen/vwInb

In such cases, you can use two workarounds to improve user experience. First, for every map embedded in your site, you can create a semi-transparent `<div>` overlay that would cover up the entire map, like a layer of ice covering a river on cold winter nights (poetic, right?). When users scroll down through the page, they will slide over the empty `<div>`. If they *do* decide to access the actual map, they need to click or tap the map first, so the `<div>` will be removed from the DOM via JavaScript. Users without JavaScript support would receive a link to the Google Map page via `<noscript>`.

A slightly better pattern to achieve almost the same experience is exhibited by adaptive maps[26], where we load a basic text link to Google Maps by default and additionally load either a static map image for small screens (preview) or a full iframe map for larger screens — preferably conditionally, so we don't have a performance overhead in either case.

Lightboxes

The same adaptive logic could also be applied to lightboxes which so often break user flow on narrow views. Quite a few websites simply squish a lightbox as a fullscreen overlay, with heavy lightbox scripts and tiny interface controls. However, this behavior goes against the logic of why lightboxes exist in the first place. As Jordan Moore so eloquently wrote[27]: "the purpose of a lightbox is to display a larger image corresponding to the selected thumbnail version while keeping the user on the same page instead of linking directly to a page showing the full image. [...] In fact you may argue that a lightbox shouldn't even exist on small displays".

Which hits the nail on the head. But if a lightbox shouldn't exist on small displays, how do we deal with it? Actions that happen in a lightbox on large views are often best handled as separate pages on smaller screens[28], so if you have an interaction that requires user input, dedicating an entire page to it in narrow views might be a good idea.

26 http://bradfrost.com/blog/post/adaptive-maps/
27 http://www.jordanm.co.uk/post/26207088124/pattern-translations
28 http://www.lukew.com/ff/entry.asp?1390

When your lightboxes contain only photos (a product gallery, for instance), you could present them within a swipeable area in narrow views, or you could simply link to the image file directly by default. Opening an image "allows the user to pinch and zoom to read what could otherwise be entirely illegible.[29]" Then you could detect the screen size and decide whether to load a lightbox script or not, and if the screen is large enough to accommodate the lightbox, inject the script on the fly. Again, no performance overhead and a better experience for everyone.

Footnotes and Sidenotes

When working with magazines publishing long reads, you might end up with situations when an article features a number of sidenotes, footnotes or pull quotes. You could try to squeeze the sidenotes within the article, perhaps right after the paragraphs which they relate to, but if they are lengthy they might interrupt reader's flow. On the other hand, with footnotes displayed as <sup>-links, users will have to jump to the foot of the page, read the footnote and then jump back to the reference, which is fine but a bit noisy and creates extra work for the user.

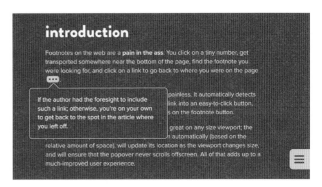

Instead of putting sidenotes within the text, or footnotes at the foot of the paragraph, we could introduce inline notes and pop-overs, enhanced with JavaScript, e.g. with BigFoot.js.

An interesting way of dealing with these issues is by using *inline footnotes* as pop-overs. You could use BigFoot.js[30] to automatically detect the footnote link and content, turn the link into a large enough button, and open a pop-over when the reader clicks on the footnote button. Of course, the pop-over has to be positioned on the top or bottom of the button automatically (based on the amount

29 http://bradfrost.com/blog/post/conditional-lightbox/
30 http://www.bigfootjs.com/

of space available), should update its location as the viewport changes size, and should never scroll offscreen. You could apply this technique to sidenotes as well: just turn them into inline footnotes at the end of every paragraph, with a different CSS styling to keep them distinguishable, and display them fully on click or tap.

PDF

Yes, you read it correctly: PDF. We spend a lot of time talking about removing all render-blocking resources from the critical rendering path, but I believe we don't spend enough time discussing how to deal with good old-fashioned PDFs. PDFs are often very heavy in file size, sometimes uncompressed, and difficult to read on a mobile screen. If your users happen to be on a slow connection, the chances are high that they won't even bother downloading a PDF file because they won't be able to read anything from it until it's been completely downloaded — unless the PDF is opened in a smart browser with an integrated PDF viewer. But what if a user knows that the content she needs is on page 17? There is no way of accessing it before the first 16 pages have been downloaded and rendered.

Interactive energy bill

Our interactive energy bill helps to explain each part of an energy bill, including the new tariff information you will be seeing on bills in the coming months. Follow the orange light bulbs to see descriptions of each area. You can also download a copy of the bill, which includes explanations of each area (PDF 2MB).

Simpler, clearer, fairer

On **31 March 2014** three new comparison tools were brought in to help make it easier for to compare energy deals:

Instead of providing only a link to PDF, we could generate thumbnail preview for all pages and make them available to users additionally to the PDF view.

Now, we *could* generate different versions of the PDF for different views and serve them conditionally to different screens, but it's inconvenient and involves unnecessary work. Instead, we could generate a (relatively) large thumbnail version of each PDF page, save it highly compressed and provide an overview of all pages to the user, as well as a PDF file. If users want to jump to page 17, they can do it via a thumbnail view. The image received will not look particularly impressive, but it will load fast and it will contain the information users need. And if they decide to download the PDF file after all, that option is always available. This is exactly what Energy Made Clear[31] does, and it does it very well indeed.

Custom Responsive Elements

Sometimes the nature of a website requires you to get quite creative when searching for a solution, so relying on more common components like the ones listed above won't really help. What if you've been asked to design a fully responsive site for living sheet music and guitar tablature with interactive notation and tabs, for example?

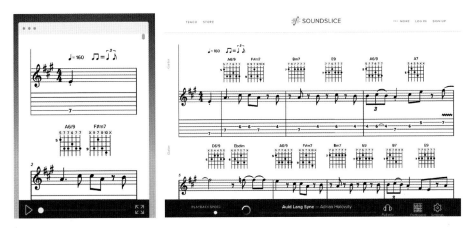

Interaction music notation, with chords and tablature adjusting depending on the screen size. With a bit of SVG, `<canvas>`, JavaScript and media queries.

Well, you start exploring. In such rare cases, you would need to figure out how to create custom responsive elements, perhaps with SVG or in `<canvas>`, and then decide how the content should be adjusted to be properly displayed at different screen resolutions. The front-end engineers behind Soundslice[32] had exactly this problem, and the way they solved it was by introducing *adaptive*

---

31 http://www.energymadeclear.com/

32 https://www.soundslice.com/

notation in which the displayed size and thickness of chords and pauses is recalculated and redrawn in <canvas> when a window is resized. I'd argue that if you can make sheet music responsive, you can make pretty much anything responsive, wouldn't you agree?

DEALING WITH COMPLEX VISUAL DESIGN

Well, you probably would agree, unless you have a very complex visual design to deal with. Coping with an abundance of visual content is often one of the reasons why responsive projects become frustrating, with the designs becoming generic, flat and oversimplified. In terms of workflow in such cases, different viewports often require intense art direction to keep the design consistent, with different visuals and different layouts for those visuals in place. In practice, it requires a bit too much extra effort, so it's generally more convenient to settle for a slightly simpler and more minimalistic design in a narrow viewport, and then add visuals only for larger viewports. It's not the only option, though.

Japanese and Chinese websites are a good primer for heavy visual responsive websites with a consistent design across viewports; in many ways they feel very advanced and thought-through. Not only hero photos or product images are art-directed; also complex infographics, step-by-step guides, video backgrounds and supporting visuals along with animations and transitions are properly directed and adjusted for tap, click and hover. Of course, these pages are quite heavy at times, but the visual consistency is very apparent in most cases.

It's not just the culture that demands a lot of visual language in Asian countries. Because web fonts would need to support thousands of glyphs, loading them just isn't viable, so text is embedded into images; and because mobile is dominating Asia, text has to be perfectly readable on narrow screens, so different versions of images are sent to different screens. Owing to this, Asian websites are almost inherently prepared for the art direction use case: there is just no way around it. Not surprising then that it's an interesting space to explore design patterns for dealing with visuals.

What if you have a number of heavily illustrated sections on a page, and these sections build up a content blob — a large area featuring all the sections at once? While you can be quite creative in your choice of visual arrangement in large views, you'll have to be more restrained in narrow screens.

Complex visual layouts on large screens can translate to slightly different layouts on narrow screens; often a list of navigation options works well, and so does a slider — but controls to move between content blocks could be helpful. Sapporo and Typekit websites as examples.

Two patterns often work well in such scenarios: you could either turn each illustrated section into a full-width block and arrange all sections vertically in one column (see Support Sapporo[33] above); or arrange all sections horizontally and use a slider to navigate through the items with a swipe (see Typekit[34]).

33 http://support-sapporo.or.jp
34 https://typekit.com/

In the first case, you could use accordions if the sections are content-heavy; in the second case, it might be a good idea to ensure that a portion of the next section is always displayed (the *overflow pattern*), or, even better, add toggles in the top-right corner to let users easily navigate to the previous and next sections without having to swipe very precisely.

Davide Calignano has recently published a simple technique[35] to keep a portion of the next section always visible with `calc`. Worth looking into.

So what can we learn from Japanese or Chinese websites? In many cases, background images have repeated patterns and are stretched for larger screens; secondary visual assets are dismissed in narrow views, but primary visual assets are more prominent than on larger views. More than usual you'll need to fit images within the container or a grid, either with `background-size` for background images or with `object-fit` for foreground images. Photography will often require art direction via the `<picture>` element, and heavy iconography might call for responsive icons.

BETTER, SMARTER RESPONSIVE WEB FORMS

Nobody loves filling in web forms; however, they are perhaps the most common yet least enjoyable interaction on the web. Going from one input field to another and typing in data feels like such an outdated paradigm, but there isn't much we can do to move away from it. Nevertheless, we could make the experience with web forms slightly better, in particular in responsive websites: we just need to figure out how to minimize user input and how to present required input fields intelligently, for narrow and wide screens.

Stacking input fields, text areas and drop-downs beneath one another for better mobile experiences isn't a particularly adventurous undertaking. But it's the micro-interactions taking place between these input fields that could improve the experience. Ideally, we'd love users to be able to focus on one thing and do it fast: typing. It shouldn't be necessary to move the mouse cursor or tap

---

35 http://davidecalignano.it/css-trick-to-reproduce-glimpse-on-native-scroll/

with a finger on an input field — users should be able to stay on the keyboard comfortably, without diverting their attention to anything else. Of course, the tabindex should still be appropriately set, so when users decide to switch to the next field via Tab on their keyboard, they can; but moving between the input fields might not necessarily require it.

Focus on Typing the Data

Swissair's[36] responsive forms are a very good example of achieving exactly this goal well. When users make a selection (in a drop-down, for example, or in a calendar), they automatically move on to the next field and can continue typing right away, unlike most interfaces where you have to manually move to the next field when you've finished with the current input field. Just such a paradigm is central to web form patterns suggested by Typeform[37]: the user always sees only one large input field at a time and can use keyboard shortcuts to make a selection or confirm input — by pressing "Enter" they move on to the next field. No drop-downs are used, no <select> menus employed — the entire experience is focused entirely on typing in data without any distractions. It works well on desktop, but it's still a bit annoying on mobile where you will see the keyboard popping up/out again after every input.

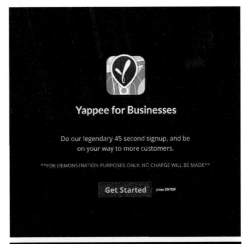

"One-input-field-at-a-time"-experience on Typeform allows users to fill in forms by focusing on only what they have to do: typing data. Everything else is taken care of automatically.

---

36 http://www.swissair.com/
37 http://www.typeform.com/

You could apply quite a few very subtle yet very handy tweaks in your form design pretty quickly:

- When a user arrives on a search page, be it related to booking flights, online shopping or a list of FAQs, activate the search box by default with the *autofocus* attribute.
- Provide valuable metadata to browsers by wisely assigning autocomplete attributes on input fields, helping browsers (and users!) prefill the entire form accurately automatically.
- Vertically adjust a textarea based on user input. Instead of reserving four rows for the input, you could stipulate just two and increase the height of the element dynamically so the scrollbar never appears.
- When a user has a lengthy address, allow them to dynamically add another input field for an optional second address line, instead of displaying it by default.
- Ask for a ZIP code first to potentially prefill state, city and sometimes even a street from it alone.
- To ensure users never lose any data, temporarily store the input during a session in localStorage. When a user accidentally hits "Refresh" or closes the window, the next time they open the window, all data will be preserved until the input has been successfully completed.

Not only the design of input elements matters, but also the choice of input elements, too. In our projects, we tend to spend a lot of time thinking about ways to remove input fields and drop-downs altogether and replace them with slightly more comfortable input methods, such as sliders, toggles or reasonably sized radio buttons.

The Right Input Element for the Right Input

Some input elements are more suited for specific inputs than others. T-shirt size might be easier to select with a few buttons rather than a drop-down menu. This could also act as a filter: once size is selected, other sizing options could disappear from the overview behind a semitransparent "All sizes" button. A price range would work better as a slider; the number of nights in a hotel, or any other discrete numerical input, would be better off with a simple *stepper* control — to increment a value, users can just keep tapping on a button instead of typing.

A flight's class with only a few options (first, business, economy) could be presented as tabs — *segmented controls* — with only one tap required to provide input. Special dietary requirements, for example, or any on/off states could be designed as a toggle. Such details make up the entire experience, so before we design (or redesign) a form, the first thing we do is conduct an interface inventory of all the input elements within the form. Chances are that the choice of input elements will have to change significantly.

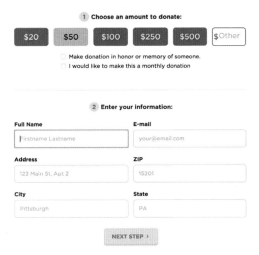

Segmented control for a donation form: with a few items provided, instead of a large drop down or input field. Image credit: Brad Frost, http://bradfrost.com/blog/post/designing-an-effective-donate-form/

Steppers and Sliders

Steppers and sliders are, however, the most convenient types of input for quantities (almost silver bullet techniques in form design!) and they could be used extensively in a variety of scenarios.

The main advantage of steppers is that they require exactly one tap to increase or decrease the value. This makes them helpful in checkouts (number of the same item in the shopping cart), or defining settings and preferences (number of travellers on a hotel booking website), or any other selection of discrete values. Steppers aren't very helpful when the range of values isn't restricted to a few items: they wouldn't be a good fit when selecting the color of a T-shirt or the brand of running shoes a customer wants; a filter list might work better in this and similar scenarios.

Steppers adjust a specific value quickly and precisely; sliders can help adjust a large set of values quickly, but not as precisely. Depending on the task, we can use a single slider with just one value (say, a specific date in history), or a double slider with a range of values (a min/max price range for a home). For predefined values, such as clothing size, we could use discrete sliders with fixed values that users can snap to easily; for indeterminate values such as price or temperature, we could use continuous sliders which don't have any fixed values at all.

Price Range

€9   €93 Average €1000+

A histogram slider on Airbnb provides some metadata about the number of available apartments at a given price range.

One caveat: if users can select any range of their choice, they might end up with empty results pages which are at best disappointing and not particularly helpful. To avoid this issue, you could extend a slider with additional metadata about the number of available products in specific ranges, creating a *histogram slider*, or *inventory slider*. You could design this by simply adding a bar chart above the slider, showing the number of available items at a given value, such as a price point. That's what Airbnb designers decided to use for the price range of available apartments. This way you clearly indicate which range is most populated with results, and where they shouldn't expect many results.

Tackling Common Pain Points in Web Forms

The patterns described above could serve as nice enhancements for specific scenarios, but there are a few common pain points that could be resolved with a few less obvious techniques.

One of them is to ask users to verify their input, be it a password or email. There is no need to ask for a password twice: you could just use a toggle button to show or hide a password if necessary, and it's a good idea to label it "Show" or "Hide" rather than relying on an ambiguous icon[38]. Instead of asking for email verification, you could use email autocomplete to autofill email addresses based

---

38 "Mobile Design Details: Hide/Show Passwords", http://www.lukew.com/ff/entry.asp?1653

on common email providers, or automatically correct them. It's also a good idea to let new users verify their email address before sending a message via the contact form, so they have a chance to correct it before sending the data, and you won't end up with incorrect or mistyped email addresses.

To tame a web form's height, we sometimes use input placeholders as labels to indicate what kind of data is required. However, if the input is lengthy or users are interrupted, they might lose the context of what exactly they were supposed to type in. That's where the *floating label pattern* is useful: the labels exist as placeholders but when users start typing, the labels float above the field in a slightly smaller font size. It's a nice way to keep both the input and context in place without losing too much space. If you can't move the label to the top but a field is wide enough to accommodate it, you could float the label to the right or left in the narrow view as well.

Some sites insist users are over a certain age to access the content. The owners of these sites honestly don't care about the actual day and month and year when users were born, they care mostly about the age. But most

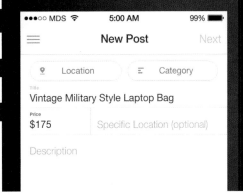

"Floating label" pattern in action: when users start typing in data, input placeholders turn into labels and float above the input field. Users see both: the label and their input. Source: http://mds.is/float-label-pattern/

visitors lie when challenged by this question, so why don't we make it easier for them to lie? Instead of asking for a specific date of birth, ask if the user was born in "1990 or earlier", or any relevant year, and use it as the input instead. It might not be feasible in every country but it's worth looking into. It also goes for credit

card input which shouldn't require card type since it can be automatically detected.

And then there is the king of <select> drop-downs: the almighty country selector. Depending on your country of residence and your current geographical location, often users just don't know where to look for their country. Will it be prioritized and displayed at the top of the list? Will it appear in alphabetical order? Will it appear in their language or in English? If you come from the Netherlands, should you look for "Holland", "Netherlands" or "The Netherlands"? As a result, the drop-down becomes an endless, tiresome journey through known and obscure countries. Not the best form of travel.

Instead of providing a drop-down, ask people to type what country they are from and show suggestions to help select the country. You could define synonyms for common input values to make your field smarter: whether a user types in "DE", "Germany" or "Deutschland", they'd get the same suggested value; the same goes for "NL", "Holland", "Nederland" "Netherlands", or "The Netherlands". More typing, but also more convenience for the user.

Less smart and smart country selector. Asking a user to type the first characters of their country might be easier than scrolling through an almost endless list of countries.

Obviously, if you care most about a specific input, such as email, or telephone input, your efforts should focus on that input. You could search for specific JavaScript libraries that would support and manage this input, like an email autocompletion library or telephone formatting library. Don't go over the top with libraries, of course, but the right tool in the right context can be just what you need to get things done well and tackle common pain points in no time.

Conclusion

Phew, that was quite a journey but, frankly, this journey wasn't particularly comprehensive. There is a plethora of good, smart solutions to be discovered — it's just up to us to look for and find them. Explore foreign responsive websites, because you'll likely be confronted with unique interactions and patterns that you haven't encountered before. Chances are high that your problem has already been solved.

In some circles, responsive design has a reputation for being difficult, complex, tiring and inefficient. Well, it isn't. It isn't if you have a good team around you, a good process in place, and a set of design patterns on which you can build your solution every now and again.

I hope you've found a few gems in this chapter that you'll be able to apply to your project right away once you flip over this page. You will fail, and you will start over, but you will eventually succeed and achieve better and smarter results much faster than you used to.

ABOUT THE AUTHOR

Vitaly loves beautiful content and complex challenges, and does not give up easily. He co-founded *Smashing Magazine* back in September 2006 and since then spends pretty much every day trying to make it better, faster and more useful. He runs responsive design training and workshops and loves solving complex UX, performance and front-end problems in large and small companies.

ABOUT THE REVIEWER

Andrew Clarke is an art director and web designer at the UK website design studio *Stuff and Nonsense*. There he designs websites and applications for clients from around the world. Based in North Wales, Andrew's also the author of two web design books, *Transcending CSS* and *Hardboiled Web Design* and is well known for his presentations and over ten years of contributions to the web design industry. He also wrote the last chapter of this book.

ABOUT THE REVIEWER

Viljami Salminen is a web designer living in Helsinki, Finland. He has worked in the web industry for over a decade and have designed websites and applications for start-ups and companies of all sizes. His core belief is that all content on the web should be accessible to anyone using any kind of device to access the internet. He has created tools such as Responsive Nav, Responsive Slides and Remote Preview.

ABOUT THE REVIEWER

Marko Dugonjić is a designer, frequent speaker, author and editor at Smashing Magazine. He co-founded *Creative Nights*, a design consultancy specialized in user experience design, typography and web standards, where he improves customers' digital experiences for international clients. He also contributed a chapter on web typography for the Smashing Book 4.

CONTENT
CHOREOGRAPHY
IN RWD

EILEEN WEBB

CHAPTER THREE · BY EILEEN WEBB

CONTENT CHOREOGRAPHY IN RWD

L ET'S START OUR JOURNEY INTO THE WORLD OF STRUCTURED CONTENT with a story about one of my clients, an international non-profit organization with a rich history and an enthusiastic staff. One fine day many years ago, their first website launched: it included a page for each of their office locations, a section describing their programs and services, staff biographies, and a brief page describing their history. The first version of the website was spearheaded by their program director, and owned and maintained by people on her team.

Over time, the organization grew: a new office in Geneva, expanded services in Chicago, a summer internship program. Each new program, event or news item meant adding pages to their website — literally creating additional HTML files. Control of the website bounced through a few departments — programs, marketing, outreach — and each group managed the files and the content slightly differently.

Enter mobile devices. This organization's users lived all over the world, and more and more of them were accessing the site on their phones or tablets. The pinch-and-zoom experience was crappy, and they came to us looking for a redesign that would make the site work across all screen sizes. They'd heard and seen how responsive web design (RWD) worked, and they were convinced that it was the solution to all their problems.

Which: yes! RWD was a great match for their needs. But adjusting the font size and column ratios across screen sizes would not actually make their users happy, because the real problem was not the early-2000's design aesthetic and inflexible images. The real problem was that the content sucked.

Content created by one department was never updated by the next. Services got renamed in the navigation but were still referenced by the old name in the body text. Important information was buried in the murky depths of flowery prose. Sidebars pointed to "Related Events" that happened in 2011. Important content like program eligibility requirements was duplicated in many places across the site, and the pages had diverged and showed inconsistent and contradictory policies. The site wasn't helping the users get the information they needed, or complete the tasks they needed to get done to do their jobs.

No one was interested in a major overhaul of just the content, but because they wanted a new look-and-feel we were able to use the responsive redesign as a scapegoat for changing their content architecture and processes. One of the major tasks was to figure out how to reduce the number of places errors could be introduced by breaking the content down into a system of reusable parts.

CONTENT IN A RESPONSIVE DESIGN

In this chapter, we'll talk about why I bother to structure your content — about what structured content lets me do on a site — and then we'll go over how to take current unstructured content and whip it into shape.

We love responsive design as a great way to approach building sites that work across all devices. As a content strategist, I love RWD because it makes it very hard to ignore glaring content problems.

At its smallest sizes, RWD isn't, generally, a festival of sound and light. When you strip the pomp and circumstance out of a beautiful desktop view, you're usually left with a very straightforward, single-column, small-screen design that puts the content front and center. If that content is poorly organized, badly written, or just generally crappy, it's very hard to ignore. If, like me, your background is in design or development, adding in a whole new phase to your projects to focus on content may seem daunting. But the alternative, which you may have already encountered, is to hope that the content fixes itself, then launch a site that doesn't help the user — despite its clever use of media queries.

What is Structured Content?

Structured content is, at its core, pretty simple: instead of storing content in a few all-encompassing content management system (CMS) fields, information is broken down into its component pieces and stored in a set of individual fields. Karen McGrane has enriched all our conversations about structured content by using the terms "blobs" and "chunks":[1] a blob is a single gelatinous field containing many different kinds of information; whereas chunks are individual, well-defined snippets of content, with clear edges and a crispy bite.

For example, here's a type of content that's common to many websites: the Event listing. In most CMSs, the default entry type includes a title field and a body field. The body field is a blob, holding all of the information about your event.

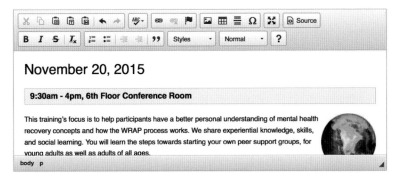

Storing all the content inside a single field is typical, but it makes it hard to reuse information across the site.

There are a few issues that often come along with this kind of setup:

- If the site has a homepage block like "Upcoming Events", it needs to be manually updated each time a new event is added. It's an extra step (and hassle) for the site administrator, and the block will quickly get out of date as events pass and need to be removed from the list.

---

1 http://karenmcgrane.com/2012/09/04/adapting-ourselves-to-adaptive-content-video-slides-and-transcript-oh-my/

- A main page like an event calendar may want to display teasers (rather than full entries) for the entries. Truncating a full body field is a recipe for confusion and poor user experience.

- If the site has multiple authors creating content, it's very hard to keep a complex body field consistent. Some people will bold the time, others will use an <h3> because they happen to look identical. Sometimes the event will include a location as the second line, and other times that information won't be included at all. An inconsistent body field is hard to style, hard to manage, and hard for a user to read.

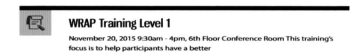

Teasers created through truncation are often confusing and missing key information.

Rather than keeping all of the information in a single field, structuring the content divides the data — components like event date, location, and teaser description — into individual fields.

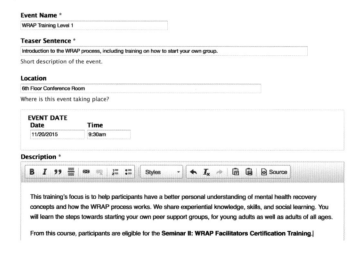

Splitting the pieces out into chunks gives me flexibility and control, setting up the site for a more consistent and customizable user experience.

What Structured Content Lets You Do

Breaking content down and storing it as individual components improves my ability to direct content quality, and it also allows me to do two things that are very relevant to RWD: I can recombine content in new forms for different uses, and I can get *really* picky about how the layout changes across screen sizes.

CONSISTENT CONTENT

When all the content lives in a single field, there's really no way to make sure any given entry contains all the pieces of information a user needs. Especially with more complex content types, there may be 15 or 20 pieces of data that need to be included in each entry — think, for example, of all of the various pieces of a product specification. From a data standpoint, it's very easy for a site author to leave out a few bits of information.

From a quality standpoint, if an author is paying attention to checking off all the data points on a list, asking them to make sure they're *also* properly representing the organization's voice and tone, communicating key messages to a niche audience, and including at least one reference to corporate environmental initiatives — it may just be a bit too much to do consistently well on each entry.

Some of those tasks listed above — speaking to a specific audience, or adhering to a corporate voice — can only be done by humans. To give those humans the space to do their jobs well, structured content lets us offload keeping track of the data-driven tasks (lists of specification numbers, or relationships to related content) to the computer. Computers love keeping track of things!

Where we used to ask authors to start on a blank page, now we're asking them to start by filling out a form. Important data fields are required, so there's no way they can get lost in the shuffle. Each field can have its own input validation for format or length. Detailed sets of information are represented in field groups, so authors don't have to remember how everything interrelates. The labels and help text for each field remind authors what the field is for, what needs to be communicated, and how they can create content that will help the user get their task done.

DIFFERENT DATA IN DIFFERENT PLACES

Once my content is stored as granular chunks instead of a single blob, I can start recombining the pieces to meet all my different data needs. I recently worked on a site that included event listings, and each entry was displayed in three places:

- Event detail page, including the title, full paragraph description, agenda, and location information.
- Upcoming events sidebar, with the title, date and time, and single-sentence description.
- Event calendar, showing just the title and time.

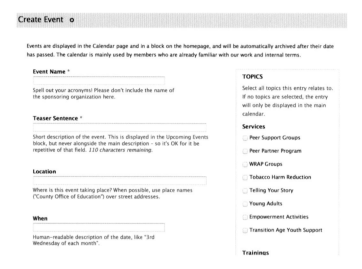

Filling out a simple form is much easier than remembering how to format elaborate content in a single WYSIWYG field.

Each event had only one entry in the CMS, and each different display pulled only the relevant information from the database. I can display different data for different screen sizes, as well. On a large screen, I may want to show an Event Location as a full address with an embedded map. On a smaller screen, I might show a simpler linked version of the address with no map. While it's important to give users on all screen sizes the same core content (because we can no longer guess context based on device[2]), it's helpful to be able to tweak the formatting and presentation across different widths.

Screen size is of course not the only variable that I want to use to control the display of content. For example, my favorite conference websites adjust the information hierarchy during the event, emphasizing which room each presentation is in, and downplaying previous days' schedules. Well-structured content allows me to do things like automatically adding a starting time `data-` attribute for each talk's `<div>`. A bit of JavaScript to attach time-based CSS classes at page load, and voilà! Clever, dynamic event listings that change styling as the day progresses.

Structured content also sets up the information for reuse in other channels. If we're creating a 100-character version of the headline for display on a small screen, that same headline could be used on Twitter, or pulled to a native app, or displayed on a smartwatch or other micro-display. Breaking content down into facets creates an ecosystem of data that can be used and reused in a wide variety of formats.

A NITPICKER'S PARADISE

Not everyone relishes the work that goes into making a pixel-perfect design. And it's true that, for the sake of their sanity, a fussy designer is generally well-served by embracing a "design system" philosophy[3] on RWD sites. But sometimes a project calls for a bit of obsessive pixel-pushing, especially at the awkward middle breakpoints (I'm looking at you, Nexus 7!), and structured content is what makes that detailed work possible. Let's look at the example on the next page:

On small screens, the date of each event is shown as a single line just above the title. Once the screen size is large enough, I want the date to display to the side in a stylized tile.

Markup-wise, this isn't a huge challenge: the entire date is in a `<div>`, and each unit has its own span with a class name of "day", "month", or "year". At

---

2   http://alistapart.com/column/windows-on-the-web
3   http://24ways.org/2012/design-systems/

larger breakpoints, CSS kicks in that shifts the date elements to stack on top of one another and floats the whole `<div>` left.

```
<div class="event-date">
    <span class="day">13</span>
    <span class="month">Jun</span>
    <span class="year">2015</span>
</div>
```

In order to style the date properly, I need the markup in every single entry to contain those exact elements, in that order. But chances are that the site admins and authors aren't comfortable in HTML. If I ask them to use that chunk of code at the top of each block of content, it won't be long before I end up with a class of "yera", a `<</span>`, and the dreaded `</div></div>`. We shouldn't require non-developers to work in HTML. It isn't kind.

Instead, I break out the event date to its own field. There are a few common interface choices for a date widget (a `<select>` list for each element, a JavaScript mask, pop-up calendar, and so on), and all of them are easier for an author than writing markup.

The site author fills out the date field in a human-readable format, and it's stored in the database in a machine-readable format (UNIX time, usually). When it's time for the date to be pulled out for display on the front-end, the CMS feeds it through a

When space is at a premium, it can be helpful to pare down to the simplest representation of the information needed.

Simple form widgets let authors enter dates consistently without having to remember how to format the information in HTML.

template that formats and marks up the data *exactly* in the way that I want. It's the same code every time, for every date, of every entry.

It's not hard to see how consistency in markup is one of the keys to the long-term viability of a responsive design. While there are a few different ways to achieve this consistency (individual fields, custom WYSIWYG buttons for marking up long-form content, and so on), the first step to standardizing markup is understanding the structure of the content itself. It's time to build a *content model*.

How To Build A Content Model

A content model is an organizational plan for all of the different content in a project. It covers both the high-level content types (like events and products) — and the individual fields and data attributes (like event date, location, and teaser sentence) that make up each type. The first step to building a model is, not surprisingly, understanding my content. I like to start by performing a structural content audit.

13 JUN 2015

Latino Empowerment Project Kickoff

The goal of the Latino Empowerment Project is to expand WRAP (Wellness Recovery Action Plan) to the Spanish speaking population in Alameda County. All of the workshops would be facilitated in the Spanish language including written materials.

Latino Empowerment Project Kickoff

13 JUN 2015

The goal of the Latino Empowerment Project is to expand WRAP (Wellness Recovery Action Plan) to the Spanish speaking population in Alameda County. All of the workshops would be facilitated in the Spanish language including written materials.

Simple form widgets let authors enter dates consistently without having to remember how to format the information in HTML.

If you know the term "content audit"[4], you're probably familiar with an editorial audit. In the editorial audit, each page or piece of content is reviewed and graded against a set of qualitative criteria, like readability, intended audience, or adherence to an existing style guide. A structural audit, in contrast, is more

4 http://www.hannonhill.com/news/blog/2012/why-and-how-to-do-a-content-audit.html

concerned with uncovering the patterns and relationships across all the content. Once I understand the content types and how they relate to one another, I can start to tease out the facets and individual fields for my content model.

STARTING THE STRUCTURAL AUDIT

When I'm faced with a huge existing site or a ton of legacy content, where do I start the audit? My take is: wherever I want. Just dive in.

(Except: don't start with the homepage. It's often a mess, and rarely has sensible ties to the rest of the site content or reuse patterns. You know what I'm talking about: the homepage is a political playground, not a structural one.)

I usually start with some of the minor content, like "Executive Bios" or "Company History". As I read through 10-15 entries or pages, I'll begin to spot patterns: these executive biographies always have a headshot, name, job title, and biography text. I may notice further nuance in some areas, like that the first paragraphs of biography text are professional background, and the last is about family and personal life.

Haydée Cuza, Ed.D. — Name
EXECUTIVE DIRECTOR — Title

Working closely with the Board of Directors, staff, and the community, Haydée is responsible for sustaining wellness and recovery programs and initiatives that eliminate stigma and discrimination. Additionally, she is committed to the overall growth and success of the mental health movement. Haydée leads with a vision of wellness and recovery, as PEERS offers empowering and innovative programs, trainings, and peer groups.

Professional Background

Combined with 25 years of professional experience working for foster care system improvements, workforce development, improving outcomes for transition age youth, and mental health; her passion for this work comes from her lived experiences as a former homeless and foster youth, struggles with mental health and wellness, personal commitment to self-reflection and healing, and being a mommy, abuelita, and multidimensional and multicultural womyn.

Personal Background

Haydée loves spending quality time with her wife, daughter, grandson, family, and close friends, and especially loves dancing and taking time to conciously connect spiritually.

Finding the patterns in existing content is the first step towards building a model.

More importantly, I'll find places where a pattern like "first paragraph: work history; second paragraph: personal history" isn't carried through, and I'll see how (or if) that inconsistency affects the user experience. I start having discussions with my stakeholders about where the new model should enforce guidelines (through required fields, help text, and so on), and what parts should be left to author discretion.

AN ASIDE ABOUT EDITORIAL CONTENT JUDGMENT

I don't specialize in editorial strategy; my background isn't in writing or editing. But even the structural audit includes some editorial judgment, because I can't look at hundreds (or even dozens) of pages without starting to recognize poor formatting, bloated text, and lack of user guidance. As I'm working through the content, I make notes about places in the site that could use editorial attention, especially sections that need design and development help (like "More prominent calls-to-action!") to be effective. This won't be as comprehensive as a full editorial audit, of course, but it's a place to start. Content strategy is about progress, not perfection.

IDENTIFYING FACETS WITHIN A CONTENT TYPE

How do I know what parts of the content should be separated into their own fields? For each chunk of information, whether it's something distinct like "Job title" or a little fuzzier like "second paragraph of the bio, holding personal history", I ask the following questions:

Is this content likely to have its own style? Audits usually happen long before design, so you won't know this for certain yet. But I'll often have a sense: a field like "Job title" is usually displayed separately from the person's name; or I may already know that the Event Location address is going to be displayed in a `<div>` that's visually-separate div from the main Event Description. Any content I think will have special display or styling requirements is a good candidate for having its own field in the content model.

Does this content have special editorial requirements? If a piece of information needs to be limited to 250 characters, or a chunk of content needs to include very specific references to corporate initiatives or internal programs, it may warrant its own field. In most CMSs, each field can have its own set of contextual help text and authoring guidelines; being able to break out content with complex or specific editorial needs allows me to customize those guidelines to help authors do their jobs well.

Is there filtering or sorting functionality based on this information? Computers are great at rearranging and customizing content, as long as we give them the tools to do it. Users may want to filter the event calendar to show only family-friendly events, or sort a list of documents to see the newest entries at the top. Any piece of data that may be useful for grouping or organizing content should go in its own field.

Will this content be displayed differently in different places on the site, or across varying screen sizes? A product may show a one-sentence description on the homepage, and a full description on the product detail page. An artist's portfolio might show an expansive photograph on a large screen, and a zoomed-in design detail on a small screen. Many responsive sites adjust content and imagery to enhance the user experience across different screen sizes; breaking information out into individual fields makes this kind of manipulation possible.

Are there other places (like an RSS feed, API, or native app) that will reuse this content? If my plans involve reusing content across different channels, what content variations do I need to support that work? Entries that will be promoted on Twitter need a sub-140-character description. Content that matches one of the special OpenGraph types[5] should include all the fields necessary to take advantage of Google and Facebook's use of that framework. When I have other plans for the content — as complex as a native app, or as simple as "internal-use-only data that we don't want to lose track of" — including fields for that information in my content model will make maintaining a consistent record much more feasible.

Once I have the skeleton of a model for a simple, minor content type — which at this point is usually just a scrawled list of content sections on a notepad — I scan another 20–30 entries to see if any of them contain information that falls outside the chunks in my proto-model. I can adjust the model to hold the new information, and also go back to my stakeholders and discuss the outliers. Some-

---

5　http://ogp.me

times outlying content (helloooooo "Photo highlights of the 2011 company golf tournament") won't make the move to the new site and so doesn't need to fit in the model.

BIGGER, MESSIER CONTENT TYPES

Finite content like biographies and calendar events are relatively easy to model. Those types tend to hold discrete chunks of information, and more importantly, people *understand* them. An executive biography is different from an event listing, and even without doing a full audit, many people could make a passable stab at modeling the information they contain. Sadly, not all content is this tidy.

The content that describes an organization's core products and services can be much more difficult to wrangle, because it's unique to the business and usually contains data and information that falls outside of my early simple models.

The most important part of modeling bigger content types is figuring out ways to group the data. Our product content might be expansive and messy, but a bunch of those fields are product specifications and can be gathered into a single section. As I list out all the pieces of data that make up the content type, I start to see smaller patterns emerge that help me make sense of the rest.

FIELD REUSE AND RELATIONSHIPS

I also keep an eye out for fields and content that are shared across content types, and relationships between types. Fields that are reused across types are the simplest to spot: the biographies for authors, artists, and staff all include headshots and URL fields. Most CMSs let me reuse the same field in different content types; I can style the field once and have that style applied everywhere that field is shown.

When the reused information is broader than a single field, that's a place where a content relationship can be helpful. I have clients with multiple offices, and different services are available at each location — I want site users to be able to look at the detail page for a single service and see all the locations where it's offered. Rather than include a text field where an author would list the offices, the content model calls for a relationship: the CMS will present a GUI (commonly an autocomplete textfield, select list, or checkboxes) that lets the author choose the locations from a list. Content relationships allow the front-end to display anything from a link to the location detail page, to a teaser of the location, to an address that will open in a native maps app on phones that support it. All without the author having to know how to create that code, because I've set the content models up to take advantage of the power of relationships.

Thinking Beyond Existing Content

Let's step back from modeling for a minute. I'm going to go out on a limb and guess that you're working on a site project because somewhere, someone is unhappy with something. Maybe the site isn't converting casual browsers to buyers, or your organization is launching an initiative and can't figure out how to integrate the new content, or you've been hearing from users that they're having a hard time finding the information they need on your site. It's rare for an RWD project to come from a place where everything is perfect except for the small-screen experience.

In the beginning of the project, I always have meetings and discussions with a bunch of stakeholders, and start to get a sense of — or explicit directions about — the kinds of improvements people want to see on the site. I have to cast my memory back, review my notes, and start to look at the existing content with an eye for identifying gaps.

DATA-DRIVEN GAPS

The gaps may be purely data-driven: if I heard from the customer service team that a lot of people call asking for the dimensions of our products, then the new version of the site should display those dimensions. If the company wants to show a more human side to their work, the new site could integrate testimonials or client stories.

I worked with a grant-funded organization that wanted to make it clear to their funders how the grants had a direct impact in the community. But there was no connection between their day-to-day program content and the foundations listed on their funding partners page. In identifying that gap, we were able to create an explicit content relationship on the new site to tie the funders and their work more closely together.

Adding the funder relationship to the content model was a small structural change that had a big impact on the way the organization presented its work.

FEATURE-DRIVEN GAPS

New site features often carry their own content needs, and it's important to identify them as early as possible. As I'm sketching out wireframes or user stories to plan the development schedule, I look for the kinds of content that the new features make use of, and see if that information is already represented in our content models.

For example, the stakeholders want the new site's event calendar to display the instructor's biography on every corporate training entry. I can add "Instructor Biography" as a new content type in our model, piggybacking on the fields and structure of the "Executive Biography" content. But the current site doesn't have instructor biographies, so who is going to write those? Will we hire copywriters, or ask people to write their own? If the listings need to include a headshot image, will a photographer be hired to take professional photos?

Sometimes the answers are simple: "We already wrote those biographies for the annual report!"; and sometimes they affect my work directly: "We don't have budget for a photographer, so design the bios without them". If you're a designer or developer, it's probably not your responsibility to figure out the answers to these questions about content gaps. But it is part of your job to raise the issues and get the team talking about how to address these content deficits long before launch day.

Giving Up: When Everything Is Just A Big Mess Forever

Not all content is precise and patterned. There are some types of content that defy organization: blobs that don't want to be chunked, or unique information that doesn't have a repeating pattern because it's the only one of its kind.

At some point in every project, I have to remind myself: some information belongs in blobs. *Data* — numbers, measurements, and taxonomy — lends itself to patterns and chunking, but *content* — essays, descriptions, and stories — is inherently blobby. Those kinds of information are already as faceted as they're going to get. When I can't break a piece down any smaller, the frustration usually leads to a realization that the information should stay as a blob. It's not a failure of a content model to include a large WYSIWYG `<textarea>` for authors to fill in with freeform content.

When I reach that point and throw up my arms and yell, "FINE. BE THAT WAY!", I circle back to reuse. What else do we need to do with this content, that having it as a blob prevents us from doing? Content models only exist to make the site better for my authors and my customers — they don't have to fit other people's use cases. Often all I really need out of a piece of content is a small summary that I can use as a teaser on other pages, or a taxonomy field to create a relationship to other sections of the site. The content model may end up being only a title, teaser, and body field. That's fine, as long it serves the needs of my site.

My approach is similar when I'm dealing with one-off content, which has no repeating patterns because it's the only instance of that information. The homepage of most sites is a perfect example — from a pure content model perspective, it doesn't make sense to build a model that will only have one entry. A single page of unique content could be hand-coded, and that's a good solution if the budget is tight and the information doesn't change very often.

But I'm not building models as an intellectual exercise, I'm doing it to support this organization and its responsive site experience. We've already talked about the cruelty of making non-coders understand HTML to make simple text updates to their content, and on the homepage the stakes are high — unclosed `<div>`s and wrongly-sized images will break the entire layout, and I will get panicked calls from executives late at night.

If authors are going to be updating the homepage content, I'll often create a "homepage" content type in the CMS, breaking down that single page into individual fields and sections to make editing the content a safe and painless experience. Sure, there's only ever going to be a single homepage, and none of that content is being reused in other channels, but guess what? There are no content model police. I will support my site experience and my authors over the theoretical ideals of what content models and content types are for any day.

Documenting And Sharing The Content Model

Content models are only useful when the whole team understands them, so it's important to get the model out of my head and onto paper or screen in a shareable format. And when I say "the whole team", I really mean it. We tend to think of the customer as the end user, and ignore the fact that the site administrators and authors are on the site more often than most users. Be persistent — annoying, even — about reviewing content models with all levels of the web team. If content entry is mostly handled by Alice the summer intern, walk through the models with Alice the summer intern. She's deep in the content every day, and has insights that others do not have.

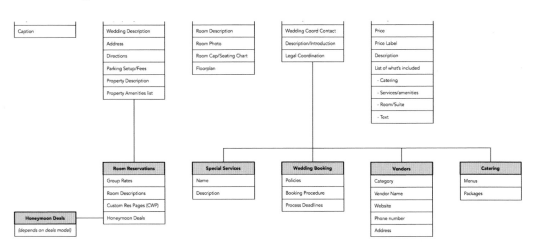

A graphic representation of the fields in the model can help people understand the overall shape of the content without diving into minutiae.

I often end up creating a few different views (a spreadsheet, diagrams, low-fidelity wireframes, and so on) of the same model in order to give a more complete picture, and to address all my team members' needs. I'm generally building a model for three different audiences: stakeholders, developers, and authors.

STAKEHOLDERS

Stakeholders want to see the big picture. They want to understand what the overall structure is, and they're very interested in what that structure allows them to do. They are generally less interested in the minutiae of implementation, and don't care if a field is represented as a boolean in the database. For stakeholders and executives, diagrams and schematics — even a very sketchy wireframe showing a user journey — are helpful.

DEVELOPERS

Developers appreciate the big picture, because who doesn't like context? But they need details about how to actually build the models in the CMS. They care about whether a field should be a text `<input>` field or a `<textarea>`, whether there's a character limit, if the field is required, and if it will need to accept HTML. The core of most content models, and the information most useful for developers, lives in a spreadsheet.

Section / Field	Format	Source System	Required	Number of Instances	Contents	Notes
Venues			Y	∞		These could be pulled as references from property data, with wedding-specific info where appropriate
Room Name	Text	EPIC	Y	1	Name of the room or hotel area available for weddings and receptions	
Room Description	Text	CMS	Y	1	Wedding-specific description	Is there a need for alternate versions of these (like "holiday-themed weddings", seasonal descriptions for ski resorts, etc)?
Room Photo	Image	MDAM	Y	1	Wedding-specific photo (decorations, place settings, etc)	
Room Capacity/Seating Chart	Text	EPIC	Y	1	Wedding-relevant only	No "classroom setup" or other meeting-focused data. The seating is already broken out by type in EPIC, so the pages just shouldn't pull the irrelevant formats.
Floorplan	Image	CMS	N	1	Floorplan of the venue, or the entire hotel grounds	Labels must match the room names!
Room Reservations						
Group Rates	Text	MARSHA	Y	1	Explanation of group rates policy and process	
Room Descriptions	Reference	EPIC	N	∞	Links to descriptions/photos for rooms available for group booking	
Custom Reservation Pages (CWP)	Boolean	CMS	N	1	If this hotel offers CWPs, this will show a brief explanation of what they are and how to request one	Could the request be a link to a form?
Honeymoon Deals	Reference	Deals	N	∞	Links to Honeymoon deals at that property	
Packages				∞		Packages as a whole may not be CMS-structured, but rather editorially structured by having strict guidelines for authors/admins to follow in the CMS.
Package Name	Text	CMS	Y	1	Name of the wedding package	
Price	Number	CMS	Y	1	Price, either flat-rate or per-person	This would allow for searching across properties, like "show me all the beach hotels who have wedding packages less than $15k".
Price Label	List	CMS	Y	1	"Flat-rate", "Per person"	
Description	Text	CMS	N	1	1-2 sentence description of the package, including any limitations (e.g. "at least 50 guests")	Limitation could be pulled out into its own field? Not sure there's enough consistency across properties for that.
List of what's included		CMS				
- Catering	Reference	CMS	N	∞	Links to catering menus	Only the relevant menus – a wedding breakfast doesn't need the dinner menu
- Services/amenities	Reference	CMS	N	∞	Links to Spa, Golf, or other relevant service pages	Hotel-internal services
- Room/Suite	Reference	CMS	N	∞	Link to included suite or room	
- Text	Text	CMS	N	∞	Any other package items	May be links (to 3rd party vendors or locations).

A spreadsheet is the perfect place to keep track of all the disparate pieces of a content model.

There's no canonical spreadsheet: every project has different needs. My basic content model spreadsheets contain the following columns:

- *Section*: groupings of fields, usually by content area like "event information" or "location data".
- *Field*: The name of each piece of data in the model.
- *Format*: the type of content stored in the field, like "Image", "Rich Text", or "Boolean".
- *Maximum length*: this is often used in RWD, where you might have 2 or 3 length variations of a single piece of content for use across different screen sizes.
- *Number of instances*: the upper limit on the number of instances of that field in each entry. For example, an event listing can only have a single location, but may have up to four instructors. This is a good time to learn how to type the ∞ symbol.
- *Required*: whether or not the field is required for each entry.
- *Contents*: a brief description of the contents of the field, like "Directions to the location, including information about where to park".
- *Notes*: any other information about the field, including thoughts about implementation, issues to discuss with stakeholders, or an explanation of what this field enables from the user experience standpoint. It wouldn't be a spreadsheet without a catch-all column.

My spreadsheets also include other columns to hold whatever information this particular project needs. Such as:

- *Source*: if we're pulling content together across systems, through APIs, or from other media like print publications, I make a note of where the information in each field will come from.
- *Example content*: especially helpful if the team is having a hard time wrapping their heads around how the current content will fit into the new model. When the model has variations on a single piece of information — like a short and long image caption that will be used on

Create Event o

Events are displayed in the Calendar page and in a block on the homepage, and will be automatically archived after their date has passed. The calendar is mainly used by members who are already familiar with our work and internal terms.

Event Name *

Spell out your acronyms! Please don't include the name of the sponsoring organization here.

Teaser Sentence *

Short description of the event. This is displayed in the Upcoming Events block, but never alongside the main description – so it's OK for it be repetitive of that field. *110 characters remaining.*

Location

Where is this event taking place? When possible, use place names ("County Office of Education") over street addresses.

TOPICS

Select all topics this entry relates to. If no topics are selected, the entry will only be displayed in the main calendar.

Services

☐ Peer Support Groups

☐ Peer Partner Program

☐ WRAP Groups

☐ Tobacco Harm Reduction

☐ Telling Your Story

☐ Young Adults

Remember our example from earlier? It's much easier for an author to create consistent content when all the guidelines are right there in the admin interface.

different screen sizes — having examples of both helps authors better understand the nuance and difference between the variations.

- *Do not include:* It can be helpful to clarify what doesn't belong in each field. "Do not include the address in this description", or "The biography should not repeat the job title (because it lives in its own field)".

AUTHORS

Authors need some of the details of the spreadsheet, like character limits and required fields, but they don't need the technical implementation data. Authors also need editorial guidelines, which help them use consistent messaging and style across the site. These guidelines are traditionally captured in a content template.[6]

The content template reminds the author who the intended audience is, the primary message that the copy needs to convey, and the purpose of the content. The content template can also include much more detailed information about what belongs in larger rich-text fields, including a paragraph-level outline, reminders of words to include (or avoid), and tips on language and style choices.

---

6 http://alistapart.com/article/content-templates-to-the-rescue

Traditionally the content template is a separate PDF, but my experience is that people don't usually remember to open those kinds of files in their daily workflow. Instead, I like to build those content guidelines directly into the CMS interface. Most CMSs allow you to customize field labels and help text for each content type. By including audience needs, voice and style reminders, and technical content guidelines directly in the CMS editing form, you're providing information to your authors exactly when and where they need it.

Good labels and guidelines:

- provide context, explaining what a field is for and how it will be used;
- are specific, encouraging accuracy and uniformity while eliminating guesswork;
- are positive and helpful, rather than hostile and prohibitive.

Field names should be specific and descriptive (think "Artist Name" and "Biography Text" instead of title and body). Help text should instruct the author about what does and doesn't belong in the field, and include guidance about how the field is being used and where it will be displayed so they understand what information it needs to contain.

If you're eager to customize your CMS (and who isn't!), I've written a whole article "Training the CMS " about improving field names and help text over at A List Apart.[7]

Working With The Model In A CMS

All of this content modeling is built on the assumption that you'll be creating the site inside a CMS. Structured content can only be used to its fullest when the data and information are kept separate from the presentation layer, and that means you need a system to manage the intersection of those layers. If you've never used a CMS before, welcome! They are a rich source of joy and frustration.

---

7 http://alistapart.com/article/training-the-cms

CHOOSING A CMS

What do I look for in a CMS? (There are of course many other considerations to choosing a CMS — technical, ongoing support needs, cost — but I'm only going to address the content issues.)

- Obviously, the CMS needs to support creating multiple content types and lots of different kinds of fields. These capabilities should be part of its core code, but a popular and well-supported add-on module is alright, too.
- It should allow me to divide and recombine all the fields in my content types for a variety of display uses, and changing the configuration for one type of display shouldn't break any of the others.
- The system should have a robust set of tools for customizing the authoring experience's layout and help text, because without that I might as well build flat HTML pages again.
- If my models or authoring workflow rely heavily on a particular type of field or functionality, I make sure the CMS has strong support for it. For example, some systems make it very easy to crop a photograph to preset dimensions from within the editing screen, whereas others require the author to upload an already cropped image. I put a high priority on choosing a CMS that makes the author jump through as few hoops as possible.

You may not have the luxury or burden of CMS choice — if you work at an agency that specializes in ExpressionEngine, or you bill yourself as a Drupal developer, or a WordPress guru*, the CMS decision has already been made. That's fine, too. You can skip right to the middle and start figuring out how to make your CMS work best for you.

Please don't.

I try to build CMS-agnostic content models to create a picture of the ideal set of fields and relationships, without any restrictions, that serve the content best. When the time comes to compromise as I map the models to a real system, having a strong sense of the ideal scenario helps me find solutions that preserve the original intent as much as possible.

GETTING CONTENT MODELS INTO THE CMS

The spreadsheet representation of the content model is built to make implementation easy. I work through it row by row, creating and customizing content types and fields until the whole model is represented in the system.

One of the most common snags I run across during implementation is when there are two nearly (or completely) identical content types. For example: "Artist Biography" and "Executive Biography", or "Training Program" and "Ongoing Education". Should I combine them, or create two separate instances? My inclination is always to combine into a single content type: perhaps "Biography" with an additional "Type" field (with the choices "Artist" and "Executive") to distinguish between the two uses. The urge is a good one, based in my desire to reuse code, simplify styling, and make the site as lean as possible. It's not, however, always the right choice.

"Training Program" and "Ongoing Education" may be identical content types with the exact same set of fields. But if they serve entirely different business purposes — say one is aimed at novice laypeople, the other at existing experts — combining them may not make sense. Are the same people in charge of both kinds of entries? If separate departments handle the two types of information, having them both use the same content type may be confusing, and may hinder my ability to customize and tweak the model and forms for each group's needs. Even if all the content entry will by handled by a single person, does that person understand these types of content to be completely different? If she says "Oh yes, I could see how those are just two versions of the same thing!", then I'll combine the content types. But if she's stuck on them being entirely unique, I either need to present a compelling reason to combine them, or be content with letting the two content types live as parallel structures.

There's a lot to be said for stakeholder education and CMS training, but it's also important that the models work with the author's understanding of the information. A model that a client is constantly fighting against is no good model at all.

Ongoing Content Maintenance

When I'm building out a content model, it's important to start conversations about governance and ongoing maintenance for each content type and section. It's tempting to ignore these questions because they're not directly related to building this fancy new RWD site, but unless I want to come back in a year and see the blog with still just that single "Welcome to our new site!" post, I have to grit my teeth and dig in.

- Owner Who's in charge of this content? This may be a specific person, or a position, or an entire department. Every type of content needs an owner who will take responsibility for its quality and accuracy.
- Approval process Does this information need to go past the legal department before it goes live? When marketing writes a compelling sales pitch, should someone in development read through it to make sure it accurately represents the product? It's important to spell out a clear path from creation to publishing that everyone understands and agrees with.
- Review schedule When will this content be reviewed, and by whom? Monthly, quarterly, annually? If revisions are necessary, who makes them? Planning for regular reviews of the site content is crucial to its ongoing quality and usefulness.

A new site often leads to changing roles and responsibilities around content. As governance and maintenance decisions get made, it's really helpful for the team to start embodying their new roles — writing blog posts on a regular schedule, having monthly meetings to review social media campaigns, editing images for the photo gallery — even though the new site isn't ready yet.

That way, new features will launch with a few months' worth of real content in them, and process issues can get ironed out before they're critical. Site launch day should never be the first day someone has to explore and learn their new tasks in the CMS.

Embracing Your Inner Content Strategist

You might notice that many of our questions and discussions are starting to roam outside the realm of development and implementation details. This is the nature of content strategy — we like to poke our noses in a lot of people's business.

Being a content strategist doesn't require you to stop being a designer, or a developer, or a project manager, or whatever your role is today. I truly believe that bad content makes it hard for you to do your job well, so when you're working solo or on a project that doesn't have a dedicated content strategist, block off some time early in the schedule to understand the current content situation. A full and robust content strategy includes a lot of information beyond a content model: voice and tone guidelines, style guides, editorial calendars, message architecture, and more. Not every project warrants all of those pieces, but I can't think of a responsive site I've seen that didn't benefit from structured content. The time spent figuring out underlying patterns, finding gaps and shortfalls, and planning for future maintenance will pay itself back before the site even launches.

ABOUT THE AUTHOR

Eileen Webb is a content strategist and co-founder of *webmeadow*, a firm that helps progressive organizations develop content and technology strategies to make the world a better place. She is also a content strategy workshop facilitator. Her background is in server-side coding and being that odd person who translates between the marketing and development teams. Her Twitter feed (*@webmeadow*) is equal parts content strategy and pictures of poultry.

ABOUT THE REVIEWER

Lisa Maria Martin is a writer, editor, speaker, and independent consultant based in Boston, MA. She practices content-driven information architecture, helping organizations plan and structure their web content logically and strategically. Lisa Maria also facilitates workshops at *www.content-workshops.com*, is the issues editor at *A List Apart*, and writes infrequently at *www.thefutureislikepie.com*.

MASTERING SVG
FOR RESPONSIVE
WEB DESIGN

SARA SOUEIDAN

CHAPTER FOUR · BY SARA SOUEIDAN

MASTERING SVG
FOR RESPONSIVE WEB DESIGN

Y OU MUST HAVE COME ACROSS SCALABLE VECTOR GRAPHICS (SVG) in
your responsive projects recently. When it comes to resolution-independent assets, SVG is one of the main contenders that we, designers
and developers alike, apply in our work. However, SVG isn't just an image file
that scales up and down in a responsive context. With SVG, you can do much
more, applying smart and nifty techniques to create both scalable and delightful
experiences.

In this chapter, we're going to go over ways to use SVG in a responsive web
design workflow. More specifically, we'll cover a workflow process from SVG
creation, to exporting and optimizing the SVG for the web. Then we'll look at
how we can embed the SVG using the different techniques available. We will
explore different techniques for creating SVG sprites and the different ways to
provide fallback, consider the performance of some of these techniques, and
discover the tools that help us automate the previous tasks. We won't forget
about accessibility and providing alternative content for people with disabilities
using SVG's accessibility features. And finally we'll go over a few clever techniques using SVG as a tool for delivering better raster graphics, that can take
your SVG knowledge to the next level.

Without further ado, let's get started.

What is SVG?

SVG is an XML-based, two-dimensional image format with support for interactivity and animation. But don't let the XML part put you off — SVG is a markup language similar to HTML, but is designed for another purpose: rendering shapes and images. These shapes and images are accessible, and can be animated and interactive. This provides us with finer control over the elements making up an SVG image, and allows us to group elements, transform them, animate them and interact with them using CSS and JavaScript.

SVG is not a new format. As a matter of fact, the World Wide Web Consortium (W3C) started work on it as far back as 1999. But the rebirth of SVG is a consequence of the rise of mobile devices and the introduction of different screen densities, which required us to look for an image format that would look crisp in all viewing contexts. SVG offers a truly resolution-independent technology for presenting graphics on the web — create the file once and use it anywhere, at any scale and resolution.

A logo in PNG format zoomed in several times looks blurry and the text content can become illegible. (Logo designed by Freepik.com)

Because SVG is vector-based, it is worth making a short detour to look at some of the differences between vector-based and pixel-based graphics.

Vector vs. Raster

Today, the majority of images on the web are pixel-based raster graphics, also known as bitmaps.

Bitmaps are images made up of pixels in a grid that contain the color information for the image rendered on the screen. They come in different formats, of which the most popular and commonly used on the web are PNG, JPEG and GIF. Bitmap images have advantages, such as their ability to recreate photographic images with high fidelity, but they suffer from a number of limitations. Obviously, the number one limitation of raster graphics is that they are not scalable — they look blurry when scaled up beyond a certain level. When a bitmap image is zoomed in to, the software or browser needs to create new pixels. It does that by estimating the color values of the new pixels based on the surrounding pixels. This approximation of color values for the new pixels leads to the blurriness of a zoomed image.

Bitmap formats also tend to be bulky, limited to a single — often low — resolution and consume large amounts of bandwidth on the web.

The nautical logo when used in an SVG format scales up while preserving the crispiness of the image.

66 *Images have been the number one obstacle to implementing truly adaptable and performant responsive pages — pages that scale both up and down, efficiently tailoring themselves to both the constraints and the affordances of the browsing context at hand."*
— Responsive Images Done Right [1]

A lot of solutions [2] were introduced, but only recently did we get a responsive images specification that provides us with a *"client-side solution for delivering alternate image data based on device capabilities to prevent wasted bandwidth and optimize display for both screen and print."* [3]

Briefly summarized, the responsive images specification introduces two new attributes to the `<img>` element — namely `sizes` and `srcset` — and a brand new `<picture>` element. Yoav Weiss wrote all about the responsive images solution

1   http://smashingmagazine.com/2014/05/14/responsive-images-done-right-guide-picture-srcset/
2   http://smashingmagazine.com/2013/07/08/choosing-a-responsive-image-solution/
3   http://responsiveimages.org/

and how you can use it in his chapter about responsive images, so we won't go into details here.

Raster images also don't come with the fine control over their content that SVGs offer, so there is no way to style or interact with individual elements of a bitmap image as we can with SVG. That said, bitmaps can be styled using CSS to some extent: CSS filter effects, blending modes, as well as clipping and masking operations can all be used to apply graphics effects to raster images, but the effects are always applied to the image as a whole.

Vector-based graphics are made up of shapes that constitute a set of lines, points, curves and colors that are drawn based on mathematical expressions. This allows SVGs to be scaled up and down while maintaining the spatial relationships between the shapes.

When using SVGs, you don't need to know about the number of pixels on the screen. This, in turn, means that you no longer have to provide @2x, @3x and @4x versions of your graphic, because the images are completely resolution-independent. You only need to serve one asset to your users without ever needing to know what their screen or window size is. As a result, SVGs allow us to balance the quality of images with the amount of bandwidth needed to download them.

More Advantages of SVG

SVG IS TEXT-BASED

Being a text-based format makes SVGs easy to edit, transform and track with version control. Their declarative nature means they often have smaller file sizes than their bitmap counterparts, especially after minification and gzipping.

Because they are XML-based, SVGs tend to contain many repeated fragments of text, which makes them a perfect candidate for lossless data compression algorithms. When an SVG image has been compressed using gzip compression, it is referred to as an SVGZ image and uses the corresponding .svgz filename extension.

- The compression ratio when the SVG is gzipped can be really high, and there are examples in the SVG specification dedicated to minimizing SVG file sizes[4] that show compression ratios as high as 84%. Note that if you host SVG files on a properly configured web server, it will compress files sent to the client by default, so compression of the SVG to SVGZ will then be unnecessary.

If it's not enabled already, you can enable SVG gzipping in your .htaccess file — thereby making sure you serve SVG/SVGZ the right way — by first adding the SVG and SVGZ media types to the list of media types:

```
# Add this to the list of Media files
AddType image/svg+xml svg svgz
```

Next, add the gzip encoding:

```
<IfModule mod_mime.c>
  AddEncoding gzip svgz
</IfModule>
```

Note that this will not gzip your SVGs. It will only make sure the server serves pre-gzipped SVGs correctly. Then, in order to enable dynamic gzipping, you need to specify AddOutputFilterByType DEFLATE and then add the image/svg+xml type to the list of other types you will probably have. For example, in the HTML5 Boilerplate .htaccess file, it looks like this:

```
<IfModule mod_filter.c>
AddOutputFilterByType DEFLATE "application/atom+xml" \
                              "application/javascript" \
                              "application/json" \
                              […]
                              "image/svg+xml" \
                              …etc.
</IfModule>
```

---

4 http://www.w3.org/TR/SVG2/minimize.html

HTML5 Boilerplate's .htaccess file contains a lot of useful reusable code snippets. To check how SVG gzipping is enabled in it, refer to the compression section of the file on Github[5].

SVGS HAVE VERY GOOD BROWSER SUPPORT

SVG 1.1 is supported by the vast majority of web browsers on desktop and mobile devices. It works everywhere except in Internet Explorer 8 (and earlier) and Android 2.3 (and earlier). SVGs are safe to use today, and there are a lot of techniques for providing fallback for browsers that don't support SVG (or even those that do support it but cannot display it for any reason) using simple feature detection techniques. We will cover many different ways for providing fallback later in the chapter.

Note that some SVG features (such as inline SVGs, referencing external SVGs in a <use> element, among others) can have different levels of browser support. Generally speaking, you will need to check support for any specific feature you use to make sure it works in all browsers you intend to reach.

SVGS HAVE BUILT-IN GRAPHICS EFFECTS

SVG comes with the ability to apply filter effects, perform clipping and masking operations, and apply background blending modes similar to those available in Photoshop and other graphics editors — all these effects can be applied to shapes and to text alike. It also comes with other advanced features like patterns and gradients.

SVG TEXT IS SEARCHABLE AND SELECTABLE

We've long used images to display graphical text in techniques for image replacement[6]. These methods are hacks that we used to get the visual result we wanted while providing alternative text for screen readers. With SVG we no longer need them, since we can apply graphical effects to text residing in a <text> element, and that text not only remains searchable and selectable, but will also be there for screen readers as well.

---

5 https://github.com/h5bp/html5-boilerplate/blob/master/dist/.htaccess#L697
6 http://css-tricks.com/css-image-replacement/

Having real text inside an SVG means that...

SVGS ARE ACCESSIBLE

SVG contains a set of accessibility features including elements that describe the graphic and make it accessible to screen readers. SVG also has a very accessible SVG DOM API that allows you to create, inspect and programmatically manipulate the contents of the SVG, which makes them a great candidate for dynamic graphics, visualizations and infographics.

SVGS ARE STYLEABLE AND INTERACTIVE

The SVG DOM API makes interactive behavior scripting using JavaScript a cinch — simply attach an event handler to an SVG node element and you're all set. It can't get any simpler than that.

SVGs can also be styled using CSS (or JavaScript). You can select SVG elements using SVG selectors like ID, class or type selectors (and even pseudo-selectors) and then apply styles to them — just like you would with HTML elements. SVGs also respond to CSS media queries, which makes it possible to adapt the graphic to different viewport sizes by controlling individual elements inside the graphic and styling them. What's more interesting about SVGs is that the *viewport sizes defined in the media query conditions correspond to the size of the SVG viewport*, not the page viewport (unless the SVG is embedded inline in the document — more about this later in the chapter). This encapsulation of styles inside SVG means that *media queries in SVG are actually element queries*, which is incredibly useful for creating modular graphics we can use anywhere, knowing that they will adapt as expected no matter where they are embedded. We'll dive into the details of making SVGs adaptive with media queries later on.

SVG IS EASY TO LEARN

As Chris Coyier says, "You can't learn JPEG", but you can learn SVG. If you're a designer who works with HTML, CSS and JavaScript then you probably already know enough to understand and work with SVGs and get up and running with them fairly quickly.

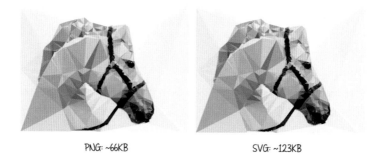

PNG: ~66KB   SVG: ~123KB

A comparison between the file sizes of an image using two different image formats. Horse illustration designed by Freepik.com.

Vector or Raster: Which Is the Better Format?

It depends. Despite all of the advantages of SVG, they are not the best candidate for every kind of image.

SVG is a great way to present vector-based line drawings, but bitmaps are better suited for continuous tone images. Raster images are the preferred format when creating or working with photographs since scanned images and photos taken using a digital camera are raster images by default. If you go with a bitmap, check out Yoav's chapter to find out how to serve the image responsively using the latest standards.

SVG is the preferred format for images like user interface controls, logos, icons and vector-based illustrations. That said, it might not always be the best choice even for those kinds of images. For example, the horse illustration above is an example of a perfect SVG candidate. Despite that, the size of the SVG version of the illustration — even after optimization — is a whopping 123KB, whereas the PNG version (saved to the web from Illustrator) is around 66KB, almost half the size.

If the difference in file size is too big, and since larger file size means more bandwidth and a negative impact on performance, you may want to prioritize performance and go with the bitmap image instead. An SVG graphic may also contain graphical effects like gradients, drop shadows, glows, and similar advanced effects. But using too many effects in an illustration may increase your SVG's size so much that a raster graphic would be preferable.

For example, the Smashing Magazine logo is a perfect candidate for the SVG format, and yet Smashing Magazine serves a PNG version. The reason is that the number of gradients and glow effects included increases the file size to more than 300KB. I personally tried optimizing the file and giving up some of the effects while preserving the overall

An SVG image containing a lot of details and paths. The illustration is designed by Freepik.com.

look; the file size dropped down to around 40KB, but that was still much larger than the 5.9KB PNG file they were (and still are) serving. As a matter of fact, by applying more optimizations[7], they could even drop the PNG size down to around 3.5KB, compared to which the 40KB size is gigantic.

Glows and the other complex graphical effects have also been proven to affect performance in most browsers at the moment.

Complex SVGs containing a lot of paths and details can sometimes also have large file sizes such that a PNG would be a better alternative. For example, the illustration above weighs around 266KB in PNG format, whereas the optimized SVG weighs around 390KB — this is due to the large amount of detail in the illustration.

It is worth noting at this point that even though an PNG file may sometimes be smaller than an SVG file, the table may sometimes be flipped if the dimensions of the image are changed. The same illustration becomes much heavier as a PNG if the dimensions are doubled before it is saved to web; in that case, the SVG format is definitely the better choice.

This is particularly relevant when you need to double the size of the image for double- (or even triple-) density screens.

---

7   http://www.netvlies.nl/blog/design-interactie/retina-revolution

Generally speaking, smaller vector images like icons are best candidates for SVG. If the images contain a lot of details, that's going to come with a cost, and a high-definition PNG could be a much better choice.

The takeaway here is that sometimes even the format that looks like the obvious go-to choice might not be — I recommend that you test and see. In most cases, you may want to provide a PNG fallback for the SVG you're working with, so you're most likely going to have both formats anyway. Also keep in mind that SVGs can be gzipped, so you might want to take that into account as well before deciding. For some images, especially simple icons and illustrations, SVG is the go-to choice. But in some cases, testing is the only way to find out which format is better. Test, compare and then choose.

There are certain things that can help you generate smaller SVG file sizes. We will cover some tips and techniques in an upcoming section, but before we do, let's do a quick overview of SVG code so that you can familiarize yourself with how exported SVG code looks. Feel free to skip to the following section if you're already familiar with SVG code.

Quick Overview of SVG Syntax and Code

An SVG graphic is made up of shapes that are marked up as human-readable XML tags. It's outside the scope of this chapter to go over all of the capabilities of SVG, and the SVG universe is too big to include in just a section of a chapter. However, we'll go over some of the basic and most important SVG elements and syntax quickly by analyzing the code for this bookshelf:

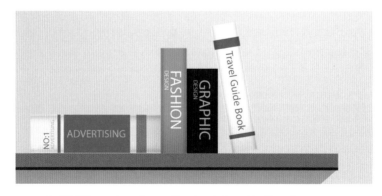

An SVG illustration of a set of books, designed by Freepik.com.

A snippet from the illustration's source code contains the following code:

```
<?xml version="1.0" encoding="utf-8"?>
<svg version="1.1" xmlns="http://www.w3.org/2000/svg"
xmlns:xlink="http://www.w3.org/1999/xlink" width="566px"
height="451px" viewBox="0 0 566 451">
  <g id="background">
    <radialGradient id="SVGID_1_" cx="218" cy="98" r="702.7084"
    gradientTransform="matrix(0 1 -1 0 504 -295.9995)"
    gradientUnits="userSpaceOnUse">
      <stop offset="0" style="stop-color:#F1F2F2"/>
        <stop offset="1" style="stop-color:#D1D3D4"/>
    </radialGradient>
    <rect y="-296" fill="url(#SVGID_1_)" width="800" height="800"/>
  </g>
  <g id="shelf-shadow">
    <linearGradient id="SVGID_2_" gradientUnits="userSpaceOnUse"
    x1="255.9995" y1="179.6211" x2="255.9995" y2="465.0788">
      <stop offset="0" style="stop-color:#414042"/>
      <stop offset="1" style="stop-color:#808285;stop-opacity:0"/>
    </linearGradient>
    <polygon fill="url(#SVGID_2_)"
    points="311,504 512,330.1 0,329.2 0,504     "/>
  </g>

  <g id="shelf">
    <rect y="307.6" fill="#414042" width="511" height="26"/>
    <rect y="307.6" fill="#808285" width="511" height="21.5"/>
  </g>

  <g id="travel-book">
    <path fill="#FFFFFF" d="M383.6,299.6c0.1,0.5-0.1,1-0.5,1.1l-38.8,
    6.5c-0.4,0.1-0.7-0.3-0.8-0.8l-33.1-196.9
      c-0.1-0.5,0.1-1,0.5-1.1l38.8-6.5c0.4-0.1,0.7,0.3,0.8,0.8L383.6,
    299.6z"/>

    <linearGradient id="SVGID_6_" gradientUnits="userSpaceOnUse"
    x1="1080.5625" y1="205.374" x2="1121.2637" y2="205.374"
    gradientTransform="matrix(-0.9861 0.166 0.166 0.9861 1398.4752
    -180.762)">
      <stop offset="0" style="stop-color:#F1F2F2"/>
      <stop offset="4.301080e-002" style="stop-color:#A7A9AC"/>
```

```
    <stop offset="0.2258" style="stop-color:#F1F2F2;stop-opacity:0"/>
  </linearGradient>
  <path opacity="0.4" fill="url(#SVGID_6_)" d="M343.4,306.4c0.1,0.5,
  0.5,0.9,0.8,0.8l38.8-6.5c0.4-0.1,0.6-0.5,0.5-1.1l-33.1-196.9
    c-0.1-0.5-0.5-0.9-0.8-0.8l-38.8,6.5c-0.4,0.1-0.6,0.5-
  0.5,1.1L343.4,306.4z"/>

  <linearGradient id="SVGID_7_" gradientUnits="userSpaceOnUse"
  x1="326.8428" y1="205.374" x2="367.543" y2="205.374"
  gradientTransform="matrix(0.9861 -0.166 0.166 0.9861
  -29.5379 59.6223)">
    <stop offset="0" style="stop-color:#F1F2F2"/>
    <stop offset="4.301080e-002" style="stop-color:#A7A9AC"/>
    <stop offset="0.2258" style="stop-color:#F1F2F2;stop-opacity:0"/>
  </linearGradient>
  <path opacity="0.4" fill="url(#SVGID_7_)" d="M383.6,299.6c0.1,0.
  5-0.1,1-0.5,1.1l-38.8,6.5c-0.4,0.1-0.7-0.3-0.8-0.8l-33.1-196.9
    c-0.1-0.5,0.1-1,0.5-1.1l38.8-6.5c0.4-0.1,0.7,0.3,0.8,0.8L383.6,
  299.6z"/>
  <linearGradient id="SVGID_8_" gradientUnits="userSpaceOnUse"
  x1="347.1924" y1="303.7969" x2="347.1924" y2="157.856" gradient
  Transform="matrix(0.9861 -0.166 0.166 0.9861 -29.5379 59.6223)">
    <stop offset="0" style="stop-color:#A7A9AC"/>
    <stop offset="0.6183" style="stop-color:#F1F2F2;stop-opacity:0"/>
  </linearGradient>
  <path opacity="0.4" fill="url(#SVGID_8_)" d="M343.4,306.4c0.1,0.5,
  0.5,0.9,0.8,0.8l38.8-6.5c0.4-0.1,0.6-0.5,0.5-1.1l-33.1-196.9
    c-0.1-0.5-0.5-0.9-0.8-0.8l-38.8,6.5c-0.4,0.1-0.6,0.5-
  0.5,1.1L343.4,306.4z"/>

  <g>
  <text transform="matrix(0.166 0.9861 -0.9861 0.166 333.0215
  148.8447)" fill="#1C75BC" font-family="'PTSans-Bold'"
  font-size="16.6835">Travel Guide Book</text>
  </g>

  <rect x="314.8" y="127.7" transform="matrix(0.9861 -0.166 0.166
  0.9861 -17.7578 57.5111)" fill="#1C75BC" width="40.7" height="14.6"/>

  <rect x="339.1" y="276.2" transform="matrix(0.9861 -0.166 0.166
  0.9861 -41.3653 63.5511)" fill="#1C75BC" width="40.7" height="6.1"/>
</g>
```

```
<g id="advertising-book">
  <!--...-->
</g>
</svg>
```

You can see a lot of <g> elements in there: this is the SVG group element, used for logically grouping together sets of related graphical elements. The <g> element serves a similar purpose to the Group Objects function in Adobe Illustrator and other graphics tools. You can also imagine a group in SVG as being similar to a layer in a graphics editor, since a layer is also a grouping of elements.

The <g> element is not the only one used for grouping elements. For the sake of brevity, I won't mention the others because those could take up an entire chapter on their own. If you're interested, feel free to check out my article I wrote about structuring, grouping, and referencing elements in SVG[8].

Groups are used to associate individual elements that make up parts of the image. For example, each book is contained within a group with an ID that defines that book. The bookshelf consists of two <rect> (rectangle) elements that are also grouped together.

Another element you see several times is the <linearGradient> element. Most SVG elements are logically named; thus, as its name shows, this element creates a linear gradient. Each linear gradient gets a unique ID. The gradients are then referenced by their IDs and used as values for the fill attribute wherever you want to use them. For instance, the shadow beneath the book shelf is made up of a <polygon> that has a linear gradient fill color. Every linear gradient is defined by two or more <stop> elements that define the colors and where these colors start (the offset). If you're familiar with CSS gradients, this syntax will look fairly familiar to you.

The text on the books is marked up as real text using the SVG <text> element. The text "Travel Guide Book" is rotated using the SVG transform attribute. As you can see, SVG code is straightfoward and easy to understand. If you come from an HTML background, you won't need a lot of time to get acquainted with SVG code.

---

8 http://sarasoueidan.com/blog/structuring-grouping-referencing-in-svg/

As we finish looking into the syntax, and before we get to the SVG workflow, let's shed some light on one of the most important yet least understood attributes in SVG: the good ol' viewBox.

Understanding the SVG Viewport and viewBox

We'll start with a look at the difference between the viewBox attribute and the SVG viewport. The viewBox attribute also has a companion attribute, preserveAspectRatio, that controls its position and size; we'll take a quick look at this attribute as we cover the other concepts as well.

Before we get into the three concepts, we need to define what the *SVG canvas* is. The canvas is the space or area where the SVG content is drawn. Conceptually, this canvas is infinite in both dimensions. The SVG can therefore be of any size. However, it is rendered on the screen relative to a finite region known as the viewport. Areas of the SVG that lie beyond the boundaries of the viewport are clipped off and not visible.

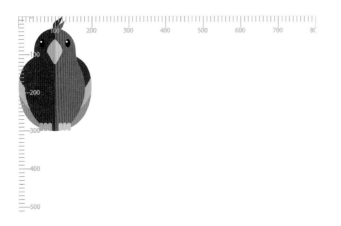

An SVG parrot illustration. The image shows the initial coordinate systems established on the SVG — these coordinate systems are initially identical, and established by the SVG width and height values.

The SVG viewport is defined by the SVG's height and width. It is to the SVG what a page viewport is to a page. Once the width and height of the outermost SVG element are set, the browser establishes an initial viewport coordinate system and an initial user coordinate system.

The initial viewport coordinate system is established on the viewport with its origin at the top-left corner of the viewport at point 0, 0; the positive *x*-axis points towards the right, the positive *y*-axis points down; and one unit in the initial coordinate system equals one pixel in the viewport.

The initial user coordinate system is established on the SVG canvas. This coordinate system is initially identical to the viewport coordinate system.

Using the viewBox attribute, the initial user coordinate system (also known as the current coordinate system, or user space in use) can be modified so that it is not identical to the viewport coordinate system.

Then, using the preserveAspectRatio attribute, the current user coordinate system (that of the canvas) can be scaled and positioned inside the viewport.

If the aspect ratio of the viewport (viewport coordinate system) is the same as that of the viewBox (the current user coordinate system), the latter will scale to fill the viewport area. And if the aspect ratio of the viewBox is not the same of that of the viewport, the preserveAspectRatio is used to specify the position of the viewBox inside the viewport, and how it is scaled. preserveAspectRatio is made up of two parts: a keyword that specifies the position of the viewBox inside the viewport; and a keyword that specifies the scaling.

I like to think of the viewBox as the "real" coordinate system. After all, it is the coordinate system used to draw the SVG graphics on the canvas. This coordinate system can be smaller or bigger than the viewport, and it can be fully or partially visible inside the viewport, too. At this point I tend to also forget the viewport coordinate system even exists and think of it as just a container for the viewBox.

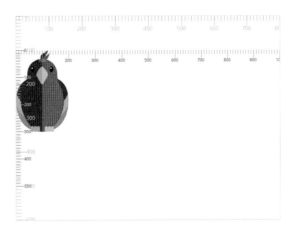

The blue coordinate system is the user coordinate system established on the SVG canvas when the viewBox value is no longer identical to the initial coordinate system (in gray). In this screenshot, the viewBox is set to "0 0 1000 500": the width and height of the user coordinate systems are 1,000 units and 500 units, respectively, with an aspect ratio that is not equal to that of the viewport. The system is positioned at the center of the viewport and scaled so that it is completely contained within it. Using the preserveAspectRatio attribute, this can be changed further.

The way the viewBox is positioned and scaled inside the viewport is similar to the way a background image is positioned and scaled inside an element's background positioning area in CSS using background positioning and sizing properties.

To dive into the syntax and meaning of each value would require an entire chapter, so I recommend that you check out my article about this subject instead. The article is extensive, really long and contains a lot of visual explanations and examples, in addition to an interactive demo to help grasp the concept of coordinate systems in SVG. You can read the article on my blog[9].

When you create an SVG in Illustrator, the dimensions of the artboard define the dimensions of the viewport, and for any exported SVG the viewBox is usually initially identical to the viewport.

Creating and Exporting SVGs in Vector Authoring Tools

There are several tools for creating and editing SVGs. The three most popular are Adobe Illustrator, Inkscape, and Sketch. Most designers' favorite editor is Illustrator, and it's the only one I've worked with, so I will refer to it throughout the chapter, but most of the concepts apply to all other vector authoring tools as well.

PICKING THE RIGHT WORKFLOW WHEN DESIGNING SVGS

Sometimes, vector editors simply fail at translating an illustration into clean SVG code. Sometimes, not only does the code look bad, but the visual result looks bad, too. Here are some useful tips for creating SVGs that can help you end up with cleaner code and overall better results.

1. Convert Text to Outlines

Converting text to outlines allows you to avoid embedding the font in the SVG. To convert your text to outlines, select your text and then go to *Type → Create Outlines*. This will convert the text into vector shapes that make up the text shape.

Note that converting the text to outlines will make it unsearchable and inaccessible. Decide whether the text needs to be accessible before you do that. If the

---

9 http://sarasoueidan.com/blog/svg-coordinate-systems/

text is part of a graphic that is not supposed to convey a specific text message (maybe it's part of a logo) then you can convert to outlines without having to worry about the text's availability to assistive technologies.

It is worth mentioning at this point that even though you can convert text to outlines while you're editing the SVG, you can skip this step altogether because you have the option to do this when you export the SVG from Illustrator — more about this in the next section.

2. Use Simpler Geometric Shapes

Neither convert these shapes to paths, nor use paths to draw simple geometric shapes such as circles, rectangles, ellipses and polygons, or polylines. The code required to draw geometric shapes is generally small. Drawing the same shapes using an SVG path usually requires extra path data in the code and hence increases the overall file size. The growth in file size may be insignificant, but if you have a lot of shapes and you convert all of them to paths, they add up.

Moreover, simple shapes are easier to maintain and manipulate by hand. Paths don't come with some of the attributes simple shapes have, such as x, y , height and width. These attributes make animating simple shapes' geometry and positions simpler; paths, on the other hand, require a more complex approach.

3. Simplify Paths

The simpler the paths, the less data is needed to represent them, hence less code and smaller overall file sizes. You can simplify a path by first selecting it and then going to *Object → Path → Simplify*. When you do that, and while

Screenshot showing the number of points our example path is initially made up of.

the path simplification panel is open, you can see a preview of the path and how it is affected by the simplification process. For example, suppose we have the path shown above. You can see the number of points it consists of (the small blue squares).

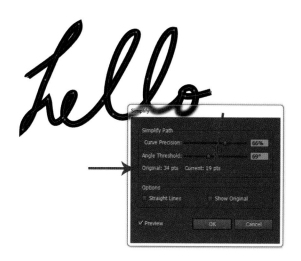

Screenshot showing the number of points the path is made up of after simplification.

If we were to simplify the path, we can specify the amount of precision we want to preserve. Here, I reduced the number of points from 34 to 19. Fewer points means less path data and consequently a smaller file size.

4. Combine or Unite Paths When Possible

Similar to path simplification, combining paths can reduce file size significantly depending on the illustration and how the elements inside it are drawn.

5. Use Good Naming Conventions and Name Files Appropriately

This is particularly important if you're going to use automated workflows such as SVG sprite creation. Most of the tools out there use the SVG file names when generating new assets. That is why using good naming conventions will save you a lot of time in later stages of your work.

In addition, the layer and group names you use in Illustrator will be translated to IDs in the SVG code. Instead of ending up with editor-generated names that make absolutely no sense at all, naming your elements and layers appropriately will save you some additional manual work. You will thank yourself for this especially if you are going to use CSS and JavaScript to style and manipulate the SVG.

6. Fit Artboard to Drawing

Ever worked with SVG and had to deal with extra white space around an icon that just won't go away no matter how you manipulate the width of it? In many cases, the white space is the result of a drawing that is drawn inside an SVG viewport — the artboard in Illustrator — that is wider than the drawing itself.

The white space will be hard to get rid of unless you know how to manipulate the SVG's viewBox attribute. If you do, you can crop the SVG to the drawing. However, if you don't want to get your hands dirty with code, you can save yourself some time by selecting your entire illustration and then going to *Object → Artboards → Fit to Selected Art*.

Adobe Illustrator comes with an options panel that provides you with a set of additional choices that allow you to optimize your SVGs further before you export them from the editor.

EXPORTING SVGS FOR THE WEB FROM ADOBE ILLUSTRATOR

Once you're done editing your image, you're ready to export it. Most editors provide several image formats to choose from.

To export your image as SVG, choose *File → Save As*. A panel will open with a drop-down select menu to choose the format you want to use. Select SVG. Below the select menu, there is a checkbox option labelled "Use Artboards". This option can be useful when you have created several symbols (e.g. icons) that you need to export as individual files. You can use this option to easily create one artboard per symbol, and output several SVG files (one per symbol) in a single operation.

Click "Save" and an Options panel will open. The screenshot below shows the best settings to choose for the web.

The export options panel in Illustrator with the best options for web chosen.

Michaël Chaize, a senior Creative Cloud evangelist at Adobe, wrote an article explaining what each option does and means[10]. Let's go over them briefly.

- The SVG Profile drop-down allows you to select different versions of SVG. The best option is SVG 1.1 as it's the version recommended by the W3C.
- In the *Fonts* section, you can choose the kind of font to use in the SVG code. There are three options: Adobe CEF, SVG and "Convert to outline". The most obvious one to choose is probably the SVG type. However, it is useful to convert the fonts to outlines in order to avoid embedding web fonts. It is also worth noting that SVG fonts do not work properly in Firefox and Internet Explorer — and may never do, so you might want to stay clear of this option. Converting text to outlines has many benefits, but know that sometimes — if you're using handwritten fonts or script typefaces, for example — converting a text to outlines may increase your file size quite a bit; you may need to test and choose what your best option is and then make sure to optimize the SVG afterward as well.
- In the *Options* section you can choose whether you want any images to be embedded inline inside the SVG or be exported as external bitmaps and referenced inside the SVG using an `xlink:href` attribute on an `<image>` element. Generally, you will want to stay away from bitmaps, so it is recommended to choose the Embed option.
- In the *Advanced Options* section, you can specify whether you want the styles to be exported and applied using Presentation Attributes or CSS Properties. Depending on how you want to use your SVG, you can choose either option — both are OK. When the styles are applied using CSS, they are embedded inside the SVG as style blocks in `<style>` elements. You can then change these styles just like you would in your style sheets for HTML elements. Presentation attributes, on the other hand, are literally attributes (e.g. `fill="#009966"`) and are set on each element in the SVG as necessary.

---

10   http://creativedroplets.com/export-svg-for-the-web-with-illustrator-cc/

Exporting the styles as CSS properties can be particularly useful if you have a lot of repetitive styles, in which case having any common styles inside one style block and applying them to multiple elements using CSS selectors would certainly save some bytes. Also, presentation attributes are overridden by any inline or external styles applied to an element — with the exception of inherited styles and user agent styles — so if you want to change the styles at any point, being able to find them in one style block will not only be convenient, but also helps avoid some cascade headaches.

It's worth noting that not all SVG attributes can be set using CSS, so you may sometimes have to edit presentation attributes as well, even if you have chosen to export the styles as blocks of CSS.

- The *Decimal Places* option tells Illustrator how many decimal places to use for point coordinates. One decimal place is usually enough — any more will bloat your file size. Note that if you choose more than one decimal place and then use an optimization tool to reduce the number to one, you may end up breaking your SVG; it's generally a good idea to set this value to 1 when you export the SVG.
- The remaining options in the *Advanced Options* section need not be checked, so you can uncheck all of them.

At this point it is worth mentioning one of Illustrator's nicest features: you can copy any shape or group of shapes to the clipboard, from Illustrator, and then paste it into your text editor as SVG code!

After exporting the SVG, it is time to optimize it even *further*.

Optimizing SVGs Using Standalone Optimization Tools

No matter what vector editing tool you use, none of them outputs perfectly clean and optimized code. Exported SVGs usually contain a lot of redundant and useless information such as editor metadata, comments, empty groups, default or non-optimal values and other junk that can be safely removed or changed without affecting the rendered SVG. Using a standalone optimization tool to optimize the code further is generally a good idea.

There are several optimization tools available. The most popular tool is *SVG Optimizer*[11] (SVGO) by Kir Belevich. SVGO is a Node.js-based SVG optimization tool. You can install and use SVGO via the terminal by first installing it using the Node Package Manager (npm):

```
npm install -g svgo
```

Then, you can optimize files by simply calling `svgo` on a single file:

```
svgo mySVG.svg
```

or an entire folder:

```
svgo -f
../path/to/folder/with/svg/files
```

Other options and arguments are available and documented in SVGO's GitHub repository.

However, optimizing files and folders manually like this can quickly become tedious. Fortunately, SVGO has many tools available that allow you to integrate it in any phase of your workflow.

SVGO TOOLS TO INTEGRATE INTO PRACTICALLY ANY WORKFLOW

The SVGO Grunt plugin

SVGO is available as a Grunt plugin[12], as well as a Gulp plugin[13]. Both plugins allow you to automate the optimization process, saving you a lot of time and effort. Links to all formats of the optimizer can be found in its GitHub repository.

To install the Grunt SVGO plugin, you start with:

```
npm install --save-dev grunt-svgmin
```

---

11   https://github.com/svg/svgo
12   https://github.com/sindresorhus/grunt-svgmin
13   https://github.com/ben-eb/gulp-svgmin

Then, in your *gruntfile*, the settings may look similar to this:

```
require(';load-grunt-tasks';)(grunt); // npm install --save-dev
load-grunt-tasks

grunt.initConfig({
    svgmin: {
        options: {
            plugins: [
                {
                    removeViewBox: false
                }, {
                    removeUselessStrokeAndFill: false
                }
            ]
        },
        dist: {
            files: {
                ';dist/unicorn.svg';: ';app/unicorn.svg';
            }
        }
    }
});
grunt.registerTask(';default';, [';svgmin';]);
```

The above example can be found in the Grunt plugin's GitHub repository.

If you haven't used Grunt before and don't know how or where to start, I recommend reading Chris Coyier's popular 24 ways article, "Grunt for People Who Think Things Like Grunt are Weird and Hard"[14].

At this point — and before we move forward — it is worth mentioning that you will not want to use all of SVGO's default optimizations. The optimizations are available as plugins that you can either enable or disable, thereby controlling which optimizations apply. Certain optimizations can do much more harm than good, and may end up completely breaking your SVG.

For instance, one optimization that you must *not apply at all* is the one that removes the viewBox attribute. You'll want to make sure the viewBox attribute is

---

14   http://24ways.org/2013/grunt-is-not-weird-and-hard/

always set, otherwise controlling the SVG and making it responsive will not be possible. We'll talk more about making SVGs responsive with CSS later in this chapter.

Whether you use SVGO or any other optimization tool, bear in mind that, sometimes, combining paths or decreasing the number of decimal points can completely break the SVG. If your SVG contains gradients, then removing IDs will break those; and if it contains blur or drop shadows that are embedded as bitmaps, then removing the xlink attribute will break these effects.

The SVGO Illustrator Plugin: SVG NOW

SVG NOW[15] is an SVG exporter for Adobe Illustrator released by Adobe's David Deraedt. It is aimed at optimizing SVG files by post-processing the generated SVG code using SVGO. It is built on top of Illustrator's SVG exporter, controls some of its parameters and default values, and runs a customized version of SVGO with an HTML GUI built on top of it to control its plugins. In essence, it is SVGO integrated into Illustrator.

Once more, the optimizations you apply using SVG NOW may end up breaking your SVG, and unfortunately there is no live feedback to tell if the checked optimizations will break the SVG or not. This means that you may sometimes end up exporting a broken SVG, and thus may need to go back to the editor, choose other optimizations, and then export again — hopefully not breaking your SVG each time.

The SVGO GUI

SVGO comes with a nice and simple drag-and-drop GUI[16] that is available for download on Windows, Mac OS X and Linux. You simply drag your images into the GUI and the SVGs are automatically optimized for you on the fly (see the image below). Notice how the file size of the SVGs decreases significantly after applying the optimizations.

15 https://github.com/davidderaedt/SVG-NOW
16 https://github.com/svg/svgo-gui

Image showing the SVGO GUI along with the results of optimizing several SVG files using the GUI. Photo Credit: SVGO GUI Github Repo.

Running your SVGs through SVGO several times can yield further optimizations with each pass. But remember, your SVG may end up completely broken and there is no way to tell whether it will be broken or not before you drop them into the GUI. I recommend you keep a backup copy for each SVG you optimize, since the GUI replaces the SVG with the optimized one by default.

SVGO OS X Folder Action

SVGO also comes with a Mac OS X folder action[17] that allows you to set up the tool for any folder and automatically optimize any files you drop into that folder.

The SVGO Web GUI: SVGOMG

Google's Jake Archibald created an SVGO-based web GUI called *SVGOMG*[18] that provides us with the feature missing from the SVGO tools mentioned so far: a live preview. Using the web GUI, you can check the set of SVGO optimizations that you want and get live feedback showing you the result of applying that optimization to your SVG.

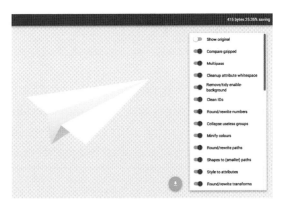

Screenshot showing the SVGO Web GUI.

---

17 https://github.com/svg/svgo-osx-folder-action
18 http://jakearchibald.github.io/svgomg/

The web GUI allows you to upload an SVG file, or input SVG code directly into the app, apply the optimizations as needed, preview the amount of savings and compare the SVG with the original one, among other options. Once you're finished, you can download the optimized SVG.

If you're not in need of automation, this tool may come in handy for some simple projects that need a quick one-time optimization.

It is also worth mentioning that the SVGOMG GUI works offline in browsers that support Service Workers.

SVGO is a great SVG optimization tool that comes with a set of extensions and apps that make it suitable for almost any kind of workflow. But you need to remember that whether you are using SVGO or any other optimization tool, your SVG's document structure and styles are likely to be changed in most cases.

You don't have to worry about optimizing your SVG with SVGO if your only intention is to use the SVG as a static image. If you want to use the SVG as a document for scripting or other animation purposes, then keep in mind that your entire document structure is going to change and this will eventually affect your animations and scripts — they might even end up not working anymore.

Choose any optimization tool, but make sure you optimize your SVG as much as possible to make sure it is ready to be embedded and used in your projects. The smaller the SVG's file size and cleaner the code, the better it is for production and performance.

Embedding SVGs

There are six ways to embed an SVG in a page, each with its advantages and disadvantages. You choose the embedding technique depending on how you're going to use the SVG and whether you need to script and style it after embedding. An SVG can be embedded in one of the following ways:

1. As an image using the `<img>` element:

```
<img src="mySVG.svg" alt="" />
```

2. As a background image in CSS:

```
.el {background-image: url(mySVG.svg);}
```

3. As an object using the `<object>` element:

```
<object type="image/svg+xml" data="mySVG.svg"><!--fallback here-->
</object>
```

4. As an iframe using an `<iframe>` element:

```
<iframe src="mySVG.svg"><!-- fallback here --></iframe>
```

5. Using the `<embed>` element:

```
<embed type="image/svg+xml" src="mySVG.svg" />
```

6. Inline using the `<svg>` element:

```
<svg version="1.1" xmlns="http://www.w3.org/2000/svg" … >
<!-- svg content --></svg>
```

USING <OBJECT>

The `<object>` element is the primary way to include an external SVG file. The main advantage of using this element is that there is a standard mechanism for providing an image (or text) fallback if the SVG is not rendered. If the SVG cannot be displayed for any reason — perhaps the specified URI is wrong — the browser will display the content between the opening and closing `<object>` tags.

```
<object type="image/svg+xml" data="mySVG.svg">
  <img src="fallback-image.png" alt="…" />
</object>
```

If you intend to use any advanced SVG features such as CSS and scripting, the HTML5 `<object>` element is your best option. You will probably want to fall back to a raster version of the SVG image using the `<img>` tag, as we did in the previous example. However, providing fallback this way has a bad consequence: browsers that support SVG will request both the SVG and the fallback image, resulting in an unnecessary extra HTTP request.

In order to avoid the double requests problem, you can provide the PNG fallback image as a background image in CSS rather than as a foreground image in HTML. To provide the fallback as a background image, instead of adding `<img>` between the opening and closing `<object>` tags, you would insert a `<div>` and then set the fallback image as a background image for the `<div>`:

```
<object id="logo" type="image/svg+xml" data="logo.svg">
  <div></div>
</object>
#logo div {
  background-image: url(path/to/fallback/logo.png);
  /* other styles here */
}
```

This workaround is used by the folks of *Clearleft*; David Bushell wrote about it in a primer to SVG[19] that he published on his blog.

Browsers supporting SVG will display the SVG referenced in `<object>` and the `<div>` will neither be displayed nor styled, thus avoiding the request for the PNG background image. Only if the browser does not support SVG does the `<div>` inside it get rendered and styled with the fallback PNG.

USING <IFRAME>

Since browsers can render SVG documents in their own right, it is possible to embed and display an SVG using an iframe. This may be a good method if you want to completely separate SVG code and script from your main page. However, manipulating an SVG image from your main page's JavaScript becomes a little more difficult, and is subject to the same origin policy, which permits running your scripts on the iframe only if the iframe and your main page originate from the main site. You can read more about the same origin policy

---

19 http://dbushell.com/2013/02/04/a-primer-to-front-end-svg-hacking/

on Wikipedia[20]. The `<iframe>` element, just like the `<object>` element, comes with a default way for providing fallback for browsers that don't support SVG between the opening and closing `<iframe>` tags.

USING `<EMBED>`

While it was non-standard in the past, the `<embed>` element is today a part of the WHATWG HTML Living Standard and the HTML5 Candidate Recommendation. Its purpose is to include content that needs an external plugin to work. The Adobe Flash plugin requires the use of `<embed>` and supporting it is the only real reason for its use with SVG. The `<embed>` element has no default fallback mechanism.

USING `<IMG>` AND CSS

Like any other image format, an SVG can be embedded using an `<img>` element. It can also be embedded as a background image in CSS.

Unfortunately, an SVG embedded as an image using either of these techniques cannot be interacted with, whether using CSS (e.g hover interactions) or JavaScript (e.g. click interactions, etc.).

Moreover, the contents of the SVG cannot be selected and styled from the style sheet, because the SVG is in another document and styles don't apply across documents. This is also why SVGs referenced externally in any of the other previously mentioned embedding techniques cannot be styled using CSS from the main page.

That said, if you are using a CSS preprocessor like LESS or Sass you may be able to modify an SVG's background fill color. Zach Schnackel wrote about a technique that uses LESS to do it[21] that you can check out.

Even though the contents of the SVG cannot be selected with CSS, you can still style an SVG image and change its overall styles and colors using CSS filters. An SVG image is an image, after all. And just as we can apply CSS filters to bitmap images, we can do the same to SVG images as well.

---

20 http://en.wikipedia.org/wiki/Same-origin_policy
21 http://zslabs.com/articles/svg-background-fill

Using CSS filter functions like `grayscale()`, `saturation()` and `hue-rotate()` among others, you can change the color, saturation, brightness and even blurriness of an SVG image. Multiple filters can be used by chaining them together, resulting in even more diverse effects. You can then use CSS transitions and animations to animate the style changes using these filters.

Animations do work in an SVG embedded as using `<img>` or embedded as a background image, but only if they are defined inside the root `<svg>`.

Generally speaking, pretty much everything that applies to an SVG embedded as a background image in CSS also applies to an SVG embedded using an `<img>` tag, CSS- and JavaScript-wise.

EMBEDDING SVGS INLINE

An SVG can also be embedded in a document inline — as a "code island" — using the `<svg>` element. Today, this is one of the most popular ways for embedding SVGs. Working with an inline SVG and CSS becomes a lot easier, as the SVG can be styled and animated by targeting it using style rules placed anywhere in the document — the styles don't need to be included between the opening and closing `<svg>` tags to work. On the other hand, the other techniques require the CSS styles and animations to be present inside the `<svg>`.

If you embed the SVG inline and apply the styles inside the SVG in a `<style>` block, these styles will affect other inline SVGs in the document. That is, if you have two `<svg>` elements in your page, and each of them has an element with an ID #paw, then if the first `<svg>` has styles applied to the element #paw, these styles will also be applied to the #paw element in the second `<svg>` — unless, of course, these styles are explicitly overridden. The takeaway here is that styles inside an inline `<svg>` can affect elements inside another `<svg>` in the same document.

Embedding SVGs as code islands in the HTML is a good choice, as long as you're willing to add to the size of the page. In addition, an inline SVG cannot be cached, and hence will require the same amount of time to render and load with every visit, unlike an image referenced using `<img>`. That adds an extra HTTP request, but browsers can then take advantage of their default caching to speed up any subsequent loads. That said, it is generally a good idea to serve resources with far-future *Expires* headers. You can do that by adding or changing a few lines in your website's `.htaccess` file. The HTML5 Boilerplate `.htaccess`[22] contains a lot of excellent ready-to-use snippets; among these snippets, you can find the few lines that specify the cache times of different file types, including media types.

```
# ---------------------------------------------------------------------
# | Expires header              |
# ---------------------------------------------------------------------

# Serve resources with far-future expires headers.
# (!) If you don't control versioning with filename-based
# cache busting, you should consider lowering the cache times
# to something like one week.
# https://httpd.apache.org/docs/current/mod/mod_expires.html

<IfModule mod_expires.c>
    ExpiresActive on
    ExpiresDefault "access plus 1 month"
  # CSS
    ExpiresByType text/css "access plus 1 year"
  # ... more file types and configurations here ...

  # Media files
    ExpiresByType audio/ogg "access plus 1 month"
    ExpiresByType image/bmp "access plus 1 month"
    ExpiresByType image/gif "access plus 1 month"
    ExpiresByType image/jpeg "access plus 1 month"
    ExpiresByType image/png "access plus 1 month"
    ExpiresByType image/svg+xml "access plus 1 month"
    ExpiresByType video/mp4 "access plus 1 month"
    ExpiresByType video/ogg "access plus 1 month"
    ExpiresByType video/webm "access plus 1 month"

  # ... more file types and configurations ...
```

Notice the `image/svg+xml` type included in the snippet.

---

22 https://github.com/h5bp/html5-boilerplate/blob/master/dist/.htaccess

- You are likely to come across a lot of inline SVG implementations. Some of these implementations include the SVG `xmlns` (XML namespace) attribute on the root `<svg>` and some don't. The truth of the matter is that if you embed your SVG inline in an HTML5 document, the `xmlns` attribute is no longer required.

The way you embed your SVG will affect any CSS and JavaScript animations and interactions that you may apply later. As a rule of thumb, SVG-as-image (an SVG embedded using an `img` tag or as a CSS background image) cannot be interacted with, and so any hover or click interactions, for example, will not work. CSS animations will only work if they are defined inside the root `<svg>` element. The `<object>`, `<iframe>`, and `<embed>` elements require CSS animations and interactions to be defined inside the `<svg>` as well, because styles do not apply across documents. And an SVG embedded inline can be interacted with and animated no matter where the animations and interactions are defined.

Using SVGs as an Icon Font Replacement
(or, How to Create SVG Sprites and Use Them as an Icon System)

SVGs are great candidates for icons. But are they good enough to replace icon fonts?

SVG ICONS VS. ICON FONTS

SVGs make a superior icon system and have lots of advantages over icon fonts or bitmap image sprites. Many articles have been written listing the advantages of SVG as an icon system[23] — here are some of the most important ones.

Scalability and resolution-independence

SVG icons are scalable and resolution-independent, which means they won't look blurry on high-resolution screens. Icon fonts, on the other hand, do not look as crisp because browsers see them as text and might apply anti-aliasing to them.

---

23 http://ianfeather.co.uk/ten-reasons-we-switched-from-an-icon-font-to-svg/

Styles and animation

SVG icons can be styled, multicolored and animated. Icon fonts can be styled like fonts can be — only their size, alignment and colors can be changed. SVG icons, on the other hand, offer finer control over individual parts of the icon, which makes it possible to create multicolor icons without having to resort to stacking techniques[24]. These techniques are used to make multi-color icon fonts possible, but for each colored part of the icon they require a different element, which are then stacked on top of one another. SVGs are also animatable, using CSS, native SVG animations, or JavaScript — which opens the door for a lot of creativity with user interface icons[25].

Semantics

SVGs are semantic. An SVG icon is a graphic — an image — so what better way to mark up an image than to use a (scalable vector) graphic tag? An SVG element (<svg>) represents an icon simply and semantically, while icon fonts usually require non-semantic markup like pseudo-elements and empty <span>s to be displayed. For people concerned about semantics and accessibility this introduces a serious issue: these elements don't accommodate screen readers well, not to mention that the markup generally just doesn't make much sense — if any — for an image.

SVGs, on the other hand, are not only semantic, but also *accessible* — even the text inside them is fully searchable, selectable and accessible, too. SVGs also contain accessibility features that allow us to make them even more useful to screen readers.

Browser support

Icon fonts have inconsistent browser support issues and quirks. Zach Leatherman has undertaken and shared a lot of research about the different issues caused by icon fonts across browsers: icons not showing up, not being loaded, or not displaying consistently across browsers; not to mention those browsers

---

24 (February 20, 2014). http://css-tricks.com/stackicons-icon-fonts/
25 http://tympanus.net/codrops/2013/11/05/animated-svg-icons-with-snap-svg/

that don't support @font-face at all. He wrote an extensive article[26] explaining what needs to be done to use bulletproof accessible icon fonts. With SVG, it's an either–or situation: the SVG is either displayed or not displayed, depending on whether the browser supports SVGs or not. If the browser cannot display your SVG icons, it will degrade gracefully and display the PNG fallback you've provided; with icon fonts, we don't have the advantage of falling back to an alternative image format.

Ease of use

SVGs are generally easier to create, use, embed and maintain. Icon fonts require a lot of work — you can either create your own icon fonts (not that simple) or use services such as Icomoon[27] to create the font. Then comes the embedding part using @font-face (and all the weird browser issues that comes with); then using CSS pseudo-elements or non-semantic elements to embed them in the page; and dealing with positioning quirks, as well as the limited styling capabilities. SVGs don't have any of these issues — they can be created and embedded more simply and you have full control of their content.

Icon fonts present browser support and inconsistency issues that require a lot of maintenance. That said, once you have applied all the necessary fixes, they work in all browsers — even old browsers like IE6! SVGs work across all browsers that support them. Support doesn't go as deep as for icon fonts, but fallbacks can be provided and even automated for non-supporting browsers.

Worth reading on these issues and more is Chris Coyier's cagematch-style article[28] comparing SVG icons with icon fonts.

The folks at the Filament Group have also shared an extensive browser support spreadsheet[29] that shows the state of browser compatibility for icon fonts versus SVG fonts created using the Grunticon icons generator they have built (we will talk more about this generator in the next section).

---

26 http://www.filamentgroup.com/lab/bulletproof_icon_fonts.html
27 https://icomoon.io/
28 http://css-tricks.com/icon-fonts-vs-svg/
29 http://goo.gl/KHaqgn

The spreadsheet clearly shows that SVG icon fonts have excellent browser support compared to icon fonts.

In the next section, we'll talk about creating and using SVG sprites, and the tools used to automate our workflows and provide fallbacks.

SPRITING SVGS

Suppose you've reached the point where you have a set of SVG files, each representing an icon, and you want to use these icons in your page. The first things that come to mind when creating icon systems are image sprites. And SVGs can be sprited, too. There are different SVG spriting techniques and tools to automate the workflow for each technique. Depending on whether you want to use the SVG icons as background images or foreground images, different tools can be used and different fallback options are available. If you want to use the icons as background images, this means they will be inserted via CSS and be included in the CSS file. An example would be to include the SVG in the CSS using data URIs:

```
.twitter-icon {
    background-image: url('data:image/svg+xml;…');
    background-repeat: no-repeat;
    background-position: 10em 10em;
}
```

The `background-position` property is used to specify which part of the sprite to display. It works by positioning the sprite in the background positioning area so that only the icon we want will be visible.

SVGs used as background images are static — you cannot add any interactions or transitions to them, and only styles and animations included inside the SVG's root element (`<svg>`) will work. If you want the SVGs to be foreground images, the SVG sprite can be either present in the HTML document or external to it. The sprite would contain all individual icons, and then you can refer to these icons anywhere in the document with a `<use>` element; for example:

```
<svg class="icon twitter-icon">
  <use xlink:href="#twitter-icon"></use>
</svg>
```

Let's go over the different spriting techniques, each of which has its pros and cons. If any of these techniques is not for you, you can certainly imagine a whole array of similar situations in which to use SVG.

SVG icon system with icons as background images

To create an SVG sprite for icons that are going to be referenced in CSS, we're going to use the Grumpicon[30] app by the Filament Group, or its sister command-line utility, Grunticon[31]. Grumpicon is the non-command-line-savvy designer's alternative to Grunticon. Among other options (which we'll mention later in the chapter), Grunticon generates an SVG sprite out of a set of SVG images, to be used as background images in CSS.

There are other[32] tools[33] for automating the creation of SVG sprites that are more or less similar to Grunticon, but it is the one I'm familiar with and I usually use it when I want to use icons as background images, so it is the one I'm going to cover in this section.

The icons we're going to see in this example are from Icomoon, an online app used to generate custom icon fonts. It allows you to pick any number of icons from a set of icon font libraries, and then download the icon font files and use them directly in your project. Icomoon also gives you an option to download the icons as images instead of fonts, and has an option for downloading CSS image sprites as well.

After picking your icons, the "Generate SVG/PNG" button at the bottom of the viewport will generate the result.

A secondary screen displays a list of the icons you picked. Once you've downloaded the files, you'll get a file containing several other files and folders — the one we're interested in is the SVG folder. The SVG folder contains the icons you selected as separate SVG files. The downloaded icons are usually of a single color, so you may want to edit them.

---

30 http://grumpicon.com/
31 https://github.com/filamentgroup/grunticon
32 http://iconizr.com/
33 https://github.com/jkphl/svg-sprite

The next step is to input your SVG folder into either Grumpicon or Grunticon. Make sure your SVG files have meaningful names: Grunticon and Grumpicon will use these names to generate class names in the CSS.

Using Grumpicon, all you have to do is drag and drop your SVG icons into the Grumpicon drop area. The app will then take your files and run them through the same Grunticon process that you would have locally if you had the Grunticon command-line tool installed.

Screenshot of the Icomoon app.

After dropping the icons, the app will then display a full list of them, and you can choose to remove any if you wish and download them.

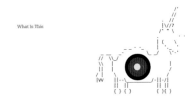

Screenshot of the Grumpicon web application.

Grumpicon will create a package containing a set of files and folders generated by Grunticon.

Icons are output: "...to CSS in 3 formats: svg data urls, png data urls, and a third fallback CSS file with references to regular png images, which are also automatically generated and placed in a folder. grunticon also generates a small bit of JavaScript to drop into your site, which asynchronously loads the appropriate icon CSS depending on a browser's capabilities, and a preview HTML file with that loader script in place." (Grunticon GitHub repository's readme file).

Before moving on to using the downloaded resources, let's go over the Grunticon setup quickly — just in case you prefer a Grunt workflow instead of the online app. The plugin is installed and enabled just like any other Grunt plugin. The minimal setup, according to the plugin's repository, requires that you fill a `files` object for the plugin to run.

The set of files and folders generated by Grumpicon. Image credit: Todd Parker.

> 66 *This files object currently requires that a cwd and a dest directory are placed, and therefore will blow up without it. This will be fixed to better fit the pattern set by Grunt for this."*
>
> — Grunticon GitHub repository's readme file

```
/* The Grunticon task configuration */
grunticon: {
    myIcons: {
        files: [{
            expand: true,
            cwd: ';example/source';,
            src: [';*.svg';, ';*.png';],
            dest: "Example/Output"
        }],
        options: {
        }
    }
}
```

The *dest* directory is the destination for the batched icons. If this directory already exists and contains other files with the same names as those output by Grunticon, it will overwrite the existing files. Either you make sure your icons are named uniquely, or simply create a new destination directory for the icons.

After finishing the setup, Grunticon will batch your SVG files whenever you run Grunt. For a full list of customization options, refer to the plugin's Gthub repository. The Grunticon plugin will output the same resources as those downloaded from Grumpicon.

Let's go back to the package download-ed from Grumpicon. The package contains a preview.html file. This file gives you a preview of the icons and their respective CSS class names.

The *preview.html* page is a working example using the resources generated by Grunticon. If you view the page's source code, you can get a clearer idea of how these resources are used. To display an icon, simply add the icon's class name in the markup. The Grunticon loader file will take care of loading the necessary CSS files that apply the icons as background images.

`.icon-github:`

`.icon-twitter:`

Screenshot of the embedded icons as shown in the *preview.html* page.

```
<div class="icon-dribbble" style="width: 32px; height: 32px;"></div>
```

Grunticon uses a special loader script (*grunticon.loader.txt*) that checks for SVG support and automatically falls back to using a PNG version if the browser does not support it. The JavaScript loader ensures that only a single style sheet is loaded instead of all three, saving bandwidth in the process. Add the loader to your page's `<head>`. Make sure the paths in the code are correct. If your style sheets reside in a CSS directory, make sure you reflect that in the paths as well.

The `<script>` loads the icons if JavaScript is enabled. `<noscript>` links to the fallback style sheet for browsers without JavaScript. You need to copy the three generated style sheets along with the PNG fallbacks folder to your CSS directory.

icons.data.svg.css contains the CSS that will load the SVG image as a back-ground. The SVGs are added inline inside the CSS file. For example:

```
.icon-dribbble {
    background-image: url('data:image/svg+xml;…');
    background-repeat: no-repeat;
}
```

The ellipsis in the snippet is actually replaced by an inline SVG expressed as a data URI, which in turn has been minified and URL-encoded.

The inline SVG background image will be loaded in browsers that support it — namely all modern browsers including IE9+, Chrome, Firefox, Safari, Opera, iOS3+, Android 4.0+ and Opera Mobile.

icons.data.png.css contains the inline data URI version of the PNG images.

```
.icon-dribbble {
    background-image: url('data:image/png;base64,…');
    background-repeat: no-repeat;
}
```

The inline PNG data is converted into base64. These backgrounds will be loaded in browsers that don't support SVG but do support data URIs in CSS (including IE8, Opera Mini, and Android 1.0 to 2.0). This style sheet will be loaded if the browser does not support SVG.

For browsers that support neither SVG nor data URIs in CSS, the *icons. fallback.css* style sheet is loaded, which references the PNG versions of the icons available in the PNG fallback folder.

```
.icon-dribbble {
    background-image: url('png/dribbble.png');
    background-repeat: no-repeat;
}
```

The PNG fallbacks are loaded in IE6–7 and non-JavaScript environments. The biggest advantage of the Grunticon workflow is that it takes care of the CSS, feature detection, and fallback assets creation for you.

The SVG spriting is established by having all the SVG images inline within the same CSS file, which allows them to be cached (as the CSS is cached). The CSS is essentially a "text sprite" with all the SVGs available inside it as plain text.

The main advantage to using minified (the white space is removed), plain text SVGs as opposed to base64-encoded SVGs in the Grunticon workflow is that the former gzips better. The reason plain text SVG gzips better is that it usually contains a lot of repeated elements that gzip can easily crunch, significantly reducing file size.

If you want to use different colors or sizes of the same icon, you'll need to export a set of SVGs for each variation in order for Grumpicon to create matching fallback PNG images. This is repetitive, of course, but necessary for universal compatibility because they are embedded as background images.

Animations also need to be defined inside the root <svg> of the original icon (the original file that Grunticon will use to generate its output) — those animations will be preserved. However, the PNG fallback will not be animated; it will be generated as though no animations were applied to the SVG.

Some Notes about SVG Data URIs

The anatomy of a resource converted into a data URI looks like this:

```
data:[<mime type>][;charset=<charset>][;base64],<encoded data>
```

The base64 declaration is only needed if you are encoding your SVG into base64. However, as you will see in the next section, it is generally better *not* to encode your SVG into base64, so we will ignore this part for now.

Without the base64 portion, the data is represented using ASCII encoding for octets inside the range of URL-safe characters and using the standard %xx hex encoding (aka percent-encoding) of URLs for octets outside that range.

Percent-encoding a character is established by converting the character to its corresponding byte value in ASCII and then representing that value as a pair of hexadecimal digits. The digits, preceded by a percent sign (%) which is used as an escape character, are then used in the URI in place of the reserved character.

Unless you are using non-ASCII characters in the SVG, set the charset declaration to US-ASCII. This is the standard URI character encoding, and it is the one used in the data URI SVGs generated by Grunticon. And because it is the standard encoding, you can skip the charset declaration entirely if you are using only ASCII characters in the SVG.

US-ASCII is a subset of UTF-8, so it is generally safe to set the encoding to that as well. However, you don't need to declare UTF-8 unless you are using non-ASCII characters in your SVG. In this case, the characters must also be percent-encoded.

Theoretically, you can just copy and paste your SVG into the URL after the character encoding (where the `<encoded data>` is in the data URI format) and have it work out of the box. Practically, however, it does not work as expected because some browsers have problems with certain characters being unescaped in the SVG. For example, the following snippet applies a background to the body of the page — it is simply a green SVG circle.

```
body {
  background: url('data:image/svg+xml,<svg
  xmlns="http://www.w3.org/2000/svg" width="200" height="200">
  <circle fill="#009966" r="100" cx="100" cy="100"/></svg>') no-repeat;
}
```

The snippet works in Chrome, but does not work in Firefox. Firefox has a problem with the hash (#) symbol being unescaped. To make it work, the snippet above would have to be encoded like this:

```
body {
  background: url('data:image/svg+xml,<svg
  xmlns="http://www.w3.org/2000/svg" width="200" height="200">
  <circle fill="%23009966" r="100" cx="100" cy="100"/></svg>') no-repeat;
}
```

Notice that the # symbol has been replaced with its percent-escaped equivalent: %23. Both Chrome and Firefox require the above snippet to be wrapped in quotation marks to work as well. But, the quotation marks need to be single not double marks. The reason is that the quotation marks used in the SVG are double, so you need to use single quotation marks to wrap the entire URI in. Thus, to avoid issues with quotation marks, use only one type of quotation marks in the SVG, and wrap the URI in the other.

The above is a simple example that can be manually fixed to work in most browsers. However, Internet Explorer still requires that you URL-encode (percent-encode) the entire SVG to make sure no unsafe characters remain unencoded. According to the specification, all unsafe characters must always be encoded within a URL, and Internet Explorer adheres to the spec more strongly, requiring that you abide with that either by base64-encoding your SVG or URL-encoding it. Therefore, it is necessary to URL-encode your SVG to make it work across all SVG-compatible browsers.

> 66 *Characters can be unsafe for a number of reasons. The space character is unsafe because significant spaces may disappear and insignificant spaces may be introduced when URLs are transcribed or typeset or subjected to the treatment of word-processing programs. The characters "<" and ">" are unsafe because they are used as the delimiters around URLs in free text; the quote mark (""") is used to delimit URLs in some systems. The character "#" is unsafe and should always be encoded because it is used in World Wide Web and in other systems to delimit a URL from a fragment/ anchor identifier that might follow it. The character "%" is unsafe because it is used for encodings of other characters. Other characters are unsafe because gateways and other transport agents are known to sometimes modify such characters. These characters are "{", "}", "|", "\", "^", "~", "[", "]", and "`".*
>
> — IETF Network Working Group Memo on Uniform Resource Locators[34]

URL-encoding the SVG from the previous snippet produces the following code:

```
body {
  background: url('data:image/svg+xml,%3C%3Fxml%20version%3D%221.0%22%20
encoding%3D%22utf-8%22%20standalone%3D%22no%22%3F%3E%0A%3Csvg%20xm
lns%3D%22http%3A%2F%2Fwww.w3.org%2F2000%2Fsvg%22%20width%3D%22200%22%20
height%3D%22200%22%3E%3Ccircle%20fill%3D%22%23009966%22%20r%3D%22100%22%20
cx%3D%22100%22%20cy%3D%22100%22%2F%3E%3C%2Fsvg%3E') no-repeat;
}
```

As a final note, if you are inlining an SVG and you only want to reference a fragment of the SVG using an identifier (we will see examples of using

---

34 https://tools.ietf.org/html/rfc1738

fragment identifiers in SVG in upcoming sections), remember that the `#identifier` needs to be included within the enclosing quotation marks, right after the closing `<svg>` tag's `>` character (or its escaped `%3E` equivalent).

Using one of many URL-encoding apps available online and as standalone apps, you can encode your SVG without having to do it manually. If you use a tool like Grunticon, it will do it for you automatically.

Data URI SVG Performance Considerations

Since we're on the subject of inlining SVGs using data URIs, it is worth spending some time looking into the performance aspects of this technique. Using data URIs in CSS as an alternative to bitmap sprites is the most typical way data URIs are being used in web design today. The performance of data URIs is important to any web designer or web application developer applying the best practice of minimizing HTTP requests.

Data URIs are most often used for small graphics that persist throughout a site. And many developers take the base64 approach to inlining graphics. However, research has shown that base64 encoded images can cause serious performance bottlenecks on mobile[35]; then again, those conclusions were refuted by other research[36]. Either way, base64 encoding needlessly inflates the content by 30%, and although gzip recovers some of this, you still end up with approximately 10% bloat for no good reason.

We also mentioned in the previous section that plain text can be a lot better than base64, so if you are ever going to use data URIs to embed SVGs, it makes sense to know why it is better not to convert them into base64[37]. There is no black or white to this — you will almost always have to test the performance of the assets at hand and compare them before making a decision as to which one to use.

Despite the many advantages that inlining images has (convenience being one of the main advantages to many developers), they are sometimes signifi-

---

35 http://www.mobify.com/blog/data-uris-are-slow-on-mobile/
36 http://www.mobify.com/blog/base64-does-not-impact-data-uri-performance/
37 http://css-tricks.com/probably-dont-base64-svg/

cantly slower than CSS image sprites, as research has shown[38], and they may have a negative impact on performance — especially on mobile.

The potential performance impact of inlining images is the main reason why inlining everything is not the answer[39]. Guy Podjarny has done quite a bit of research in an article he shared on the Performance Calendar blog. Based on Podjarny's and other research, it is recommended that you limit the use of inlining to small image files. According to Podjarny, "the HTTP Overhead of a request & response is often ~1KB, so files smaller than that should definitely be inlined. Our testing shows you should almost never inline files bigger than 4KB." Complementary to Guy's research, a study conducted by Peter McLachlan shows that "15–20kB for max data URI size, and no more than 3–5 instances seems like a good rule of thumb for mobile".

Remember that the content of the page will not render before the CSS is parsed, so the bigger the CSS file (due to a possibly large amount of images in it), the longer it is going to take to render the page. Inlining inside CSS is a render-blocking procedure that can easily have a visible impact on performance that your users may definitely see and feel. That is, unless you serve the images in a style sheet that is loaded asynchronously.

At this point is it worth mentioning that the loading script used in Grunticon is asynchronous by default, so you don't have to worry about render blocking when you use it. Also remember that CSS is usually shared across multiple pages. If your CSS-inlined images are not used across all pages, you might be delaying the rendering of the page and loading unnecessary resources in those pages.

Inline SVGs injected in the CSS have an advantage over HTML-inlined SVGs: SVGs inlined in HTML cannot be cached and will be loaded every time the page is loaded. Not to mention the overhead caused by loading the inline SVGs in browsers that may not be able to render them. CSS-inlined SVGs, on the other hand, can take advantage of browser caching along with the rest of the styles. You should keep in mind, though, that CSS-inlined SVGs will be downloaded every time the CSS changes — although this may not happen very often.

38 http://www.mobify.com/blog/css-sprites-vs-data-uris-which-is-faster-on-mobile/
39 http://calendar.perfplanet.com/2011/why-inlining-everything-is-not-the-answer/

Guy also recommends that page images (images referenced within the page, not CSS) rarely be inlined: *"Page Images tend to be big in size, they don't block other resources in the normal use, and they tend to change more frequently than CSS and Scripts. To optimize image file loading, load images on-demand instead."*

Inlining has its advantages and disadvantages — you should be careful not to abuse it. If your images are not critical for above-the-fold rendering, they don't need to be inlined either. If, for any reason, you do inline them, try to load them asynchronously.

HTTP/2[40] brings some important performance optimizations to HTTP requests. The main advantage of inlining (saving that extra HTTP request) will no longer apply because HTTP/2 enables the server to send multiple responses in parallel for a single client request — what's known as server push. This removes the concern about the additional HTTP request from the equation. HTTP/2 server push makes inlining obsolete.

These are just notes and considerations to keep in mind when working with SVG (or other images, for that matter). Always, always test your page's or app's performance before settling for a particular technique. Don't rush into prioritizing maintainability or convenience over performance.

SVG Icon System with Icons as Foreground Images

In the previous section, we discussed a workflow for providing SVG icons as background images via CSS. But what if you want your icons to be document images, actually part of the HTML content? There are ways to do that, too.

When an SVG sprite is to be used in a document, it can be embedded in the document and then parts of it are referenced throughout the document, either by using fragment identifiers or the SVG `<use>` element.

Once more, you need a set of SVG icons, obviously. The first step is to create the SVG sprite by combining the individual icons into one `<svg>` and then injecting that SVG into your document.

---

40   https://http2.github.io/

Inside the `<svg>`, we're going to define the icons using the SVG `<defs>` element. The `<defs>` element makes sure the icons are not going to be rendered unless they are referenced somewhere in the document.

Inside the `<defs>` element, a group is going to wrap every icon — if you have five icons, define five `<g>` elements. The `<g>` (group) element will contain the code for an individual icon; it will also get a unique ID that describes the icon.

```
<svg style="display: none;">
  <defs>
    <g id="icon-twitter">
      <!-- Twitter icon markup -->
    </g>
    <g id="icon-github">
      <!-- Github icon markup -->
    </g>
    <!-- more icons -->
  </defs>
</svg>
```

An even better alternative than the above template is using the SVG `<symbol>` element to wrap the markup of an icon. The `<symbol>` element combines the features of the `<defs>` and `<g>` element, and adds to them the ability to be scaled and positioned inside any containing viewport by using its `viewBox` and `preserveAspectRatio` attributes. `<symbol>` can also be made accessible using SVG's accessibility elements, `<title>` and `<desc>`, so that whenever the symbol is referenced in `<use>`, all its instances will also be accessible since the accessibility elements will be transferred as well. We'll talk more about making SVGs accessible in the accessibility section later in the chapter.

Replacing the `<defs>` element from our previous snippet with `<symbol>`s means the code would look like this:

```
<svg version="1.1" xmlns="http://www.w3.org/2000/svg"
style="display: none;">
    <symbol id="icon-twitter" viewBox="0 0 35 35">
      <title>Twitter</title>
      <desc>Icon linking to author's Twitter account</desc>
```

```
    <!-- Twitter icon markup -->
  </symbol>
  <symbol id="icon-github" viewBox="0 0 35 35">
     <!-- icon contents -->
  </symbol>
     <!-- more icons here... -->
</svg>
```

The inline style declaration `style="display: none;"` on the `<svg>` element is used to hide the `<svg>` to prevent it from being rendered. Without it, there would be an empty white area where the SVG would normally be displayed.

It is best to inject the SVG at the top of the document because doing so later may cause some weird behavior in some WebKit browsers that prevents this method from working. Until the bugs are fixed, injecting on top is the way to go.

Now that the SVG is available in the document, the icons (`<symbol>`s) inside it can be referenced using the `<use>` tag:

```
<svg class="icon-twitter">
  <use xlink:href="#icon-twitter" />
</svg>
```

If you use the `<defs>` plus `<g>` approach, you will need to specify a `viewBox` on the `<svg>` containing the reference to the icon (the `<use>`), as opposed to specifying it on the `<symbol>`. Note that the value of the `viewBox` will depend on the size of the icon. In our example here, since each icon is 35×35px, instead of specifying the `viewBox` on the `<symbol>`, you just specify it on the root `<svg>` instead, and then use your icon:

```
<svg class="icon-twitter" viewBox="0 0 35 35">
  <use xlink:href="#icon-twitter"></use>
</svg>
```

Creating the SVG sprite by combining the icons you have can get tedious or at least time-consuming. Fabrice Weinberg created a Grunt plugin called *grunt-svgstore*[41] that automates the merging process. The plugin takes a folder containing a set of SVGs and merges them into an SVG file with each icon wrapped in a `<symbol>` with the `viewBox` and a generated ID prefix that you can specify in the plugin options. For example:

```
grunt.initConfig({
  svgstore: {
    options: {
      prefix : 'icon-', // This will prefix each ID
      svg: { // Will add and override the the default xmlns="http://www.
w3.org/2000/svg" attribute to the resulting SVG
        viewBox : '0 0 100 100',
        xmlns: 'http://www.w3.org/2000/svg'
      }
    },
    default : {
      files: {
        'icons/SVGSprite.svg': ['SVGIcons/*.svg'],
      },
    },
  },
});
```

The plugin will merge all the icons in the *SVGIcons* folder into an SVG file named *SVGSprite* that it generated and output into the icons folder. Next step would be to inject the SVG into your document and reference the individual symbols with `<use>`.

Ideally, we would reference an external SVG sprite to take advantage of browser caching. Instead of referencing an SVG fragment that resides in an SVG embedded inline, we would be able to reference a fragment of an external SVG sprite. For instance, the previous example would look something like this:

```
<svg class="icon-twitter">
  <use xlink:href="socialIcons.svg#icon-twitter"></use>
</svg>
```

---

41 https://github.com/FWeinb/grunt-svgstore

The sprite could be hosted on a CDN, too. And you need to remember to add the xmlns attribute in this case because the SVG would no longer be inlined. This technique has one major advantage over HTML inlining: the browser will be able to cache the SVG, making subsequent loading times much faster. However, it also has one big drawback: IE does not support referencing an external SVG in <use> — and this applies to all versions of IE.

To use an external SVG sprite, you will need to provide a fallback for IE. Jonathan Neal has made a plugin called *svg4everybody*[42] that fills the gap between SVG-capable browsers and IE. The plugin makes it possible to use an external SVG in IE9+, and provides markup for IE6–8 to fall back to a PNG version of the icons. The plugin does not automate the generation of the PNG icons, though, so you would have to take that on yourself. There's more about *svg4everybody* in the fallback sections coming next.

The Grunticon plugin we used earlier for creating SVG icons as background images also comes with an option that allows you to generate one or more of those icons as foreground icons in the HTML. You can use the enhanceSVG option to tell Grunticon that you want to generate selected icons as inline SVG embedded in the document:

```
grunticon: {
  foo: {
    files: {              // Handle files here
    },
    options: {
      enhanceSVG: true
    }
  }
}
```

After you've done this, you can have any icon embedded in the page and ready for styling just by adding a data-grunticon-embed attribute to an element with that icon's class name:

```
<div class="icon-burger alt="" data-grunticon-embed></div>
```

---

42 https://github.com/jonathantneal/svg4everybody

This will generate the icon you want and embed it inside the `<div>` element, and then you can select and style the SVG from your CSS, and script it using JavaScript.

```
<div style="background-image: none;" class="icon-burger alt">
  <svg class="svg-source" xmlns="http://www.w3.org/2000/svg" width="32"
height="30" viewBox="170.6 12.6 32 30" enable-background="new 170.6 12.6
32 30">
    <!-- SVG icon content -->
  </svg>
</div>
```

With this option, you can generate one or many of your icons as inline SVGs in the document if you want or need to script and style them with CSS.

The above example and more information about this can be found in Grunticon's repository on GitHub.

STYLING THE ICONS AND APPLYING TRANSITIONS TO THEM

HTML-inline SVG can be styled and animated with CSS, SMIL and JavaScript. You can select individual icons and apply styles to them. That said, this only works because the source SVG is embedded inline as well; if the SVG were referenced externally, styling the contents of each icon from the main document wouldn't be possible.

When the source SVG sprite is not inline, and the icons are embedded in the document using `<use>`, styling the contents of the icons is not straightforward anymore.

When an SVG element is referenced or "copied" using `<use>`, the new instance and its contents are not cloned into the normal DOM — they are cloned into a shadow DOM. Selecting elements in the shadow DOM requires other approaches.

Styles applied to the `<use>` element will be inherited by all of its contents. This might be useful, but it does not give us the control we need over the individual shapes and contents of an icon. To target the shadow DOM and style elements inside a `<use>` element, the `/deep/` combinator[43] can be used but does not currently have good browser support.

Fabrice Weinberg came up with a trick that uses the CSS `currentColor` variable along with the `color` property[44] to leverage inheritance in SVG to "leak" upper-level styles down to the elements inside the shadow DOM. Using this trick along with other SVG attributes that can be used to style a `<use>` element, a limited amount of styles can be applied to the content of `<use>`.

Fabrice's technique allows you to change two colors inside the contents of a `<use>` element by using the `fill` and `color` properties in CSS, and then using `currentColor` inside the original contents of the SVG element. For example, suppose you have defined a two-color logo and you want to create a modified version of that logo by changing its two colors. A good example is the Sass logo made up of a circular background and a path making up the letter "S".

```
<svg style="display:none;">
  <symbol id="logo">
    <circle id="logo-background" cx="…" cy="…" r="…" fill="currentColor" />
    <path id="logo-letter" d="…" />
  </symbol>
</svg>
<svg class="logo logo--blackOnWhite"><use xlink:href="#logo" /></svg>
<svg class="logo logo--whiteOnBlack"><use xlink:href="#logo" /></svg>
```

By injecting the `fill="currentColor"` attribute inside the original logo code, we're making sure the circle will inherit the current color specified using the `color` property in CSS.

Then, we're taking advantage of the fact that when we apply a `fill` color to the `<use>` element, all the descendents of `<use>` will inherit that fill color as well. Then, in CSS, we specify both the `fill` and `color` values that we want:

```
.logo--blackOnWhite {
```

---

43   http://www.html5rocks.com/en/tutorials/webcomponents/shadowdom-201/#toc-style-cat
44   http://codepen.io/FWeinb/blog/quick-tip-svg-use-style-two-colors

```
    color: black; /* will be used as a fill value by the circle element */
    fill: white;  /* will be inherited by the path from use */
}
.logo--whiteOnBlack {
    color: white; /* will be used as a fill value by the circle element */
    fill: black;  /* will be inherited by the path from use */
}
```

Thus, using inheritance in CSS and SVG, we're able to change two colors inside the contents of <use> which would otherwise not be possible.

Amelia Bellamy-Royds has taken this idea of color inheritance and variables further by using CSS variables to achieve the same thing. She has written about it on the CodePen Blog[45]. The idea is to define some color variables in an upper level and then access those variables by using them as values for attributes like fill in the original SVG code. For example, if an icon is referenced by <use>:

```
<svg class="bird">
  <use xlink:href="#bulbul"></use>
</svg>
```

...the CSS could contain something like:

```
use {
    color: gray;
    fill: currentColor; /* this will be the base fill color inherited by
all elements inside <use> */

    /* define variables here */
    --secondaryColor: yellow;
    --tertiaryColor: black;
}
```

Then, in the original SVG fragment being referenced (the <symbol> which contains the contents of the Bulbul bird illustration), we use the variables as values for the fill attribute:

---

45 http://codepen.io/AmeliaBR/thoughts/customizable-svg-icons-css-variables

181

```
<symbol id="bulbul" viewBox="0 0 300 200">
    <path id="body" d="…" />
    <path id="tail" fill="var(--tertiaryColor)" d="…" />
    <path id="head" fill="var(--tertiaryColor)" d="…" />
    <path id="vent" fill="var(--secondaryColor)" d="…" />
</symbol>
```

We're practically injecting the styles into the shadow DOM *before it* becomes shadow DOM. That's brilliant.

Amelia's technique only works in browsers that support CSS variables, which at the time of writing is only Firefox. And neither Weinberg's technique with currentColor nor Amelia's technique with variables work on an SVG embedded as a CSS background image.

PROVIDING AND AUTOMATING FALLBACK FOR HTML-INLINE SVG SPRITES

There are several ways to provide fallback for SVG sprites — each way has pros and cons. Some techniques provide background images in CSS; others provide an HTML-inline fallback. Depending on your needs and the way you reference the SVG sprite, you may find any of these techniques useful.

SVG fallback as foreground images

If you reference an external SVG sprite, and if you prefer providing fallback in the form of foreground images, Neil's *svg4everybody* plugin is a good option.

To use *svg4everybody*, add it in the <head> of your document.

```
<script src="/path/to/svg4everybody.ie8.min.js"></script>
```

According to the plugin's GitHub repository, IE6–8 require the script to run this early to "shiv" the <svg> and <use> elements.

If running the standard script in IE9–11, be sure to set X-UA-Compatible higher than IE8. This can be done with a response header or the following <meta> tag:

```
<meta http-equiv="X-UA-Compatible" content="IE=Edge">
```

Then, in SVG-capable browsers and in IE9+, the external SVG sprite can be referenced in <use>:

```
<svg class="icon-twitter">
  <use xlink:href="socialIcons.svg#icon-twitter"></use>
</svg>
```

In IE6–8, the document markup is modified to fallback to PNG images.

```
<svg class="icon-twitter">
  <img src="socialIcons.svg.codepen.png">
</svg>
```

Note that fallback PNGs point to the same location as their corresponding SVGs, only with the hash (#) replaced by a dot (.), and with an appended *.png* extension. This means that you need to make sure the PNG fallbacks follow this naming convention as well.

SVG fallback as background images

If you're going to provide the SVG fallback in the form of a background image, automating the process will be a good idea.

Yulia Bukhvalova created a Grunt plugin called *svg-fallback*[46] that automates the generation of the PNG fallback sprite for a set of SVG icons and generates a style sheet to apply these fallbacks. The plugin also generates the SVG sprite (similar to Fabrice's grunt-svgstore process). The generated CSS will contain class names used to provide fallback for non-supporting browsers. For example:

```
.ie8 .icon { /* Load the sprite when the document has a class 'ie8' */
    background-image: url(fallback-sprite.png);
}
.icon-twitter {
    width: 32px;
    height: 32px;
```

---

46 https://github.com/yoksel/svg-fallback

```
    background-position: -192px 0;
}
.icon-github {
    width: 32px;
    height: 32px;
    background-position: 0 0;
    fill: green;
}
/* .etc */
```

The plugin is customizable and has a set of options that you can specify yourself. With the above CSS fallback ready, the SVG sprite would be used as we saw earlier:

```
<svg xmlns="http://www.w3.org/2000/svg" class="icon icon-twitter">
    <use xlink:href="#icon-twitter"/>
</svg>
```

It is important to note here that the xmlns attribute is necessary for this to work, otherwise IE will ignore the entire SVG code and not apply the fallback background at all. If you need to reach browsers that the plugin does not cater for, then it will be necessary to do some extra browser sniffing or feature detection, and manually add other class names to the CSS — that is, unless you fork the repository and customize the plugin to your liking.

SVG Fallback Using SVG Conditional Processing (SVG Fallback as Background Image)

The SVG Document Structure specification[47] defines elements and attributes — namely the <switch> element and its requiredFeatures, requiredExtensions and systemLanguage — that give us the ability to specify alternate viewing depending on the capabilities of a given user agent or the user's language. Conditional processing attributes only affect the direct rendering of elements and do not prevent elements from being successfully referenced by other elements (such as via <use>), so they are similar to the display property in that respect.

---

47 http://www.w3.org/TR/SVG/struct.html#ConditionalProcessing

The three attributes act as tests and return either true or false results. The <switch> renders the first of its children for which all of these attributes test true. If the given attribute is not specified, then a true value is assumed.

This conditional processing feature can be used to provide inline fallback for IE, for example. David Corvoysier wrote an excellent article explaining the technique[48] back in 2009 — the logic is embedded inside the <svg> and uses the <foreignObject> element to insert the non-SVG fallback. Using <switch>, SVG-capable browsers will render the first markup they understand (the SVG) and ignore the rest (the contents of the <foreignObject>). IE will do the opposite: it ignores the SVG it does not understand and renders the contents of the <foreignObject> because it is plain HTML.

```
<svg xmlns="http://www.w3.org/2000/svg">
  <switch>
    <use xlink:href="#icon-twitter"></use>
    <foreignObject>
      <div class="fallback icon-twitter-fallback"></div>
    </foreignObject>
  </switch>
</svg>
```

The CSS looks something like:

```
.icon-twitter-fallback {
    background-image: url(../icons/icon-twitter.png);
}
```

The .icon-twitter-fallback <div> will be rendered in IE but not in SVG-capable browsers. However, some SVG-capable browsers will still download the fallback image or background image even if not needed.

The folk behind HighRobotics came up with an interesting technique to avoid the double download issue[49]. The idea is to add another <svg> in the main document containing styles that hide the fallback <div> and remove its back-

---

48 http://www.kaizou.org/2009/03/inline-svg-fallback/
49 http://developersdev.blogspot.ru/2014/10/svg-fallback-pure-css-can-i-use-part-5.html

ground, thus preventing it from being rendered and its background from being downloaded.

```
<svg xmlns="http://www.w3.org/2000/svg" width="0" height="0"
id="hide-fallback">
 <style>
 <![CDATA[
  .fallback { background: none; background-image: none; display: none; } >
 </style>
</svg>
```

The above SVG would be added in the same document. This works because styles inside an `<svg>` can be used to style the contents of another `<svg>` in the same document. So, the `.fallback div` will neither be rendered nor its background downloaded in browsers that support SVG. IE, which does not understand SVG, will simply ignore this style declaration and will render the fallback as expected. This technique using the extra `<svg>` is also useful for preventing double downloads when an SVG is embedded using `<object>`. Instead of providing an `<img>` fallback between the opening and closing `<object>` tags, a `<div>` with a background image would be used, and that `<div>` would be hidden and not rendered in SVG-capable browsers.

```
<object type="image/svg+xml" data="icon-twitter.svg">
  <div class="fallback icon-twitter-fallback"></div>
</object>
```

In the same document, the `#hide-fallback` SVG would be added to make sure the fallback is not downloaded in SVG-capable browsers.

Other Fallback Techniques

An SVG might often be embedded as an image using an `<img>` element. Providing fallback in this case would be different. Using Modernizr[50], you can check for browser support for SVG and provide a PNG alternative in browsers that

---

50　http://modernizr.com

don't support SVG, either by adding or changing markup, or by simply swap-ping our the image src URI. Something like the latter would be fairly simple if the SVG and PNG versions of the images are in the same folder and have the same names for each image respectively.

```
if (!Modernizr.svg) {
  $("img[src$='.svg']")
    .attr("src", fallback);
}
```

Alexey Ten came up with a no-JavaScript technique[51] for providing fallback for SVG using an <image> element. The technique is based on research[52] done by Jake Archibald that showed that browsers treat <image> and <img> almost the same, so that if you provide <image> with both an xlink:href and src attributes, SVG-capable browsers will use xlink:href and ignore src, while non-SVG browsers will do the opposite.

For example, if we have the following declaration:

```
<image xlink:href="svg.svg" src="svg.png" width="300" height="250"/>
```

SVG-capable browsers will read it as:

```
<image xlink:href="svg.svg" width="300" height="250"/>
```

Browsers that don't understand SVG will read it as:

```
<img src="svg.png" width="300" height="250"/>
```

Using this technique to provide fallback for an inline SVG icon, for example, we could just insert the <image src="icon-twitter.png"> into the <svg> and have non-SVG browsers fall back to it. Ten's technique is clever and works as expected in almost all browsers, but it comes with a major drawback: both the

---

51 http://lynn.ru/examples/svg/en.html
52 http://jakearchibald.com/2013/having-fun-with-image/

SVG and the PNG images are requested and downloaded in IE9+, which has a direct impact on performance.

Of course, an SVG embedded as an <img> can be treated like other image formats referenced like that. Fallback can be provided using the <picture> element with an <img> element inside it — the <picture> <source> would point to the SVG, and the <img> would point to a set of PNG fallback sources (using srcset). You can read more about this in Yoav's chapter.

Another interesting fallback technique is one that allows you to provide fallback for an SVG used as a CSS background image, by taking advantage of the fact that all browsers supporting SVG background images also support multiple background images. Because of this, we can do the following:

```
.logo {
  background: url('logo.png');
  background: none, url('logo.svg');
}
```

The above snippet will display the SVG background image in browsers that support multiple background images in CSS — these same browsers also support SVG background images. SVG-capable browsers are going to display the SVG background and override the previous declaration using the PNG image. Any browser that does not support multiple background images (for instance, IE8) will display the PNG image and ignore the second background declaration. Browsers will make only one HTTP request for the image they want to display — win!

This technique was documented by Ben Schwarz[53] and, in the same blog post, Schwarz shares a Sass mixin that makes reusing this technique throughout your CSS easier:

---

53 http://germanforblack.com/post/43975575422/protip-all-browsers-that-support-svg-background

```
$public_path: "./";
 @mixin vector-bg-with-fallback($name) {
  background-image: url('#{$public_path}images/#{$name}.png');
  background-image: none, url('#{$public_path}images/#{$name}.svg');
}
```

Note that Android 2.x browsers will not display any of the images when using this technique. This may or may not be a problem, depending on how important that background image is for your design on mobile.

BETTER SVG SPRITING USING NATIVE SVG FRAGMENT IDENTIFIERS

SVG comes with a native way to link to portions of an image using fragment identifiers. This makes using SVG sprites much easier once this feature is fully supported across browsers. Fragment identifiers are used to link into a particular view of an SVG document. A view is a region of the SVG graphic that is bound by a view box. The box defining the view is specified using the viewBox attribute. The idea of specifying and displaying a view in SVG is practically the same as cropping an image to a specific region and hiding the parts of the image that are clipped out.

In SVG, we can crop a graphic by changing the values of the viewBox attribute. The viewBox attribute allows us to specify the position of the top-left corner of the view and its width and height, thus defining the bounds of the view area, and then crop the SVG to that area. Using this concept, we can crop an SVG sprite to only show a particular icon inside it. Assume we are working with the SVG sprite on the right:

An SVG icons sprite. Icons from Icomoon.

If we want to crop the sprite to the settings icon, it would be useful to know the coordinates of the top-left corner of the icon's bounding box, and its width and height; these values can be used to specify the viewBox that we need to crop the SVG. To determine these values we can use the Transform panel in Illustrator — the panel shows these values for each element when it is selected (see the screenshot on the next page).

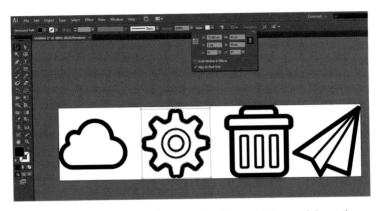

Screenshot showing the Transform panel in Illustrator. The panel shows the coordinates and dimensions of the bounding box of the icon.

Using the SVG as an image, we can then reference the settings icon by specifying its view like so:

```
<img src='uiIcons.svg#svgView(viewBox(72.5, 2, 60, 59))' alt="Settings
icon"/>
```

Alternatively, you can define the views inside the SVG source code using the `<view>` element and the `viewBox` attribute. The `<view>` element requires at least the `viewBox` attribute and a unique identifier.

```
<view id='icon-settings' viewBox='72.5 2 60 59' />
```

You can then reference that view in the `<img>` `src`:

```
<img src='uiIcons.svg#icon-settings' alt="Settings icon" />
```

Note that you need to explicitly set the dimensions of the `<img>` to make this work — some browsers may not crop the SVG to the specified view box otherwise. Support for SVG fragment identifiers[54] is not bad, but it's neither perfect nor reliable. At the time of writing, the technique is buggy in some

---

54 http://caniuse.com/#feat=svg-fragment

browsers, and it requires a workaround to function properly in Safari. Adobe's Bear Travis documented the issue and its solution[55] in a small experiment he shared, which is worth checking out.

A similar technique to SVG views using fragment identifiers is called SVG stacks, a technique thought out by Erik Dahlstrom. It works by first giving each of your icons in the SVG file a unique ID and the same class name, adds some CSS to hide all icons and only display the one that gets selected with the `:target` pseudo-class. Then you could use a hash in the URL to pass the ID into the SVG file, like `background: url(icon.svg#ID)`.

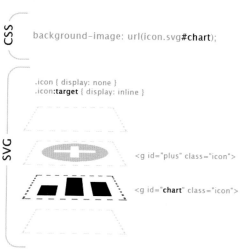

Illustration explaining how SVG stacks work. Image credit: Simon (Simurai).

SVG stacks have pretty much the same browser compatibility as SVG fragment identifiers. Simon "Simurai" wrote a blog post about the technique[56] that is well worth a read if you're interested in knowing more about it.

Making SVG's Cross-Browser Responsive with CSS

Icons don't need to be fluid; they don't have to respond to their container's width. But if the illustration is embedded as a regular image or object, or even a background image, we need to make sure that it responds to layout changes as expected. Using CSS, an SVG image can be made fluid and adaptive.

MAKING SVGS FLUID WITH CSS

When an SVG is exported from the editor, it always has `height` and `width` attributes that are equal to the size of the canvas in the editor — unless you removed these attributes during your optimization process.

---

55 http://betravis.github.io/icon-methods/svg-sprite-sheets.html
56 http://simurai.com/blog/2012/04/02/svg-stacks/

In order to make the SVG fluid, you need to either remove these attributes completely, or override them and make them fluid in CSS. Keeping these attributes is good for backwards compatibility and will make sure the SVG renders at its intended size if CSS is disabled. Moreover, some browsers will not handle the SVG correctly if it is used as a background image in CSS unless it has width and height attributes. But if you're just embedded the SVG inline in the document, make sure its dimensions are fluid. Any fixed height and width will restrict the SVG to those dimensions, preventing it from responding to changes in its container's width.

Do not remove the `viewBox` *attribute*. It also comes by default. Keep it. Without the `viewBox`, the SVG is not going to be responsive.

You may have to set the `preserveAspectRatio` attribute to `xMidYMid meet`. If the attribute is not present, you don't need to do that because it will default to this value. If it is set to another value, then — unless you have deliberately set it to that value — you should change it. The value `xMidYMid` meet scales the SVG canvas up as much as possible while keeping it inside the bounds of its viewport and maintaining its aspect ratio.

Next, depending on the embedding technique you used, you may need to apply a fix or use the padding hack to make your SVG fluid. We'll talk more about how this hack works shortly.

If the SVG is embedded as a CSS background image, no fixes or hacks are needed — it will behave and respond to CSS background properties as expected.

If the SVG is embedded using `<img>`, `<object>` or `<embed>`, the SVG will be fluid and scale as expected in all browsers except Internet Explorer — IE requires a fix to scale it correctly. IE has a problem scaling the image: it scales the `<svg>`'s width correctly (the SVG viewport width) but the height is fixed at 150px, the default height for replaced elements in CSS. IE is smart enough to set the width of the SVG to 100%, which means that the SVG will scale horizontally but not vertically, thereby producing an amount of white space on either side (left and right) of the image. The white space on either side of the image is due to the SVG viewport extending horizontally but not vertically, which results in the SVG `viewBox` being restricted by the height; with the aspect ratio of the viewbox preserved by default, this ratio will no longer match that of the viewport, hence the white space.

To fix that, you need to explicitly set the width of the SVG to 100%. For example, assuming you have `<img src="mySVG.svg" alt="Banner image" id="banner"/>` in your markup, you can make it fluid by adding this rule to your CSS:

```
#banner {
    width: 100%;
}
```

As the image container's width changes, the image will respond as expected. Note that the dimensions of these elements will establish the viewport for the SVG canvas. If you embed the SVG using `<iframe>` — and like all other elements embedded as iframes — most browsers will set the size of the iframe to the default size of replaced elements in CSS: 300×150px.

The only way to make an iframe responsive is by using the padding hack. The padding hack was pioneered by Thierry Koblentz in 2009[57]. Koblentz's technique makes it possible to create intrinsic ratios for videos and iframes.

To make the iframe fluid, you first need to wrap it inside a container:

```
<div class="container">
    <iframe src="my_SVG_file.svg">
        <!-- fallback here -->
    </iframe>
</div>
```

Next, we apply some styles to the container following these rules:

```
.container {
    height: 0; /* Collapse the container's height */
    width: width-value; /* Specify any width you want (a percentage
value, basically) */
    /* Apply padding using the following formula */
    /* This formula makes sure the aspect ratio of the container equals
that of the SVG graphic */
    padding-top: (svg-height ÷ svg-width) × width-value;
```

---

57 http://alistapart.com/article/creating-intrinsic-ratios-for-video/

```
    position: relative; /* Create positioning context for SVG */
}
```

The idea here is to establish a height-to-width ratio on the container that is the same as the height-to-width ratio of the `<svg>`. We make use of the `padding-top` (or `padding-bottom`) property in CSS to do that.

First, we collapse the container's height. Since padding specified as a percentage is calculated relative to the width of the element — even if the padding is at the top or bottom of the element — we're going to apply padding to expand its height again. The new height of the container will be equal to the padding; any additional height will throw off the aspect ratio we need.

The padding is applied to the top (or bottom) of the container, following the formula shown in the code snippet. This formula uses the values of the `height` and `width` attributes of the `<svg>` (the ones we removed earlier) to specify a padding value that allows the intrinsic ratio of the container to match that of the `<svg>`.

If we were to make the logo from the first section of this chapter fluid, the container's CSS would look like the following code. The height of the SVG logo is 214px, and its width is 182px.

```
.container {
    width: 50%; /* Or any width for that matter */
    height: 0;
    padding-top: 42.5%; /* (182px ÷ 214px) × 50 */
    position: relative;
}
```

Because the container's height has been collapsed and a fairly large amount of padding is applied to the top of it, its content — the SVG iframe— is pushed down so that it no longer sits inside the container anymore. In order to pull the SVG back up, you need to position the iframe absolutely inside the container. This is why we used `position: relative` on `.container` — it will establish a positioning context for the SVG.

Finally, and now that we have a positioning context, you position the iframe absolutely inside the container, and scale it so that it gets the container's height and width:

```
iframe {
    position: absolute;
    top: 0;
    left: 0;
    width: 100%;
    height: 100%;
}
```

Note that you will probably need to remove the default iframe border; override it with your own or remove it completely with `border: none;`.

If you've embedded the SVG inline as a code island inside the HTML document, it will work as expected in all browsers except IE; the height of the SVG will again be fixed to 150px as in the case of `<img>`, `<object>` and `<embed>`. But the solution to this issue is different this time: instead of applying `width: 100%` to fix this, the padding hack is required again. Wrap the `<svg>` in a container and use the CSS hack mentioned earlier to make the SVG fluid. Note that, unlike the `<iframe>`, the `<svg>` does not need a `height` and `width` to inherit its container's size. It won't hurt if you add them, but they're not required.

MAKING SVGS ADAPTIVE WITH CSS

Because SVG content is made up of XML tags that render graphics, we can select individual elements and apply specific styles to them, just like we can select HTML elements, using CSS selectors.

Like changing the styles of an HTML element — like background color, borders, and so on — you can also change certain styles of an SVG element using CSS. SVG elements are usually styled using presentation attributes like `fill`, `stroke`, `transform` and many others. However, only a subset of all presentation attributes can be set using CSS. You can find a list of SVG styling properties that can be set using CSS[58] in the SVG Styling specification. Note that in SVG 2, this list is extended to include more properties.

SVGs also accept styles specified inside CSS media queries — just like HTML. However, there is one important difference between the way an HTML element responds to media queries and the way an `<svg>` does: the sizes specified in

---

58 http://www.w3.org/TR/SVG2/styling.html#SVGStylingProperties

the media queries refer to the size of the SVG viewport, not the size of the page viewport, unless the SVG is embedded inline in the document (using `<svg>`).

If an SVG is embedded using an `<img>` or `<object>`, the sizes in the media queries will correspond to the sizes of these elements. On a practical level, this is like having element queries[59] in SVG. But if the SVG is embedded inline, the viewport sizes in the media queries refer to the size of the page viewport instead.

To apply media queries to the SVG, add them inside a `<style>` block inside the root `<svg>` element.

```
<svg xmlns="http://www.w3.org/2000/svg" version="1.1" viewBox="0 0 182
214">
    <style>
        /* CSS styles and media queries here */
    </style>
    <!-- SVG elements here -->
</svg>
```

Suppose we want to make the earlier nautical logo adaptive, hiding parts of it on smaller viewport widths so that it doesn't take up too much screen real estate.

An adaptive logo created using CSS media queries. (Logo designed by Freepik.com)

An adaptive logo — or any image illustration for that matter — can be useful for hiding extraneous detail on small screens, removing small text that may not be readable, or styling certain parts of the image in different screen contexts.

---

59 http://responsiveimagescg.github.io/eq-usecases/

To do that, we're going to select the parts that we want to hide and then we set their `display` to `none`. Of course, you can also style elements differently rather than hiding them. The code for the adaptive logo looks like this:

```
<svg version="1.1" xmlns="http://www.w3.org/2000/svg" viewBox="0 0 182
214">
    <g id="horizontal-rule"><!-- shape content --></g>
    <g id="rope"><!-- shape content --></g>
    <g id="log-title"><!-- shape content --></g>
    <g id="top-anchor"><!-- shape content --></g>
    <g id="logo-subtitle"><!-- shape content --></g>
    <g id="rescue-wheels"><!-- shape content --></g>
    <path id="boat-wheel" d="…" />
</svg>
```

Adding the media queries:

```
<svg version="1.1" xmlns="http://www.w3.org/2000/svg"
    viewBox="0 0 182 214">
    <style>
      @media all and (max-width: 400px){
         #rescue-wheels, #rope {
            display: none;
         }
         #logo-title, #boat-wheel, #horizontal-rule, #logo-subtitle {
            transform: translateY(-15px); /* nudge elements up to
fill
white space resulting from removing the elements in the middle */
         }
      }

      @media all and (max-width: 250px){
         #boat-wheel, #horizontal-rule, #logo-subtitle {
            display: none;
         }
      }

      @media all and (max-width: 210px){
         #logo-title {
            display: none;
```

```
      }
    }
  </style>
  <!-- SVG content -->
</svg>
```

You can make images adapt any way you want — it's as simple as making HTML elements adaptive.

Similarly, you can create responsive icons in a spritesheet-like method by defining several icons inside your SVG and then using CSS media queries to only show the icon that you want based on the viewport size. The icons and the logic used to show and hide them would all be encapsulated inside the SVG as well. First, the icons are arranged inside the <svg>:

```
<svg>
  <g id="home_icon_0" class="icon">
    <!-- paths and shapes -->
  </g>
  <!-- … -->
  <g id="home_icon_8" class="icon">
    <!-- paths and shapes -->
  </g>
</svg>
```

Then, CSS is used to hide the icons and show only the icon we want based on the conditions specified in the media queries:

```
<svg>
  <defs>
    <style>
    /* Hide all of the icons first. */
    .icon {
      display: none;
    }
    /* Display the first one. */
    #home_icon_0 {
      display: block;
    }
```

```
    /* Display the desired icon and hide the others according to the
viewport's size. */
    @media screen and (min-width: 25em) {

      #home_icon_0 {
        display: none;
      }

      #home_icon_1 {
        display: block;
      }

    }
    @media screen and (min-width: 30em) {
      #home_icon_1 {
        display: none;
      }

      #home_icon_2 {
        display: block;
      }
    }
    /* And so on */
    </style>
  </defs>
<!-- Icon groups go here -->
</svg>
```

Ilya Pukhalski wrote about this technique in his article for Smashing
Magazine, "Rethinking Responsive SVG"[60].

Making SVGS Accessible

Responsive web design is about more than just adapting your website's layout
to different device sizes. It's also about making sure your content responds to
your users' needs so they can access it from any device no matter the context —
this content also includes any and all images. No website or application is truly
responsive if it is not accessible.

---

60 http://www.smashingmagazine.com/2014/03/05/rethinking-responsive-svg/

SVG comes with a set of accessibility features[61] to make the images more accessible to a wider group of users, including those with disabilities. A number of these SVG features can also increase usability of content for many users without disabilities, such as users of personal digital assistants, mobile phones or other non-traditional web access devices.

In the SVG specification, two elements exist to make SVG images more accessible: <title> and <desc>. These elements are used to provide a text alternative to the graphic.

The <title> element is similar to the alt attribute of the <img> tag. It provides a human-readable title for an SVG container (such as an SVG <g> element), or graphics element, or the root <svg> element. The <title> has to be the first descendant of its container and is not rendered by default. However, it may be rendered by a graphical user agent as a tooltip. It may be rendered as speech by a speech synthesizer if styled to do so.

```
<svg viewBox="0 0 100 100">
    <title>Company logo</title>
</svg>
```

The <desc> (description) element provides a longer, more complete description of an element that contains it. It is useful for complex content that has functional meaning.

```
<svg viewBox="0 0 500 300">
    <title>Chemical Reaction</title>
    <desc>Animated illustration showing the stages of a chemical reaction
in a laboratory.</desc>
</svg>
```

These accessibility elements are part of SVG 1.1 — but SVG 1.1 accessibility support is limited in browsers and screen readers.

Leonie Watson, digital accessibility consultant and member of the W3C HTML Working Group and HTML Accessibility Task Force, conducted and

---

61 http://www.w3.org/TR/SVG-access/

shared research[62] indicating that the `<title>` and `<desc>` elements, and the role of the `<svg>` element are not represented consistently in browser accessibility APIs and screen readers.

According to Leonie[63], it is possible to enhance the information exposed through the browser accessibility APIs with a handful of ARIA attributes — specifically `role` and `aria-labelledby`.

To take advantage of these attributes, the `title` and `desc` are given IDs that are referenced by `aria-labelledby`, and the `role` attribute is used to specify a role for the SVG — which in most cases is `img`.

```
<svg viewBox="0 0 500 300" role="img" aria-labelledby="title description">
    <title id="title">Chemical Reaction</title>
    <desc id="description">Animated illustration showing the stages of a
chemical reaction in a laboratory.</desc>
</svg>
```

If the graphic contains interactive elements, such as a link (`<a>`), the `role="img"` may not be appropriate anymore. Giving a `role` to the `<a>` element in this case would allow screen readers to more correctly recognize it as an interactive element. Wrapping plain text in a `<text>` element helps make that text accessible. As we mentioned earlier, text that is outlined is converted into SVG shapes and hence will not be recognized as text.

These are small details and simple measures that have a significant effect on the accessibility and usability of our websites.

Using SVGS to Optimize the Delivery of Other Image Formats

SVGs have uses that go way beyond simply displaying icons or illustrations. In this section, I want to go over some of the clever techniques and tips that can take your SVG knowledge and usage to the next level.

---

62 http://www.paciellogroup.com/blog/2013/12/using-aria-enhance-svg-accessibility/
63 http://www.sitepoint.com/tips-accessible-svg/

USING SVG MASKS TO OPTIMIZE RASTER GRAPHICS

JPEGs have better compression rates than PNGs for photographic data. Wouldn't it be awesome if we could get the compression rate of a JPEG while preserving the transparency of PNGs? Using SVG's masking capabilities, we can do just that.

The idea behind this technique is to use an SVG mask to clip out or mask the areas of the JPEG that we want to be transparent. We end up serving a JPEG image with simulated alpha channels, thus combining the transparency of a PNG with the compression of a JPEG. The SVG serves as a mere container to display the image and apply the mask to it. This technique was first written about[64] by Dirk Weber.

Peter Hrynkow also wrote about the same technique[65] but in reverse: Peter started out with a PNG without transparent areas (kind of like a JPEG version of the PNG), and then used a PNG mask to achieve the transparency.

Suppose we have the PNG image shown on the right. The pigeon PNG with a transparent background weighs around 133KB.

The first step to optimize the image is to convert it into a JPEG. I did that by saving the image in Photoshop as JPEG instead of PNG. By saving to JPEG, the transparent areas become white and the image size drops from 133KB to 19.3KB for a high-quality JPEG, and 10.3KB for medium

A pigeon photo on a transparent background. Image credit: Francisco de la Vega

quality. The next step is to prepare a luminance mask to use as an SVG mask. The SVG <mask> element that we are going to see uses luminance masks (not alpha masks) to mask elements.

---

64 http://w3.eleqtriq.com/2014/08/applying-alpha-channels-to-jpgs/

65 http://peterhrynkow.com/how-to-compress-a-png-like-a-jpeg/

To achieve the transparency of the original image, we need to hide the white background and only keep the bird image. Using a luminance mask, we can do that by using a mask as shown below: the white (luminant) areas of the mask represent the areas of the JPEG that we want to keep; black areas in the mask represent areas we want to mask out.

JPEG   Mask

The JPEG image on the left, and the luminance SVG mask on the right.

Now that we have the mask and JPEG ready, we use SVG to apply the mask and serve the JPEG with transparent areas. The JPEG can be included inside the SVG using the SVG `<image>` element.

```
<svg version="1.1" xmlns="http://www.w3.org/2000/svg" xmlns:xlink="http://
www.w3.org/1999/xlink"
viewBox="0 0 400 530">
  <defs>
    <mask id="mask">
      <image width="400" height="530" xlink:href="pigeon-mask.png">
      </image>
    </mask>
  </defs>
  <image width="400" height="530" xlink:href="pigeon.jpg"
mask="url(#mask)"></image>
</svg>
```

The `<svg>`, `<mask>` and `<image>` have the same dimensions. And that is all you need to serve a PNG with the high compression rate of a JPEG. The SVG serves as the container holding the masked image.

Of course, since this technique relies on SVG and SVG masks to work, it will only work in browsers that support SVG, which means that it does not work in IE8 (or earlier) and older versions of Android. In addition, it is recommended that you inline the SVG to make it work in most browsers. Referencing an external SVG containing the images, using an `<img>` tag, for example, does not work in all browsers. You can refer to the CodePen demo[66] for test results loading the SVG in different ways.

USING SVG AS A CONTAINER FOR SERVING RESPONSIVE IMAGES

Another technique that uses SVG as a container for serving raster graphics is the Clown Car Technique by Estelle Weyl.

Estelle's technique takes advantage of SVG's ability to include raster images with `<image>`, and the CSS `background-image` property's ability to respond to CSS media queries.

The idea behind the Clown Car Technique is to include multiple images inside the SVG, and then use CSS media queries to display the image we want depending on the size of the viewport.

Using `<image>` to include the raster images inside the SVG, hiding them with `display: none;` and showing them on demand has one major drawback: all of the images will be requested and downloaded even if they are not displayed. So, instead of using foreground images, Estelle uses CSS background images to include the images in the SVG.

```
<svg xmlns="http://www.w3.org/2000/svg"
     viewBox="0 0 300 329" preserveAspectRatio="xMidYMid meet">
  <title>Clown Car Technique</title>

  <style>
    svg {
      background-size: 100% 100%;
```

---

66 http://codepen.io/shshaw/details/IDbqC/

```
      background-repeat: no-repeat;
    }
    @media screen and (max-width: 400px) {
      svg {
        background-image: url(images/small.png);
      }
    }
    @media screen and (min-width: 401px) and (max-width: 700px) {
      svg {
        background-image: url(images/medium.png);
      }
    }
    @media screen and (min-width: 701px) and (max-width: 1000px) {
      svg {
        background-image: url(images/big.png);
      }
    }
    @media screen and (min-width: 1001px) {
      svg {
        background-image: url(images/huge.png);
      }
    }
  </style>
</svg>
```

The above SVG is then either included inline or referenced as an external
SVG using <img> or any other embedding technique.

```
<img src="responsiveImage.svg" alt="Responsive image" />
```

In our responsive SVG, we include all of the images that we might need to
serve and then show only the appropriate image based on media queries. Using
CSS background images, only the image that is needed is going to be requested
and downloaded. Although clever, this technique has a lot of drawbacks: browser
support inconsistencies; security issues that require <object> instead of
<img> to load the image; and using conditional comments to provide fallback
for Internet Explorer, in addition to performance considerations that make
this technique neither as ideal nor simple as it looks. You can read all about

the technique, its gotchas, implementation options and drawbacks by reading Estelle's article on Smashing Magazine[67]. Make sure you read the comments section below the article for more insight about the technique's pros and cons.

In light of the advances made in the area of providing responsive images using the responsive images specification (`<picture>` and `srcset`) that Yoav talks about in his chapter, we have a more semantic, performance-optimized solution to deliver responsive images today and in the future.

That said, the Clown Car Technique is still worth mentioning as a way to show how SVG can be used to provide alternative solutions, by taking advantage of the encapsulation of resources and styles in an SVG that make it similar to iframes in some of its characteristics. This fact can be leveraged such that SVG becomes a tool and a means to an end, not just another image format.

Where To Go From Here?

SVG represents a very large and diverse universe with lots of capabilities. Using it allows us to bring together the best of two worlds — HTML and SVG — to achieve visual effects and optimizations that would otherwise not be possible without graphics editors.

One of the most powerful and impressive features of SVG lies in its animation effects. SVGs can be animated in a way similar to HTML elements using CSS animations[68] and JavaScript. The animations range from simple transition effects (for icons and logos) to two-dimensional and even three-dimensional animations including complex transformations.

More complex animations involving shape tweening and shape morphing currently require JavaScript or SMIL to work, but SMIL is soon to be deprecated in favor of the Web Animations API.

Using SVG, you can also move elements along arbitrary paths, but this ability will also be available to us via CSS some time soon. Certain SVG attributes like `stroke-dashoffset` and `stroke-dasharray` can be animated to obtain

---

67 http://www.smashingmagazine.com/2013/06/02/clown-car-technique-solving-for-adaptive-images-in-responsive-web-design/

68 http://www.smashingmagazine.com/2014/11/03/styling-and-animating-svgs-with-css/

animated line drawing effects. You may have come across this effect on the Vox Product blog[69], where they explain how they used these attributes in SVG to animate illustrations of an Xbox and PlayStation 4 on their respective review pages on the Polygon website. Jake Archibald wrote an excellent introductory article[70], including an interactive demo that explains how this concept works.

SVG can also act as a web font format. However, SVG fonts are deprecated or not supported in most browsers. Do not use them. That said, there is a proposal[71] that may bring SVG back to the web fonts scene as a way to bring color, gradients, animation and other aspects of SVG's rich graphics model to web fonts. Bram Stein has written all about web font formats and their performance aspect in his chapter about web font performance.

SVG is an exciting world with lots of potential, and it provides us with a bunch of new tools to add to our workflows that are certainly worth exploring and getting more creative with. I hope this chapter has been useful in helping you integrate SVG into your responsive web design workflow.

ABOUT THE AUTHOR

Sara is a Lebanese freelance front-end web developer, writer and speaker, focusing on HTML5, SVG, CSS and JavaScript. She writes and speaks and gives workshops on front-end web development, mostly about CSS and SVG, and has authored *Codrops' CSS Reference*. When she's not speaking or writing, she builds and delivers websites for small and medium businesses around the world, while sipping a cup of fruit-flavored green tea.

---

69 http://product.voxmedia.com/2013/11/25/5426880/polygon-feature-design-svg-animations-for-fun-and-profit

70 http://jakearchibald.com/2013/animated-line-drawing-svg/

71 http://www.w3.org/2013/10/SVG_in_OpenType/

ABOUT THE REVIEWER

Jake Archibald works in *Google Chrome*'s developer
relations team, working on specs, testing
implementations, and ensuring developers have tools
to make their jobs less painful. He's a big fan of time-to-
render optimizations, progressive enhancement, and all
of that responsive stuff.

ABOUT THE REVIEWER

Dmitry Baranovskiy started his career in 2000 as a back
end developer, then shifted to design and then to front-
end. He used to work in such a companies as Atlassian
and Sencha as a JavaScript developer, nowadays he is
toggling zeros and ones at *Adobe*. Dmitry has a big passion for SVG and JavaScript that he utilized by creating
Raphaël and Snap.SVG JavaScript libraries. When he is
not coding and not spending time with his family — he is
probably doing pullups.

BUILDING ADVANCED
RESPONSIVE MODULES
WITH FLEXBOX

ZOE M. GILLENWATER

CHAPTER FIVE · BY ZOE M. GILLENWATER

BUILDING ADVANCED RESPONSIVE MODULES WITH FLEXBOX

I CAN REMEMBER WHEN I FIRST HEARD you could create a web page layout without tables — just CSS. I was rather confused, but intrigued. There was this new thing called CSS floats, and you could use it to place boxes beside each other in columns without having to struggle against massively nested table markup, spacer GIFs, rowspan and colspan, and all the other junk that made tables so ill-suited for web layout. I dived into float-based layout headfirst and didn't look back, but along the way I discovered, as I'm sure *you* have, that floats have their own shortcomings that can sometimes make them tricky to work with — after all, they weren't actually designed to control overall page layout.

For one thing, you always have to plan for some sort of float containment method so that the floats don't hang out of the bottom of their parent containers. You also need to be careful that your floats don't wrap when you didn't intend for them to do so. Plus, although floats don't suffer from the rigid structure of tables, you're still somewhat dependent on the HTML source order, since floats don't move up, only over to one side (at least not without all sorts of negative margin madness). And, of course, there are the usual complaints that you can't make separate floats the same height, and you can't center a float horizontally or vertically. Most of these things can be worked around in various ways, sure, but the techniques can be messy and confusing. They're complications that have to be worried about and fiddled with every time, instead of features that just work.

Add to the mix the requirement that your float-based layout be responsive, and these limitations become even more obvious and frustrating. Being able to move something just left or right isn't good enough when you need the same box to appear at various places on the screen at different viewport sizes. Plus, now that you're using percentages to size your floats, there's an even greater likelihood that a miscalculation on your part, or a rounding error on the browser's part, will send a float wrapping. Using good old `display:table` or `display:inline-block` solves some of the issues with float-based layout, but with one big limitation: the source order has to match the visual order, even more so than with floats.

The CSS Flexible Box Layout module[1], called *flexbox* for short, solves a lot of these shortcomings and makes building responsive layouts much easier than our current layout methods. Flexbox gives you more control over the things you care about in a responsive layout — like order, alignment, and the proportional sizes of your boxes — and lets the browser figure out the rest, the math-y stuff that computers are good at, like the exact dimensions needed for the boxes to perfectly fill the available space. You can create much more complex and reliable layouts with flexbox than you can with floats, table display, or `inline-block` alone, all with far less CSS.

When To Use (And Not Use) Flexbox

That doesn't mean flexbox is a silver bullet. It's one of several new layout mechanisms that CSS3 offers us, and each is well-suited to different uses.

GO FOR IT!

Flexbox is strongest when used to lay out, size, and align the components within a section on a page, or the content within a component. For instance, flexbox would be great for laying out the links within a menu, the fields within a complex form, or the story boxes within a main content area. We'll look at several component layout examples like these throughout this chapter.

Even though a couple of browsers still in use today don't support flexbox (basically IE9 and earlier), you can still use it today as a way to progressively

---

1   http://www.w3.org/TR/css3-flexbox/

enhance the responsiveness of your UI components. Non-supporting browsers may render alignment, spacing or sizing a little differently from flexbox browsers, but we'll make sure they don't display anything broken, weird or ugly. Flexbox is a great progressive enhancement tool when fine-tuning the appearance of your components.

If you're building a responsive site, flexbox can be especially useful in making your components more adaptive to the changing dimensions of their containers. The browser can automatically resize and move chunks of content as needed, often without you having to add any media queries. If you want to maximize the responsiveness of your content, flexbox is the way to go.

Flexbox is also a great option for creating the overall page layout on narrow mobile screens. That's because mobile layouts are usually much simpler than desktop layouts, and because browser support is excellent among mobile browsers — all the major mobile browsers support it.

For up-to-date stats on which browsers support flexbox, head to http://caniuse.com/#feat=flexbox.

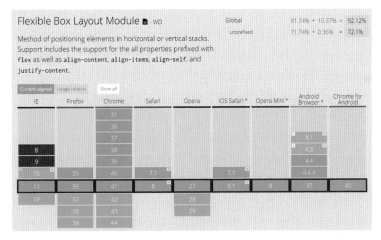

Can I Use shows that all major browsers support flexbox, or over 92% of browsers in use globally (as of spring 2015).

HOLD UP

Apart from mobile, flexbox is not terribly well-suited to handling the overall page layout, unless that layout is relatively simple. There are a number of reasons for this. For one thing, flexbox rather depends on items being siblings to one another. If you have a complicated HTML structure, you may not be able to get different pieces at different levels within the hierarchy to work together in the way you want. For instance, if you have two sibling elements, one with child elements nested inside, you can use flexbox to make those siblings match each other in width and height, but you can't get the children to automatically match the width and height of their parent's sibling.

Flexbox is not a true grid system. Within a single row or column, flexbox can make all the items have equal widths or heights, or proportional dimensions, which seems very grid-like. But for every new line, flexbox will start over on its calculations, resulting in items that don't necessarily line up with the items in the lines before or after. Relative sizing is an awesome feature of flexbox, but the sizes of items are relative only to siblings in the same row or column.

Another reason flexbox isn't the best for overall page layout is that you don't have complete freedom over the visual placement of your content without regard for HTML source order. That's the holy grail of page layout, and it's something that CSS Grid Layout[2] will give us, once it's fully developed and more widely supported. Flexbox can do some reordering, but it's still a bit source-dependent, as we'll see in more detail later on with the `order` property.

The final reason to avoid flexbox for overall page layout for desktop (at least for the time being) is that browser support for flexbox on desktop still has a couple of holes: IE9 and earlier versions of IE don't support it, and all other major desktop browsers do. While this means that flexbox *does* actually have great support on desktop browsers — enough to use it to lay out individual page components — depriving users of the overall page layout is a lot more problematic than them not seeing the exact sizes and alignment within a page component. I'm completely fine with users of IE9 and earlier seeing something a little different from other browsers. But not seeing any layout at all? That's going a bit far.

---

2   http://www.w3.org/TR/css-grid-1/

Apart from desktop page layout, flexbox is also not the right choice for flowing content into multiple columns. That's the job of the CSS Multi-column Layout module[3]. Flexbox can lay out blocks of content beside one another, creating multiple columns, but each of those columns has to be a separate element in the HTML.

So again, use flexbox for what it's been designed to do and is good at: laying out individual components and their chunks of content. Like any tool, it has its strengths and weaknesses.

DIVING INTO THE CODE

Once you've decided that flexbox is appropriate for the layout task you want to complete, you'll be ready to get coding. Before diving deep into the code, keep in mind that since flexbox is a totally new layout mechanism, it introduces a lot of new CSS properties, as well as some new layout concepts like main axis and cross axis. All these new terms may sound daunting at first, but they do make sense — and once you start actually playing with them in real pages, you'll be able to really understand what exactly they do, and flexbox stops looking so daunting.

Let's dive deeper into flexbox and slowly find our way through all the (fancy and not so fancy) properties it has.

FLEXBOX ACTIVATE!

To turn on flexbox, set `display:flex` or `display:inline-flex` on a wrapper element to make it a *flex container* and indicate that you're using the new visual formatting model on its children, called *flex items*. Only the children become flex items, not all descendants of the flex container. The `flex` value makes the flex container a block-level element, while the `inline-flex` value makes the flex container an atomic inline-level element (an inline box that doesn't break across lines, like `inline-block` elements).

---

3   http://www.w3.org/TR/css3-multicol/

```
<div class="container">
    <div><p>Lorem ipsum dolor sit amet, consectetur adipiscing elit.</p></div>
    <div><p>Nulla at purus ipsum.</p></div>
    <div><p>Aliquam lacinia non risus eu rhoncus.</p></div>
    <div><p>Nulla blandit erat ac nunc malesuada pellentesque.</p></div>
</div>

.container {
    display: flex;
}
```

If you're also using the vendor-prefixed versions of flexbox, add the prefix to the `display` *value*, not on the `display` property itself. For example, `display:-webkit-flex`.

Well, would you look at that — by setting that one little property I've already achieved a multi-column layout! The flex items, each one a `<div>`, change from their default stacking behavior to sitting side by side.

By default, flex items sit side by side as soon as you turn their parent into a flex container.

SETTING ORIENTATION

The items lay out side by side because when you create a flex container, the browser automatically sets its `flex-direction` property to the default value of `row`. This property, set on the flex container, sets the flow direction of the flex items within it.

In a nutshell, `flex-direction` lays out the items in rows or columns, horizontally or vertically. It's setting the direction of the axis along which the flex container's children (flex items) will be displayed. In flexbox terminology, the direction you set is called the *main axis*, with the other direction being the *cross axis*. Our flex items are flowing horizontally right now, so that's the main axis; width, the horizontal dimension, is the *main size* of its child flex items. If we had set `flex-direction` to `column` this would all be reversed.

Plus, flex items can start their layout journey from any side of their container — not just top-to-bottom and left-to-right, but also bottom-to-top and right-to-left, depending on what you tell the flex container to do and the writing mode of the page (the direction in which text flows). The origin point for the flex items along their main axis is called the *main start side* of the container, and they will flow from there to the *main end side*. See image below for all of these orientation-related flexbox terms.

Although these axes just sound like W3C mumbo-jumbo syntax detail that you can ignore, it's actually important to remember which axis you're dealing with every time you work with a flex container. That's because the axes affect all of the other flexbox properties that will come later. Flexbox is so flexible because its properties can make items lay out and align in any direction, but it needs to know at what point it's supposed to start and move out from, and in which direction.

Flex items can be laid out side by side, running from left to right or right to left, depending on the value you choose as well as the writing direction of the language of the page, or stacked vertically, running from top to bottom or bottom to top.

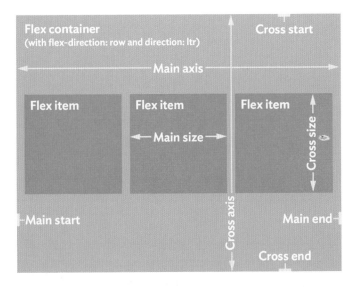

Flexbox is direction-neutral, which is why it uses generic terms like main start instead of absolute terms like top.

flex-direction

Specifying the direction in which to lay out the container's flex items.

row (default)	Lay out the items horizontally in the same direction as the text direction: left to right for ltr languages and right to left for rtl languages.	
row-reverse	Same as row but flipped, so right to left for ltr and left to right for rtl.	
column	Lay out items following the block direction of the current writing mode; usually this means vertical from top to bottom.	
column-reverse	Same as column but flipped, so usually vertical from bottom to top.	

These diagrams are all based on a language that runs from left to right and top to bottom.

As you can imagine, this makes flexbox great for RWD, since you can change orientation easily at different screen sizes. If you want these same boxes to stack on narrow screens, for instance, you can change flex-direction to column.

```
.container {
    display: flex;
    flex-direction: column;
}
```

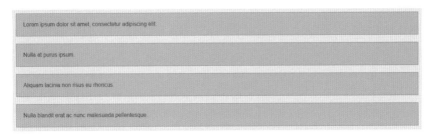

Changing the `flex-direction` value to `column` changes the `<div>`s layout from side by side to vertically stacked.

The margins of adjacent flex items don't collapse together. So, if you have a bunch of vertical flex items with 10 pixels of top and bottom margin each, you'll end up with 20 pixels of space between them.

In the real world, however, layouts are rarely as simple as this. Most of the time, you'll probably have a mix of horizontal and vertical elements in all but the narrowest of views. Fortunately, with flexbox you don't have to pick just one orientation or the other — you can turn a flex item into a flex container itself and give its children a different layout than the parent has.

```
<div class="container vertical">
    <div><p>Lorem ipsum dolor sit amet, consectetur adipiscing elit.</p></div>
    <div class="container horizontal">
        <p>Nulla at purus ipsum.</p>
        <p>Aliquam lacinia non risus eu rhoncus.</p>
    </div>
    <div><p>Aliquam lacinia non risus eu rhoncus.</p></div>
    <div><p>Nulla blandit erat ac nunc malesuada pellentesque.</p></div>
</div>
```

```
.container {
  display: flex;
}
.horizontal {
  flex-direction: row;
}
.vertical {
  flex-direction: column;
}
```

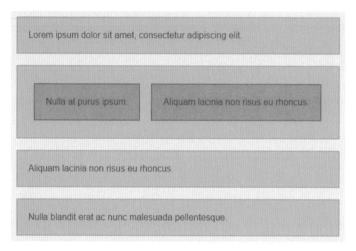

The second green box is both a flex item and a flex container to its child orange boxes, which are laid out horizontally not vertically like their parent and its siblings.

CHANGING ORIENTATION AUTOMATICALLY

So far, flexbox perhaps doesn't seem all that exciting. "I can stack boxes? I already have display:block for that. I can put boxes side by side? Already have display:inline-block, float, and all sorts of things for that." You're right. But by adding another flexbox property, flex-wrap, we can let the browser decide for us when to switch from vertical to horizontal orientation, based on when there's enough space for the items to fit comfortably side by side.

Technically, the browser isn't changing orientation — flex-direction will be set to row all along. It's just that with flex-wrap added and set to the wrap value, the browser is allowed to wrap the flex items onto multiple rows, stacked on top of one another. That's what the flex-wrap property does: it doesn't *force* wrapping to happen, it merely tells the browser whether wrapping is *allowed* when needed (similar to floats or inline-block elements); or whether it should never happen but allow overflowing instead (similar to table-cell elements).

flex-wrap

Specifying whether the container's flex items can wrap if needed and which direction the new lines stack in.

Value	Behavior	flex-direction: row	flex-direction: column
nowrap (default)	Lay out the items in a single line (row or column) regardless if they have to overflow.		
wrap	Flow the items onto multiple lines if needed (following the writing direction) to make the items fit without overflowing.		
wrap-reverse	Same as wrap but stack the new lines in the opposite direction to the writing direction.		

There's a small percentage of browsers still out there that don't support `flex-wrap` but do support the rest of flexbox, such as Firefox 27 and Android 4.3. Check your own usage logs and Can I Use[4] to decide whether this will be a problem for your users and the way you're using flexbox.

By default, flex items always stay on the same line together, whether that be a row or a column, thanks to `flex-wrap` being set by default to `nowrap`. Sometimes you want this rigidity. But when you do want wrapping to happen, you can simply set `flex-wrap` to `wrap`, as I'm doing here to allow items to stack on narrow screens. Even though the orientation isn't set to `column`, what we'll see is vertical stacking on narrow screens, where everything can't fit on one line.

```
.container {
    display: flex;
    flex-wrap: wrap;
}
```

I could also have used the shorthand `flex-flow: row wrap;` here, to set both `flex-direction` and `flex-wrap` at the same time.

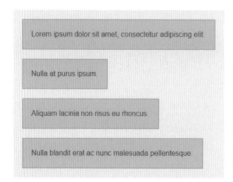

With `flex-wrap:wrap`, the row-oriented flex container is allowed to make multiple rows when needed, instead of just keeping all the flex items in one row.

If `flex-wrap` was instead left at its default value of `nowrap`, the browser would keep the flex items on one single row — no matter what.

4 http://caniuse.com/#feat=flexbox

Widen the viewport and your single-column layout will switch to two columns per row automatically, and then more, when there's enough room for them to fit and without you having to add different layout styles with media queries. Of course, this doesn't look so hot when the blocks don't stretch to fill the width of their container.

As you widen your viewport, items will begin to sit side by side.

What we have right now looks no different from using `display:inline-block`. We need to do something to specify the widths of these blocks. That's where the `flex` property comes in, which makes setting dimensions in responsive layouts much easier.

Sizing Boxes

You're probably familiar with Ethan Marcotte's famous RWD formula for coming up with the proper percentage widths for columns in a responsive layout: *target ÷ context = result*. As far as math goes this is pretty simple stuff. But it's still math and any time math gets involved in design I feel like there has to be a simpler way. Plus, this only accounts for widths. Throw margin, padding and border sizes into the mix and you've got an even trickier equation to solve. Combining different units of measurement in a single layout is called a *hybrid layout*; and when you've got a hybrid layout, you've got a headache.

Setting `box-sizing:border-box` takes care of the problem of mixing pixel- or em-based padding and borders with percentage widths, since the pixels or ems will just get subtracted from the declared width values automatically by the browser. But this doesn't affect margin. If you want to have 20 pixels of space (gutters) between your columns but you want those columns to have percentage widths, how do you get everything to add up to 100%?

There are clever tricks to work around the problems of hybrid layouts, but none are as simple as what flexbox provides: the `flex` property. It lets us specify proportional sizes that take margin, padding and border into account so that items can automatically resize to fit the available space perfectly. It's pretty awesome and powerful, but also really easy to misunderstand and screw up. (Believe me, I've learned this the hard way.)

UNDERSTANDING THE FLEX PROPERTY

The `flex` property is set on flex items directly and affects either their width or height, whichever is the main dimension along the main axis. (See, there are the axes I told you about!)

There are three components to `flex`, which is a shorthand property: `flex-grow`, `flex-shrink`, and `flex-basis`. Here's an example of what a `flex` value might look like, with these three pieces in order:

```
.stretch-and-squish {
    flex: 1 1 200px;
}
```

The `flex-grow` value means how much the flex item will grow relative to other items if there's extra space available on a line; you can think of it as the number of shares of extra space that a flex item gets. In the example above, `.stretch-and-squish` would get one share of any extra pixels in its line, due to the first value of 1 in the three-part `flex` value.

The `flex-shrink` value means how much the flex item will shrink relative to others if there's not enough space. It's basically the proportion of the overflowing pixels that it will have lopped off to get everything to fit again.

If the `.stretch-and-squish` element or its siblings are overflowing, it will get one share of the overflowing pixels deducted from its size, due to the second value of 1.

Both `flex-grow` and `flex-shrink` are set to unitless integers (0, 1, 2, etc.) since they're specifying a proportion, not an absolute value. If you set them to 0, you're saying that you don't want them to grow or shrink at all. But grow or shrink compared to what? That's where the very important third component of the `flex` shorthand comes in, `flex-basis`.

The `flex-basis` property is the initial starting dimension before free space is added on or taken away from the item. It can be set to any standard `width` or `height` unit (`.stretch-and-squish` is set to 200px) and these values act the same as their width or height equivalents. For instance, a percentage value for `flex-basis` is relative to the size of the container, and it affects the size of the content box unless you've changed the box model using `box-sizing:border-box`. The `flex-basis` property can also be set to one of two special keywords, `auto` or `content`, which I'll explain with an example in a moment.

Browsers first size each of the flex items according to its `flex-basis` value. If wrapping is turned off, it puts all of them along the same line (row or column). If wrapping is on, it puts as many items along a line as can fit before wrapping and starting a new line. Now that the items are on lines and have starting dimensions, and possibly some padding, border and margin taking up space too, the browser can see how much space is left over or how much space is overflowing on each line. The browser then divvies up this excess space in whatever ratio the `flex-grow` and `flex-shrink` values specify.

If `flex-grow` and `flex-shrink` are off (set to 0), then `flex-basis` acts just like standard `width` or `height`, setting the flex item to a specific size. If `flex-grow` is on (set to some positive number) and `flex-shrink` is off, then `flex-basis` acts a bit like `min-width` or `min-height`: "You can get bigger than this, but no smaller." Swap that around (`flex-grow` off, `flex-shrink` on) and `flex-basis` acts like `max-width` or `max-height`: "You can get smaller than this, but no bigger." And if both are on, well, `flex-basis` is like something we've never had before! It's a starting point, and everything else that can affect dimension — margins, padding, border, even just extra pixels on the line — can be flexibly added or removed from that starting point to make everything fit nicely.

If the `flex` property and process still sound confusing, you aren't alone: it's definitely confusing when you first read about it. It took me many attempts to get my head around it. But once you look at real examples, as we will in a moment, and play around with it yourself, you get a clearer sense of how all the pieces work together.

By default, flex items have a `flex` value of `0 1 auto`, which means they won't grow to fill space but instead size to their content and can shrink to their minimum size (by wrapping text, for instance). If you want your flex items completely inflexible (`0 0 auto`), you can use `flex:none`. It's also acceptable to use only one or two values within the `flex` shorthand instead of all three, such as `flex:1`, which the browser would interpret to mean `flex-grow:1`. See table below for more information on these values.

	flex-grow	flex-shrink	flex-basis
Default value*	0	1	auto
Value when omitted from **flex** shorthand	1	1	0%

* Also equivalent to `flex:initial`

FULL-WIDTH AND EQUAL-WIDTH MADE EASY

These `flex` property components probably don't make a lot of sense without some real examples to look at. Let's start with the basic colored blocks we were just looking at. What we want to happen is for each item to stretch to fill the full width of the container when there is only one item per line, but when there are multiple items per line, they should have equal widths.

A `flex-grow` value of 1 will accomplish both of these things. Since it makes items grow when there is extra space in a line, it will stretch each single-line item to take up any space left over on its line. And since all the items have the same `flex-grow` value of 1, they will each take up one equal share of the extra space when there is more than one on a line together.

The `flex-shrink` value isn't that important here, since our items aren't over-flowing from their gray parent box, which would be the only time `flex-shrink` would come into effect. Setting it to 0 (no shrinking allowed) or 1 (all items can shrink by one share) is fine. But the value of `flex-basis` is very important because the initial dimension determines when the items will wrap, as I described in the browser's layout process above. Let me show you what I mean.

The first `flex-basis` value we'll try is `auto`. This tells the browser to use whatever the main size is already set to, via the `width` or `height` property; if the main size isn't explicitly set, it will size the items according to their content.

Setting `flex-basis:content` directly indicates that you want to size flex items based on their content. But it's one of the few new additions to the flexbox spec since it became a candidate recommendation and therefore doesn't yet have good support. For now, you can use `auto` for `flex-basis` and get the same effect if `width` or `height` are also set to `auto`, their default values.

```
.item {
    flex: 1 1 auto;
}
```

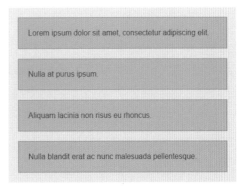

You can see that thanks to the `flex-grow` value of 1, the items do stretch to fill the full width when they are alone on a line; when there are several on a line, they stretch proportional to their initial width, based on the length of the text block that each contains. The first item is the widest because it has the widest content, for example.

Because `flex-grow` is set to 1 on every box, they each grow to fill the extra space on their line.

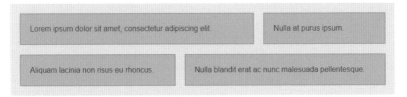

At a wider viewport width, two can fit on each line and they still grow to fill the extra space on the line. But they aren't equal width because their starting dimensions, `flex-basis`, are based on their content width.

If you don't want the items to size according to their content but instead match each other in width, you'll need to give them each the same starting width. That will mean that when browsers add on extra pixels to make them stretch, they will be adding those extra pixels to blocks that are already all the same width. Thus, they will all grow by the same amount and remain equally wide. Let's start simple and just set the `flex-basis` for all of them to 0px.

```
.item {
    flex: 1 1 0px;
}
```

This gives the boxes equal width when they're on a line together, but if you narrow your viewport you'll see that they never wrap. The text just overflows without a care in the world.

When the starting width is **0px** for all the boxes, they all grow the same amount and end up of equal width.

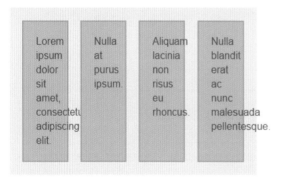

The `flex-wrap` property is still on, but with `flex-basis` set to **0px** the boxes never have a reason to wrap.

This happens because of that 0px value; that's the starting dimension of each item. The `flex-grow` property will let the items get bigger than this if there's room, but if not, there's nothing stopping them from shrinking all the way back down to their initial size of zero.

Instead, we need to set `flex-basis` to some value that we never want the items shrinking below — just like `min-width`, but with flexibility.

```
.item {
    flex: 1 1 10em;
}
```

With this change, browsers put as many 10em-wide items as they can on a line, then wrap when room runs out, and then go back to distribute the extra pixels on each line. No more text overflow!

Note that flex-basis doesn't always act like min-width. It does in this case because flex-wrap is on; once browsers can't fit items, they just wrap them and so never have to shrink the items smaller than their starting width. If flex-wrap is off and flex-shrink is on, browsers have permission to go smaller than the flex-basis value.

Even with this simple example, you can see how dramatically a layout can change without having to create different versions of that layout within multiple media queries. These four blocks might be four feature stories on your home page that you want to sit in four columns on wide screens, two columns on medium screens, and one column on narrow screens. You don't have to work out where to put the breakpoints and what crazy percentage widths to assign to your boxes within each breakpoint — browsers do all that.

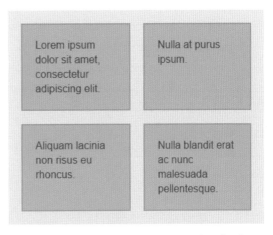

At narrow widths, the boxes will now wrap when they hit the flex-basis value of 10em.

In fact, I don't have to put any of this in a media query — I can put it in the default styles outside any media queries and each layout change just kicks in whenever space allows. It's as if browsers figure out content-driven breakpoints for you. This doesn't make media queries obsolete, of course (I still love you guys, MQs!), but it's nice any time you can automate things and keep your CSS simpler.

A non-flexbox fallback for this sort of full-width grid layout that does involve the use of media queries would be to use text-align:justify in combination with percentage widths. Patrick Kunka explains how in "Text-align: Justify and RWD"[5]. We'll talk later about the specifics of combining different layout techniques with flexbox layout.

REAL-WORLD RWD USES FOR THE FLEX PROPERTY

I've already mentioned that you shouldn't place your entire page layout in the hands of flexbox, but the flex property does make laying out many responsive components a lot simpler and enables flexible behavior you can't achieve with any other CSS. Let's look at a few examples, starting with a form.

It's not uncommon for forms in responsive web pages to switch between at least two layouts: one with the labels stacked over the fields on narrow screens; and another with the labels beside the fields on wider screens. Switching between these layouts is quite easy to do by writing two sets of layout styles, each in its own media query; but flexbox allows you to write one set of layout styles to control both — no media queries needed. Here's how that CSS might look:

```
.label-field-pair {
    display: flex;
    flex-wrap: wrap;
}
.label-field-pair label {
    flex: 0 0 8em;
    margin-right: 10px;
}
.label-field-pair input {
    flex: 1 1 12em;
}
```

5 http://www.barrelny.com/blog/text-align-justify-and-rwd/

Let's look closer at what's happening here. Setting both `flex-grow` and `flex-shrink` to 0 on the labels means they will stay stuck at their `flex-basis` starting width of 8em. But because I've set `flex-grow` to 1 on the inputs, each will always stretch to fill whatever space is left on its line; their `flex-basis` value of 12em acts like a minimum width. At wider viewport sizes, there's room for an 8em label, 10px margin and 12em input all on the same line. As the viewport narrows, browsers figure out when the components can no longer fit beside one another and automatically wrap the input at this point.

This form is just one simple example of a full-width component with a hybrid layout. The `flex` property comes in handy any time you want a component to stretch to the full width or height of its container and you don't have all the inner pieces of the component in the same unit of measurement. You can size some of the pieces with pixels or ems, or just leave them at their initial content-driven size, and then use the `flex` property on the remaining pieces to get them to stretch and fill up whatever space is left over.

Full name:

Email address:

Comments:

When there aren't enough pixels to place the input next to the label, the browser can wrap the input and then stretch it to fill its container.

Full name:

Email address:

Comments:

This wider form layout was created with the same CSS as the narrow version. The inputs always stretch to fill the remaining space on a line, making full-width forms easy.

Creating a page with an off-canvas menu can be a more complex hybrid layout to achieve. Let's say you want the menu to slide in from the left, and instead of pushing the content area off the right side of the screen you want the content area to contract in width to let the menu fit. No big deal if the menu is

With most off-canvas menus that appear on the left, the content gets cut off on the right.

set to a percentage, but tricky if it's set to any other unit of measurement — even more so if it has no explicit width at all but rather is sized to its content.

What we need is `flex-grow`. Remember, for a full-width hybrid layout, set some pieces to a fixed or content-driven width (the menu) and set the remaining pieces to flex (the content area). In this case, I'll start out with the menu set to 0 in width since I want it to be hidden by default, and set the content area to `flex:1` to take up all the remaining width. (We'll talk about why this is better than setting it to `width:100%` in a minute.)

```
html, body {
    height: 100%;
}
.container {
    display: flex;
    min-height: 100%;
}
.content {
    flex: 1;
    padding: 100px 40px 40px 40px;
    transition: all .3s;
}
.menu {
    overflow: hidden;
    width: 0;
    height: 0;
    transition: all .3s;
}
```

To toggle the menu's width from 0 to auto and make it visible, I'll use the :checked pseudo-class on an invisible checkbox to toggle the showing and hiding of the menu without JavaScript. This only works, though, if that checkbox is a sibling of the menu and content blocks, not nested within one of them. Plus, I'll need a visible label for the checkbox, to act as the menu trigger when clicked; the label can contain a hamburger menu icon using an icon font or image.

```
<div class="container">
  <input id="hamburger" type="checkbox" class="hamburger-checkbox">
  <label for="hamburger" class="hamburger-label" role="button"
       aria-labelledby="menu">&#xf0c9;</label>

  <nav role="navigation" class="menu">
    <ul class="menu-list">
      <li class="menu-item">Publications</li>
      <li class="menu-item">Shop</li>
      <li class="menu-item">News</li>
      <li class="menu-item">Events</li>
      <li class="menu-item">Your Account</li>
      <li class="menu-item">Contact Us</li>
    </ul>
  </nav>
  <main role="main" class="content">
    ...
  </main>
</div>

.hamburger-checkbox {
  position: absolute;
  opacity: 0;
}
.hamburger-label {
  position: absolute;
  top: 40px;
  left: 40px;
  z-index: 1;
  display: block;
  width: 42px;
  height: 42px;
```

```
font: 42px/42px FontAwesome;
text-align: center;
cursor: pointer;
}
```

The `.hamburger-label` element is both a flex item and absolutely positioned. This is totally fine — the absolutely positioned flex item will be placed relative to the main start corner of the content box of the flex container[6]. We'll talk more about how flexbox interacts with other layout methods near the end of the chapter.

> Explaining the `:checked` pseudo-class in detail is beyond the scope of this chapter, but if you're not familiar with using it in this way, read more about how it works at http://css-tricks.com/almanac/selectors/c/checked/ and http://css-tricks.com/the-checkbox-hack/. There are also some issues with its use in older mobile browsers, which you can learn how to address, if needed, at http://timpietrusky.com/advanced-checkbox-hack.

To make the menu appear when the user clicks or taps on the label, simply change its `width` from `0` to `auto` (or 10em, or 200px, or whatever width you want it to be once it's visible) when `hamburger-checkbox` is `:checked`.

```
.hamburger-checkbox:checked ~ .menu {
    width: auto;
    height: auto;
    padding-top: 6.5em;
}
```

If I had set the content block to `width:100%` instead of `flex:1` to make it stretch to fill the viewport width, it would now be hanging off the right side of the viewport by whatever amount the menu is now taking up. But the `flex` property on the content block keeps this from happening. The content block instead shrinks from 100% to whatever space is left next to the menu, allowing

---

6   http://www.w3.org/TR/css3-flexbox/#abspos-items

them both to fit perfectly side by side.

I could even take this a step further by changing the placement of the menu at different viewport widths. Perhaps on very narrow screens I don't want the content block to get so contracted when the menu appears, so I could switch `flex-direction` from `row` to `column` to stack the menu above the content block and make it appear to slide in from the top instead of the left. On very wide screens I might not hide the menu at all but instead have it as an always visible sidebar menu or top nav bar. All of this is trivial to accomplish with a few flexbox properties and some media queries. Full-width hybrid layouts no longer have to be a headache to build.

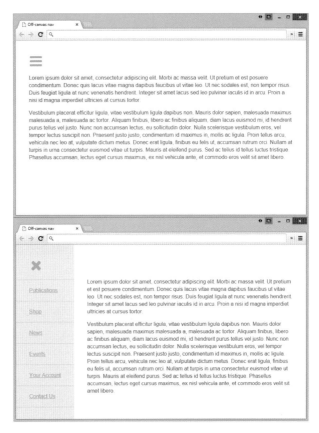

Because it's set to `flex: 1`, the main content area fills the space in the viewport perfectly, contracting when the menu is visible despite the menu having no explicit width.

Making a layout or component stretch to full width can sometimes be hard even when you're not using a hybrid layout but are using the same unit of measurement all the way across a line. Think of a gallery with an unknown or variable number of items in it, each item set to a certain pixel or em width. In a fluid layout, it's ideal to have a gallery without hardcoded rows, so that the items can simply wrap as needed, varying the number on a line depending on how many can fit in a given viewport width. Using `display: inline-block` makes this easy. But the problem with `display:inline-block` is that it won't stretch the items equally to make each row take up the full width of its container. This can be accomplished with `display: table-cell` instead, but then you lose the wrapping ability of `inline-block`.

The `flex` property combined with `flex-wrap` gives you the best of both worlds. Give each item a `flex-basis` in pixels or ems, so it starts out at that width; set `flex-grow` to 1 and items can then stretch farther if needed, as though its width was set to a percentage and filled the full width of its row with its siblings.

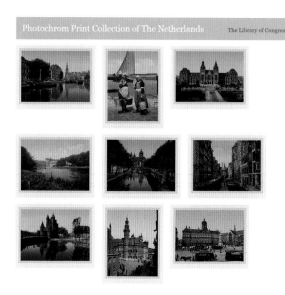
Photochrom Print Collection of The Netherlands   The Library of Congress

Using `display:inline-block` is an easy way to make a gallery where the items wrap when needed, without having to hard code percentage widths into media queries. But it doesn't allow the rows to stretch to the full width.

```
.gallery {
    display: flex;
    flex-wrap: wrap;
    margin-right: -20px;
}
.gallery-item {
    flex: 1 0 250px;
    box-sizing: content-box;
    margin: 0 20px 20px 0;
    padding: 10px;
    border: 1px solid #dddddd;
    text-align: center;
}
```

The items wrap when needed, then stretch to fill their row.

While I'm normally a big fan of box-sizing:border-box, I've overridden it here with box-sizing:content-box; then I can set my flex-basis to the width of my largest image (250px), ensuring that it will be the minimum width of the *content* area of the box, not the total space that the box takes up with padding and border included.

> Remember, flex-basis sets the size of whichever box is being used by the box-sizing property, the content box or the border box. IE10 and 11, however, always make flex-basis size the content box, even if you have box-sizing:border-box set, adding padding and border onto the flex-basis size. This is not a big deal if you have flex-shrink on, because it will simply subtract the padding and border away again if needed, but it can cause overflows if flex-shrink is 0. To work around this bug, you can set width/height to the value you want flex-basis to be, since IE treats box-sizing correctly with the width property, and then set flex-basis to auto so it inherits that width, but with the benefit of box-sizing respected.

Advanced Alignment Control

You may have noticed that in all the examples I've shown you so far (or rather, for all the `flex-direction:row` examples), the boxes are all equal in height with others on their line, similar to how `display:table-cell` makes side-by-side boxes equal in height. This is due to the flexbox `align-items` property, which is set on the flex container and has `stretch` as its default value. You get equal-height columns for free with flexbox!

> For a non-flexbox fallback for equal-height columns, you can use `display:table-cell`, of course, but you can also use some JavaScript. Osvaldas Valutis explains how to use flexbox with JavaScript for equal height gallery items at http://osvaldas.info/flexbox-based-responsive-equal-height-blocks-with-javascript-fallback.

This is only one of a bevy of alignment options that flexbox provides, through the use of four new properties:

- The `align-items` property on the flex container determines how flex items are laid out along the cross axis on the current line. For instance, when `flex-direction` is set to `row`, the cross axis is vertical, and thus `align-items` affects the flex items' vertical alignment; if `flex-direction` was set to `column`, it would affect their horizontal alignment. Not only is this handy for equal-height columns, but it also makes vertical centering a breeze (using `align-items:center` for horizontal flex items).

- The `align-self` property on an individual flex item establishes how that item is aligned on the cross axis, overriding the default specified by `align-items`. If you wanted all of your items across a line to be vertically centered with each other via `align-items:center` on the container, but you also needed just one of those items to be bottom-aligned instead, you could set `align-self:flex-end` on it to override the centering on that item alone.

- The justify-content property on the flex container stipulates how the flex items are laid out along the main axis on the current line. It basically takes any free space left in the line and distributes it between, before or after the flex items. It's particularly handy for spacing items out across the full width of a line, as we'll see in a moment.

- The align-content property on a multi-line flex container determines how the container's lines are laid out when there is extra space in the cross axis. It's similar to justify-content in that it affects where the gaps go, but it applies to entire lines of flex items, rather than items themselves within a single line.

align-items

Specifying the alignment of the container's flex items along its cross axis*

flex-start	Place the cross-start margin edge of the items on the cross-start line.	
flex-end	Place the cross-end margin edge of the items on the cross-end line.	
center	Center the items' margin box in the cross axis.	
baseline	Align the items along their baselines.	
stretch (default)	Stretch the items to fill the cross size of the line (but still respect width and height constraints).	

*align-self uses these same values, but you apply it to a single flex item, not a flex container

justify-content

Specifying the alignment of the container's flex items along its main axis, distributing the extra space in the line outside the flex items.

`flex-start` (default)	Pack the items starting at the main-start edge of the line.	
`flex-end`	Pack the items at the main-end edge of the line.	
`center`	Place items in the center of the line.	
`space-between`	Evenly distribute the items across the line, with the first item flush with the main-start edge and the last item flush with the main-end edge.	
`space-around`	Evenly distribute the items across the line, but with equal spaces on each side of each item, so that the empty space before the first and after the last items equals half of the space between two adjacent items.	

align-content

Specifying the alignment of a container's lines when there is extra space on the cross-axis, distributing the extra space in the container between or to the lines.

flex-start	Pack the lines starting at the cross-start edge of the container.	
flex-end	Pack the lines at the cross-end edge of the container.	
center	Place lines in the center of the container's cross axis.	
space-between	Evenly distribute the lines across the cross axis of the container, with the first line flush with the cross-start edge and the last line flush with the cross-end edge.	

space-around	Evenly distribute the lines across the cross axis, but with equal spaces on each side of each line, so that the empty space before the first and after the last lines equals half of the space between two adjacent lines.	
stretch (default)	Split the free space evenly between the lines and stretch each by that amount to take up remaining space in the cross axis.	

Without flexbox, many of these alignment options are tricky to achieve, and some are just outright impossible. Alignment can become even trickier in responsive layouts, where shifting and resizing content can knock it out of whack at any moment.

Flexbox gives us much more control and precision with alignment. Because alignment is usually a purely aesthetic enhancement rather than an integral part of the meaning or usability of our content, it's the perfect piece of flexbox to layer on as a progressive enhancement, regardless of whether or not you're using flexbox more broadly to control layout.

For instance, remember the off-canvas menu, and how I mentioned it could become a top nav bar on wide screens? Here's some CSS that could do that, hiding the hamburger icon and making the menu visible by default:

```
@media (min-width: 70em) {
  .container {
    flex-direction: column;
  }
}
```

```
.hamburger-label {
    display: none;
}
.sidebar {
    width: auto;
    height: auto;
}
.hamburger-checkbox:checked ~ .sidebar {
    padding-top: 0;
}
.menu {
    display: flex;
}
}
```

Once the links are laid out on a single line as a nav bar, it would be nice to stretch them across the full width of the viewport, with equal spaces in between. I can do this by setting justify-content to space-between (with text-align:center as a simple fallback for non-flexbox-supporting browsers.)

```
@media (min-width: 70em) {
    ...
    .menu {
        display: flex;
        justify-content: space-between;
        text-align: center;
    }
}
```

| Publications | Shop | News | Events | Your Account | Contact Us |

Lorem ipsum dolor sit amet, consectetur adipiscing elit. Morbi ac massa velit. Ut pretium et est posuere condimentum. Donec quis lacus vitae magna dapibus faucibus ut vitae leo. Ut nec sodales est, non tempor risus. Duis feugiat ligula at nunc venenatis hendrerit. Integer sit amet lacus sed leo pulvinar iaculis id in arcu. Proin a nisi id magna imperdiet ultricies at cursus tortor.

Vestibulum placerat efficitur ligula, vitae vestibulum ligula dapibus non. Mauris dolor sapien, malesuada maximus malesuada a, malesuada ac tortor. Aliquam finibus, libero ac finibus aliquam, diam lacus euismod mi, id hendrerit purus tellus vel justo. Nunc non accumsan lectus, eu sollicitudin dolor. Nulla scelerisque vestibulum eros, vel tempor lectus suscipit non. Praesent justo justo, condimentum id maximus in, mollis ac ligula. Proin tellus arcu, vehicula nec leo at, vulputate dictum metus. Donec erat ligula, finibus eu felis ut, accumsan rutrum orci. Nullam at turpis in urna consectetur euismod vitae ut turpis. Mauris at eleifend purus. Sed ac tellus id tellus luctus tristique. Phasellus accumsan, lectus eget cursus maximus, ex nisl vehicula ante, et commodo eros velit sit amet libero.

The links are equally spaced across the width of their container.

Note that this is not stretching the links in the menu *themselves*, as the `flex` property or `display:table-cell` would do, but rather it stretches out all the extra space *in between* the links to distribute it equally across the line. I can't get equal spaces between items using `display:table-cell`, even if I set `table-layout:fixed`, because that only makes each cell equal in width, regardless of its content. If the cells have different amounts of text in them, that means that the gaps inside the cells will vary, too.

Let me show you what I mean. Here's the table-layout version of our full-width nav bar:

```
.menu {
   display: table;
   table-layout: fixed;
   width: 100%
}
.menu-item {
   display: table-cell;
   padding: 10px;
   border: 1px solid #5d9fa3;
   text-align: center;
}
```

With borders on, you can see that each link is of equal width, so they look equally spaced (image below, top). Turn borders off, however, and you'll see the spaces between the end of one link's text and the start of the next are not equal in width (image below, bottom). Flexbox's `justify-content` property fixes this unattractive little annoyance for us.

| Publications | Shop | News | Events | Your Account | Contact Us |
| Publications | Shop | News | Events | Your Account | Contact Us |

Using `table-layout:fixed` on the nav makes each link equal in width, but that doesn't mean that the links' text blocks are equally spaced.

COMBINING ALIGNMENT PROPERTIES

You can combine multiple flexbox alignment properties to get more fancy. Let's say you have an article heading component that includes a photo, title, category and date (you may also use this pattern on a blog post heading, blog comment, or e-commerce product listing).

```
<header class="article-header">
    <figure class="article-header-image">
        <img src="img/snow-day.jpg" alt="Kids happily sledding">
    </figure>
    <section class="article-header-text">
        <h2 class="article-title">Another School-free Snow Day
for Hillsborough Kids</h2>
        <span class="article-category">Weather</span>
        <span class="article-date">28 January 2015</span>
    </section>
</header>
```

Another School-free Snow Day for Hillsborough Kids

Weather   28 January 2015

The starting point of the article header, before adding any layout CSS.

At narrow widths, you want the photo full-width, followed by the title on its own line and the category and date on a line below, pinned to opposite sides. At wider widths, the photo will go on the left, and, just to make this a good challenge, you need the category and date to be aligned with each other on the baselines of their text, but the whole line to be aligned with the bottom of the photo.

Another School-free Snow Day for Hillsborough Kids

Weather   28 January 2015

The narrow-screen header layout we're going for.

Another School-free Snow Day for Hillsborough Kids

Weather   28 January 2015

The widescreen version of the article header layout.

There are a couple of ways you could tackle this with flexbox, but I think the most straightforward is to use `flex-wrap` and row orientation on the wrapper for the photo and text block. With smart `flex-basis` values (essentially minimum widths here), this method lets these two items stack on narrow screens and move side by side on wider screens — without using a media query. I'll also adjust the margins and padding so there's a gap to the right of the photo only when it is on the left of the text block, not on its own line.

```
.article-header {
    display: flex;
    flex-wrap: wrap;
    margin-left: -20px;
}
.article-header-image {
    flex: 1 1 320px;
    padding-left: 20px;
}
.article-header-text {
    flex: 1 1 20em;
    padding-left: 20px;
}
```

Another School-free Snow Day for Hillsborough Kids

Weather　28 January 2015

With flexbox added, the layout switches to two columns on wider screens without a media query.

Now I need to turn the text block itself into its own flex layout. I want the three items inside to wrap as needed, so I'll make the whole text block a multi-line flex container with horizontal flow. Giving the title a `flex-basis` value of 100% makes it take up a full line by itself, leaving the following two flex items (category and date) to sit beside each other on the next line.

```
.article-header-text {
    display: flex;
    flex-wrap: wrap;
    flex: 1 1 20em;
    padding-left: 20px;
}
.article-title {
    flex: 1 1 100%;
}
```

Since the category and date are horizontal flex items, the vertical axis is their cross axis. That means `align-items` will affect their vertical alignment and `justify-content` will affect their horizontal alignment. I want them vertically aligned on their baselines.

```
.article-header-text {
    display: flex;
    flex-wrap: wrap;
    align-items: baseline;
    flex: 1 1 20em;
    padding-left: 20px;
}
```

For their horizontal alignment, I want one on the left and one on the right. Since `justify-content:space-between` moves the first flex item to the start of the line and the last to the end before equally distributing the remaining space in between, it's perfect for pinning two items to opposite ends of their line.

```
.article-header-text {
    display: flex;
    flex-wrap: wrap;
    align-items: baseline;
    justify-content: space-between;
    flex: 1 1 20em;
    padding-left: 20px;
}
```

Without flexbox, I could instead use `display:table-cell` to pin them to opposite sides, but then they won't wrap if the viewport is too narrow, or content too long, to fit both on the same line. Floating them in opposite directions will let them wrap if needed, but then I'll end up with a weird mismatch between the alignment when they go to two lines. Flexbox allows them to display under each other, neatly aligned on the left, when the space requires them to wrap.

Another School-free Snow Day for Hillsborough Kids

Hillsborough News

28 January 2015

Using floating or `inline-block`, the date stays right-aligned when it wraps to a second line, which looks awkward.

Another School-free Snow Day for Hillsborough Kids

Hillsborough News

28 January 2015

Using `justify-content` or the `flex` property, the date wraps to the left side under the category, which looks a lot more natural.

Finally, to move the line containing the category and date down to the bottom of the image, I'll set `align-content` to `space-between` to move the first line to the top and the last line to the bottom. This is so much better than absolute positioning, because if the content is taller than the image, nothing overlaps — it just goes back to the normal alignment, where the second line follows immediately after the first. The `align-content` property only kicks in when there's extra height in the block that can be distributed between the lines.

```
.article-header-text {
    display: flex;
    flex-wrap: wrap;
    align-items: baseline; /* items' vertical alignment */
    justify-content: space-between; /* items' horizontal alignment */
    align-content: space-between; /* lines' vertical alignment */
    flex: 1 1 20em;
    padding-left: 20px;
}
```

Each of these flexbox additions tweaks alignment in a small way, but taken together the layout is much more responsive to the viewport size and text length, allowing the content to wrap more elegantly and remain more readable in different circumstances.

Record-breaking Winter Brings Another School-free Snow Day for Hillsborough Kids

Weather   28 January 2015

When there's no extra height in the text block, `align-content` does nothing and you get normal line stacking.

Record-breaking Winter Brings Another School-free Snow Day for Hillsborough Kids

Weather   28 January 2015

Once there's extra height available, `align-content: space-between` places it between the two lines, pushing the second line to the bottom.

MAGICAL MARGINS

In addition to these flexbox alignment properties, there's another small detail of how flexbox works that can be a big help in aligning content. Flexbox redefines how `margin:auto` works. If you set a `margin` in the main axis to `auto`, it will take up all the remaining space left in that line. It's great for pinning items without having to resort to absolute positioning.

Returning to the nav bar example, let's say at wide sizes you want a logo to sit in the middle of the nav bar, with half the links on the left and half on the right. Most people would cheat and break the list of links into two `<ul>` elements. But you're not a cheater! You're going to do this right, just like your mama taught you.

Each link in the nav bar is already a horizontal flex item, thanks to `flex-direction:row` on their container. But none of the links have been set to actually flex their widths. That means each is only as wide as its text, and with `justify-content:space-between` removed, that leaves a bunch of extra room on the line after the last link.

The starting point of the horizontal nav bar, before being split on the left and right sides of the logo.

To move that extra room in between the News and Events links, just give the Events link (the fourth link) `margin-left:auto`. That moves all the extra space on the line to the left side of Events, effectively pushing it and all the content that follows it as far right as they can go.

```
.nav-item:nth-child(4) {
    margin-left: auto;
}
```

With `margin-left:auto` on the fourth link, all the extra space on the line is devoted to its left margin.

This works because the main axis is horizontal and the auto margin is also along the horizontal axis.

Now the nav bar is visually divided into two pieces, so all that's left is to move the logo into the gap. There are a few ways you could do this, but I think the simplest is to center the logo and then shift the nav bar up around it using a negative top margin.

Publications   Shop   News

Events   Your Account   Contact Us

Lorem ipsum dolor sit amet,
consectetur adipiscing elit. Nulla at
purus ipsum. Aliquam lacinia non
risus eu rhoncus.

Lorem ipsum dolor sit amet, consectetur adipiscing elit. Sed sed laoreet quam. Etiam vehicula vel enim non
commodo. Integer quis eros sed ante semper ultricies id at justo. Integer vel cursus dui. Duis vitae rhoncus
sem. Donec sed odio sodales, mollis ante id, dapibus dolor. Curabitur feugiat metus vel nisi vestibulum
faucibus. Nunc iaculis felis eu arcu malesuada hendrerit. Duis vehicula dictum magna eu hendrerit. Vestibulum
mauris nibh, hendrerit eget nisl suscipit, congue gravida urna. Morbi a eros aliquet, dictum sem vel, commodo
neque. Phasellus sit amet nulla risus. Curabitur tempor lacinia nibh ac eleifend. Nam egestas et est tincidunt
suscipit. Fusce facilisis venenatis erat, vitae varius lectus. Maecenas commodo, urna vitae tempor vulputate,
lectus justo malesuada enim, non tincidunt ipsum arcu eget sem.

The final nav has the appearance of being split in two, but it's still a unified `<ul>` in the HTML.

```
.logo {
    text-align: center;
}
.menu {
    margin: -40px 0 40px 0;
}
```

Thanks to flexbox, this nav bar can undergo several layout changes at different viewport sizes without much trouble.

REORDERING BOXES

A slightly more complex (and perhaps cooler) way to get the logo in the middle of the list of links is to move it there with the flexbox order property.

The order property specifies the order in which browsers lay out flex items in their container. You can think of it like assigning the items a position number in a line. By default, all flex items are in position zero, and since they're in the same position they simply follow the source order. But, if sibling flex items have different order values from each other, browsers will lay them out in ascending order of those values.

To use order on the nav bar, the logo needs to become a sibling flex item of the links; in other words, it has to go in the `<ul>` too. I think this is fine, semantically-speaking, as the logo is functioning as a home link.

```html
<nav role="navigation">
   <ul class="menu">
        <li class="logo menu-item"><a href="index.html"><img
src="img/logo.png" alt="Home"></a></li>
        <li class="menu-item"><a href="...">Publications</a></li>
        <li class="menu-item"><a href="...">Shop</a></li>
        <li class="menu-item"><a href="...">News</a></li>
        <li class="menu-item"><a href="...">Events</a></li>
        <li class="menu-item"><a href="...">Your Account</a></li>
        <li class="menu-item"><a href="...">Contact Us</a></li>
   </ul>
</nav>
```

Now I can divide up the nav bar into order groups. The first three text links need to come first, so they'll need the lowest order value; I'll just keep them with the default of 0. The logo needs to

The logo is the first item in the list in the HTML.

come next, so it gets the next highest order value, 1. The last three text links need to come after the logo, so they get the next highest order value, 2.

```css
.menu-item {
     order: 0; /* default */
}
.logo {
     order: 1;
}
.menu-item:nth-child(n+5) {
     order: 2;
}
```

This does indeed move the logo into the middle of the list, but I haven't added the auto margin to one of the links to split the nav bar at that spot. I can't simply add the margin to the fourth text link, as I did in the last nav bar example, because with every last bit of extra space on the line to its left, the logo will be stuck with the first three links on the left side, rather than in the middle.

With `margin-left:auto` on the fourth link, all of the extra space in the line goes to its left, leaving the logo squished on the left side.

To fix this, I can use two auto margins and browsers will simply divide the extra space on the line evenly between the two items with those margins.

```
.logo {
    order: 1;
    margin-left: auto;
}
.menu-item:nth-child(5) {
    margin-left: auto;
}
```

Half the extra space goes on the left side of the logo, half on the left side of the Events link, and therefore the logo is moved to the center.

A SOLUTION FOR RWD'S STACKING ORDER PROBLEM?

Not being tied to source order any more makes responsive layout so much easier. Sometimes, the order you want your content to stack in vertically on narrow screens is not the same order that you need the boxes to be in to make floating or `display:table-cell` work for wider screen layouts.

Using a very simple example, let's say you want your content to stack in the order of: header, main, sidebar, subnav, and footer on mobile. That needs to be your source order, then. But, perhaps on a wider screen layout, you need either the subnav or sidebar element (or both) to come *before* the main element, not after it, so that you can float it to the side of the main box and create a three-column layout.

Since this is a simple example, this source order problem can be worked around in various ways, such as using negative margins with floats. But

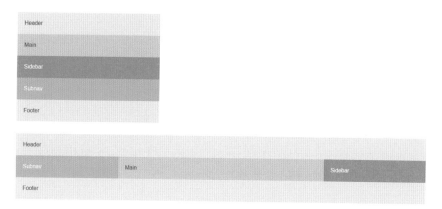

We want Main to come before Sidebar and Subnav when narrow, but be in between them when wide.

most layouts in the real world are far from this simple and can require quite tricky maneuvers to make a single source order work for all layouts across all viewports.

The flexbox order property affords more source-order independence, making this problem a lot easier to solve. You can pick the source order that makes the most sense for your content, from a semantic and accessibility point of view, and then adjust the visual order that the boxes appear in as needed.

Since flexbox currently has better support on mobile than on desktop browsers, and because simple mobile layouts are more suited to flexbox, I'd advise placing your major content blocks in the source order that's needed for the wide layout — provided it's a logical, accessible order — and continuing to use non-flexbox layout methods there. The desktop layout will just use the default HTML source order. But on mobile, you can turn to flexbox and use the order property to override the source order and get the stacking order that you're after.

Using the simple three-column layout example again, here's how I could structure the HTML to make the desktop layout easy to create with floats or display:table-cell.

```
<body class="container">
   <header class="header">Header</header>
   <nav class="subnav" role="navigation">Subnav</nav>
   <main class="main" role="main">Main</main>
   <aside class="sidebar" role="complementary">Sidebar</aside>
   <footer class="footer">Footer</footer>
</body>
```

In the mobile styles outside the first media query, I can turn on flexbox, then simply turn it off in the widescreen media query.

```
.container {
   display: flex;
   flex-direction: column;
}
@media (min-width:50em) {
   .container {
       display: block;
   }
}
```

With flexbox on for mobile, there are a couple of ways I could use the order property to rearrange the default stacking order. One would be to explicitly assign each box a position number.

```
.header  { order: 0; }
.main    { order: 1; }
.sidebar { order: 2; }
.subnav  { order: 3; }
.footer  { order: 4; }
```

I don't think this is wise to do, however. What if I later add another box to the HTML? I'll need to renumber all the order values for all the boxes so that I can assign the new one its proper place in line. This is similar to how people used to use tabindex to give every link and form field an explicit, hard-coded tab-stop position in the tabbing order of a page. It's inflexible and not very future-proof. A better approach, I think, is to keep as many items using the default order as possible and only assign order properties to the few items that need to move out of the default order. In this case, it's really just the subnav box that I need to pull out from its native place line and place lower in the stack. I can keep the header, main and sidebar boxes in this same order by simply keeping them all with the default order value of 0, and assign order:1 just to subnav and footer.

```
.subnav,
.footer {
    order: 1;
}
```

Header, main, and sidebar are in the first group, and subnav and footer are in the second group. Since I've only assigned two of my five boxes an explicit order, if I later add more boxes, there's much less chance that I will need to renumber the existing boxes to accommodate them in the stacking order.

POTENTIAL PITFALLS WITH THE ORDER PROPERTY

Your mind may be spinning with all of the possibilities brought to web layout by being able to move content anywhere, regardless of source order. But before you get too excited, let me point out a few issues with the flexbox order property that might make you think twice about using it widely.

The first issue is that the flexbox order property can only reorder sibling elements — flex items directly within the same flex container. This means that the source order still has some hold on your visual order. You can't use the flexbox order property to move content literally anywhere; it's limited and more suited to smaller layout shifts. Other CSS layout modules like Grid Layout are going to do the heavy lifting when it comes to visual reordering.

As an example of the sibling restriction on flexbox reordering, consider a flex container with four child items. You could rearrange these four with one another to your heart's content, but you couldn't pull out the sidebar-item-highlight block from within <aside> and place it above <main> using order:-1, or any value. The sidebar-item-highlight block is simply not a sibling of <main>.

```
<div class="flex-container">
   <header>...</header>
   <main>...</main>
   <aside>
        <div class="sidebar-item">...</div>
        <div class="sidebar-item sidebar-item-highlight">...</div>
        <div class="sidebar-item">...</div>
   </aside>
   <footer>...</footer>
</div>
```

Even if <aside> is a flex container too, the order count basically starts over within each flex container. Only the children of that flex container can be reordered in relation to one another.

Even when you don't have a sibling issue and can achieve the layout shift you're after using order, you'll have to be very careful to make sure that the layout degrades well in older browsers without flexbox support. When you use flexbox to center some content vertically, for instance, it's not a big deal if the small minority of users with old browsers see it top-aligned instead: it's purely aesthetic. But if you use flexbox to rearrange entire sections of content, it could potentially be confusing or less usable if the content appears in a different order from the one you intended; order is often tied to meaning, not just aesthetics. You'll need to make sure that both orders — the default HTML one and the visual one you've created with flexbox — are logical and usable, so that users both with and without flexbox all have a good experience.

This can be tricky to achieve when you factor in accessibility. Flexbox only changes the order visually, but screen readers still read out content in its HTML order. Plus, most browsers keep the tabbing order based on the HTML, not the visual order. (The exception to this, currently, is Firefox, which does change the tabbing order to match the visual order, although this violates the spec.)

That means that sighted non-mouse users, such as people who use a keyboard or other device because of mobility limitations, might have a really confusing time trying to navigate through the page, depending on how you've used the order property. For instance, in the earlier example where I moved the subnav <div> above the footer, a user tabbing through the page would first go through all the links in the header, then jump down to the subnav, then jump back up to the main and sidebar sections, and then jump back down to the footer. Seeing the focus outline jump around the page in a seemingly arbitrary way as you tab through the content would be a very confusing experience.

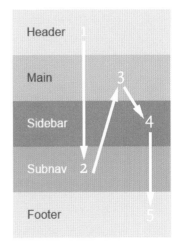

The tab order would follow this illogical path since I've moved the `<div>`s only visually, not in the HTML.

This layout is just for narrow mobile screens, where tabbing isn't used nearly as much, which minimizes the problem a lot. But we can't consider it a non-issue and write it off entirely. People *do* use keyboards on mobile devices, as well as other input devices that simulate tabbing. You still need to ensure keyboard navigation is usable on mobile sites.

These accessibility issues are why the spec states explicitly that you must use the order property only for visual, not logical, reordering of content[7].

Using order Progressively and Accessibly

I probably seem like a complete tease right now. A wet blanket, ruining your beautiful dreams of being able to move content around the page willy-nilly, without care or consequence.

But don't despair. It *is* possible to use order in a way that doesn't affect accessibility and degrades gracefully in old browsers. Let me give you one example of using order in a progressive enhancement sort of way.

Here's a recipe, with its photo placed in the middle of the text so that on wider screens I can float it next to the ingredients list. But perhaps on the single-column narrow view I don't want the photo above the ingredients. I could use the order property to move the photo above the recipe title on mobile only.

In the styles outside any media queries, I set flex-direction to column to stack all the pieces of the recipe in a single column, and then set the order value of the image to -1. All the other flex items inside the recipe container have the

---

7 http://www.w3.org/TR/css3-flexbox/#order-accessibility

Thai Shrimp Salad

SERVES 3-4 AS A SIDE DISH

PREP TIME	COOK TIME	TOTAL TIME
15 MINS	5 MINS	20 MINS

Ingredients

- 400 grams shrimp, peeled and deveined
- 1 tsp vegetable oil
- 3 tbsp sweet thai chili paste
- juice of a lime
- 1 stalk lemongrass, only white parts
- 2 medium shallots
- 1/2 cup fresh mint, lightly packed and chopped
- 3-4 kaffir lime leaves

Directions

1. Sauté the shrimp in vegetable oil over until cooked through, about 3-4 minutes. Drain any liquid and place in a mixing bowl.
2. Add chili paste and lime juice until combined.
3. Remove the stem from the kaffir leaves. Cut the leaves, lemongrass stalks, and shallots into very thin slivers.
4. Add kaffir, lemongrass, shallots and mint leaves to the shrimp and toss until combined.
5. Serve immediately or chilled.

I need to place the photo before the ingredients list to float it to the right of the list (Recipe and photo courtesy of Della Cucina Povera: http://dellacucinapovera.com).

Thai Shrimp Salad

SERVES 3-4 AS A SIDE DISH

PREP TIME	COOK TIME	TOTAL TIME
15 MINS	5 MINS	20 MINS

Ingredients

- 400 grams shrimp, peeled and deveined
- 1 tsp vegetable oil
- 3 tbsp sweet thai chili paste
- juice of a lime
- 1 stalk lemongrass, only white parts
- 2 medium shallots
- 1/2 cup fresh mint, lightly packed and chopped
- 3-4 kaffir lime leaves

Directions

1. Sauté the shrimp in vegetable oil over until cooked through, about 3-4 minutes. Drain any liquid and place in a mixing bowl.
2. Add chili paste and lime juice until combined.
3. Remove the stem from the kaffir leaves. Cut the leaves, lemongrass stalks, and shallots into very thin slivers.
4. Add kaffir, lemongrass, shallots and mint leaves to the shrimp and toss until combined.
5. Serve immediately or chilled.

The default stacking order based on the HTML order, with the photo before the ingredients list, is shown in the narrow mobile view before flexbox is added.

default order value of `0`. `-1` is smaller, so the image will come first; that is, move up to the top of the stack.

```
.recipe {
    display: flex;
    flex-direction: column;
}
.recipe-photo {
    order: -1;
}
.recipe-photo img {
    width: 100%;
}
```

In the wide media query for the desktop view, I simply turn off flexbox by setting the recipe's `display` back to `block`. That puts the image back in normal flow order, where I can then float it to the right of the ingredients list.

```
@media screen and (min-width:800px) {
  .recipe {
    display: block;
  }
  .recipe-photo {
    float: right;
    width: 50%;
  }
}
```

Thai Shrimp Salad

SERVES 3-4 AS A SIDE DISH

PREP TIME   COOK TIME   TOTAL TIME
15 MINS   5 MINS   20 MINS

Ingredients

- 400 grams shrimp, peeled and deveined
- 1 tsp vegetable oil
- 3 tbsp sweet thai chili paste
- juice of a lime
- 1 stalk lemongrass, only white parts
- 2 medium shallots
- 1/2 cup fresh mint, lightly packed and chopped
- 3-4 kaffir lime leaves

Directions

1. Sauté the shrimp in vegetable oil over until cooked through, about 3-4 minutes. Drain any liquid and place in a mixing bowl.
2. Add chili paste and lime juice until combined.
3. Remove the stem from the kaffir leaves. Cut the leaves, lemongrass stalks, and shallots into very thin slivers.
4. Add kaffir, lemongrass, shallots and mint leaves to the shrimp and toss until combined.
5. Serve immediately or chilled.

RECIPE AND PHOTOS COURTESY OF DELLA CUCINA POVERA. ALL RIGHTS RESERVED

There's no need to worry about desktop browser support for flexbox since I'm not using it there, and any mobile browsers that don't support flexbox will simply see the image before the ingredients — a little different in appearance, but not wrong or confusing. Plus, there are no accessibility problems in moving the photo because the reordered content doesn't have any text or links within it. Both reading order and tabbing order will be the same with and without flexbox. This is a visual enhancement that doesn't hurt user agents that can't interpret it.

The photo has the lowest order value, so it is placed before its siblings and displays before all the text.

You can use the order property in this same progressive way on articles, product listings and other similar page components that include decorative content that can appear in multiple places and still make sense. It's fine to have text within the reordered content as long as the text makes sense when read in both the HTML order and the visual flexbox order, such as a photo caption that could be read before or after an introductory paragraph. And if you can avoid having any links or form fields in the reordered content, your accessibility will be even better.

OTHER WAYS TO CHANGE VISUAL ORDER

We've made it through all the flexbox properties now (yay!), but before we wrap up, I wanted to mention that it's also possible to affect the visual order of your content using the `flex-direction` and `flex-wrap` properties that I covered near the start of the chapter. Both of these have reverse values which place the content in the opposite direction than the default flow.

For instance, the Guardian's responsive website[8] uses `flex-direction: row-reverse` in its widescreen layout to place story blocks side by side, but run them from right to left instead of left to right (see below). This creates a different visual order from the one you see on narrow screens, where the content stacks in its default HTML order (see image on the next page); the topmost content doesn't become the farthest left content as you might expect.

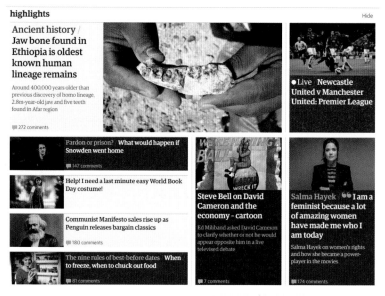

The Guardian widescreen layout uses `flex-direction:row-reverse` within the main story and on the bottom row to place blocks from right to left.

---

8 http://www.theguardian.com/

You face the same accessibility issues when reordering with `flex-direction` and `flex-wrap` as you do with the `order` property, but they give you a couple of other options for manipulating visual placement in a simple way.

HANDLING BROWSER VARIANTS

Near the start of this chapter, I mentioned that flexbox has great browser support. It's just that different browsers support different versions. Before flexbox became a candidate recommendation in 2012, its syntax went through a lot of changes, so the properties and values changed names a couple of times. Fortunately, most of the behavior stayed the same, so for the most part you can feed the different property and value names without a problem.

If you want to, of course. Here are the approaches you could choose to take:

The narrow layout keeps the content in the default HTML order. For instance, the main story photo comes before its text block, not after it, as you might expect from looking at the widescreen layout.

- *Use only the non-prefixed, current, standard syntax.* This is the purest approach, but browser-prefixed properties are perfectly fine to use, provided you do so before the non-prefixed properties. I wouldn't recommend this approach.

- *Use the non-prefixed and browser-prefixed versions of the standard syntax.* This is a safe approach, and it's what you'll need to do if you want to add Safari support on both desktop and iOS, which I'm guessing you do.

- *Use the above plus the -ms- prefixed 2011/2012 syntax.* This will get you support in IE 10, so this is a pretty good idea.

- *Use the above plus the -webkit- prefixed 2009 syntax.* This gives you older versions of Safari and the Android browser. However, it's a lot slower to render than the current flexbox syntax[9]. Plus, the browsers it benefits no longer have much market share. Your audience may vary, of course, so the choice is up to you. But, personally, I don't tend to add this syntax.

Current syntax, no prefixes	Current syntax but browser prefixed	2011/2012 syntax	2009 syntax
Chrome 29+	Safari 6.1+	IE 10	Safari 3.1–6
Firefox 22+*	iOS Safari 7.1+	IE Mobile 10	iOS Safari 3.2–6.1
IE 11+	Blackberry 10+		Android 2.1–4.3
IE Mobile 11+			
Opera 17+			
Opera Mobile 12.1+			
Opera Mini 8+			
Android 4.4			

*Firefox 22–27 did not support the `flex-wrap` and `flex-flow` properties.

It can be hard to keep track of which properties from which syntaxes correspond, and adding the various browser variants can be messy and time-consuming. If you can avoid doing it manually, you'll save yourself a lot of confusion and errors. There are lots of Sass and LESS flexbox mixins that can create all the variants for you, or you can customize them to add just the variants you want.

If you're using Sass, check out https://github.com/mastastealth/sass-flex-mixin, https://gist.github.com/cimmanon/4461470, or https://github.com/thoughtbot/bourbon/blob/master/app/assets/stylesheets/css3/_flex-box.scss. If you're using LESS, check out https://github.com/annebosman/FlexboxLess.

---

9   http://updates.html5rocks.com/2013/10/Flexbox-layout-isn-t-slow

Another tool you can use to add prefixes is the *Autoprefixer* library that, naturally, adds browser prefixes, including various flexbox versions. It uses the Can I Use database to determine which prefixes are needed, and can be customized to target specific browsers. Autoprefixer can be used in a wide variety of development environments; go to https://github.com/postcss/autoprefixer#usage to learn how to use it in conjunction with your tool of choice.

A potential downside to using Autoprefixer for flexbox is that you can't prevent it from adding just the 2009 syntax, for instance. If you make it exclude the browsers that use the 2009 syntax, it will exclude them from all prefixed CSS properties, not just flexbox properties. To work around this, you could write a PostCSS plugin to remove the 2009 properties after Autoprefixer does its work; see https://github.com/postcss/postcss.

The bottom line is this: go ahead and use whichever variants you want, or none of them. Throughout this chapter, I've shown you only the non-prefixed properties, but this was just to keep the CSS I showed you from being super long and hard to read and understand. That doesn't mean I'm saying you shouldn't use any prefixed versions in the real world. Just as you need to decide whether flexbox is appropriate for the layout task you want to complete, you need to decide which browser variants you're going to use for each individual project.

Using Flexbox With Fallbacks

Until browser support for flexbox becomes universal, or unless you're working on a site for a specific browser, I recommend using flexbox for progressive enhancement, like the recipe photo example. Your layout should be clear, usable and (hopefully) attractive without flexbox, so that users of non-supporting browsers still have a good experience; then you can layer flexbox on top to improve responsiveness even further. So how do you handle the layout for the non-supporting browsers?

I don't have a single answer to this question. There's currently no flexbox polyfill that will magically make all your flexbox effects happen with JavaScript instead of CSS. But there are a few ways to provide a good fallback experience for non-supporting browsers, and the one you choose will depend on the way you're using flexbox.

ONE APPROACH: DO NOTHING

The simplest fallback approach is to do nothing for non-supporting browsers. If I'm using flexbox only for cosmetic enhancements, not essential layout, I think it's perfectly fine for different browsers to display different things.

That's already happening anyway. I don't provide any fallbacks for `border-radius`, `box-shadow`, `text-shadow`, gradients, multi-columns, transitions, or any number of other aesthetic enhancements I can add with CSS3 — you probably don't either. Most folks in our industry have accepted that all browsers and devices are going to display our webpages somewhat differently no matter how hard we try for things to look identical between browsers. When you're using flexbox just to fine-tune alignment, change a photo's placement, or other purely cosmetic enhancements, it's completely acceptable and sensible to provide no fallback to attempt to imitate the effect in old browsers.

For instance, if I'm using flexbox just to nicely center a couple of items together, it's not a big deal if instead they're top-aligned in IE7, 8 and 9. This appearance will be different, but it's not wrong; it won't look broken and it won't provide a bad experience for users of those browsers. This use of flexbox is progressive enhancement, pure and simple.

COMBINING FLEXBOX WITH ALTERNATIVE LAYOUT METHODS

If you're using flexbox to control layout, meaning the placement and sizing of items, you might decide this is a more essential part of the design and want to provide a fallback. In this case, you can use any layout CSS you normally would as your flexbox fallback, because most of the time both layout methods can coexist.

Using `display:table-cell` is a great alternative to flexbox because it affects boxes in much the same way that flexbox does. For instance, it can do equal-height columns, make boxes stretch and shrink to fit their content, vertically center content, and make a single box on a line take up all the remaining space after the fixed-width boxes have been sized.

However, one of the big differences between flexbox and `table-cell` display is that table-cell doesn't allow boxes to wrap when needed. At narrow widths, content in adjacent "cells" may overflow and overlap one another. Plus, IE7 doesn't support `display:table-cell`, so it won't work as a fallback for that browser, if you still support it.

If this is a possibility for your content and you need wrapping, inline-block or float are other good fallbacks for flexbox layout. Just as with `display:table-cell`, you can use either of these layout methods at the same time as flexbox.

In the article header example we looked at earlier, I can use both table-cell and inline-block to control the layout before adding flexbox as a progressive enhancement. I'll use table-cell to lay out the image and text block beside each other; and then inline-block inside the text block, since the three pieces of content in there have to be able to wrap if needed.

```
@media (min-width: 70em) {
  .article-header {
    display: table;
    display: flex;
    width: 100%;
  }
  .article-header-image {
    display: table-cell;
    flex: 1 0 auto;
    padding-right: 10px;
  }
  .article-header-image img {
    width: auto;
  }
  .article-header-text {
    display: table-cell;
    display: flex;
    align-items: baseline;
    justify-content: space-between;
    align-content: space-between;
```

```
    width: 100%;
    vertical-align: middle;
  }
  .article-title {
    flex: 1 1 100%;
  }
  .article-category {
    display: inline-block;
  }
  .article-date {
    display: inline-block;
    text-align: right;
  }
}
```

See how I have both table and flex `display` values on `article-header` and `article-header-text`? Both conflicting values can be declared on the same element, because non-supporting browsers just ignore the flex stuff that they don't understand, and browsers that do understand it use whatever value comes last to override the earlier value.

The same thing happens with `display: inline-block` and the `float` and `clear` properties. When you use both inline-block or floating as well as flexbox on the same element, flexbox overrides them. This means that non-supporting browsers use the inline-block or float positioning; supporting browsers use the flexbox positioning; and neither layout method needs to be hidden from either set of browsers: they don't conflict — they coexist.

There are a few other standard CSS properties that get overridden or work differently in conjunction with flexbox; see http://www.w3.org/TR/css3-flexbox/#flex-containers for the brief list.

But, there are a few tricky issues you may run into when you combine floating with flexbox.

First, if you're using the 2009 flexbox syntax for older versions of Safari and the Android browser (by setting `display` to `-webkit-box` rather than `-webkit-flex`), those browsers exhibit a bug where a flex item that is also floated will disappear. Luckily, the fix is simple: just add position:relative to the floated flex item to make it reappear. (Illogical, yes, but that's a bug fix for you!)

Second, some float containment methods can clash with certain flexbox effects. For instance, the classic clearfix class adds generated content at the end of the parent of the float, and this new piece of content will be counted as a flex item just like the other boxes within that parent. Since it has zero width and height this is normally not a problem, but if you're using the justify-content property to equally distribute the flex items, this invisible flex item gets distributed too and takes up space. You may want to avoid using the clearfix class when using flexbox in conjunction with your floats, or move it to another container element without display:flex on it.

The invisible piece of content that clearfix adds is at the right edge of the nav bar after Contact Us, thanks to justify-content:space-between pushing it to the end of the line. It takes up no space itself, but since it's a flex item it gets aligned like the rest of them and ends up with space around it, leaving a big gap and making the nav not appear full-width.

A third issue is that when you float you often give the content following the float a large side margin to get it out of the way. But flex items don't need this margin to sit side by side, so adding it only introduces a huge gap between flex items. This is when you need to break out the Modernizr feature-detection script[10] and have it add the flexbox-supporting or non-supporting classes to the opening <html> tag element of your page. Then you can use these classes to add the margin only when flexbox isn't supported and floating is used instead.

For instance, if I was using both flexbox and floating to place a sidebar to the left of a main content block, I could add the 300-pixel left margin on the main content block only when flexbox is unsupported and Modernizr has added the no-flexbox class to the <html> tag.

---

10   http://modernizr.com

```
.container {
   display: -webkit-box;
   display: flex;
}
.sidebar {
   float: left;
   position: relative;
   width: 300px;
}
.no-flexbox .main-content {
   margin-left: 300px;
}
```

Most of the time, you don't need Modernizr to separate out the flexbox and non-flexbox fallback styles, as flexbox can just override in browsers that understand it, but sometimes you do need to isolate certain properties, and luckily Modernizr makes that easy.

The main CSS layout method that doesn't work in conjunction with flexbox is absolute positioning. Flexbox doesn't override it, so if you're using it as your non-flexbox starter styles, you'll need to isolate it with Modernizr. See http://www.w3.org/TR/css3-flexbox/#abspos-items for the details.

Let me give you one final example of using flexbox as progressive enhancement on top of other layout methods, but this time across the entire page layout. My friend Chris Weiher's existing website, Watch Me Work[11], didn't have a mobile version and wasn't responsive. He told me that he wanted the mobile version of the site to have live video streams at the top of the page so that users could get viewing right away — the main purpose of the site.

I knew I could do this with responsive web design, rather than creating a separate mobile site, so I first created a wireframe of his existing desktop design with live streams added to the bottom of the page. Then, in the narrow mobile version, I moved the live streams to the very top, even over the hero banner. In both versions, the layout was pretty simple — a series of stacked bars — so

---

11 http://www.watchmework.com

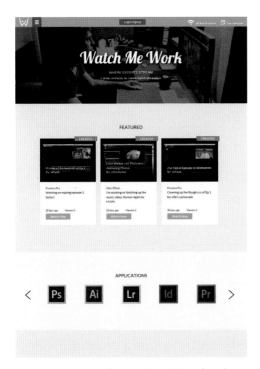

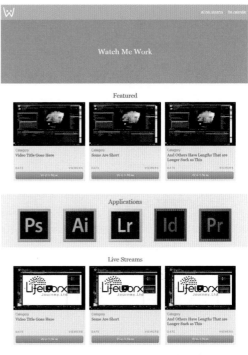

The existing design of Watch Me Work, with no live streams section and no narrow mobile version of the layout.

My widescreen wireframe of the revised layout, with a Live Streams section at the bottom so I could make it available for the mobile version.

I could rely on the default block stacking of <div>s to lay out the major page sections. I simply needed to use the order property to move the live streams section up from its native HTML position at the end of the page on narrow screens.

```
.watch-me-work {
    display: flex;
}
.header {
    order: 0;
}
.section {
    order: 2; /* all of the sections, including Live Streams */
}
```

My narrow-screen wireframe re-orders the page sections to place Live Streams at the top.

```
.section-live {
    order: 1; /* override to move Live Streams
above others */
}
@media (min-width: 40em) {
  .section {
      order: 0; /* back to default source order */
  }
}
```

That was all the flexbox I needed for the overall layout of the major page sections. I then used flexbox (on top of simpler layout CSS) inside these sections to size and align the chunks of content. For instance, to put the video stream blocks (inside the featured and live sections) beside one another in the wider layout, I used floating as a starting layout style, but added flexbox as well so I could make them have equal height. The flex value simply overrides the width value that the floating layout will use.

```
.stream-list {
    display: flex;
    flex-direction: column;
}
@media (min-width: 40em) {
  .stream-list {
      flex-direction: row;
  }
  .stream-item {
      float: left;
      width: 32%;
      margin-right: 2%;
  }
  .flexbox .stream-item {
      flex: 1 1 33%;
      margin-right: 20px;
  }
}
```

```
.stream-item:last-child {
    margin-right: 0;
  }
}
```

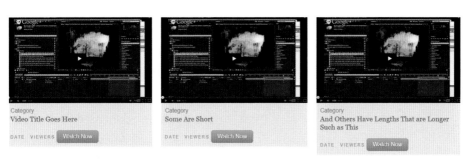

Without flexbox, the stream items are not equal height across their row, but they still look fine as a basic style for older browsers.

Using flex on the gray box within each stream item makes them stretch to fill the full height, so you can see the stream items are of equal height across the row.

With the stream items having equal height across their row on wide screens, I could then pin the date, viewers and button to the bottom of each block, making them align with one another across the row. To do this, I first needed to turn each stream item into a `flex` container itself, and stack the video (`stream-video`) on top of the gray text block (`stream-info`). I made the video not flex so `stream-info` could take up the rest of the height inside `stream-item`.

```
.stream-item {
    display: flex;
    flex-direction: column;
}
```

```
.stream-video {
    flex: 0 0 auto;
}
.stream-info {
    flex: 1 1 auto;
}
```

Next, I needed the children of stream-info to be flex items too, so I could use the new auto margin pinning behavior on them. That meant stream-info needed to be a flex container with vertically stacked children.

```
.stream-info {
    display: flex;
    flex-direction: column;
    flex: 1 1 auto;
}
```

Finally, I added an auto margin on the top of the wrapper for the date and viewers text (stream-meta), pushing it and everything after it to the bottom of its container. I also made it a flex container so I could use justify-content to push its children, date and viewers, to opposite sides of their line.

```
.stream-meta {
    display: flex;
    justify-content: space-between;
    margin: auto 0 10px 0;
}
```

And I didn't have to do anything to make the button fill the width of its container — it did that by default thanks to align-items:stretch on the stream-info, which makes flex items' widths, not heights, stretch when the flex container is set to vertical alignment.

In the applications logo list, I used inline-block and text-align:center to lay out the logos in the middle of a single line, but I added flexbox on top to make the logos stretch to fill the line.

The date, viewers and button are now pinned to the bottom of their stream item and full-width within it.

```css
.app-list {
    display: flex;
    text-align: center;
}
.app-item {
    display: inline-block;
    flex: 1 1 auto;
    margin-right: 20px;
    text-align: center;
}
.app-item:last-child {
    margin-right: 0;
}
.app-item img {
    max-width: 100%;
}
```

The page is full of small flexbox enhancements like this that make the layout more responsive to the space available, helping it to look more polished in between the breakpoints.

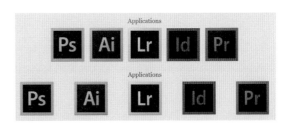

The applications list without flexbox (top) and with flexbox (bottom).

Conclusion

Flexbox is not necessarily a replacement for all the other layout mechanisms that we've been using for a while, but rather is an addition to our box of tools to help create responsive layouts. Try layering flexbox on top of simpler layout CSS to enhance the sizing, alignment and ordering of content within your UI components. We've looked at real-world examples of components that can be made more responsive, more easily, thanks to flexbox's powerful and flexible properties.

We've looked at lots of code along the way. But using flexbox is about a lot more than memorizing new syntax. It's about shifting the way you think about web layout problems and visualize their solutions. When I made the switch from table layout to float layout, there was a certain point where I just started thinking in floats, and table layout actually became harder for me because I no longer thought about web layout from that perspective and within its limitations.

You can experience that same sort of mental shift with flexbox today. To start thinking from a direction-neutral flexbox point of view, you just have to use it. So play around with it! The more you use it, the more easily you'll be able to understand how to manipulate layout with it, and the more ideas you'll gain of how flexbox can be used to enhance your daily work.

ABOUT THE AUTHOR

Zoe is a web designer and developer specializing in responsive design, UX and accessibility. She loves creating sites that work for as many people and devices as possible, and she loves achieving it with the shiny new flexbox. Zoe currently works as a senior designer for *Booking.com*, living in Amsterdam, but she is originally from the Chicago area in the USA. She's got a fantastic husband and two adorable and energetic little kids.

ABOUT THE REVIEWER

James Williamson is a senior author for *lynda.com* and an Adobe Certified Instructor. He has many years of web, print, and digital video experience, and has been a featured speaker at Flashforward as well as a regular speaker at Adobe MAX. James also blogs (infrequently) about all things web at his site, Simple Primate, which can be found at *www.simpleprimate.com*.

WEB FONTS
PERFORMANCE

BRAM STEIN

CHAPTER SIX · BY BRAM STEIN

WEB FONTS PERFORMANCE

T HE RAPID ADOPTION OF WEB FONTS has enriched typographic diversity on the web but also created a new and major bottleneck in terms
of performance. Browsers that block rendering while downloading
web fonts add a significant and unnecessary delay to displaying a web page
even though the DOM and CSSOM may already be available. Users should be
presented with readable text as soon as possible instead of having to stare at a
blank or partially rendered page while fonts are downloading.

The only way to make content accessible as soon as possible is by treating
web fonts as a progressive enhancement. This doesn't mean web font performance is not an issue. You still need to load web fonts as quickly as possible so
that users experience your site exactly how you designed and built it.

Let's fix this. But before we can, it is important to understand web fonts: the
formats, how browsers load them, and which existing and new CSS features
are useful to control font loading and rendering. We'll then move on to basic
and advanced font optimization techniques that will help you make the right
trade-off between performance, usability and design.

Web Fonts & Formats

What exactly is a web font? A web font is nothing more than a font downloaded from a web server instead of one read from the local file system. The CSS @font-face rule lets you define and use custom fonts on your site. You're probably familiar with the basic syntax.

```
@font-face {
  font-family: My Font;
  src: url(myfont.woff);
}
```

The src property will accept multiple comma-separated formats. The browser will pick a format that it supports using a format hint listed after a font file's URL. The following @font-face rule uses three different font formats.

```
@font-face {
  font-family: My Font;
  src: url(myfont.woff) format('woff'),
       url(myfont.otf) format('opentype'),
       url(myfont.ttf) format('truetype');
}
```

In the above example, woff, opentype and truetype are all format hints. Formats are selected by browsers based on support and the order in which they occur. Given the above example and a browser that supports OpenType and TrueType fonts, the OpenType file will be used.

If we had placed the TrueType file before the OpenType file, the TrueType file would have been used instead. Alternatively, a browser with support for all three formats would use the WOFF file, which is the first format it encounters.

Unfortunately, there isn't a single web font format that covers every browser you might want to support. There are currently six web font formats, each with their own advantages and disadvantages.

- TTF (TrueType)
- OTF (OpenType)

- EOT (Embedded OpenType)
- WOFF (Web Open Font Format)
- WOFF2 (Web Open Font Format 2)[1]
- SVG fonts (Scalable Vector Graphics)

So which format(s) should you use? This depends entirely on which browsers you support. The WOFF2 format offers the best compression rates, but is only supported by the most recent browser versions[2]. The WOFF format has much wider browser support but isn't supported by older Android and iOS versions.

However, older Android and iOS do support TrueType and OpenType fonts. If you need to support Internet Explorer 6, 7 or 8 you'll also need to use EOT because it is the only supported format in those browsers.

The bottom line is that you should pick the formats that are most suitable for the browsers you support *and* give you the best compression rates. The only exception to this rule will be made for the SVG font format. SVG fonts do not support any of the OpenType features required to properly display text, such as kerning, ligatures and advanced positioning. Browser support for SVG fonts is limited; it's been removed from Chrome, and have never been supported on IE or Firefox. The combined lack of OpenType features and limited browser support means there really is no reason to use SVG fonts either now or in the future[3].

When researching `@font-face` on the web, you may have seen the so-called "bulletproof" `@font-face` syntax[4] mentioned. This particular syntax is designed to support all browsers and font formats. It employs a special hack to work around `@font-face` bugs in older versions of Internet Explorer.

---

1 WOFF2 is a fairly new file format and there isn't much public information on how to create them. A good place to start is Google's WOFF2 repository (https://github.com/google/woff2). FontSquirrel's Web Font Generator also generates WOFF2 files.

2 *State of Web Type* provides a reference for current support of type features. http://www.stateofwebtype.com

3 To clarify: this doesn't mean you shouldn't use SVG at all; it is great for many uses, which you can read all about in Sara Soueidan's chapter on SVG. In fact, SVG may even have a future use in fonts, because Mozilla and Adobe are working on a specification to use SVG in OpenType as a way to specify color and animations in fonts (http://www.w3.org/2013/10/SVG_in_OpenType/). It just doesn't work so well as a web font format.

4 http://www.fontspring.com/blog/the-new-bulletproof-font-face-syntax

```
@font-face {
  font-family: My Font;
  src: url(myfont.eot?#iefix) format('embedded-opentype'),
       url(myfont.woff2) format('woff2'),
       url(myfont.woff) format('woff'),
       url(myfont.otf) format('opentype'),
       url(myfont.svg#myfont) format('svg');
}
```

Internet Explorer 6-8 do not support multiple urls for the `src` property. These versions of Internet Explorer will take the entire value of the `src` property as the URL. That means that they won't just use *myfont.eot*, but the entire value including the other URLs, format hints, whitespace, and so on. You'll see a fix for this issue in the first line of the `src` property. The query parameter and the fragment identifier (`?#iefix`) prevent this issue from happening by tricking Internet Explorer's URL parser into thinking the remainder of the URL can be ignored.

Other browsers will ignore this because the `src` property is valid and the EOT format is only supported by Internet Explorer. The other formats are specified in order of preference so that browsers pick the most efficient format (e.g. in order of compression rate: WOFF2, WOFF and TrueType/OpenType).

With usage of IE 6–8 at an all-time low and careful selection of fallback fonts, you can consider removing the EOT format from the `src` stack altogether. Put them in the wastebasket along with SVG fonts. This drastically simplifies the `@font-face` syntax and gets rid of the ugly IE-specific hack.

Format	IE8	IE9	IE10	IE11	Chrome	Firefox	Safari	Safari (iOS)	Opera	Android WebKit
WOFF2	No	No	No	No	Yes	No	No	No	Yes	No
WOFF	No	Yes	Yes	Yes	Yes	Yes	Yes	Yes	Yes	Yes
TTF/OTF	No	Yes	Yes	Yes	Yes	Yes	Yes	Yes	Yes	Yes
EOT	Yes	Yes	Yes	Yes	No	No	No	No	No	No

Browser support for the the simplified `@font-face` syntax. Add the EOT font format if you want to support older Internet Explorer versions.

```
@font-face {
  font-family: My Font;
  src: url(myfont.woff2) format('woff2'),
       url(myfont.woff) format('woff'),
       url(myfont.otf) format('opentype');
}
```

Now we have coverage for Internet Explorer 9 and above and all modern browsers on both desktop and mobile. You can find up to date browser support tables for all web font formats at *The State Of Web Type*[5].

Font Loading

You're probably familiar with how the CSS font stack works: the browser tries to load the first font in the stack that matches a given family name, weight, style and variant. If that isn't available, it continues with the next fallback font until it finds one that is available.

There's one caveat here: a browser's font-matching algorithm will return fonts that match only on family name but not on weight, style, or variant. Consider this scenario: the browser has found a match for family name but not the required variation (bold, bold italic, etc.). Instead of rendering the text in a fallback font the browser will use the variation it already has and attempt to generate the required variation. This is the cause of so-called "faux bold", "faux italic" and "faux small caps", also officially known as *font synthesis*, described in great detail by Laura Franz in her article "*Setting Weights And Styles With The @font-face Declaration*"[6].

Type designers spend a lot of time making beautiful, specialized variations of their typefaces; auto-generated faux variations are less desirable than their designed counterparts. You can avoid this by always including web fonts for all the styles you use on your site. Let's say your site uses

---

5 http://stateofwebtype.com
6 http://www.smashingmagazine.com/2013/02/14/setting-weights-and-styles-at-font-face-declaration/

thin, thin italic, thin bold, regular, and bold styles for a web font. In order to avoid faux styles you must include separate @font-face rules for that particular font for each of those five styles.

Faux styles can occur for both web fonts and locally installed fonts. However, you're unlikely to see faux styles for locally installed fonts because most installed versions include bold and italic variations by default.

The font fallback mechanism is a bit more complicated than simple selection based on font family, weight, style and variant. Web browsers have to take into account that not every font includes all characters. They will need to find fonts that either fully or partially match the character support for a given piece of text.

```
<p>hello world!</p>
```

Let's say you're using two fonts which each only support a select number of characters. Font A supports the characters "h", "e", "l" and "o" and font B supports "w", "r", and "d". The CSS font stack contains both web fonts and the generic sans-serif fallback font.

```
p {
   font-family: A, B, sans-serif;
}
```

In this seemingly contrived example (which is actually quite common for content written in multiple languages) browsers will use

The browser uses three different fonts for a single paragraph because the fonts only contain a limited number of characters.

three different fonts — Font A, Font B and the generic sans serif — to render the "hello world!" string. Sans serif is used because neither Font A nor Font B include the "!" character.

Using web fonts does not significantly change the fallback mechanism. However, when a font family name is used in a font stack it is first matched against all `@font-face` rules in the document before the browser will look at local fonts; if a match is found within the document's `@font-face` rules, the browser will start downloading the web font. (Older Internet Explorer versions are an exception: they start downloading fonts for all `@font-face` rules regardless of whether they are used or not.) While fonts are downloading, browsers will not examine other families in the font stack because they need to know which characters are in the web font before they can fall back to other fonts.

This means that browsers will go through the following three steps for each font family name they try to match, before giving up and using a fallback font (which in turn goes through the same steps).

1. The font family matches a `@font-face` rule, but the font file is not in cache. The font is applied once it is downloaded.
2. The font family matches a `@font-face` rule and the font file is cached. The font is applied immediately.
3. The font family matches a locally installed font and is applied immediately.

There are several drawbacks to this mechanism. Browsers need to have enough information from both the CSSOM and the DOM before they can start downloading a web font. The benefit of this approach is that if a web font is not used by any CSS selector that matches an element in the DOM, browsers can

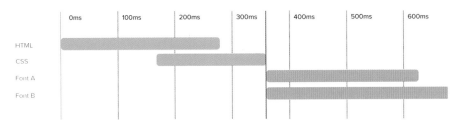

This waterfall shows that fonts only start downloading once both the DOM and CSSOM are available, because only at that point does the browser know it needs to load web fonts.

prevent unnecessary downloads. In practice this could very well mean that font downloading is blocked by both your HTML and CSS.

Another drawback is that browsers can only know which characters are included in a font after they have finished downloading it. If a font doesn't include the characters required to render the content it will have been downloaded for nothing!

This can be avoided by using the unicode-range property in your @font-face rules. The unicode-range property tells browsers which characters are part of the font so that they can decide whether or not to download the font. If the font supports some of the characters required to render text, browsers will download the font. The font is not downloaded if none of the required characters are listed in its Unicode range. In the upcoming section on subsetting we'll take a closer look at browser support for the unicode-range property and also demonstrate how to exploit it to optimize font downloads.

The final drawback is the amount of time it takes to download a web font compared with locally installed fonts. This is an important difference between locally installed fonts and web fonts. Browsers solve this problem in two different ways. Some browsers attempt to show the content to the user as soon as possible by applying a fallback font while web fonts are loading. This will result in users seeing the text in a fallback font for a (hopefully brief) moment of time before it is replaced by the web font. This is usually referred to as the *Flash of Unstyled Text* (FOUT).

	IE8	IE9	IE10	IE11	Chrome	Firefox	Safari	Safari (iOS)	Opera	Android WebKit
Font loading	FOUT	FOUT	FOUT	FOUT	FOIT	FOIT	FOIT	FOIT	FOIT	FOIT
Timeout	n/a	n/a	n/a	n/a	3 sec.	3 sec.	∞	∞	3 sec.	∞

Font loading behavior in browsers. Internet Explorer uses FOUT while others use FOIT with an optional timeout.

However, most browsers assume the FOUT is undesirable and hide any text that uses a web font while that font is loading. When it has finished loading, the text will be rendered using the web font. This is referred to as the *Flash of Invisible Text (FOIT)*. This is especially noticeable when a paragraph combines web fonts and locally installed fonts. The sections of the paragraph that use the locally installed font will render, but the sections that use the web font will be invisible.

The FOIT is usually accompanied by a timeout that renders the text in the fallback font if a certain amount of

A common sight with browsers that use the flash of invisible text: content that uses web fonts are hidden while the rest if the content is visible.

time has passed. In recent versions of Chrome, Opera and Firefox this timeout is set to three seconds. The three second timeouts are based on research by both Mozilla and Google which has shown that most fonts load within three

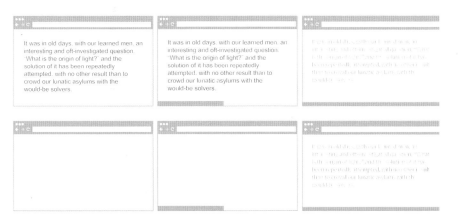

The Flash of Unstyled Text (top) shows the content immediately and swaps out the fallback font once the web font has loaded. The Flash of Invisible Text (bottom) hides the content while the web font is loading (possibly with a timeout).

seconds[7]. If the web font loads after these three seconds, the text will be re-rendered using the web font.

This means that users that have slow downloading fonts (for whatever reason) first get a FOIT, followed by the FOUT, and then finally the web font. Safari and older Android browsers have no timeout, so they will not render text while web fonts are still loading (for however long that takes).

No matter which approach you prefer, we need a better vocabulary to discuss, control and implement custom font loading behavior. It is confusing to talk about a combination of FOUT, FOIT, FOUT followed by FOIT and timeouts that may or may not happen. This is where the proposed `font-rendering` property[8] comes to our rescue. It introduces a vocabulary to talk about font loading behavior and proposes a new CSS property to customize this behavior.

CSS font-rendering Property

Browser vendors are currently trying to standardize and control font loading behavior with a new CSS property. The `font-rendering` property, if accepted as a standard and implemented by browser, will let you customize the font loading and rendering behavior.

The proposal describes three parameters that can be combined to implement any font loading approach. Font loading is said to be "blocking" if it blocks the page from rendering. If a font is replaced with another font, this is called a "swap". An example of swapping is when a fallback font is replaced by a web font. Finally, a web font can be said to be "optional": the font will be shown immediately if it is available; if not, the fallback font is shown indefinitely.

The `font-rendering` property accepts the same three parameters:

- `block`: block the rendering of the text while the font is loading, with an optional timeout;
- `swap`: use a fallback font and render the font if it becomes available, with an optional timeout;

---

7 https://www.igvita.com/2014/01/31/optimizing-web-font-rendering-performance/
8 https://github.com/KenjiBaheux/css-font-rendering

- `optional`: show the font if it is available (for example, if it is cached) and otherwise the fallback font. Do not re-render the page, even if the web font becomes available.

The proposed `font-rendering` property is intended to be used as part of a `@font-face` rule.

```
@font-face {
    font-family: My Font;
    src: url(myfont.woff);
    font-rendering: block;
}
```

It is also possible to customize the default behavior of both `block` and `swap` by specifying a timeout value in seconds. By combining `block`, `swap` and `optional`, you can create any desired custom font rendering scheme.

```
@font-face {
    font-family: My Font;
    src: url(myfont.woff);
    font-rendering: block 5s swap 3s;
}
```

This will block the rendering of the page for five seconds. If the web font loads within those five seconds, it's used immediately. If it fails to load within five seconds, the fallback font is used instead. There is also a three-second grace period where the web font can still load and be swapped in. If the font loads after the combined timeout of eight seconds (5s + 3s) it will not be swapped in and the fallback font will continue to be used. However, if the font loads after these eight seconds it will be stored in the browser cache and used on the next request.

The `font-rendering` property lets you simulate the FOUT with a value of `block 0s swap infinite`, and the FOIT with a three-second timeout with `block 3s swap infinite`.

```
/* FOUT using the font-rendering property */
@font-face {
  font-family: My Font;
  src: url(myfont.woff);
  font-rendering: block 0s swap infinite;
}

/* FOIT using the font-rendering property */
@font-face {
  font-family: My Other Font;
  src: url(myotherfont.woff);
  font-rendering: block 3s swap infinite;
}
```

Unfortunately, at the time of writing, the property has not yet been implemented by any browser (nor accepted as a standard, and is likely to undergo
significant changes). Once the font-rendering property (or something like it)
has been adopted, it will be a great way to control font loading and rendering
without using JS. Until then we need to rely on the CSS Font Loading API.

CSS Font Loading API

The CSS3 Font Loading Module[9] defines a new interface for managing the web
fonts in your document. The interface lets you load fonts on demand and gives
you JavaScript events for various load states. The module introduces a new
FontFace object to represent @font-face rules. It can be used to programatically
create new web fonts or modify existing ones, and serves as a complement to
the CSS font-rendering proposal.

You can create a new instance by calling the FontFace constructor with
three arguments: the first argument is the font family name; the second is
either a string or a typed array; and the third argument is an object describing
the web font.

```
var myfont = new FontFace('My Font', 'url(myfont.woff)');
```

---

9 http://www.w3.org/TR/css-font-loading/

The string format used for the second parameter is the same as the
@font-face src property so it to supports multiple font formats. Use the third
parameter to give the web font various properties such as weight, style and
which Unicode characters it supports.

```
var myfont = new FontFace(
  'My Font',
  'url(myfont.woff) format("woff"),' +
  'url(myfont.otf) format("otf")',
  { weight: 'bold', unicodeRange: 'U+0-7ff' }
);
```

This creates a new FontFace instance, but it does not load. To load the web
font, call the load method on the FontFace instance. This method returns a
promise[10] which will be fulfilled when the font has loaded, or rejected if it fails
to load.

```
myfont.load().then(function () {
  console.log('load success');
}).catch(function () {
  console.log('load failure');
});
```

This makes a network request to download the font from the server, or
retrieve it from cache, but it does not add it to the document. An element with
this web font in its font stack wouldn't trigger a font load either. The web font is
not available to CSS until you add it to a FontFaceSet.

Each document has its own FontFaceSet that contains FontFace objects for
all the @font-face rules in that document. You can use this set to add or remove
fonts from the document. The set also contains some methods to explicitly
load fonts or to check if fonts are in the set. The set for the current document is
available as the fonts property on the document context.

---

10 http://people.mozilla.org/~jorendorff/es6-draft.html#sec-promise-objects

```
> document.fonts
< FontFaceSet { size: 2, status: "loaded", … }
```

This set already contains two FontFace objects that are loaded. These could have been @font-face rules in the document's style sheets, or FontFace objects explicitly loaded by some other script.

We can make our font available by adding it to the set.

```
document.fonts.add(myfont);
```

This does not necessarily make the font available right away. The font is only swapped in if it is used in a CSS selector (that matches a DOM node), or if it is explicitly loaded using the set's load method. If the document contained a CSS selector that referenced this font — and the font was preloaded — it would replace the fallback font right away. If the font wasn't loaded, browsers would download the font first and then use it to replace the fallback font.

```
p {
    font-family: My Font, sans-serif;
}
```

It is also possible to explicitly make the font available without having a font stack trigger the loading by using the set's load method. This function will make the font available whether it is preloaded or not. A font being available means that even though the font might not be used in the page, it is ready to be swapped in. The load method takes a CSS font shorthand property value as input.

```
document.fonts.load('16px My Font');
```

This will load My Font and make it available. If there is an element in the page that uses "My Font" in its font stack, its fallback font will be replaced with "My Font" immediately. If there isn't, nothing will happen. Reusing the font shorthand property value offers a convenient method of loading several fonts that match the variation and font family names used in the shorthand.

```
document.fonts.load('bold 16px My Font, My Other Font');
```

This will load the bold variation of both "My Font" and "My Other Font" (if they match a @font-face rule). An unfortunate side effect of reusing the font shorthand property is that you are required to specify a font size. The font size is only used to make the shorthand font value syntax legal, but it isn't used for font matching.

Like the load method on FontFace, the set's load method also returns a promise which you can use to be notified when the fonts in the set are loaded (or fail to load).

```
document.fonts.load('16px My Font').then(function () {
  console.log('My Font has loaded and is applied.');
});
```

If you want to check the availability of a font without triggering a load you can do so using the check method.

```
document.fonts.check('16px My Font').then(function () {
  console.log('My Font is available');
});
```

The CSS Font Loading API is still under development but you can already use it in the latest versions of Chrome, Opera and Firefox (behind a flag). If you are targeting modern browsers you can use a polyfill I've written[11]. The polyfill supports Internet Explorer 9 and later, Firefox, Safari, Android, and iOS. Included with the polyfill is a small promise library, so it is possible to use the polyfill to implement all the examples from this chapter.

---

11 http://github.com/bramstein/fontloader

If you need support for older browsers you can achieve the same results using the Web Font Loader[12]. The Web Font Loader is a collaboration between Typekit and Google, and it gives you the ability to load custom fonts as well as fonts from several web font services. It also provides font load events so you can use custom styles or scripts when a font loads (or fails to load).

Basic Optimizations

Before moving on to advanced font loading methods, you should first check if you have the basics right. Often, the most performance can be gained by doing some simple optimizations, such as caching, compression and subsetting.

Another simple, and often overlooked, optimization to consider is to reduce the number of fonts you're attempting to load. For the best performance you should aim to load a maximum of three or four variations. Carefully evaluate your content and design before attempting to load more than that.

FALLBACK FONTS

One of the best ways to give the appearance of improved performance is to define proper fallback fonts for your web fonts. You should aim to find a font with a similar x-height (the height of the lowercase characters) and em-width (the width of characters) so as to reduce the visually jarring reflow that happens when a fallback font is replaced by a web font.

Nathan Ford wrote an excellent article on how to construct a good font stack[13]. He recommends giving font stacks for body text and headlines a different structure. For example, a font stack for body text consists of four types of font families.

```
font-family: Ideal, Fit, Common, Generic;
```

The "Ideal" font is the one you wish to use, while all the others are fallback fonts. "Fit" is something that is close in both style and metrics to your

---

12 http://github.com/typekit/webfontloader
13 "Better CSS Font Stacks" by Nathan Ford: http://artequalswork.com/posts/better-css-font-stacks/

"Ideal" font, and available on a significant portion of your visitors' devices and operating systems. "Common" is a font family that is common on most platforms and still (roughly) matches your design. Generic is one of the generic font family names: serif, sans-serif, monospace, etc. Font stacks for headlines are similar, but differ in the qualities that should be looked at when selecting a headline font (for example, in headlines, style should be favored over metrics).

Selecting fallback fonts is no easy task. Blindly copying and pasting "known" font stacks is never a good idea. Each platform and device has a different set of locally installed fonts. Some fonts are included with the operating system while others are installed by applications that every user may not have.

Good tools for finding out which font families are available on a given platform are *fontfamily.io* by Zach Leatherman[14] and *Tinytype* by Jordan Moore[15]. Combining these tools with the usage statistics of your website will let you simplify your fallback stack by using the fallback fonts that most of your visitors will have. This simplifies testing your font stack. Always test your site with web fonts disabled so you can test the fallback behavior and user experience (like any other progressive enhancement). Go through each fallback font in your stack and test them on the operating systems and devices that your target audience uses.

Another important issue to keep in mind is the difference in variations (weight, style, etc.) between locally installed fonts and web fonts. For instance, consider what would happen if you load a web font with a thin weight, but your fallback font only supports regular and bold weights. If your web fonts fail to load you might be in for quite a design surprise.

Theoretically, the best way to avoid the visual discontinuity between web fonts and fallback fonts is to use metric-compatible fonts. Metric-compatible fonts are fonts designed to have identical metrics to another font so they can be used as a substitute without affecting page layout.

---

14 http://fontfamily.io
15 http://www.jordanm.co.uk/tinytype

Each character in a metric-compatible font has the same width and height as the same character in another font (the font whose metrics it is compatible with). Several such fonts have been designed.

Perhaps the most famous example is Arial, which is metric-compatible with Helvetica. If your web font is Helvetica, an excellent fallback font (from the point of view of minimizing metrical changes) would be Arial. However, in practice, metric-compatible fonts are of limited use. There simply aren't enough of them available as either locally installed fonts or as web fonts to serve as good fallback fonts.

CACHING

The simplest way to improve caching is to set HTTP response headers with a long cache expiration time. This works really well until you need to update the resource (cache invalidation). A common way to solve this is to give each resource a unique filename based on a hash of its content. Each time the contents of the files change, the hash and thus the filename will also change. Once the HTML or CSS file that references the resource falls out of cache (which should have a shorter cache expiration time) the latest resource versions will be downloaded. This lets you set long expiration times on resources and have the ability to update them. To learn more about this approach to caching read the Google Web Fundamentals caching guide[16].

This approach also works really well for fonts, because they change infrequently. Setting an HTTP `Cache-Control` response header with a long `max-age` value for both the CSS and font files is an easy way to significantly improve the performance of your site. It is a good idea to cache both the CSS and font files for at least one week by setting the `Cache-Control` header with a `max-age` value of 604800 (60 seconds × 60 minutes × 24 hours × 7 days).

```
Cache-Control: public, max-age=604800
```

---

16 https://developers.google.com/web/fundamentals/performance/optimizing-content-efficiency/

A useful HTTP cache control extension is `stale-while-revalidate`[17]. If this property is set on a resource, browsers will use the cached version of a resource even though it has already expired (and should technically be retrieved from the server). They will then asynchronously make a request to the server to retrieve the latest version of the resource, and update the cache so the latest version of the resource is used on the next request. Like the `max-age` property, `stale-while-revalidate` takes a number of seconds that indicates the amount of time the response can still be used even though it has expired.

If you cache your resources for one week, a good `stale-while-revalidate` value would be two weeks or `1209600` seconds (60 seconds × 60 minutes × 24 hours × 14 days). This will keep your resources reasonably up to date and the longer grace period will make sure returning visitors do not block on downloading content they already have in cache.

```
Cache-Control: public, stale-while-revalidate=1209600, max-age=604800
```

This property can be used for all HTTP resources, but it is especially useful for font files, which — even though they might be stale — can still be used to render content, and thus not block your page. At the time of writing only beta versions of Chrome and Opera support this property. Older browsers will ignore the property, so it is safe to set the property on your resources.

COMPRESSION

There are two ways to compress fonts: compressing the data inside font files; and compressing fonts when they are sent from the web server to browsers. Most web servers can compress assets using gzip and all modern browsers will decompress them transparently. You should turn on this feature for font files as well, but it isn't necessary to do so for all font formats.

The WOFF2 and WOFF formats are already compressed so they don't gain anything by having the web server compress them again. The OpenType and TrueType formats do not have compression built in, so they should always be

---

17   http://tools.ietf.org/html/rfc5861

compressed by your web server. Even though the EOT format supports compression, many tools do not generate compressed EOT files, so they should be compressed by your web server.

You can gain even better compression rates by compressing your font files (and other assets) using Google's Zopfli compression algorithm[18]. Zopfli generates gzip-compatible output, so it can be used where gzip is supported. In fact, Zopfli can also be used as an algorithm for compressing the font data inside WOFF files using my own modification of Jonathan Kew's *sfnt2woff*[19], called *sfnt2woff-zopfli*[20].

Using this sfnt2woff-zopfli to compress your WOFF files will result in an average of two to six percent additional savings compared to the standard compression used by WOFF.

Inlining

A common trick for reducing load times is to inline fonts in a separate CSS file by using base64-encoded data URIs. This avoids the additional overhead of an extra HTTP request for each font variation. While this might seem like an attractive option, there are many reasons why inlining fonts is not a good idea. Guy Podjarny's Performance Calendar article, *"Why Inlining Everything Is NOT The Answer"*[21], is a great resource on the disadvantages of inlining resources.

The most obvious reason not to inline is that it limits you to a single font format. Inlining multiple formats in the same CSS file is a bad idea because browsers will downloaded the entire file whether or not they support the formats. You could work around this problem by using a different style sheet for each font format and switching between them based on the user agent string, but this is error-prone (user agent strings often lie). Inlining also doesn't work for formats that cannot be inlined; for example, Internet Explorer does not support inlining EOT files as data URIs.

---

18 https://code.google.com/p/zopfli/
19 http://people.mozilla.org/~jkew/woff/
20 https://github.com/bramstein/sfnt2woff-zopfli
21 http://calendar.perfplanet.com/2011/why-inlining-everything-is-not-the-answer/

Inlining also runs counter to browsers' ability to download multiple assets in parallel. It is more efficient to download multiple font files in parallel than as part of one big file. The base64 encoding also adds a 20–30% overhead to your font's file size, which further reduces the benefits of inlining (though this can be negated by applying gzip or Zopfli compression to your CSS files as described in the previous section). Last, but not least, check your font license before deciding to inline fonts: inlining is often explicitly prohibited.

As a general rule, you should not inline fonts in CSS files unless you have a very specific use case, such as supporting only a single web font format or browser, storing fonts in localStorage, or low-bandwidth and high-latency connections.

SUBSETTING

Most fonts support glyphs (characters) for several languages and scripts. The more glyphs included in a font, the larger its file size will be. Unlike locally installed fonts, web fonts need to be downloaded over (possibly) unreliable or slow network connections each time they are used. We have an interest in keeping the file size as small as possible, so the next optimization after selecting font formats is to subset the font, by removing characters and features you don't really need.

For example, if your site is written exclusively in English you don't need the glyphs for other languages and scripts in your web font. Removing them will reduce the file size of your web font significantly.

A good tool for creating static subsets is FontSquirrel's *Web Font Generator*[22]. Its expert mode lets you define any custom subset and it will automatically generate the correct subsets and font formats for you. Be careful when subsetting a font: names and places often contain characters you normally wouldn't use in English. Another thing to be mindful of is the license agreement that comes with the font. It often does not permit custom subsets. Contact the font foundry if your license doesn't permit subsetting or if you have any questions about subsets — they're often happy to help.

---

22 http://www.fontsquirrel.com/tools/webfont-generator

Subsetting works well for languages and scripts that have clearly defined boundaries. Nevertheless, subsets are not the answer to all large font files, because browsers treat subsets as two separate fonts. This means that OpenType layout features (such as ligatures and kerning) that span multiple glyphs stop working across subsets. For example, scripts like Arabic are difficult to subset because they contain a large number of characters that can be used in almost any order, and often include (required) ligatures and kerning information for many character combinations. Creating subsets for these scripts at the wrong point could result in failure to display a required ligature or incorrect kerning because the characters are in different subsets. Be careful when you subset your fonts. It is usually better to first load a minimal subset followed by a larger superset, than two or more complementary subsets.

You can help browsers choose which subset to download based on your page content by using the `unicode-range` property in your `@font-face` rules. This property tells browsers which characters are included in the font, so they can only download the fonts when they are needed (because the characters are used on the page). For example, if most of your content is written in English and a couple of your pages contain Cyrillic you can create two subsets.

```
@font-face {
  font-family: My Font;
  src: url(myfont-english.woff);
  unicode-range: U+20-7E;
}
```

IE8	IE9	IE10	IE11	Chrome	Firefox	Safari	Safari (iOS)	Opera	Android WebKit
No	Partial	Partial	Partial	Yes	No	Partial	Partial	Yes	Partial

Browser support for the `unicode-range` property. Full support indicates browsers use Unicode ranges to selectively download and display fonts. Partial support indicates browsers that only display the characters listed in the range, but do not use the information to optimize font downloads.

```
@font-face {
    font-family: My Font;
    src: url(myfont-cyrillic.woff);
    unicode-range: U+0400–U+04FF;
}
```

The browser will look at which characters are used on the page and if a match is found within one of the @font-face rule's Unicode ranges, the font is downloaded. If a page only used characters within the Unicode range for the English subset, it will only download the English font file and not the font containing all Cyrillic characters. Likewise, if a page only contains Cyrillic, the English subset will not be downloaded. Both subsets will be downloaded if the content is mixed English and Cyrillic.

Unfortunately, this useful property is only supported in a handful of browsers. While most WebKit-based browsers support the syntax, only Chrome and Opera download fonts selectively based on the unicode-range property. At the time of writing, Firefox and Internet Explorer do not support the unicode-range property (though Firefox has an implementation in progress and the Internet Explorer team has shown signs of interest as well).

The fallback behavior when this property is not supported is not ideal, but workable: browsers will download all font files that match the font family required to render the content (even though some of them may not be used).

If the content on your site is mostly or entirely static it is possible to create a perfect subset for your content. This requires finding all characters in your content and using them to create a subset. This works great for sites that are rarely (if ever) updated, but is problematic for dynamic sites because a new subset needs to be created each time the content introduces characters that are not in the existing subset. You'll need to find a trade-off between character support, file size and cacheability.

Besides static subsetting, there are two additional subsetting approaches: dynamic subsetting, and dynamic augmentation. Both work by examining the content on a page and creating the perfect subset for it. The difference between these two methods lies in how they handle updates to existing subsets.

The idea behind dynamic subsetting is to create new subsets for any content not covered by existing subsets. For instance, let's say you run a blog network. There is no way to anticipate what kind of web font character set support you need — people might write and publish content in all sorts of languages. Using dynamic subsetting you can load subsets based on the content of a page instead of deciding on the subset beforehand (i.e. statically). Subsets can also be created for content that is dynamically inserted into the page (a news widget, etc.). This has been described in great detail by Nathan Ford in his article, *Adventures in Dynamic Subsetting*[23].

Dynamic augmentation is very similar to dynamic subsetting. It also dynamically creates subsets based on the content, but instead of creating new subsets, it will update the existing subset so that it covers the characters required by the new content. Dynamic augmentation does this by adding the new characters to the existing subset (thus creating a new subset). So instead of having multiple subsets on a page as with dynamic subsetting, dynamic augmentation will always only have a single subset that is updated as required.

While the end result for both methods is the same (one or more subsets that cover all the content on a page) there is an important distinction. Recall that browsers treat subsets as separate font files, and that OpenType features will not work across multiple subsets. While this is a minor inconvenience for Latin-based languages, it is a major problem for complex scripts (such as Arabic) where OpenType features are required to display text properly. This is where dynamic augmentation shines. Instead of creating complementary subsets, it will update an existing subset with new characters and OpenType features. The result is that OpenType features work correctly because the subset is a single font file.

23 http://artequalswork.com/posts/adventures-in-dynamic-subsetting/

Dynamic augmentation is also a necessity for scripts that are too large to be served as a single subset. Typically, you should try to keep your individual font files below 100KB — but the average Asian font is several megabytes. Dynamic augmentation would, for example, let you load the characters for your primary content in a single and small request so it can be displayed quickly. You can then asynchronously update the subset to include character support for all your content. Because these fonts are dynamically constructed client-side using JavaScript, it is difficult to cache them. This is where technologies like Service Workers[24] could be helpful by enabling a background process to explicitly cache a dynamically augmented font.

Google has released the source code for their font utility *sfntly*[25] which can be used as a base for dynamic subsetting. There are currently no open source subsetting engines that can perform dynamic augmentation. This means that — for now — you'll need to rely on font service providers to do this for you. Currently only Google Fonts, Typekit and Fonts.com offer dynamic subsetting.

Font Loading Strategies

You've squeezed the most out of your font formats, set the correct caching headers, and generated the smallest possible subsets. Now it's time to load fonts efficiently by applying a font loading strategy suitable to your performance and design requirements.

APPLYING FONTS SELECTIVELY

A simple approach to improving web font performance is to only use web fonts selectively. Remember that a web font is loaded on demand; it isn't loaded if there is no CSS selector (using that web font) that matches an element in the DOM. This makes media queries a great tool for responsive typography.

---

24 http://www.w3.org/TR/service-workers/
25 https://code.google.com/p/sfntly/

A good example is the web site for A List Apart, which uses media queries to apply a condensed version of their typeface (Georgia Pro) on smaller viewports[26].

Implementing the same behavior is straightforward. Start by setting the default web font and use media queries to apply a different font stack when the viewport matches your desired dimensions. If the media query doesn't match, the condensed font won't be downloaded and the regular font will be used.

```
@font-face {
  font-family: My Font;
  src: url(myfont.woff);
}

@font-face {
  font-family: My Font Condensed;
  src: url(myfont-condensed.woff);
}

body {
  font-family: My Font, Arial, sans-serif;
}
@media (max-width: 400px) {
  body {
    font-family: My Font Condensed, Arial, sans-serif;
  }
}
```

Media queries let you selectively use custom font stacks. They should not, however, be used to enable or disable web fonts based on device pixel ratios or viewport dimensions. With ever increasing resolutions on modern handheld devices, your media queries might get executed even on devices that are often on unreliable and slow cellular connections. Likewise, mobile devices with small viewports may be on high-speed connections (such as Wi-Fi). Screen sizes or device pixel ratios don't say much about whether or not the device's internet connection is fast (the deciding factor for loading fonts or not). Use media queries as a way to load fonts based on your design and not simply to reduce page load.

---

26 http://alistapart.com/blog/post/a-list-apart-5-01

Another example of this is Type Rendering Mix[27], which adds classes based on your browser's text rendering engine and the antialiasing method.

```
<html class="tr-coretext tr-aa-subpixel">
```

Using these classes you could switch to a different font weight based on the text rendering engine your visitors are using. For example, Mac OS X's Core Text renders text slightly heavier than Microsoft's DirectWrite text rendering engine. You could solve this discrepancy by applying a lighter weight of your font in case your visitor is using Mac OS X with subpixel antialiasing.

```
html {
    font-family: My Font, Arial, sans-serif;
    font-weight: 400;
}

html.tr-coretext {
    font-weight: 300;
}
```

These are just two examples of this useful technique. Using JavaScript and classes you could enable, disable or change your fonts based on any condition.

SIMULATING SWAPPING AND BLOCKING BEHAVIOR

If you prefer the swapping behavior (as used in Internet Explorer), it is possible to simulate it in browsers that do not have native support. We do this by creating a helper function that returns a promise and resolves after a given amount of time.

```
function timeout(ms) {
    return new Promise(function (resolve, reject) {
        setTimeout(reject, ms);
    });
}
```

---

27 http://typerendering.com

We can use this promise to race against the font loading promises. If the font loading promise resolves before the timeout, we know the fonts have loaded. If instead the timeout fires, the promise will be rejected and we can display the fallback font. First, we add a class to the `<html>` element to indicate fonts have started loading. Later we can use this to style against.

```
var html = document.documentElement;
html.classList.add('fonts-loading');
```

Next, we create an instance of `FontFace` for each font we want to load and add them to the document's `FontFaceSet`.

```
var myfont = new FontFace('My Font', 'url(myfont.woff)');
document.fonts.add(myfont);
```

We then start the race between the font loading and the timeout. If the promise is resolved, the `fonts-loading` class is replaced by the `fonts-active` class; and if the promise is rejected (because of the timeout), it is replaced by the `fonts-inactive` class.

```
Promise.race([
  document.fonts.load('16px My Font'),
  timeout(3000)
]).then(function () {
  html.classList.remove('fonts-loading');
  html.classList.add('fonts-active');
}, function () {
  html.classList.remove('fonts-loading');
  html.classList.add('fonts-inactive');
});
```

We can use these three classes to style the page and to simulate swapping and blocking behavior. The first step is to always apply the fallback font to the page. This will ensure that the browser won't wait for web fonts to load and will display the text as soon as possible.

```
html {
    font-family: Arial, sans-serif;
}
```

Once the fonts load, the fonts-active class will be added to the <html> element. We can use this to apply the web font.

```
html.fonts-active {
    font-family: My Font, Arial, sans-serif;
}
```

Because the browser has already loaded the font it will not trigger the browser's default font loading behavior and so applies the font immediately. If the font fails to load for some reason, nothing happens because the fallback font will remain active. We can use the same three classes to simulate blocking behavior in all browsers. Again, we use the fallback font for all content, but instead of showing the text immediately we hide the content while the fonts-loading class is on the <html> element. The reason we hide the text on the fonts-loading class and not the html selector itself is to prevent the page from being invisible on clients that do not support JavaScript.

```
html {
    font-family: Arial, sans-serif;
}

html.fonts-loading {
    visibility: hidden;
}
```

Like before, if the fonts load, the fonts-active class will be added to the <html> element. We use this to add the font to the font stack and make the content visible.

```
html.fonts-active {
  font-family: My Font, Arial, sans-serif;
  visibility: visible;
}
```

If the timeout triggers, the content will still be invisible. To fix that, we use the `fonts-inactive` class to reset the visibility.

```
html.fonts-inactive {
  visibility: visible;
}
```

With both methods it is possible for the fonts to load after the timeout has triggered. This won't actually affect your page in either case because the web font will never be applied to your page unless the `fonts-active` class is set. Remember, a timeout is important to reduce the reflow that happens after a user is already engaged in reading the content on the page.

Asynchronous Loading and Caching

If your primary goal is to have your website's content visible as soon as possible — regardless of whether it is using web fonts or a fallback font — you might consider asynchronously loading fonts and explicitly managing the cache. This technique was used by the Guardian newspaper to optimize its front-end performance. The approach, as described in Smashing Magazine's performance case study[28], is to explicitly cache fonts in `localStorage` after they have been retrieved for the first time. On the first request the fonts are loaded through an AJAX request. Once the fonts have finished downloading they are stored in `localStorage` and also inserted into the DOM. On the next request the fonts can be retrieved from `localStorage` and inserted into the DOM right away instead of making another network request.

---

28 www.smashingmagazine.com/2014/09/08/improving-smashing-magazine-performance-case-study/

This approach to asynchronous loading and explicit caching is fairly easy to implement. To start, we'll create a reusable method to insert the content of a style sheet in the document. We'll use this method to insert the style sheet after it has been retrieved from the server or from localStorage.

```
function insertStylesheet(css) {
  var style = document.createElement(style);
  style.textContent = css;
  document.head.appendChild(style);
}
```

The following logic is executed on every page request and checks if the style sheet containing the fonts is present in localStorage. This check should preferably be included in the <head> section of the page in order to prevent the browser from applying its default font loading behavior.

If the style sheet with the fonts is stored in localStorage it is directly inserted into the page using the insertStylesheet method. If there is no entry for the fonts in localStorage it will make an AJAX request for it. The result of that request will be stored in localStorage and then also displayed.

```
if (localStorage.fontStylesheet) {
  insertStylesheet(localStorage.fontStylesheet);
} else {
  var request = new XMLHttpRequest();
  request.open('GET', 'myfonts.css');
  request.onload = function () {
    if (request.status === 200) {
      var stylesheet = request.responseText;
      localStorage.fontStylesheet = stylesheet;
      insertStylesheet(stylesheet);
    }
  };
  request.send();
}
```

A variation of this technique does not render the fonts after retrieving them; instead, the first request always uses the fallback fonts and first-time visitors do not experience swapping behavior. Subsequent requests will then find the font in localStorage and render the fonts immediately. In essence this is the "optional" behavior as described in the CSS font-rendering proposal. You can do this by removing the insertStylesheet call after storing the font in localStorage.

The most commonly cited reason for using this technique is to optimize both the initial load from a clean cache (by loading the fonts asynchronously), and the load time for frequent visitors. While this may seem like a good approach on paper, it doesn't buy you much in practice. The main benefit of this approach is that it takes fonts off the critical path by loading them asynchronously. However, this benefit isn't unique to this method, and many other font loading techniques are asynchronous.

A problem with this approach is that it requires fonts to be inlined in the style sheet to be efficient. While this avoids multiple requests, it also comes with all the downsides of inlining fonts that were discussed in the "Inlining Fonts" section above. Tests have also shown that localStorage is slightly slower than reading from the browser's cache, though this overhead is insignificant compared to parsing a font and re-rendering the page.

The caching benefits of storing fonts in localStorage for frequent visitors are also uncertain. Visitors who could benefit from this approach are your most frequent visitors. They are also the most likely to have many of the assets of your website already present in their browser cache. Treating fonts differently from other resources takes up extra storage in the browser (or device), most likely violates your font licence, and forces you to recreate caching behavior that is already well implemented and understood: the browser cache.

A much better approach is to load fonts asynchronously, and as soon as possible using the browser's cache. This is easily achieved using the native Font Load API (or the polyfill)[29]. The following code creates a new FontFace instance, and then preloads it. During loading, the font is not available to the document so the fallback font will be shown immediately. If the font loads successfully we

---

29 http://github.com/bramstein/fontloader

add it to the document by calling `document.fonts.add`. This will make it available to the page and trigger a rerender of the fallback font to the desired web font.

```
var myfont = new FontFace('My Font', 'url(myfont.woff)');

myfont.load().then(function () {
  document.fonts.add(myfont);
});
```

The nice thing about this approach is that it transparently reuses the browser's cache. On the first load the fallback font will be used until the font is retrieved from the network and stored in the browser's cache. On subsequent requests the font is already cached, after which the `load()` method returns immediately. This in turn causes the font to be added to the page immediately.

The downside of this approach is that the fonts are always swapped in when they load. This is desirable early in the page load cycle, but becomes distracting for your users once the fallback font has been shown for a while. A better approach would be to show the font if it loads within a certain period of time and continue to show the fallback font if it fails to load during that time. On subsequent requests, the font will be cached and thus shown immediately. We can do this by reusing the timeout function we created earlier.

```
function timeout(ms) {
  return new Promise(function (resolve, reject) {
    setTimeout(reject, ms);
  });
}
```

As before, we create a new `FontFace` instance for our font. Instead of calling `then` directly, we use the `Promise.race` method together with the `timeout` function. In this case we race the font load promise against the timeout promise with a value of three seconds.

```
var myfont = new FontFace('My Font', 'url(myfont.woff)');

Promise.race([
  myfont.load(),
  timeout(3000)
]).then(function () {
  document.fonts.add(myfont);
});
```

The race promise could settled by either the font loading or by the timeout being triggered. The promise will only be resolved if the font has loaded within the timeout. In this case we add the font to the document and make it available for the page. If the promise is rejected, nothing happens and the fallback font will continue to be used. On subsequent page loads the browser will go through the same process again, but this time the font is already cached and can be loaded and rendered quickly.

It is also possible to combine this approach with your preferred font rendering approach. By default, this method uses a fallback font until the web font is swapped in, but by adding loading, active and inactive classes you can simulate any font loading approach.

```
var html = document.documentElement;
html.classList.add('fonts-loading');
var myfont = new FontFace('My Font', 'url(myfont.woff)');
myfont.load().then(function () {
  document.fonts.add(myfont);
  html.classList.remove('fonts-loading');
  html.classList.add('fonts-active');
}).catch(function () {
  html.classList.remove('fonts-loading');
  html.classList.add('fonts-inactive');
});
```

If you prefer blocking behavior, you can hide content while fonts are loading, and show it again if your fonts are loaded (or fail to load, an equally important case to cover).

```
html {
  font-family: My Font, Arial, sans-serif;
}

html.fonts-loading, html.fonts-inactive {
  visibility: hidden;
}

html.fonts-active {
  visibility: visible;
}
```

This approach is very flexible. It lets you simulate any loading strategy with very little code *and* takes advantage of the browser's cache for the best performance. This approach isn't limited to a single font either, as the next section on prioritized loading will show you.

PRIORITIZED LOADING

For sites that need to load a lot of fonts, there's another strategy that works really well. The basic idea is to divide the fonts into several groups with different priorities. The first group should contain fonts that are used more often on the site and are necessary to render the most important content. The next font groups contain fonts of decreasing importance.

We can do this by waiting for the first group to load and only then start loading the second group, and so forth. If we have four fonts to load, but only the first and second are the primary ones, we could load them in two groups (1 and 2, and 3 and 4).

```
var font1 = new FontFace('Font1', 'url(font1.woff)'),
    font2 = new FontFace('Font2', 'url(font2.woff)'),
    font3 = new FontFace('Font3', 'url(font3.woff)'),
    font4 = new FontFace('Font4', 'url(font4.woff)');
```

Like before, we use the promise `all` method to create a group consisting of multiple fonts. When all fonts in that group have loaded we add them to the document and start loading the second group.

```
Promise.all([
  font1.load(),
  font2.load()
]).then(function () {
  document.fonts.add(font1);
  document.fonts.add(font2);

  Promise.all([
    font3.load(),
    font4.load()
  ]).then(function () {
    document.fonts.add(font3);
    document.fonts.add(font4);
  });
});
```

The benefit of this approach is that it forces the browser to prioritize the first group (because it doesn't yet know about the second group). This prevents cases where, for example, fonts from the second group load before the fonts in the first group. With a larger number of fonts it also prevents blocking the browser's download queue which has a limited number of connections per host. The failure mode of this approach is straightforward owing to the default behavior of the promise all method. If one or multiple fonts in a group fail to load, the promise will be rejected and none of the subsequent groups will be loaded. This avoids cases where a partial group or lower-priority group is loaded before the group with the highest priority.

Prioritizing can also be used to reduce the distracting reflow caused by swapping. By loading only the regular style of a font in the first group, the browser will generate faux bold and italic variations while downloading the second group containing the real bold and italic variations. Because the browser is using the regular variation to generate the faux ones, the reflow caused by loading the true variations will be much less distracting than waiting for all variations (including regular) to load all at once. This technique has been described in Zach Leatherman's article, "Flash of Faux Text—still more on Font Loading"[30].

---

30 http://www.zachleat.com/web/foft/

This is surprisingly easy to implement using the Font Load API. First, load the regular style and add it to the document. Once it has been added, trigger downloading the other variation(s) of the same font (in this case, bold). Since we added the regular style to the document before loading the bold variation, the browser will swap in the font and generate a faux bold style until the real bold has loaded.

```
var myfontRegular = new FontFace('My Font',
                     'url(myfont-regular.woff)', { weight: 400 }),
    myFontBold = new FontFace('My Font', 'url(myfont-bold.woff)', {
    weight: 700
});

myFontRegular.load().then(function () {
  document.fonts.add(myFontRegular);

  myFontBold.load().then(function () {
    document.fonts.add(myFontBold);
  });
});
```

Another example of prioritizing is to load complementary subsets or supersets of a single font. A subset without any special characters and no OpenType features loads much faster than a superset of the same font with all characters and OpenType features. You can exploit this by loading the minimal subset first and using it to show your content as soon as possible. You can then asynchronously load the superset and insert it into the page with the same name. Reflow will still happen, depending on which OpenType features are included in the superset, but this should be minimal considering it is a superset of the same font.

```
var myfont = new FontFace('My Font', 'url(myfont.woff)');
myfont.load().then(function () {
  document.fonts.add(myfont);

  var fontAllChars = new FontFace('My Font',
  'url(myfont-all-chars.woff)');
  fontAllChars.load().then(function () {
    document.fonts.add(fontAllChars);
  });
});
```

It is possible to vary loading and rendering strategies per group as well. For example, with carefully chosen timeout values and assuming a small primary group, you could consider adopting blocking behavior for the primary group, while subsequent groups use fallback fonts until the web fonts are swapped in.

Closing Thoughts

Serving web fonts quickly and reliably is no easy task. It requires knowledge of font formats, the fallback mechanism, networking, caching, and how browsers load fonts. Performance also depends on a lot of (external) factors: your visitor's browser and bandwidth, how many fonts your design requires, which languages you need to support, and so on.

However, it is possible to improve performance with minimal effort by applying some simple optimizations such as caching, compression and subsetting. Combining those with the new CSS Font Loading API and the advanced techniques in this chapter you'll be able to optimize and customize font loading in all browsers.

It's hard to single out a preferred optimization, but if there is one thing you should take away from this chapter it is the following: treat web fonts as a progressive enhancement and don't place them on the critical path of your web page. They are, after all, optional.

ABOUT THE AUTHOR

Bram is a web developer working on web font serving at *Adobe Typekit*. He cares a lot about typography and design on the web, and is happiest working at the intersection between design and technology. In his spare time he runs the *State of Web Type* and maintains a collection of JavaScript libraries for improving web typography. Bram regularly tweets about web typography at *@bram_stein*.

ABOUT THE REVIEWER

Zach is a front-end engineer / web developer with Filament Group. He has given talks at Smashing Conference, CSSConf, and The White House. He also herds NebraskaJS (a JavaScript meetup) and its eponymously named NebraskaJS Conference. He previously held the title of User Interface Architect for Union Pacific Railroad.

RESPONSIVE
IMAGES

YOAV WEISS

CHAPTER SEVEN · BY YOAV WEISS

RESPONSIVE IMAGES

ALMOST FROM ITS VERY BEGINNING, responsive web design has had one thorny issue that has proved extremely difficult to get right: responsive images. In this chapter we will discuss the different responsive images use cases and what native solutions we may need to create performant responsive websites. We will also look at ways to make these solutions easier to deploy and maintain. But first, let's take a walk down memory lane, and see how we got here.

How it All Began

Our story starts in ancient times, when WURFLs roamed the wilderness and mobile-only websites were a thing. Back in these pre-2007 days, a developer who wanted to provide mobile users with access to their website created a simpler, dumbed-down version of the real website and served that based on UA detection. That method was never truly reliable, but it was necessary to serve tailored content to mobile devices.

But the mobile landscape was revolutionized by Apple's iPhone. The proliferation of devices that followed, with a myriad of form factors and functionality, called out for a better way to target mobile (and not so mobile) users. Responsive web design combined new browser capabilities and CSS techniques to create websites that adapted to the device displaying them, and maintained their good looks everywhere. Developers could stop worrying about unreliable device detection and think of their websites in terms of viewport dimensions.

RWD is based on three pillars: media queries, fluid grids and flexible images. But even in RWD's early days it was obvious[1] that the flexible images part was not holding to its promise.

Even though RWD sites *looked* different on each device, underneath, they continued to download the same resources everywhere. And since images comprised the major part of the bytes that websites were downloading, and where lots of savings could be made between different devices, that meant a lot of wasted bytes for low-end devices and narrow viewports, and eventually, bloated mobile websites.

And so, the issue of responsive images was born.

The realization that something had to be done about those pesky responsive images started creeping up across the developer and web performance community. From the four corners of the world, developers gathered and started discussing possible solutions. Hacking around the problem seemed like the obvious answer but, as we soon discovered, it was a poor one[2]. All hacks had issues either with double downloads, delays, or trouble serving the first site load, creating their own share of performance issues while trying to solve a performance problem.

Slowly but surely, more and more developers reached the conclusion that a native solution was required to resolve this problem, and that it could not come soon enough.

Some of us formed the *Responsive Images Community Group* (RICG), which took on the uphill battle of defining the various use cases of the responsive images problem; convincing browser vendors that it's a problem worth solving; specifying, along with browser vendors, the solutions to these use cases; and pushing the implementation in browsers, with the help of the community[3].

---

1 http://blog.cloudfour.com/css-media-query-for-mobile-is-fools-gold/
2 http://blog.yoav.ws/responsive_images_hacks_wont_cut_it/
3 https://www.indiegogo.com/projects/picture-element-implementation-in-blink

What Is The Responsive Images Problem?

In short, it's the problem of efficiently loading appropriately sized content images that fit the page's design. The emphasis here should be on "efficiently". More than anything else, the responsive images problem is a performance issue. We want to load high-density images on high-resolution devices, and load images with larger dimensions on devices with wide viewports that need them; but just as importantly, we want to avoid the download of these images on devices that do not need them. We also want to do all that without introducing delays to the image download process, so as to not introduce regressions at page-load time.

The source of the problem is that to make a decision regarding the ideal resource to load, browsers need to take into consideration the screen's device pixel ratio (DPR), the viewport dimensions, the image's dimensions, and the final display dimensions of the image — and they need all this info pretty early in the page's load.

While browsers can easily know the DPR and viewport dimensions at this stage, the image's dimensions are only available to it *after* it downloaded the image. Its display dimensions are available only after all the relevant CSS is downloaded, parsed and the page is laid out. The image's display dimensions can also be affected by the image's physical dimensions, and by the dimensions of images around it in the page.

All these factors mean that a native solution to the responsive images problem has to provide browsers with the missing info as part of the markup.

Of course, in some cases you can use an SVG resource instead of a raster image and have it scale infinitely as far as needed. That option is thoroughly covered in Sara Soueidan's chapter. Be sure to check it out.

However, SVG only makes sense for some images (e.g. computer-generated ones), and even then raster images may eventually be smaller than their equivalent vector-based images. In other cases, it may make sense to use a technique dubbed *compressive images*[4], where a single high-definition but heavily compressed image is sent to all devices.

---

4   http://www.filamentgroup.com/lab/compressive-images.html

This image is then scaled down when viewed on normal-definition devices, where the compression artifacts tend to disappear in the process. When viewed on high-definition device screens, the device pixels are relatively small, so the compression artifacts are not highly visible. The downsides of that approach are that it only works for images displayed as fixed-width regardless of the responsive breakpoint, and it has a negative memory impact on non-Retina devices.

WHAT IS A PIXEL ANYWAY?

This may sound like a philosophical question, but there are multiple types of pixels that we need to be aware of to fully understand responsive images. A *pixel* (funnily enough, short for "picture element") was originally defined as a single dot that a screen can display in a certain color, and it was originally dictated by the screen's physical characteristics.

A *CSS pixel*, on the other hand, is defined in the CSS spec as an equivalent to the way a pixel of a device with 96dpi is seen from an arm's length[5]. That's a rather complex way of saying that CSS pixels may vary in size according to the intended viewing distance, but should not vary according to the device's screen characteristics. Therefore, when high-resolution (or "Retina screens") were introduced, they brought with them the concept of device pixel ratio (DPR), which was defined as the ratio between a CSS pixel and a device pixel.

On non-Retina screens, CSS pixels are probably the same dimensions as the *physical device pixels* (which means we have a DPR of 1). On higher-resolution screens, CSS pixels are larger than device pixels, which results in higher DPR values. Typical DPR values for today's devices can range from 1 for low-end devices and up to 3 and even more for higher-end devices.

It is important to understand that when we're discussing pixels in browsers, we are almost always referring to CSS pixels and not device pixels.

Now, since we defined DPR as the ratio between CSS pixels and device pixels, it is influenced by desktop browsers' zoom (which changes layout and so increases the size of CSS pixels). That is the reason it is not rare on a desktop to see all kinds of fractional DPR values. On mobile, where the dominant zoom

---

5   http://dev.w3.org/csswg/css-values/#reference-pixel

method is pinch zoom (which doesn't have an impact on layout, but acts as a magnifying glass), DPR is not affected by zoom, and is determined by the device's characteristics.

Another definition we need to get familiar with is of the image's intrinsic size. Every raster image has its native dimensions which are defined by the number of pixels it has in its rows (width) and columns (height). It's important to note that these physical image pixels are displayed in the same dimensions as CSS pixels, unless we tell browsers otherwise.

The Different Use Cases

Pretty early on, the community recognized that when people talk about responsive images, they often refer to different things. In an effort to have a productive conversation, the community defined the major use cases for responsive images, and even had them stamped as an official paper[6].

In the following sections we will get an overview of the different use cases, and see what's the best way to tackle each one of them.

FIXED-WIDTH IMAGES

The *fixed width use case* had a pivotal role in making the need for responsive images apparent. With the release of the iPhone 4 and its Retina screen, developers became painfully aware that different devices need to be served with different image resources.

Imagine that the website you're building has images that are always of the same dimensions regardless of viewport size — it could be a large, prominent photo in a magazine's article, or mid-sized thumbnails in an image gallery, or small profile pictures in a dashboard. "Responsive" behavior of images in this case basically means that you want them to look good on high-end devices with a higher DPR but you don't want to send Retina images to devices that don't need them .

For example, let's say you want to write an article with a layout that looks something like the following outline:

---

6   http://usecases.responsiveimages.org

An article with a fixed-width image in a wide viewport.

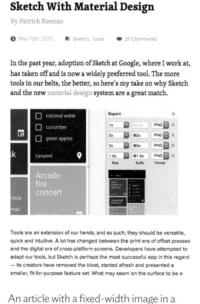

An article with a fixed-width image in a narrow viewport.

That's a fairly simple layout and if we ignore DPR, it can be achieved with a simple `<img>` element and the `src` attribute. But we're not here to ignore DPR, are we?

One thing worth noting is that the various responsive images syntax constructs that we'll discuss below can all be seen as extensions to the good old `<img src>`, and can be seen as progressive enhancement, where legacy browsers just download the `src` resource, and supporting browsers download the responsive, better adapted resource. Since the image in our example is of a fixed width of 500 CSS pixels, the syntax we would use to achieve that would be:

```
<img src="sketch_500px.jpg"
     srcset="sketch_750px.jpg 1.5x, sketch_1000px.jpg 2x,
     sketch_1500px.jpg 3x"
     width="500" alt="Sketch With Material Design">
```

Short and sweet, right? No need for too many explanations there. This is just like the good-old `<img>` element, with the addition of the `srcset` attribute. Inside `srcset`, all we do is give browsers a comma-separated list of resources and their x descriptors (describing the image's pixel density), and the browsers pick the best fit, by matching these values with the screen's DPR.

How do browsers choose the best resource? That, intentionally, is up to the browsers. It enables browsers to apply optimizations regarding which resource to pick if there's no resource that perfectly fits the DPR, as well as future optimizations that relate to the user's preferences, bandwidth considerations, etc.

Currently in Blink, the rendering engine behind Chrome and Opera, browsers pick the resource that is closest to the current screen DPR. In order to do so, browser sorts all the image candidate resources according to their density (which the web developer defines using the x descriptors, as we've seen above). Then it calculates the geometric mean of the densities of each neighboring sorted candidate pair. If the DPR is smaller than the geometric mean, the smaller neighbor gets picked. Otherwise, if the DPR is smaller or equal to the larger candidate's density, the larger one gets downloaded.

The important thing to note here is that you should not rely on these calculations. They may vary between browsers and between browser versions. You just need to provide browsers with a set of resources in varying quality levels, and let them do their thing.

Note that the 1x image resource is defined in the `src` attribute, where it doubles as a fallback resource. There's no need to write the same resource twice!

That part of the syntax, usually referred to as the `srcset x` descriptor, was one of the earliest proposals for a standard to tackle part of the responsive images problem. At the moment of this writing, it is implemented and shipped in Safari, as well as Chrome and Opera.

Since this part is fairly simple and has been around for a while, it has become what many people talk about when they say `srcset`. However, as we'll soon see, it is not the most useful part of the `srcset` syntax when it comes to RWD, since it mainly tackles fixed-width images.

VARIABLE-WIDTH IMAGES

Assuming your site is a responsive website with images whose dimensions vary based on the viewport dimensions, the above technique is not enough. It's better than nothing, sure, but a 1,920px wide screen and a 360px screen with the same density will get the same image, which means you'll be making significant UX compromises, either on blurriness or on load speed.

What you really want is to define the image resources in a way that allows browsers to pick the right one for the current DPR *and* viewport size. But how can we do that?

Ideally, we'd want to define the set of available image resources along with their physical dimensions (i.e. their width in pixels), and have browsers download one based on the image's display dimensions.

But there's a problem: browsers don't know what the image's display dimensions will be when they need to choose which resource to download. The image's display dimensions depend on the final page's layout, which often relies on external CSS and can be influenced by the image's dimensions, as well as the dimensions of other images on the page. That's some circularity madness right there!

So, if we want the browser to download the right resource, we need to provide it with a hint regarding the final display dimensions — there's just no way around that. Depending on our design, the image's dimensions can vary at the various layouts. So, yeah, we have a complex problem on our hands here. Let's see if we can break it down to smaller pieces.

We can start out by adding a header image to our article from earlier on. Something that would look like the following (see the image on the next page).

The syntax to define that header image would be:

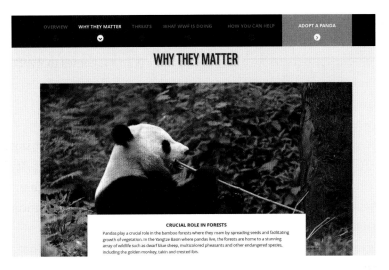

An article featuring a panda header image over a wide viewport.

An article featuring a panda header image over a narrow viewport.

```
<img src="panda_fallback.jpg"
    srcset="panda_360.jpg
        360w, panda_540.jpg 540w,
        panda_720.jpg 720w,
        panda_1080.jpg 1080w,
        panda_2160.jpg 2160w,
        panda_3240.jpg 3240w"
    alt="A panda eating bamboo.">
```

Note: Of course, the image resource file names can be just about anything. They include the resource's width in px here only for illustrative purposes.

As you can tell, the srcset attribute here functions very much like the srcset attribute we've seen in the previous example, only that instead of having x descriptors that describe the image resource's density, they have w descriptors that describe the image resource's "physical" width in pixels. Now, you may ask yourself why we only have means to describe the image's width, but not ones to describe its height. In fact, we are planning on adding h descriptors in the future, that will enable just that, but due to height based selection being a weaker use-case, it was decided that handling of that as part of the specification and the native implementations would have to be part of the next phase, rather than the current one.

But, didn't we just say that the browser cannot wait for the image's display dimensions to be calculated because doing so would result in significant delays and possible double downloads? And if the browser cannot wait for the display dimensions, how can it use the image's physical dimensions to determine which resource to download?

Well, since the image needs to be displayed as 100% of the width of the viewport (it is our header image, after all), we don't care much that the browser doesn't know anything from our markup regarding its display dimensions.

By default, the browser would assume that we need the largest image for our viewport. That would be the image that is as wide as our viewport's width, and therefore the browser will download the image it actually needs to properly display our header image. As we'll see later, we also have a way to indicate the browser that we need images that are smaller than that.

Now, let's say we also want to add an image gallery where each one of the images takes up about a third of the viewport's width. How can we do that?

Well, changing the CSS so that the image's container is as wide as 33% of the viewport is not a problem, but how do we tell the browser that the image it needs to load won't be as wide as the viewport, but a third of that size?

The proper way of doing that would be:

```
<img src="tiger_500px.jpg"
     sizes="33vw"
     srcset="tiger_200px.jpg 200w, tiger_500px.jpg 500w,
             tiger_800px.jpg 800w, tiger_1000px.jpg 1000w,
             tiger_1500px.jpg 1500w, tiger_2000px.jpg 2000w"
     alt="Tiger">
```

`srcset` here is not at all different than what we've seen earlier in our header image. The main difference here is the `sizes` attribute. It is our way of telling browsers, "This image will be displayed with roughly the width of the CSS length indicated."

What happens behind the scenes is that browsers take the provided `w` descriptors and use them along with the `sizes` value to calculate each provided resource's image density. You can think of it as browsers translating all the `w` descriptors into `x` descriptors internally. Then they perform the same (browser-defined) calculation we saw earlier with `x` descriptors to find the resource with the density that is closest to the current DPR. That means that `w` descriptors take DPR into account as well as their sizes-defined CSS length (which is often dependent on the viewport width, by using the `vw` CSS units). When your screen's DPR is higher (or when you zoom in), larger images are more likely to get picked.

If you're not familiar with `vw` units, they are relatively new CSS units, which represent percentages of the viewport width, after taking the vertical scrollbar into account. A `50vw` CSS length, then, translates to 50% of the viewport's width.

But, you're not limited to using `vw` units as part of your sizes CSS lengths. You can use any one of the supported CSS length units such as `px`, `em` and others. It is worth noting that relative CSS length units, such as `em`, behave inside of `sizes` exactly like they do inside media queries, and are calculated in relation to browsers' *initial* font size[7], rather than the current font size of the parent container (a common cause for confusion and misunderstandings!).

Just like other places that accept CSS lengths, you can also use CSS's `calc()` functions to represent lengths that are combined from multiple expressions. For example, `calc(50vw - 30px)` is a length that represents 50% of the viewport width minus 30 CSS pixels, which can be very useful when adjusting the image's dimensions to paddings or margins. Note that even though it is often used in CSS, `%` is not a valid unit inside of `sizes`. The reason is the confusion that it created among developers when encountering it at first ("Percentage of what, exactly?"). With `vw` being an exact and clear equivalent, support for `%` as a unit

---

7   http://dev.w3.org/csswg/mediaqueries-3/#units

was dropped. Since browsers use the `sizes` info only to calculate the image density, which in turn affects the resource picked as well as the image's intrinsic dimensions, the CSS length we provide to browsers doesn't have to be totally accurate, as long as the image's display dimensions are defined elsewhere. An image's display dimensions are still defined using the same CSS rules, or by using the `width` and `height` attributes.

Using `width` alongside `sizes` is permitted, although somewhat redundant, but it's worth noting that `width` doesn't affect the resource selection algorithm, so it cannot be used as a `sizes` replacement.

In our case, we defined the image as relative to the viewport width by choosing the `vw` units. But we could have used `px` or `em` to define fixed width images, or even the `vh` (percentage from viewport height) units, if we really wanted to complicate things.

That would give us a result that looks something like:

An example of an image gallery where each image is a third of the available viewport width, on medium viewport.

Now we're trying to tackle a different part of the page that contains a bunch of thumbnails. While trying out different layouts, we realize that if we maintain the thumbnails as wide as a fixed percentage of the viewport width, they'd be too large on wide viewports and too small on narrow ones. RWD to the rescue!

We come up with a new implementation plan. The thumbnails will be displayed at four columns on wide viewports, as a fixed percentage of the viewport width or up to a certain width. On narrow viewports, they should be displayed in a two-column layout, under similar constraints. Like this:

Animal thumbnails in a wide viewport, displayed in a 4-column layout.

Animal thumbnails in a medium-sized viewport, still in a 4-column layout.

Animal thumbnails in a medium-sized viewport, now in a 2-column layout.

That's great as far as the design goes, but how do we notify browsers about all of that, so they don't download images that are too large for what's needed? The way to do that is by defining the image's *sizes* attribute with our breakpoints:

```
<img src="thumb.jpg"
    sizes="(min-width: 1200px) 235px,
           (min-width: 641px) 24vw,
           (min-width: 470px) 235px,
           50vw"
    srcset="thumb100.jpg 100w,
            thumb200.jpg 200w, thumb235.jpg 235w,
            thumb300.jpg 300w, thumb470.jpg 470w"
    alt="A rad animal.">
```

Here we can see that the `sizes` attribute becomes slightly more complex than what we saw earlier. It is comprised of comma-separated value pairs, where the first (optional) value is a media condition (a media query without the media type), and the second value is a CSS length.

Browsers go over the media conditions and look for the first one that matches the current environment. While we can use any arbitrary media feature here, it probably makes the most sense to use viewport dimension media features (such as `max-width` and `max-height`), since they are the most likely to have an impact on your design's breakpoints and, therefore, your image dimensions. Note that for the values themselves, we can use relative CSS length units, like `em`, as well as `px` units.

The second, non-optional value of the pair, is a CSS length. That CSS length describes the estimated display dimensions of the image. This is the hint the developer has to give browsers for them to know which resource to pick.

Once browsers find a matching media condition (or there is no media condition at all), the matching CSS length is then used to calculate the density of the various resources inside `srcset`.

The image's density for resources with `w` descriptors is calculated by dividing the resource's width (as defined by the `w` descriptor) with the CSS length picked from `sizes`. If sizes is `400px` and the resource is defined with `800w`, this resource has density equivalent to a resource defined with `2x`.

Browsers can then use the resource density, along with the screen's DPR (and possibly other factors), to figure out which resource would be the best to download and display.

Going back to our code example above, assuming we're running with a browser viewport of 1,320 pixels, the browser will go over the `sizes` pairs and pick the first one: `(min-width: 1200px) 235px`. That would indicate to it that the image is likely to be displayed at a width of 235 pixels. Therefore, assuming the browser's DPR value is 1, it will likely try to download the resource closest to 235 pixels and it would end up downloading `thumb235.jpg`. If the DPR value is 2, in order to match the screen's density the required resource needs to be twice as large, so the browser will probably download the resource closest to 470 pixels, which is `thumb470.jpg`.

Now, if our viewport is 660px wide, the `(min-width: 641px) 24vw` pair matches, and the image is likely to take up slightly less than a quarter of the viewport's width. That means browsers will try to download the image that's closest to 158px wide for a DPR value of 1, and closest to 317px wide for a DPR value of 2. The actual resource picked is likely to be different here between browsers, since there's no exact match. In Chrome, the picked resource for the first case would probably be `thumb200.jpg`, and for the second case the picked resource would probably be `thumb300.jpg`. Future versions may modify the selection algorithm, so again, this is not something you should rely on.

As we've seen in our first example of this use case, if the `sizes` attribute is missing, a default value of `100vw` is used as the effective size instead, as it represents the largest display dimensions the image might be displayed in without horizontal scrolling.

Why did I use all of those "likely"s and "probably"s in the sections above? Again, they're there because for the resources *inside* `srcset` browsers are free to pick whatever resource their algorithms see fit. That means that you can't rely on browsers downloading and displaying the exact resource you want them to. That's a Good Thing™, since it leaves browsers room to innovate in this space, by adding user preferences, network considerations and other future optimizations to the decision-making process. And since all the different resources should only differ in quality, differing resource choices shouldn't have any impact on your page's layout.

But what happens if you want to see slightly different images on different layouts, showing images whose proportions are different, whose subject is more visible, or anything else your creative self desires? Well, that's what the art direction use case is all about!

Art Direction

The term *art direction* with regard to responsive images was first coined by Jason Grigsby[8]. It refers to cases where you want to tailor the displayed image to a specific responsive layout breakpoint. Art direction should be used when your image resources differ not only in their quality, but also in their proportions, crop area, copy text location, shot angle, and so on. The possibilities are limitless!

In these cases, you need to make sure that the image displayed to your users at a certain design breakpoint is in fact the image you intended they'd see. Using srcset for these cases won't do the trick, since, as we saw, with srcset it is browsers that have final judgement regarding the downloaded resource. Here, we need to have the final say about the downloaded resource, otherwise the page's layout might be broken, or the image's subject won't be displayed clearly.

A panda header image, cropped when viewed from a narrow viewport

An example of a page displaying a header image in its full context when space is available, and focused on the subject when it is scarce.

---

8   http://blog.cloudfour.com/a-framework-for-discussing-responsive-images-solutions/

The art direction syntax goes something like:

```
<picture>
    <source media="(min-width: 45em)" srcset="large.jpg">
    <source media="(min-width: 32em)" srcset="med.jpg">
    <img src="small.jpg" alt="A panda climbing up a tree.">
</picture>
```

Here again we hand out a grocery list of resources to browsers. The difference is that this is a list of `<source>` tags, and *their* selection algorithm is well-defined by the spec[9]. Browsers follow that algorithm to the letter and pick the `<source>` tag that you intended, every time.

Very much like they do when using the `sizes` algorithm, browsers go over the list of sources and pick the first one that matches. A match can happen based on both `media` and `type` attributes. (Why `type`? We'll see that in a bit.)

When both `media` and `type` attributes of a `<source>` either match or are missing (including if one of them matches and the other is missing), that source is picked. In other words, the `<source>` is picked for either case of:

```
<source media="matching media query" srcset>
<source type="supported MIME type" srcset>
<source media="matching media query" type="supported MIME type" srcset>
<source srcset>
```

If none of the `<source>`s match, the `<img>` is picked. And once we have an element that's picked as the source for this image, the resource that will be downloaded is chosen using the `<source>`'s `srcset` and `sizes` attributes, according to the same mechanisms we discussed earlier.

A few things to take note of:

* `<source src>` does nothing, and is ignored during the selection process. Make sure you use `<source srcset>`.

---

9   http://www.whatwg.org/specs/web-apps/current-work/multipage/embedded-content.html #select-an-image-source

- Even though `<picture>` is the parent element, the element doing all the heavy lifting here is the `<img>`. The `<img>` uses its `<picture>` parent and its older `<source>` siblings to pick a resource to load, but eventually it is the `<img>` that is used to display the resource. That means that the `<img>` must be there or no image will be displayed on screen. That's also good for fallback purposes: the `<img>` needs to be there to provide a fallback for older browsers, so it should be there anyway. Regardless, if the `<img>` is not there, nothing will display.

- Last but not least, if you want to style your image, you need to style `<img>` like you always have. In the immortal words of Tab Atkins, you should think of `<picture>` as a "magical span" around your `<img>`. Same goes for alt text. It should go on your `<img>`, like it always has.

The last point becomes fairly intuitive once we realize that `<picture>` is simply an extension to the good old `<img>` tag, and not a replacement. `<img>` still works as it always has, and is not going anywhere.

WHY CAN'T WE DO ART DIRECTION WITH SIZES/SRCSET?

By design, the `sizes/srcset` syntax takes into account the viewport's width as well as the screen's DPR. Art direction does not take DPR into account, since DPR doesn't matter much for layout purposes. Therefore, adding art direction into the same syntax would have meant that web developers had to explicitly specify all the DPR and viewport width combinations in the markup.

That would have made the developer's job much more difficult and would have made the syntax much harder to grasp and significantly more verbose.

Of course, web developers can abuse `srcset` by including multiple resources that are not the same image at different quality levels, but images that represent different crops or angles of the same subject. However, doing that would pretty much guarantee that at some point browsers will not pick the image intended, and the site's layout will be broken, or the image will get skewed.

The other way around is also possible. Web developers can abuse `<picture>` and use it for use cases which aren't exactly art direction per se. The problem here will be less obvious, but the result would be unnecessary downloads in some cases (e.g. when the viewport is downsized, and the image to be displayed is smaller than the one already displayed), and it would mean that browsers won't be able to download smaller images in case of network problems, or if the user has set a preference for smaller images at the expense of quality.

WHY CAN'T IT BE BASED ON CONTAINER SIZE?

As we've already discussed, both `<picture>`'s source selection and the `sizes` attribute are based on media queries and media conditions that are often evaluated based on the viewport's dimensions.

Web developers often state that it would have been more convenient for them to select the image source (as well as CSS in general) in a way that is based on the container's dimensions, rather than the viewport's. The concept is often referred to as *element queries* (EQs).

The reason current responsive images solutions are not based on element queries is a fairly simple one: the concept is not well defined, at least at the time of this writing. There are multiple obstacles to defining element queries; all of them can be overcome with time and effort, but there is no real reason to hold off responsive images until such a time when these issues will be resolved.

It is not yet clear how EQ-based responsive images would work, nor if they would have to sustain some delay in order to be loaded only after layout is calculated. Time will tell.

If you want to experiment with element queries today, there are several polyfill-like JavaScript libraries that implement them. In case you also need to lazy-load some of your page's images, libraries such as *lazysizes*[10] can enable both lazy loading and loading of the appropriate image resources according to their display dimensions.

---

10 https://github.com/aFarkas/lazysizes

A standards-based alternative is the *Clown Car Technique*[11]. One of the advantages of SVG here is that, very much like an iframe, media queries inside it refer to the dimensions of the SVG, rather than the dimensions of the entire page's viewport. That means that when using this technique, the image resource is picked according to its display dimensions. On the flip-side, that's also a disadvantage here. Image download would start much later than it would using the native responsive image techniques. For further details on that technique (and all things SVG), be sure to go over Sara Soueidan's excellent chapter.

The Responsive ~~Images~~ Issues Community Group (*RICG*[12]) is currently pushing towards defining element queries, mainly by gathering up the use cases for it. But it is still at a very early stage, and will need a lot of refinement before it is something that's ready to be implemented in browsers. If this is something you feel strongly about, we could use all the help we can get.

WHAT ABOUT SEPARATION OF CONCERNS?

The introduction of `<picture>` and `sizes` adds more CSS-based syntax to HTML. Even though media attributes have existed for a long while now, and HTML5 incorporated[13] the media query from CSS into HTML, their use inside HTML isn't very common, and they aren't as widespread across the document as `<picture>` and `sizes` media queries are likely to be.

There have been some voices expressing concerns that this is likely to violate the separation of concerns principle, and may create a maintenance problem once web developers want to change design breakpoints and have to modify these media queries across multiple pages and in multiple places in every page. Not good.

What is the plan to tackle this obvious problem?

Well, the short-term plan is simple: web developers would be better off using some templating system (either dynamic or as a build step) and keeping their

---

11   http://www.smashingmagazine.com/2013/06/02/clown-car-technique-solving-for-adaptive-images-in-responsive-web-design

12   http://ricg.io, the new website of the RICG.

13   http://www.w3.org/TR/html5/document-metadata.html#attr-link-media

design breakpoints in a single place. If any design breakpoint changes are applicable to multiple pages, they can be changed at a single location and be applied to multiple pages.

But since "The tools will save us" is rarely a good answer in web standards discussions, there's also a long-term plan. That plan involves an addition to the media queries standard called *custom media queries*[14]. It's more or less an equivalent to CSS variables for media queries, and would enable us to define the page's breakpoints in a single, inline `<style>` tag in the HTML's `<head>`.

Why inline? Because of performance reasons (which is the ultimate goal here), we would still need browsers to be able to evaluate these media queries before any external resources have finished downloading, like they do today.

Image Format Fallback

One more thing you may want to do with images (not necessarily responsive ones) is to serve different file formats to different browsers, according to browser support for them. As well as traditional file formats that browsers support (PNG, JPEG and GIF), there are several newer file formats that browser vendors are trying to encourage developers to use. These formats usually perform better than the traditional ones, since they include all kinds of algorithmic improvements that make image compression more efficient. Specifically, Google is pushing the *WebP*[15] format and Microsoft is promoting *JPEG-XR*[16].

Unfortunately, these new formats lack the traditional formats' level of ubiquitous support, which means that if you serve these formats as your `<img src>` value, even though the browsers that support them will exhibit an improved user experience, the ones that don't won't show any image at all. That's hardly good.

Up until today, the only way to serve such formats without breaking the user experience in non-supporting browsers was content-negotiation, using the Accept HTTP header or UA sniffing. While that mostly works fine, there are

---

14 http://dev.w3.org/csswg/mediaqueries-4/#custom-mq
15 https://developers.google.com/speed/webp/
16 http://msdn.microsoft.com/en-us/library/windows/desktop/hh707223.aspx

some caveats. It requires server-side fiddling, which some developers can't do, or aren't interested in doing; and it also introduces difficulties with making these images publicly cacheable.

With the `<picture>` syntax, we finally have a way to define a client-side fallback mechanism. By using the type attribute on `<source>` we can provide the browser with multiple image URLs, and let browsers pick the one they support. Such mechanisms have been available for other resource types for years (e.g. fonts and videos). Now a fallback mechanism is also available for images.

The syntax for client-side format fallback looks something like:

```
<picture>
    <source type="image/webp" srcset="president.webp">
    <source type="image/vnd.ms-photo" srcset="president.jpxr">
    <img src="president.jpg" alt="The president fistbumps someone.">
</picture>
```

Just as we've seen for media, browsers go over the various `<source>` elements and pick the first one that matches; that is, the first one which has a supported image MIME type as the value of its type attribute.

Accessibility

As far as accessibility goes, that's easy. Nothing has changed in image accessibility with the introduction of `srcset`, sizes and `<picture>`. Since `srcset` and `<picture>` are simply enhancements of the `<img>` element, browsers can continue to use the good old alt attribute inside of `<img>` and get the text alternative to the image from the attribute's value.

Some people have called[17] for support of multiple `alt` values and multiple `figcaption` values that depend on the picked resource. For now the consensus within the RICG is that such usage is an edge case and is best addressed using JavaScript. If this is something you need to do, there's a prollyfill (a `polyfill` for a not yet standard API) called *picturecaption*[18] that can let you do just that.

---

17 https://github.com/ResponsiveImagesCG/picture-element/issues/254
18 https://github.com/iandevlin/picturecaption

Did You Think Of Using CSS?

One of the earliest hacks to resolve responsive images was to turn content images into background images, and control the image resource using CSS media queries. In that technique, the `<img>` is replaced by a `<div>` and the image displayed is controlled using `@media` rules.

An example of that would be the following HTML and CSS:

```
<div id="content_image"></div>

#content_image {
    background-image: url("cropped.jpg");
}
@media screen and (min-width: 50em) {
    #content_image {
        background-image: url("uncropped.jpg");
    }
}
```

Only the required image[19] will be then downloaded and displayed, enabling a hacky way to get art direction in place. There are problems with that approach:

- CSS becomes part of the content, and may incur frequent changes as content changes, rendering it non-cacheable in the long term.
- Accessibility is harmed, since there's no way to define accessible alternatives to background images.
- Search engines will not recognize these images as content images, and will not include them in an image search.
- Performance is (often) harmed, since background images, usually defined in external CSS, require the entire CSS to be downloaded and parsed in order to be discovered by browsers.

That last point is also what prevented the adoption of any CSS-based responsive images proposal. Content images have always been discoverable at the early

---

19 http://timkadlec.com/2012/04/media-query-asset-downloading-results/

stages of the page's loading cycle, and adding an extra delay for all the external CSS files to finish downloading and be applied will incur an excessive performance hit.

Did You Think Of Using JavaScript?

For obvious reasons, most of the initial hacks to tackle the responsive images problem were based on JavaScript.

The problem when using JavaScript to resolve this is that you have two less-than-ideal options: either delay the loading of images by eliminating their original src attribute; or incur a double download, where the initial src resource is downloaded and then replaced by a higher resolution or better fitting image.

That means that JavaScript-based solutions suffer from a performance penalty, one way or the other.

Why Not A File Format?

A file format would be a great solution to most of the responsive images use cases, and I have given a lot of thought[20] to how such a format might look, how would it work, and how can it be fetched by browsers.

Unfortunately, the downside of introducing a new file format is that it's an excruciatingly slow process. Google has been pushing WebP for over four years now, with very little cross-browser adoption. Microsoft has been promoting JPEG-XR for even longer and with even worse results.

File formats (even if they're just a wrapper around existing file formats, like the one I proposed) still need an ecosystem of authoring tools in place. It is also a field filled with intellectual property and patent claims, and the resulting FUD makes it difficult to introduce new formats without the backing of very large corporations. And even then, it's *slow*.

With that said, I'm not ruling out a future in which a responsive file format can be incrementally fetched, with the help of HTTP/2.0, and resolve most of the use cases in an elegant way. It's just not the world we live in today.

---

20 http://www.smashingmagazine.com/2013/09/24/responsive-image-container/

What About Background Images?

As we explored at the start of this chapter, the responsive images problem mostly referred to content images, because the background images angle was mostly covered. For art direction we had CSS media queries, which had no specific performance issues. They weren't loading unnecessary resources, and didn't have any delay penalty when compared to regular background images.

To address high-density screens, we had two options: either use media queries with the `resolution` media feature (or its non-standard predecessor `device-pixel-ratio`); or use the (WebKit-prefixed) `image-set` property. All in all, these were way more than what we had in the content images world (which was nothing), so the community didn't put much focus on background images.

How, then, can we handle responsive background images today?

Say you need to add to your website a Retina background image (that would be loaded only on devices that need it, of course). You can get that done in supporting browsers by doing something like:

```
.hero-image {
    background-image: -webkit-image-set(url(1x.jpg) 1x, url(2x.jpg) 2x);}
```

The (prefixed) property is only supported by Safari, Chrome and Opera. The property is not currently supported by IE or Firefox. Alternatively, if you need to art-direct the background image to specific breakpoint layouts, you can achieve that by using media queries and the `@media` rule:

```
.hero-image { background-image: url(narrow_viewport_crop.jpg); }
@media (min-width: 800px) {
    .hero-image { background-image: url(wide_viewport_crop.jpg); }
}
```

Many have used the above technique over the years as a way to hack together some form of responsive images. As we've seen, we no longer need to do that, since nowadays we have proper responsive content images, and mixing our content images and our CSS is a bad practice for multiple reasons: performance, maintainability, accessibility, and SEO, to name a few.

But now, when the work on getting responsive content images support has calmed down, some focus is bouncing back[21] to responsive background images, and matching their capabilities to those of content images. Specifically, there's no way today to define a set of resources by their width and letting browsers pick the best one for the required display dimensions (like we do with *w* descriptors in `srcset`).

MIME type switching is also a neglected use case in the background images world. Tab Atkins has proposed[22] to add these use cases into the image-set specification, and it looks like no one is opposing that.

It is too early to tell how far along that is in practice, or what would be the adoption rate from browser vendors once that becomes part of the spec.

The Importance Of Image Optimization

The savings that can be achieved by responsive images don't reach their full potential unless you properly optimize your images. Image optimization techniques have been available for a long while now, yet many web developers don't apply them and let their users download excessive image data.

What can we do to change that? Covering the whole subject of image optimization is beyond the scope of this chapter, but I feel I should cover the basics. Consider this Image Optimization 101.

IMAGE FORMATS

The web has traditionally had three universally supported raster image formats: JPEG, PNG and GIF. In modern browsers, it also has a vector-based format: SVG.

GIF is the most limited format, and aside from being the universal way of showing short animations of cats, there's not much else it is particularly good at, so we won't expand any further on it here.

JPEG is over 20 years old and is pretty good at handling photography. It is what is called a "lossy" image format, which means that when an image is compressed into a JPEG, *some* quality is lost along the way. That is due to its

---

21   http://blog.cloudfour.com/the-forgotten-responsive-images-spec-image-set/
22   http://lists.w3.org/Archives/Public/www-style/2014Oct/0439.html

nature, which mimics the way humans perceive imagery — it gets rid of data that represents changes in the image that are barely visible to the human eye. The format doesn't do as well for computer-generated graphics with very sharp edges, since the lossiness of the format can cause visible artifacts. Another feature lacking is support for transparency, not to mention a full-fledged alpha channel.

PNG has also been around for a while (since 1996). Unlike JPEG, it is best used for images that have sharp color differences, such as computer-generated graphics. Also unlike JPEG, it is a lossless format, meaning that encoding a PNG does not reduce the image's original quality. It is an improved and patent-free version of GIF, and has multiple modes that enable it to display photography with true colors (usually referred to as PNG24, as opposed to PNG8 which can only have up to 256 colors). However, since it is not well-adapted to that, these files often tend to be significantly more bloated than their JPEG counterparts. On the other hand, it has a full alpha channel, which means that you can have transparent or semi-transparent parts in your images.

SVG is extensively covered in Sara Soueidan's chapter, but in short it's a mark-up-based format that represents images as mathematical vectors, enabling them to keep their original sharpness when scaled up or down. Sounds like the perfect solution for the responsive images problem! Unfortunately, like PNG, it is best suited to computer-generated images, and when the images in question have many small details, or are not extremely large, it is possible that the SVG version would be larger than the PNG counterpart.

The main takeaway here is that you should pick the best format for the image you want to display. If it's a photo, chances are that the best format is JPEG. If it's a computer-generated image with sharp edges, it's likely that SVG or PNG are best. And if you need your photo to have a transparent or semi-transparent alpha channel, your choice is between using a PNG or using a glorious hack[23] combining a JPEG and a PNG alpha mask inside an SVG!

---

23 A JavaScript library that converts a PNG with a transparent background into a JPEG and a PNG-based alpha mask, stuffed up inside an SVG. http://quasimondo.com/ZorroSVG/

MOAR IMAGE FORMATS!

While the formats described above are supported by all modern browsers, we've already discussed other image formats on the web that are only supported by a subset of browsers; specifically the WebP and JPEG-XR image formats, promoted by Google and Microsoft respectively.

JPEG-XR is mainly a JPEG replacement with some additional features (such as an alpha channel) and improved compression algorithms. It is designed to efficiently represent high definition photography.

WebP, on the other hand, is trying to answer the use cases of all other raster image formats. It has a lossy mode designed for photography (that sports an alpha channel as well), a lossless mode designed for computer-generated images, and an animated mode, designed to tackle animated GIFs. The format is based on the VP8 video format.

Both these formats provide compression benefits over the older image formats: both cite around 30% compression improvements over JPEG in various benchmarks. As we discussed, JPEG-XR is only supported by IE, and WebP only supported by browsers that are built on Chromium, so Chrome and Opera.

IMAGE OPTIMIZATION

Once you've determined the best format for the image in question, you still need to convert it to the appropriate format, resize it and optimize it. Let's take a look at how that's done.

Resizing

Manual image resizing can often be done by using the built-in resizing utilities in your favorite image editor. Some of these utilities even provide a GUI for performing batch conversions, so avoiding some of the manual hassle. There are also command-line utilities (e.g. ImageMagick) that enable you to handle image resizing tasks. They are often more adapted for batch conversions, using scripts.

Which image dimensions should you pick? Ideally, the various resources that you provide in `srcset` should not be that far apart when it comes to byte size. In this way, the browser can pick a resource whose dimensions are as close to ideal as possible. What do I mean by "not that far apart"? Well, that depends on your performance budget[24], your server storage space, server CPU costs, and so on. The best way to go would be to test your site over typically used viewports (which you can probably get from your analytics data), and see if the amount of wasted image data fits within your performance budget. If it doesn't, then decreasing the steps between the image resources inside your *srcset* and adding some intermediate sizes may help. These intermediate resources would enable browsers to download images closer in size to their actual display dimensions.

Testing how far off are you from ideal image dimensions can be done using a command-line utility I wrote called *Sizer-Soze*,[25] which the good folks at the RICG later turned into a web service at *sizersoze.org*[26]. You can use it to test the wasted image bytes on your website for popular layout breakpoints, and figure out how far you are from ideal image dimensions. The main downside with the utility is that you must include a polyfill in your pages to see the benefits of `srcset` and `<picture>`, since the utility is based on PhantomJS, which itself is based on an old WebKit engine lacking support for these features.

Optimization

Image optimization techniques are divided into two kinds:

- Lossless optimization: an optimization technique that doesn't result in any quality loss as far as the image goes. This can be comprised of elimination of irrelevant metadata, as well as lossless recompression of the image data, crunching the data some more. This type of compression is, as it were, free (i.e. the image quality is unharmed, the only cost for it being server CPU) but is often limited.
- Lossy optimization: an optimization technique that results in some quality loss: either the loss of some precision, the introduction of subtle artifacts, or the loss of some colors.

---

24 http://timkadlec.com/2013/01/setting-a-performance-budget/
25 https://github.com/yoavweiss/Sizer-Soze
26 http://sizersoze.org

Despite its name, lossy compression often goes unnoticed by users. But it does come with a quality price and the lossier the compression engine settings are, the worse image quality will be.

The best tool for lossless image optimization out there is Kornel Lesiński's *ImageOptim*[27] (and its *command-line version*[28] is something you should definitely add to your build/back-end flow). By its very definition, lossless optimization doesn't result in a quality loss, so this is something you should always add to your image processing pipeline. It is also important to always add it as the last phase of the image processing pipeline, since some of the other tools may add some useless noise to your images that lossless compression will get rid of.

The best tool for lossy compression? Well, that depends on the format.

For the common case in which the image you want to optimize is a JPEG, you can apply moderate and controlled form of lossy optimization by running through a script called *cjpeg-dssim*[29], a script that runs the JPEG multiple times through a highly optimized encoder called *MozJPEG*[30], making sure that the level of compression applied will only have a very small visual effect. In the future, MozJPEG may get that functionality integrated into the encoder, eliminating the need for an external script. If the image you have on your hands is a PNG, your best bet is to run it through a lossy optimizer such as *ImageAlpha*[31], or the command-line equivalent *PNGQuant*[32], to reduce its number of colors or its precision, and thereby its byte size.

Deployment Concerns

I know what you're thinking — all of the above means a lot of work. Resizing and optimizing every image and then adding multiple resource URLs in the markup to match them can be very cumbersome. Fortunately, that's not the only way to provide your users with the best performance. One might even say that

---

27 https://imageoptim.com
28 http://jamiemason.github.io/ImageOptim-CLI/
29 https://github.com/technopagan/cjpeg-dssim
30 https://github.com/mozilla/mozjpeg
31 http://pngmini.com
32 http://pngquant.org

it's a sure way to a) go mad and b) mess it up from time to time. We humans are not very good at tedious, repetitive tasks. Computers, on the other hand, are great at just that. What you need to create is an automatic process that would make sure all your images are responsive and optimized, and let the computers take care of that from that point on.

Now, there's no one-size-fits-all solution here, since what you need to automate your image pipeline varies according to your choice of back-end, the source of your images, and what your site even does.

But there are some rules to live by:

- Static assets should be optimized using a build process. There are many build frameworks out there, such as Grunt and Gulp. Many of them have rich ecosystems of plugins to enable you to add an image optimization step into your build process with very little work. *Use them.*

- User-uploaded images should be optimized as part of the upload process. Keeping the original around is probably a good idea, in case you'd one day want to reprocess them to bump up your image quality.

- Markup creation of srcset should be automatic. It can be part of a templating framework, a build-time solution, or part of your dynamic HTML generation, but adding multiple resource URLs to the HTML by hand is nobody's idea of a good time. Automate it away.

- sizes still requires manual work. sizes is brand-new, and we don't yet have the tools to automatically generate sizes on the server side. Until we do, the extra optimization that sizes provides requires manual intervention, at least in classifying the different images on your page to their corresponding sizes value.

- Art direction using `<picture>` requires manual intervention as well, at least for now. Hopefully with time, CMSs and back-end frameworks will find the UI language to enable their users to define art direction with simple means.

If you are using a CMS, the RICG is working with Drupal as well as WordPress to integrate responsive images support into the CMSs themselves, to make sure that CMS users get their benefits with as little work on their part as possible. Hopefully, other CMS and server-side frameworks will soon have the proper plugins in place to enable easy responsive images deployment.

I believe the simplest way for CMSs to support the basic use cases of user-generated responsive images would be to ask the users and editors to upload the highest-quality images possible, and have back-end code that resizes these images automatically and creates the `srcset` syntax that comes with them. I'm hoping that this part will soon be a standard part of major CMSs.

If art direction is required, you'd probably have to get creative and set up a process in which users can define different crops or points of interest for each uploaded image, so that you could then automate the creation of the various crops. At the moment we have not yet created such easy-to-use tools, but I hope they'll show up soon and get integrated into the major CMSs.

As far as automation goes, there are many open source utilities that can help you. To name a few, *grunt-responsive-images*[33] and *gulp-responsive*[34] seem very useful to get a build process in place and automate the responsive asset creation of your site's static assets.

Common Pitfalls

As with any new piece of technology, there are a few things that may confuse you at first. Here's a list of things you should look out for when starting to use `srcset` and `<picture>`.

---

33 https://github.com/andismith/grunt-responsive-images
34 https://github.com/mahnunchik/gulp-responsive

SOURCE ORDER MATTERS

Both the source selection and the source size selection algorithms are *first-match* algorithms. That means that the first `<source>` that matches is the one that gets picked. The same goes for the first media condition that matches inside the `sizes` value. Therefore, you should be careful to order media queries and media conditions included there from the narrowest to the widest. If you use `max-width` media queries, you should arrange them from the smallest value to the largest. If you use `min-width` media queries, it should be the other way around, from the largest value to the smallest. Failing to do so would mean that the wider media query will always get picked, while the narrower ones below it never will.

SRCSET DOES NOT PROVIDE GUARANTEES

Many developers try out `srcset` and are disappointed when browsers don't react to their resizing of the screen and reload the image. The thing is, that's exactly the point of `srcset`.

Browsers may reload the resource when the user's environment changes (browser is resized or reoriented, usually), but they don't have to. And in some cases, it makes no sense to do so (think about what should happen if a browser is downsized, and the image is as well). That behavior is not really documented anywhere outside of browsers' source code, and as we said, may change between browser versions. In short, you should not assume anything about any browser's resource download behavior when it comes to `srcset`.

DON'T LIE TO THE BROWSER

If you provide a browser with the wrong information regarding `srcset`'s resources, the browser will act on that false information. That means the wrong resource may get picked to be downloaded and displayed, but it also means that the intrinsic size of the downloaded resource — which is the actual resource dimensions, corrected according to the provided descriptors — will get skewed.

If the image's display dimensions are not defined in CSS, the image's display size will be incorrect. Therefore, make sure you provide the correct values of w and x descriptor when writing out srcset.

Should I Use <picture> Or srcset?

We've already discussed this, but since it's a question that comes up a lot, I think it's a point worth repeating. <picture> is for art direction; it should be used when you need absolute control over which image resource is loaded at each design breakpoint. Otherwise, you're better off using srcset to provide the browser with multiple alternative resources, and let it pick the one that best fits the user's current conditions. Of course, <picture> can also be used for client-side MIME type fallback, regardless of responsiveness.

Can I Use It Today?

Native support for most of the features we've discussed is not yet complete across all browsers, but you can certainly start using these features right now.

Full support for <picture>, srcset and sizes has shipped in Chrome and Opera since versions 38 and 25 (released in October 2014) respectively.

Firefox has implemented the responsive images features alongside the implementation in Blink, and it has reached the stable branch with Firefox 38.

The srcset x descriptor is already supported in Safari 8. The implementation for sizes and srcset's w descriptor is complete in WebKit (the rendering engine behind Safari) but, unfortunately, it did not ship in Safari 8. Since it's already implemented, there's reason to be hopeful that it will get shipped in a future version. Support for <picture> is not yet in WebKit (due to some missing infrastructure), so it is likely that having full <picture> support in Safari will take longer.

Regarding IE, srcset x is in development and hopefully will be part of a preview release soon. <picture> is still under consideration, but the IE development team has shown positive signs regarding the possibility of starting its development. Let's hope its status will switch to in development shortly.

<picture> element support has also been implemented in the W3C's validator[35], so you can use that to spot mistakes in your markup, should you run into trouble with it.

On top of that, the feature has a standards-compliant polyfill called *picturefill*[36], which you may want to use if you're using variable-width images or art direction and want to port the benefits of that back to legacy browsers.

For fixed-width images (so the x descriptor of srcset), native support is widespread enough that a polyfill is often not necessary.

Even without picturefill, the inherent < img> fallback makes it so that legacy browsers will still download and display the fallback image, meaning that the user experience in these browsers won't be any different than if you simply use an < img> element.

The Proposal Left Behind

Those of you who followed the responsive images saga closely may remember yet another proposal, called *Client Hints*. That proposal suggested solving some of the use cases by using HTTP request headers to tell the server about a browser's environmental conditions, and letting the server adapt the images it sends accordingly. That kind of solution is generally referred to as *content negotiation*.

For a long time, this proposal stagnated because some browser folks were reluctant to add new content negotiation-based solutions, owing to past bad experience[37] with this kind of solution. Without support from these browser vendors, progress on Client Hints stalled for a long while. However, recent interest in the proposal have lead to its revival. In fact, it's currently one of the issues I'm working on in Blink, and hopefully work in Firefox, WebKit and IE won't lag behind.

---

35 http://validator.w3.org
36 https://scottjehl.github.io/picturefill/
37 https://wiki.whatwg.org/wiki/Why_not_conneg

Community

We cannot sum up the responsive images effort without mentioning that unlike the development process behind most web platform features, it was a community-driven one. It was championed by the RICG, supported by the developer community, and taken home when browser folks got involved too. One big happy standards-writing family.

In the same spirit, the feature's implementation in Blink (the rendering engine behind Chrome and Opera) also set something of a precedent. Defuse initial[38] implementation[39] concerns from the Blink project, I devised an implementation plan[40] with the Blink team and started to work on related infrastructure. At first, I worked on that during my free time, but later on, after I realized how long that was going to take, I completed the feature's implementation as my day job.

The effort was financed by the community via a crowdfunding campaign which was put together with the help of the RICG gang (particularly Mat Marquis and Geri Coady).

Web developers and agencies, as well as Google and Opera, contributed to the campaign, making it possible for me to work full-time on the implementation, and bring it to where it is today.

Overview

In this chapter, we went over the various responsive images use cases and how to solve them with the native tools provided by browsers.

The main things you need to remember from it all are:

- If you need art direction or specific control over the images loaded in different environments, use `<picture>`. Otherwise, `srcset` is better, since it delegates that control to browsers, and lets browsers optimize the resource downloaded to the user's conditions.

---

38 http://lists.whatwg.org/htdig.cgi/whatwg-whatwg.org/2014-January/041833.html
39 http://lists.whatwg.org/htdig.cgi/whatwg-whatwg.org/2014-January/041910.html
40 https://groups.google.com/a/chromium.org/d/msg/blink-dev/9xIjDTOwbeI/1mL2lDYaHFYJ

- sizes is an optimization, hinting to browsers about the image's final display dimensions. It doesn't have to be there, nor does it have to be extremely accurate. But when it's there, it enables browsers to download even smaller images.

- Optimize your images! Images are the number one resource when it comes to byte size. Don't send excessively large images for no good reason. But also, make sure that regardless of dimensions, your images are optimized, in the appropriate format, and don't contain excessive metadata.

- No one can remember to do all of the above manually for each image on a site. Automate these things as far as you can. Bake them into your CMS, your image upload process, or your build system. Make sure that once you've done the hard work of getting that in place, it will be automatically applied to all future images in your site.

One more thing: if you find the entirety of the subject slightly overwhelming, that's probably because it's a complicated subject, and it's not easy to get it all in one sitting. If that's the case, you'll probably do better by simply starting out with `srcset`, get some savings in place and extend your solution from there. sizes can be added later on, as an extra optimization, and `<picture>` can be added when your content needs force you to.

Responsive images have been a pain point when developing responsive websites for quite some time. Now, finally, a native solution is here, shipped in Chrome and Opera.

You can start using it today, with or without *picturefill*, and start saving your users time and money!

This chapter is loosely based on an article commissioned by Opera's developer relations team and includes screenshots from www.worldwildlife.org.

ABOUT THE AUTHOR

Yoav doesn't get discouraged easily and is not afraid of code. He is a web performance and browser internals specialist, especially interested in the intersection between responsive design and web performance.

He has implemented the various responsive images features in Blink and WebKit as part of the Responsive Images Community Group, and is currently working at *Akamai*, focused on making the web platform faster. When he's not writing code, he's probably slapping his bass, mowing the lawn in the French countryside or playing board games with the kids.

TESTING AND
DEBUGGING
RESPONSIVE
WEB DESIGN

TOM MASLEN

CHAPTER EIGHT · BY TOM MASLEN

TESTING AND DEBUGGING RESPONSIVE WEB DESIGN

I USED TO BE A TERRIBLE WEB DEVELOPER. I thought I was really good at my job but looking back now I can see that while I was fast at completing tasks, the code I produced was unmaintainable. Despite having a very good knowledge of how browsers worked, I regularly produced buggy code. And after years of regularly working in teams I was still very precious about my own work and I lacked the intellectual humility to accept better ideas.

Fortunately for me, making websites was easy. Web development used to be simple: four browsers, all running on desktop computers, two kinds of input and one static design to build. I could get away with creating unmaintainable, buggy code because it was simple to debug and fix. Today this is no longer the case because responsive web design has made our jobs so much harder than it used to be.

Wow. Writing that out feels quite therapeutic. Unfortunately, there are no Web Developers Anonymous help groups for me to continue letting all of this out. If this was a help group and I was introducing myself to you I'd say, "Hi, everyone. My name is Tom Maslen and I've been practicing web development for about 17 years. Recently I've started taking responsive web design. It all started in 2011 when I joined the BBC to work on the new responsive version of the BBC News website. Initially, there were too many browsers and devices for me to support, so I came up with a technique called '*cutting the mustard*'[1] to help me cope. This technique has caught on now and is becoming more widely used throughout the industry. Since joining BBC News four years ago, I've dealt with a large responsive codebase on a daily basis. Typical issues are always to do with how developers and designers work together, the maintainability of our codebase, debugging in the massive amount of devices we now support and working out the best way to test these devices to suppress the amount of bugs that make it to the live site." *Thanks for sharing, Tom.*

I've spent a long time building up a way of working that minimizes the pain points that responsive web design now presents us with. I want to go through this with you: to show you how you can build future-friendly CSS structures that will scale up to support large responsive websites; get you to take testing seriously, but not over-complicate your workflow (responsive web design has now made manual testing almost impossible); and finally, how to sanely prioritize and debug problems in all types of devices and browsers.

Despite what my project manager may say, I'm very happy to tell you that I'm no longer a terrible web developer. The journey from terrible to good is actually quite a typical one; maybe there'll be some parallels with your own career. I've structured this chapter into three parts that roughly cover three phases of different attitudes and ways of working I've passed through in my career:

1. *How you shouldn't do it:* work fast, make stuff up as you go along, test the day before a release, and constantly release bugs and regressions to the live site.

2. *Getting better at making, testing and debugging responsive websites:* get burnt by being too pragmatic, get taken under the wing of a wiser developer, be introduced to testing and become a dogmatic follower of the practice, realize the importance of writing maintainable code and start to improve oneself.

3. Expertly applying testing to your development workflow: get burnt by

---

1 See page 375 for explanation. http://responsivenews.co.uk/post/18948466399/cutting-the-mustard

being too dogmatic, decide what works for me, and learn how to write tests correctly and define an optimal workflow.

Phase 1: How You Shouldn't Do It

Before the iPhone, Chrome, preprocessors, code linting and Sublime Text, my web development setup was quite simple: Microsoft Notepad and Firefox. It seems almost impossible now to think that I was able to create entire websites with such a simple setup, as well as fix and debug CSS rendering and JavaScript syntax errors using only `window.alert` and my own custom debug tool. Before web browsers had internal dev tooling, we'd fix layout issues by adding debug CSS like this:

```
td {
    border: 1px solid green;
    padding: 10px;
}
div {
    border: 1px solid red;
    margin: 10px;
    padding: 10px;
}
h1,h2,h3,h4,p {
    border: 1px solid blue;
    margin: 10px;
    padding: 10px;
}
```

This simple piece of CSS would help me to find typical CSS rendering issues like unclosed tags, and the double margin bug[2] and the peek-a-boo bug[3] in older versions of Internet Explorer.

I'd then have to go into the CSS to find the offending selectors or properties and work out where to apply a fix. There was never really any planning put into CSS; typically one CSS file would be used for an entire site. The CSS file would

---

2 http://www.positioniseverything.net/explorer/doubled-margin.html
3 http://www.positioniseverything.net/explorer/peekaboo.html

often be over 1,000 lines long. If there were more than one of you working on the single CSS file then it would quickly become a mess of contrasting styles with no obvious order.

The main issue with CSS is that every selector, no matter where in the file it is located, has the potential to globally apply any CSS property. To combat this I used to use a very obvious selector style:

```
body div#header          { /* ... */ }
body div#header h1        { /* ... */ }
body div#header p#strapline { /* ... */ }
```

Yes, I was THAT guy. The selectors here are way too verbose but they helped me to maintain the CSS: it made the order of selectors obvious, created regions for you when you wanted to add a new selector, and implied an order of styling *(important when trying to follow the cascade)*.

Unfortunately, below all of my perfectly structured CSS would be quick fixes, patches to bugs and additional new styling added by other developers or myself when I was in a hurry. Over a long enough period of time the CSS would become ordered chronologically, the latest changes would be at the bottom of the file. Monkey-patching specific browsers with extra CSS files loaded only for them would exacerbate this anti-pattern. Trying to work out the cascade by a series of selectors that are constantly overriding each other and then being overridden themselves by an additional CSS file was very hard.

There was no care or thought put into the maintainability of the codebase. All of the value was placed into how fast I could complete tasks. Web development was different ten years ago than it is today. Back then we had four web browsers (IE6, IE7, Firefox and Safari) with rendering engines that were very different from each other. It took a lot of effort to get a webpage looking the same and for the JavaScript to work across all of the browsers we supported.

Today, most browsers are very standards-compatible (go pay some respect to the devs who worked on WaSP[4]: you can write CSS and JavaScript and expect it to more or less behave the same in every browser). The challenge today is with

---

4   http://www.webstandards.org

responsive web design: we need to create interfaces flexible enough to fit into any viewport size and aspect ratio.

Testing was even more chaotic. For most of my professional life I've done most of my own testing. Before responsive web design I'd develop a website on a PC using Chrome (or Firefox before Chrome was born). When the page was at a certain stage or even finished I'd check it in the following browsers in this order:

- Firefox
- IE8
- IE7
- IE6
- Safari
- Opera

Then I'd go over to a Mac in the corner of the office and check Safari, Firefox and Opera again. It was common for developers in my team to test each other's work or for the project manager to test for us. We'd do this testing a few days before we were due to release, it would often be a tense and stressful period where somebody else would be going through my work, pointing out where I'd made mistakes.

Some sites were complex JavaScript applications, holiday booking sites or warehouse applications. Making changes to these codebases was not simple and once the code was released we'd find that we had broken parts of the functionality we hadn't touched, or that what we made didn't work in certain circumstances; or, even more typically, that the JavaScript threw an error in IE6. I'd always refer to these as "bugs" when really what I meant was "mistakes in my code".

It took a long time for me to work out that my blasé attitude toward testing was responsible for all the quality issues we had. "It works on my computer" became a cliché in our industry, and I was one of the biggest sinners for repeating this.

I used to be very precious. I wasn't a good developer until about five years ago. I didn't like other developers telling me what to do or testing my code.

The one thing I hated more than anything — and this sounds crazy — was releasing code. I would get physically nauseated as a release date came closer. And when we did release, I wanted to run away. Looking back, I think it's because I knew there would be issues; that once the thing I had been carefully crafting in my personal office space was exposed to the world, people would find problems with my work and I'd be open to criticism.

I don't know if this fear of releasing is common, but I do recognize preciousness in other developers. It's a trait I always try to expel from members of my team. An important part of being a good developer is acknowledging that you don't always get things right, and you should be open to other developer's opinions. I take inspiration from Brad Frost in this respect, who once said: "It's not a criticism, they're helping me to make my website even better!" This expresses an incredible amount of intellectual humility. We should all adopt the same outlook.

We should see testing in the same way. It's not there to catch you out or to prove you're not good at your job. Because responsive web design has made front-end development harder to practice, our understanding of JavaScript, browsers, devices and CSS now has to be of a very high standard. This mental model of how everything works together is very hard to keep track of and testing can help you. To define what things should do, how they do it, and then make sure no regressions appear.

Knowing when to apply testing and how to do it hasn't been a typical part of a web developer's skill set. It's time for this to change.

Phase 2: Getting Better At Making, Testing And Debugging Responsive Websites

I don't know any single developer who thinks responsive web design has made everything easier. I do know great front-end developers who have had enough and retreated to working only on back-end, server-side programming. The complexity of front-end development has increased to keep up with the diversity we have to support. Like all types of programming, though, the easier your front-end code is to understand and work with, the easier it will be to debug.

You have to fight the constant creep of complexity; you have to put effort into maintaining and structuring it sensibly. I always try to apply two key programming principles when building websites: simplicity, and predictability.

Simplicity is the opposite of complexity. This means creating HTML, CSS and JavaScript that are modular, scalable and consistent. Predictability means that the outcomes of any changes you make are obvious and expected. When you make a change to a complex system, the outcome can be unpredictable and hard to control.

Here are some of the ways that you can improve how you practice responsive web design:

- Building predictable, simple CSS with easy-to-follow naming conventions, directory structures and media queries
- Keeping clear separations of concern
- Use testing to stop bugs getting on to your live site
- Use visual regression tools to speed up testing responsive websites

BUILDING PREDICTABLE, SIMPLE CSS: EASY-TO-FOLLOW NAMING CONVENTIONS

The key to making anything easy to maintain and debug is to concentrate on keeping it simple to understand, and ensuring any outcomes from changes are predictable. Pain points with CSS come from the global nature of the language. It's very easy to build a complicated cascade of inherited styles which then causes problems with the priority of selectors.

BEM (block, element, modifier)[5] is a technique for naming selectors that addresses this problem. It's a popular way to implement CSS, and as a reader of a Smashing book I'd expect you to have heard about it already. At the BBC we use an adaptation of BEM:

```
.block__element--modifier
```

Using double delimiters allows us to use hyphens within each part of the

---

5   https://en.bem.info/

naming convention and still maintain readability. We also add modifiers directly to the block:

```
.comments-and-analysis { /* ... */ }
.comments-and-analysis--highlighted { /* ... */ }
.comments-and-analysis__para { /* ... */ }
.comments-and-analysis__para--bottom { /* ... */ }
```

Using BEM notations gives us some solid benefits:

- As all selectors use class names, every selector has the same specificity. Hijacking styles higher up the cascade becomes much harder.
- The cascade in your CSS structure becomes obvious, making it easier to maintain and understand what is going on.
- A predictable, modular pattern for extending existing CSS emerges.

A valid criticism of BEM is that it adds more noise to your HTML; elements' class name values are much more prominent than other parts of the markup. I agree that BEM isn't perfect, but I strongly believe that it's much better than any other current alternative. When it comes to HTML and CSS, you need a certain number of hooks to define the relationship between element and style. These hooks can make either your HTML or CSS more complicated. It's better to add this complexity to your HTML because a BEM style selector acts like a unique key in both your HTML and CSS, making it easy to trace the relationship in either direction. The verbosity of BEM is what makes it predictable and easy to work with.

BEM's verbose use of class names always attracts strong opinions. Here are three opposing ideas about how to use class names.

1. Class names should describe the content semantically

Traditionally thought of as best practice, this naming convention actually provides very few benefits and affords us no room to maneuver to create maintainable CSS structures. Before responsive web design I was a firm believer in deriving semantic meaning from class names, and I would always highlight the CSS Zen Garden website[6] as an example of the ability to use semantically appropriate class names while maintaining a firm control over the design. But I was wrong. The truth of the matter is CSS Zen Garden is just a tech demo; its designs are derived from what is possible within the confines of the markup.

Nobody makes CSS separately from HTML. In a development team you don't have the HTML guy sat next to the CSS guy delivering their responsibilities in isolation of each other. HTML and CSS are always written together at the same time. It serves no real purpose either, as web browsers, search engines and screen readers will ignore the values in the `class` attribute. The only computational benefit is for microformats.

2. Purely semantic HTML without class names should be used

It sounds impossible, right? A great argument for this has been written by Heydon Pickering in his article on *Semantic CSS With Intelligent Selectors*[7]. Heydon's argument is that if you write your markup semantically enough then you don't need classes and can use intelligent selectors instead. Here's an example:

```
// HTML
<a href="/previous-article-snippet/" rel="prev"
class="prev">previous page</a>

// CSS
a[rel=prev]:before {
  content: '2190'; /* encoding for a left-pointing arrow ("←") */
}
```

Because the hyperlink in the code above has been given a `rel` attribute, we can use a selector that is unique enough to target and style this element. `rel="prev"` gives us the same hook as the class name alternative `class="prev"` for our styling, but it gives the hyperlink contextual value. Again, I think this approach is a little too idealistic. It works at the atomic scale of a design (naviga-

---

6 http://www.csszengarden.com
7 http://www.smashingmagazine.com/2013/08/20/semantic-css-with-intelligent-selectors/

tion elements and forms, for example), but when it comes to building the layout of a page there aren't enough unique elements and properties to hook your CSS to. If you take a design like the Guardian newspaper's homepage, there will be promos to story pages that semantically are identical, yet they will be presented very differently.

This approach also doesn't lend itself well to some of the advantages afforded to us by *progressive enhancement* (PE). Using PE we can change a hyperlink into a button and use AJAX to pull the linked content directly into the page. In this case we may want to make the hyperlink look like a button.

Heydon correctly criticizes BEM methodology for being too verbose, adding too much noise to the HTML document, and breaking the single responsibility principle (HTML for content, CSS for presentation).

3. Class names are for describing the semantics of presentation

The BEM approach. All class names have semantic meaning, but that meaning is not applied to the content[8]. The primary goal for an element's `class` attribute is a hook for the developer to apply styling and interaction. Classes are there purely for developers to take advantage of. I'm not suggesting that we start using class names like `big-bold-header` — we should still use semantic names, but the names should give us presentational semantic value. Using BEM's naming convention to define modular HTML and CSS components is the best naming strategy.

BUILDING PREDICTABLE, SIMPLE CSS: ORGANIZING SASS FILES

Following conventions in your code is one thing, but even if your classes are well named, you need to order them properly to make sense of the structures you create. Defining your CSS as modules has many advantages. It promotes re-use throughout your code, meaning you can reduce the amount of CSS required (as you accurately guessed, this is referred to as being DRY — don't repeat yourself — in programming) and it makes the structure of your CSS highly maintainable. Thanks to CSS preprocessors like Sass we can separate CSS into logical

---

8   http://nicolasgallagher.com/about-html-semantics-front-end-architecture/

divisions and keep them in separate files. If you follow BEM methodology it will give you an obvious idea of how to break your CSS into separate files. Each block that you define with BEM can become a CSS module and live in its own file.

When devising your file structure it's important to think about how other developers (and you in six months' time) will use it. Deeply nested directories with vague sounding names will make searching for code and interpreting your intent difficult. For example, here is a limited example of the current responsive BBC News Sass directory structure:

```
sass/
    partials/
        components/
            _block-e/
            _block-f/
            _block-g/
            _block-h/
        fixes/
            _old-ie-fixes.scss
        helpers/
            _horizontal-divider.scss
            _url64.scss
        pages/
            elections/
                _colors.scss
                _election-results.scss
                _layout.scss
            live/
                _base.scss
        views/
            partials/
                _block-a/
                _block-b/
                _block-c/
                _block-d/
            _compact.scss
            _core.scss
            _shared.scss
            _tablet.scss
            _wide.scss
        services/
```

```
news/
      _config.scss
      feature.scss
      smart.scss
      tablet.scss
      wide.scss
arabic/
      _config.scss
      feature.scss
      smart.scss
      tablet.scss
      wide.scss
```

It all seems a bit random, doesn't it? We never intended this, but as the codebase has evolved over time, more features and developers have been added to the project. Managing this growth has been hard. Of all the different parts of the responsive news codebase (which includes large amounts of PHP, Ruby, HTML, JavaScript and CSS) we've refactored the CSS the most. This is because it's very hard to build large amounts of CSS.

To be fair to my development team, we do go through periods of mass feature development followed by a technical debt catch-up, where necessary refactors will be undertaken. At the time of authoring this chapter, we are once again refactoring our CSS to be more component-focused. A shallow-nested, wide file structure is a better strategy than the one exhibited above, as it will make it easier to scan the structure of your CSS. We could further change the list above:

```
sass/
   browser-fixes/
      _old-ie.scss
   components/
      _block-a/
      _block-b/
      _block-c/
      _block-d/
      _block-e/
      _block-f/
      _block-g/
      _block-h/
```

```
content-sections/
    elections.scss
mixins/
    _horizontal-divider.scss
    _url64.scss
services/
    news/
        _config.scss
        feature.scss
        smart.scss
        tablet.scss
        wide.scss
    arabic/
        _config.scss
        feature.scss
        smart.scss
        tablet.scss
        wide.scss
```

The example is a little contrived as the number of subdirectories within *components/* would be much higher, but you should get the gist of what I'm trying to achieve. The *fixes/* and *helpers/* subdirectories are moved to the top and renamed to *browser-fixes/* and *mixins/*. The vague-sounding *partials/* is removed completely and replaced with *components/*, which is much more obvious. Another vaguely named *directory, pages/*, is correctly renamed *content-sections/*, which denotes additional styling that is not based on page type but, rather, content. Changes like this have helped the BBC News development team in the following ways:

- We've moved towards working with a living style guide. When we first started the site in 2012, it was fairly simple. The CSS was structured to work with just three page types, each containing a small number of components. As the amount of page types and components have increased, the importance of components has come to the fore and we are now structuring our CSS around that.
- As more developers joined the team we've had to make the structure much more modular to allow multiple contributions. A developer is

now much more likely to work on a component than a page type, so atomizing the CSS into components also matches how we work.

- Swapping out or replacing components with new versions is easier now there is a single, obvious place to edit the CSS for each component.

There's one final important thing to note. A Sass convention is used for naming files that are not to be changed into equivalent CSS files. Any file name that starts with an underscore (e.g. `_horizontal-divider.scss`) will never be converted into a CSS file. This handy visual indicator immediately tells you if a Sass file is to be consumed by other Sass files.

BUILDING PREDICTABLE, SIMPLE CSS: USING MEDIA QUERIES

When building a responsive site there are elements of your design that you need to consider when the layout adapts to a change in viewport size:

- Typography: size, leading and measure of the text all need to stay relative to one another.
- White space: margins and padding will need to change to help you specify the relationships of elements in your interface as well as the intended content hierarchy.
- Positioning: you need to make the most of the space available to your content.

By using media queries in our CSS we control when styles are applied at specific viewport widths. Although media queries are an essential part of realizing a responsive design, the declaration of selectors is too verbose. Look at the example below. Applying a default value to a style and overriding it at two viewport sizes requires us to declare the selector three times:

```
body {
```

```
        background: red;
}
@media (min-width: 320px) {
        body {
            background: white;
        }
}
@media (min-width: 768px) {
        body {
            background: blue;
        }
}
```

A nice feature of Sass is the ability to nest media queries within selectors themselves. This syntax isn't available in native CSS but it's really useful because it reduces the amount of code you need to write. Using Sass we can make the example above much terser and more readable using nested media queries:

```
body {
    background: red;
        @media (min-width: 320px) {
            background: white;
        }
        @media (min-width: 768px) {
            background: blue;
        }
}
```

Don't repeat yourself (DRY) is a good programming principle being applied here: the body selector is used only once. The physical space on the screen between the media query and the style properties is reduced. If you think about it, we're using a visual design affordance: implying a relationship by placing two items closer together, and so making the brain work less to decipher the code.

When you start to interpret a responsive design you should put a good deal of effort into thinking about how you are going to build the site. There are typically two strategies you can pursue when using media queries:

• Define breakpoints up front and apply them globally across a site. This strategy effectively builds vertical silos of designs for you to apply styling to. We can refer to this technique as using macro media queries.

- Add media queries into your CSS as and when you need them. This can be thought of as using micro media queries.

These two strategies map nicely onto two different mental models designers use to shape a responsive design:

- Content out: adding breakpoints as and when they are required.
- Device first: Defining the canvas size of devices and adding content to fit into these predefined constraints.

While the first is a much more holistic approach to responsive web design, it's a much harder paradigm to understand. Designers and developers coming from a typical desktop-only background often struggle to come to terms with the content-out approach. Pointing at two different designs and saying, "This is what mobile users will see, and this will be what tablet users will see" is a very simple and easy to understand way of communicating to customers, project managers and other potentially non-technical stakeholders.

At BBC News our designers have typically created four versions of every design: feature phone, smartphone, tablet, and desktop designs. Using a device-first approach works for us as there are many people involved in the initial design stage. Having documents we can refer to and have conversations around is essential.

Unfortunately, the four designs don't translate into code as easily as we hope (see the aside "Changing How We Work" for more information about this). A good developer will use the four designs as guides to how they are supposed to work rather than interpreting them as strict instructions.

Aside: Changing how we work

As we learn more about responsive web design and improve how we practice it, the BBC News development team has started to change how designers and developers work together. We've come from a typical development practice that meant designers spent a long time working out a design before presenting it to a developer to build. While it's important for everyone to get an understanding of what will be built, we've found it can be detrimental to your productivity to do too much design work before developers get involved.

Static designs do not consider many of the challenges the web brings us. Static designs won't tell you how to deal with:

- Hostile experiences in browsers: there are many different rendering engines and loading conditions we have to cater for.
- Massive variation of screen sizes: defining four breakpoints up front before the problem has been fully explored means you put form before function.
- Connection speeds: balancing performance against the amount of content and functionality in a design is impossible to do if the design is finished before any development concerns have been thought about.
- The variability of interaction types: the correlation between screen size and input type is quickly blurring. There is no longer any guarantee that small screens equal touch and large screens equal mouse.

To combat these challenges we're slowly changing to a more collaborative way of working. In some teams designers work directly with developers, quickly mocking up designs for developers to turn into code. It's only then that the team decides which parts of the design work in browsers. Other teams have found it easier to produce the largest and smallest designs in Photoshop and Illustrator, and hand over only those to development, allowing the developer to work out the designs between.

The most interesting approach has been in the BBC News visual journalism team. Some journalists have produced very rough working prototypes to explore an idea. This prototype is then handed over to a designer who improves the interaction and layout. Once the journalist and designer are happy, the prototype is handed to a developer, who rebuilds the prototype to create a robust and responsive codebase that works across the entire spectrum of supported browsers and devices.

These different ways of working depend not just on the type of work being done (creating templates for CMSs as well as quickly built interactive infographics), but also on the skill sets available to each team. Some designers at BBC News will have good HTML and CSS abilities and will be able to create prototypes or even fully functioning, production-ready code; others will be comfortable working purely in Photoshop and Illustrator. The same, too, goes for developers. I like to use the term "UX developer" (which I consider myself to be) to describe a developer who has an appreciation for UX and can interpret designs and use them as a guide.

Other developers will be most comfortable translating a design directly into code without trying to interpret it. Of all the different changes responsive web design has forced on us, the largest and hardest one to adapt to has been the change to how we all work together. When we first built the responsive version of the BBC News site in 2012, we adapted how we worked as a small team very quickly. But since then, we've had to integrate these changes in working practices with the rest of the business. In a business as large as BBC News, this transition can take a long time.

When translating designs into code, you can continue to follow either of the two approaches mentioned earlier:

- Define your media queries up front, splitting the output into separate width-based files. Using Sass @if statements to break each CSS component becomes a distinct pattern in your code. This can be thought of as using macro breakpoints.

- Or, add media queries to each component as and when needed. Think of these as micro breakpoints.

Device-centric (Macro) Media Queries

A device-first approach to your CSS will require some up-front thinking and Sass plumbing. You'll need to decide what your macro breakpoints are going to be. Typically, people think of these around device types: mobile, tablet and desktop. You'll need to use some Sass syntax to get this to work. Here's an example:

```
// tablet.scss
$tablet: true;
@import 'components/block-a';

// _block-a.scss
.block-a {
    background: gainsborough;
        @if $feature {
                width: 240px;
                font-size: 18px;
        }
        @if $smart {
                width: 320px;
                font-size: 20px;
        }
        @if $tablet {
                width: 768px;
                font-size: 24px;
        }
        @if $desktop {
                width: 1008px;
                font-size: 20px;
        }
}
// outputted tablet.css
.block-a {
    background: gainsborough;
    width: 768px;
    font-size: 24px;
}
```

While this approach still allows you to share styling across each macro break-point (look at the properties with @if statements in the example above), you will need to think about how each generated CSS file is loaded into the browser. A good rule of thumb with responsive web design is to only download what you are going to use, so we can use a JavaScript function to help us do this:

```
function decideWhichCSSToLoad () {
    var width = document.clientWidth;
    if (width >= 1008) {
        loadCSS('desktop.css');
        return;
    }
    if (width >= 600) {
        loadCSS('tablet.css');
    }
    if (width =< 599) {
        loadCSS('smart.css');
    }
}
```

Lazy loading content into the page

One technique the responsive BBC News website executes well is loading non-primary content into the page using AJAX. We refer to this process as *transclusion*. To transclude is to load one hypertext document into another. We label content as primary if it's related to the URL of the document. Any content on the page that is not related to the URL is secondary.

The secondary content is fetched from endpoints linked to from the page. JavaScript scans through the DOM, replacing any hyperlink with its linked to document if it has the class .fetch. This works well for old, feature-poor browsers. Because we don't serve these browsers any JavaScript, the page they render is much lighter and simpler. The users of these browsers can still see all of the content, but they need to make additional clicks.

Making multiple subsequent requests, especially for small fragments of HTML can have a negative impact on performance. To tackle this we do what we call a *super transclude*. If we know what all of the requests for secondary content are going to be, we create an additional endpoint for the JavaScript to pull down all the extra content in one request. JavaScript can then break the single response up into its constituent parts and add them to the correct areas of the DOM.

When executed at page load, the JavaScript function mentioned above will correctly load the right CSS file to match the user's viewport size. However, as soon as a user changes the orientation of their device, the width of the viewport may increase or decrease dramatically (especially as 16:9 aspect ratios are very common on smartphones) and will require a different CSS file. We could handle this using JavaScript to listen for changes in orientation:

```
window.addEventListener('resize', decideWhichCSSToLoad);
```

Loading the newly required CSS via a JavaScript event will produce a noticeable delay as the browser will need to wait for the requested resource to download and be rendered. This lag will be even more noticeable on a mobile connection because first, they are typically slower than broadband; and second, to reduce battery drain mobile devices will disable their radio connection to the mobile network (i.e. the closest mobile phone mast) once a page has finished downloading, so requests made after the fact have to wait for the device to re-establish an internet connection.

Caching

One way to deal with having to make requests for external asset files (CSS, JavaScript, etc.) is to get the browser to cache the responses once they've been downloaded. Browsers now have various strategies you can use for caching other than setting the expiry date on the file; for example, throwing the content of files into localStorage or using the Service Worker API. Regardless of how you cache the file it's important to understand how long you will need to cache the contents for and also what content to cache.

With non-responsive, small sites we can normally store all of the required styling for a site into one CSS file. Users will need to download the file on the first page they visit, but subsequent pages and visits will benefit as the file will be loaded from the cache. This may not be the best strategy for a responsive site, however, as the amount of styling needed for an entire responsive site may be very large. Deciding how to cut up your CSS into separate files always involves balancing the benefits of caching for subsequent pages versus the download time for the initial page.

Personally I'd always opt for downloading payloads as small as possible for the following reasons:

- The initial impression your user gets when they first come to the site is important. If this experience is too poor then they won't continue around your site, so you won't benefit from caching anything up front.
- The size of caches varies massively on mobile devices and they're much less reliable than caches on desktop browsers. Even if you do tell mobile browsers to cache a file, there's no guarantee it will actually happen.
- When a new version of the site is available, you need to break the browser cache and force the user to re-download any cached assets. If you work on a product that practices continual delivery (i.e. you are releasing multiple versions of your CSS or JavaScript every day), then you're more likely to need to break the cache more frequently than the frequency of your users' visits.

Macro breakpoints do have advantages. I find that the four designs I am handed by a designer give me around 80% of the layout that I will end up needing in browsers. However, I am an experienced developer with a good knowledge of UX and can generally work out the last 20% on my own. Less assertive or inexperienced developers might struggle with this approach.

A device-first approach is also becoming less relevant to our industry. Two years ago you could definitely place all devices into one of three buckets: mobile phone, tablet, computer; but today the distinction is less obvious. Phones, tablets and laptops are diverging every year, diluting the differences between them.

The tipping point is the iPhone 6 Plus. It's a very popular device that is somewhere between a phone and a tablet. It doesn't really fit into either category and if we were to use our device-first media query strategy it wouldn't match any of the macro breakpoints.

The wrong reaction to the iPhone 6 Plus would be for designers to start producing five designs, because sometime in the next 18 months a new device we don't know about will come out that won't fit into any of the five macro breakpoints. The only way to stay future-friendly is to be device-agnostic; that is, always take into account the massive variance of combinations of browser, connection speed, screen size and input type our users have.

Trent Walton wrote an excellent blog post on this issue called "Device-Agnostic"[9]. Trent writes about this topic so elegantly that I highly recommend that you read his article right now before carrying on with this chapter. While I think it's still good practice for designers to produce four designs to help the team understand the intent of the design, when these designs are implemented they need to be coded in a way that doesn't use the designs as constraints.

Content-Out (Micro) Media Queries

Designing content out means thinking about your design without the constraints of a device. This is hard to do as we typically contextualize our designs by thinking of the way they work on a phone or tablet. The responsive web doesn't really have edges, there's no set width or consistent fold; defining your layout from your content is the only way to be truly responsive. However, designing in this fashion is hard if you are used to working only in Photoshop or Illustrator, as the only way to see when the layout starts to break is by looking at the design as code in a browser.

---

9   http://trentwalton.com/2014/03/10/device-agnostic/

If you are able to work in this fashion then you will be able to code each CSS module to its own specific requirements independent of other modules. For example, width properties can be set to the exact pixel values required by the layout for each module separately:

```scss
// _block-a.scss
.block-a {
   width: 100%;
   @media (min-width: 320px) {
     width: 320px;
   }
   @media (min-width: 768px) {
     max-width: 768px;
   }
   @media (min-width: 1008px) {
     width: 1008px;
   }
}
// _block-b.scss
.block-b {
   width: 100%;
   @media (min-width: 575px) {
      width: 575px;
   }
   @media (min-width: 768px) {
      width: 768px;
   }
   @media (min-width: 977px) {
      width: 882px;
   }
}
```

While the device-first approach creates a uniform consistency of breakpoints across all of your modules that may seem preferable (especially as you can define them using variables to reposition a breakpoint with one quick edit), over time, treating each component with its own targeted breakpoints becomes more maintainable. There are two reasons for this:

- As you have to support an ever increasing diversity of device screen sizes, a content-out approach means you would already have thought about and catered for your design at viewport sizes that aren't currently popular.

- Giving each component its own breakpoints effectively decouples components from one another. You could update and release a small portion of your CSS to cater for new devices, without having to make large, global changes to your CSS (as we will discuss later on: small changes are easier to test than large changes).

Structuring your CSS content out lends itself nicely to some increasingly popular front-end strategies. Development teams are starting to create living style guides of HTML and CSS: pattern libraries that are maintained and contributed to independent of the pages that consume them. Think of these as an organization's own version of Twitter Bootstrap. The ability to develop components in isolation becomes critical as the number of components in a library increases. A component's ability to remain consistent regardless of the others in the page is essential as it reduces the complexity of the overall system.

Another increasingly popular strategy is to place inline a certain percentage of the CSS required for a page, typically the CSS that defines the beginning of the content (see the aside "Defining the Fold in a Responsive Design" for an explanation of this). While putting JavaScript and CSS assets inline is generally considered bad practice (owing to the decrease in caching capability and a blurring of separations of concern), this strategy takes into account and prioritizes the *perceived* rendering performance of a page over the actual rendering performance. De-normalizing a selection of your CSS by inlining it allows the user to immediately start consuming the content and not notice that the page is still loading (see "CSS and the critical path" by Patrick Hamann for more information on this technique[10]).

---

10   https://speakerdeck.com/patrickhamann/css-and-the-critical-path-cssconfeu-september-2014

Defining the Fold in a Responsive Design

Typically, the fold is the line in a webpage defined by the bottom of the user's screen. Before responsive web design this was quite clear-cut: a 1,024×764 monitor resolution meant the fold was somewhere around the 650px mark. The name of this cut-off point derives from print design. When presented in a newsstand, a newspaper will usually be folded in half. It became a standard design practice for newspapers to place attention-grabbing content above the fold.

The idea of a physical fold is incompatible with responsive web design. The context of a fold is too dependent on the user's device and so is meaningless in a world of multiple devices. Prioritizing the rendering of the beginning of the content is an interesting idea though, especially considering the complex nature of performance that responsive web design gives us. If we thought of the fold as a limit in size of content rather than rendered length of content on the screen, then we can actually define a fold across all devices for us to target.

You could measure this responsive fold in either kilobytes or time to render. Once you have an idea of where your responsive fold is, you can then de-normalize the loading of your CSS (i.e. place it inline) to speed up the rendering of the beginning of your content.

How you decide to use media queries in your CSS is up to you. Personally, I'd opt for a content-out approach as it's the most future-friendly, but I'd lean towards a device-first approach under the following conditions:

- Your team has well-defined development and design roles, does large amounts of design work up front, and works with external stakeholders.

- The interface is very simple and straightforward, lending itself to stretching out across viewport sizes. Large bodies of text work well in this respect, as large changes in whitespace on either side of a collection of paragraphs won't distract someone from consuming the content.

- When you know you definitely only have to cater for a limited number of devices. If the business proposition was only for smartphones, then you're looking at viewport sizes ranging from about 320px up to 480px in portrait mode, and 600px to 700px for landscape mode — so you can make assumptions about required breakpoints. Be careful, however; browser and device support requirements often change throughout the life cycle of a project. Even if you think you only have to support iPhones, then this is already non-trivial as iPhones 4, 5, 6 and 6 Plus all have different viewport sizes.

A nice compromise between the two approaches is to instruct your designer to create designs at the two extremes of the device widths you want to support, and then let the developer work out how the design adapts between them. Producing designs for the smallest screen size and the largest will allow you to split your workflow into two distinct design and development phases, giving your designer the time to go and explore the problem, without spending too long on designs that might not work at medium viewport sizes at all.

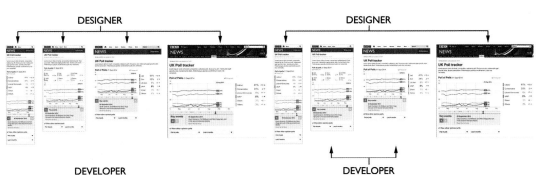

Designing for multiple viewports takes up valuable time without giving you feedback on the feasibility of the design.

An alternative to this is to design at the extremes and let the developer (with your assistance) work out the design for the viewports between the extremes. This will work well if your developer has an understanding of UX.

When starting a new project I always try to make big decisions based on the lifetime of a codebase. In my experience a codebase lasts roughly three years before it's considered legacy and will need to be replaced wholesale.

Think about how your users will behave over that three-year period. Will they still be using IE8? Will they try to access your site via an Apple Watch or a kind of device that hasn't even been invented yet? In three years' time the only certainty is that the problem will be even more complex, so a content-out approach to structuring your CSS is definitely the best strategy. However, it is the hardest way of designing and building websites.

Designing in the browser is a great way to work if you can do it, but don't be dismayed if you struggle. Web development is a multifaceted discipline often involving teams of people. It's much more important to be able to work together in this mixed discipline team. Whether you are designing in Photoshop or browsers, the essential thing to do is look at how your webpage behaves in browsers and then make a definitive design choice. Dan Mall (a co-author of this book) coined the phrase "decide in the browser" as a better way to describe this approach: design wherever you want, but don't make the final decision until you've seen a working prototype in a browser.

KEEPING CLEAR SEPARATION OF CONCERNS

The Sony Experia Tipo comes with a recent version of Android. With a screen resolution of 320×480px, it's one of the smallest smartphones available.

Presentational logic at the extremes of responsive web design can get complicated. When you're designing content to work on massively different screen dimensions — say, a Sony Experia Tipo phone (320×480 pixels) and a 27" iMac (2,560x1,440 pixels) — the layout can change radically. It's easy to fall into the trap of quickly appending a CSS fix into JavaScript to deal with an obscure edge case or bug that crops up towards the end of a project. Such fixes quickly build up and make your code hard to manage. Keeping a clear separation of concerns — JavaScript for behavior and CSS for style — is vital to keep your code maintainable.

An all-rounder who works on websites almost entirely on their own might not see a clear separation in what they build. By mixing these concerns in your code, not only are you hurting maintainability but the code also becomes difficult to test. With a small change to your coding style we can very quickly make your code much more testable. Here are a few lines of JavaScript, for a button that makes an element appear on the screen:

```
$('.button').bind('click', function () {
    $('.element').show();
});
```

This is a perfectly valid way to apply this logic, and you could test it appropriately like so:

```
$('.button').trigger('click');
expect($('.element')[0].display == 'block').toBeTruthy();
```

But the JavaScript here is mixing up different concerns. Not only is it applying interaction, it's also directly adding styles to the element in the DOM. Another code smell is the need for the test to trigger a DOM interaction. What we really want to test is the code we write, yet to initiate our code we have to get the browser to fire an event. Here's a better way:

```
function showElement () {
    $.('.element').addClass('show');
}
$('.button').bind('click', showElement);
```

We'd now test our functionality like this:

```
showElement();
expect($('.button').hasClass('show')).toBeTruthy();
```

This is much nicer code because:

- There is a true separation of concerns. JavaScript applies no styling, but a hook for CSS is added.

- Our code uses an event to bind our business logic to an interaction in the DOM, yet we can test our business logic separately without ever worrying about the browser's event logic.

- The code reads much more clearly.

This change makes our code less implicit and more declarative. Declarative code is better because we state what we want, rather than implicitly try to apply it (the execution is extracted away in the function showElement).

This separation makes the application of our business logic more concise and easy to read. The execution of our business logic is isolated into a single function that can be reused but, more importantly, is easier to test. Concise, predictable and easy to read code should be a core objective when you are writing JavaScript. Ideally, you should only add comments to your code when you need to. Note the following line:

```
$('.button').bind('click', showElement);
```

It almost sounds like an English sentence. When you read it ("button bind click show element"), you can understand what it is doing, so you don't need to comment it. The line in our test reads even better: "expect button has class show to be truthy".

Code can get complex quickly. if statements and looping control blocks aren't really important and get in the way of understanding the real purpose of coding: what you're trying to achieve. By writing JavaScript in a style that separates our three concerns (content, style and interaction) we can improve the maintainability of our JavaScript.

This change in how we write JavaScript is very relevant to responsive web design. For example, I built a responsive version of the "clickable guide" format for the BBC News website.

Because the proposition of the content is very much dependent on the background image, it doesn't really scale down to mobile phone sizes very well.

When viewports are wide enough, the clickable guide renders a large image with hotspots. Clicking a hotspot reveals additional content.

Viewports smaller than the main image still get all the content, but it's listed on the page.

This interactive element essentially has two modes that we call "interactive" and "list". When the viewport is too small to display the background, we list the content in the page.

Switching between the two layout modes is done via JavaScript by adding and removing two classes on the top-level element:

```
function switchLayoutMode () {
  if ($(window).width() >= 976) {
    clickableGuideElm.addClass('interac-
tive-mode');
    clickableGuideElm.removeClass('list-
mode');
  }
  else {
    clickableGuideElm.adClass('list-mode');
    clickableGuideElm.removeClass('interac-
tive-mode');
  }
}
window.addEventListener('resize', switch-
LayoutMode);
```

At no time do we directly manipulate a style via JavaScript. We keep a strict separation of concerns using classes as hooks between JavaScript and CSS. We use BEM methodology in our CSS. When it comes to switching between layout modes we break with the general BEM convention of not nesting classes within each other:

```
.interactive-mode {
  .clickable-guide__main-image-holder {
    display: block;
  }
}
```

```
.layout-mode {
  .clickable-guide__main-image-holder {
  display: none;
  }
}
```

Developing and debugging the different modes of this responsive interactivity was simple because I could switch between them by changing the width of the browser window. However, debugging other types of responsive interactive content, like a quiz with different interface states that can take up to 10 clicks to reach, can be more tricky. Making a small change, hitting the refresh button and then having to go through a sequence of 10 clicks to see that change can be very time-consuming and frustrating. Being able to use JavaScript to quickly change the setting of your quiz to its end state will solve this frustration. You can add a line of debugging JavaScript to help you default the quiz to its end state:

```
$('.quiz').addClass('end-page');
```

Debugging the end state now becomes much simpler.

IMPROVE YOUR KNOWLEDGE OF TESTING

It's important to get a feel for when testing becomes a necessity and what types and levels of testing need to be implemented. There are two conditions that guide my decision about when to start testing.

First, the most important factor is how much trouble you are likely to get into if a bug creeps its way onto your live site. The more severe the outcome is for a bug, the more important it becomes to write tests. If you're making a banking website where users pass sensitive information, start writing tests. If the income of your company depends on the website, start writing tests. But if you're making fluffy stuff, say an interactive map that highlights the most popular breed of dog in a particular area, then testing becomes less important.

Second, the bigger a project becomes, the more invested I would be in testing. This is true for size when it comes to the amount of code, features and team members. When constantly iterating through a site's features it's easy to create regressions, breaking or altering pre-existing functionality. It's vital to have a suite of automated tests you can run to prove previously created features still work as expected. Members of development teams change, people take knowledge with them when they leave. A suite of tests will provide your team with documentation of how features are supposed to work.

Once you've decided that it's time to create tests for your product, you then have to decide how you want to test. The testing discipline offers many different techniques — it's easy to become dogmatic and write too many tests.

Testing takes time and energy, so you aren't going to deliver code as fast as you used to. The trade-off is that the quality of your work improves immensely. You need to find the right balance between code quality and time to deliver. Again, think about the potential severity of an outcome.

For instance, if I were responsible for an e-commerce site, I would probably put more effort into testing the payment processing web forms than the search listings. Releasing small rendering errors to a listing page will result in the user's search experience becoming slightly worse. We could create high-level visual regression tests (explained in more detail below) to compare the current version of the page with its previous iterations. This would be a quick and cheap way to tell you if something has changed without you having to write complex code tests.

But an error for the checkout form might result in the user paying too much by accident, or not being able to purchase at all, so I'd make sure that the web form was covered by unit and functional tests. These are harder to create but prove that the web form works every time you run them.

After you've identified what you want to test, it's time to look at the different ways we can test code and layout. Once we've done this we can start to put together a test plan. Here are some typical ways a responsive site may be tested.

Manual Testing, or Browser and Device Testing

This is as basic as we're going to get with testing. Responsive web design makes this different, though, as we now have multiple types of devices to test. Having a list of all the features or pages of your site and their functions is important.

The list informs the tester of what it is they actually need to test and whether your site is achieving its objectives. If you don't have any kind of requirements list then the tester won't know if anything is missing or whether the site matches your intentions. Responsive web design makes this type of testing hard because you need to check everything several times in different devices as well as different browsers.

Exploratory Testing

Instead of going through your site confirming that specific parts of it work as expected, with exploratory testing we randomly go through the site looking for problems. Professional testers will be particularly good at exploratory testing as they will know of common issues or patterns to test for: does your payment system web form work with negative numbers? Will your webmail client work if you right-click on a link and open in a new window? Will the JavaScript library for parallax scrolling cause IE8 to burst into flames? Does anything work in the Nokia Ovi browser?

Functional Testing

Functional testing takes a more formal approach to manual testing. It involves creating test use cases to verify specific functionality. Functional testing introduces us to the concept of testing frameworks: programs or online services that will run our functional tests against a website or codebase to confirm that the tests are passed. (*Selenium* is a popular testing framework.) Functional testing shouldn't cause too much trouble in responsive design if you follow the content parity paradigm, meaning that all functionality is provided at some level to all visitors of your site. However, you will run into issues if you do not provide the same functionality to all users irrespective of their device.

Unit Testing

Here we look at the absolute smallest testable part of an application and test it in isolation: testing components of the page instead of the whole page itself. A framework will be used based on the programming language you want to test.

For example, JavaScript has many different unit testing frameworks, the most popular being *Qunit*. Because we are testing parts of our application in isolation, there may be other parts of the code that are required for the unit of code to be tested. These dependencies can be substituted for mocked alternatives. You can use unit testing to visually test individual parts of CSS using *PhantomCSS*.

Visual Regression Testing

Comparing two screenshots of the same URL and visually highlighting the difference between them is visual regression testing. It quickly shows you what changes have happened to the page. This is a great way to test for changes or regressions in the layout of a webpage, especially if there are subtle differences in your layout depending on viewport size. Even minor changes like a 1px difference in whitespace can be picked up. When you think about how much time manually testing a responsive website could take then you can start to see the benefits of this way of testing.

AUTOMATED TESTING

The ultimate goal of all testers, and it should be yours too, is to automate as much testing as possible. You can't automate manual or exploratory testing, but you can automate functional, unit and visual regression testing.

Most of these testing techniques can be defined and implemented by a tester. Unit testing is slightly different, though, as it is highly dependent on the structure of code. It's more typical for a developer to create their own unit tests using development techniques like TDD (test-driven development) and BDD (behavior-driven development). An outcome of TDD is a suite of unit tests that can be automated. An outcome of BDD will be a mixture of unit and functional tests that can also be automated.

The ideal situation to be in is to have a suite of tests you can run automatically to ascertain that your code and the layout of your site are in good working order. It's unrealistic to expect this test suite to give you full coverage of code and layout. There are just too many variants when it comes to responsive web design: multiple browser rendering engines, devices with different default font and viewport sizes, and users who change the default settings (like zoom, for example). Even if you could test all of the different variants, it would make your test suite take too long to run. And if it takes a long time to test your code, you'll be less inclined to test.

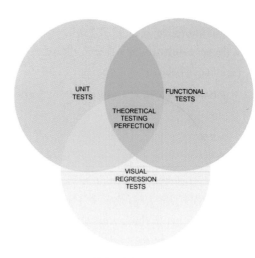

Holy trinity testing

You'll never be able to automatically test all of the different circumstances webpages face in the wild, but you should try to get yourself into a situation where you have a minimum amount of tests that give you a high enough level of confidence that you won't deploy any more than minor mistakes.

Confidence is the key to all this. Make the change, then run the tests. If we automate as much as possible then it frees up more time to spend manually testing aspects of our codebase that are hard to automate. Elements of your codebase that you should try to automate testing for are:

- layout (in a single browser rendering engine)
- code
- business logic

We can automate the testing of layout, code and business logic using what I like to call the holy trinity of automated testing. You'll find a convenient Venn diagram explaining it on the next page. Mapped to client-side technologies, this roughly translates to:

- functional tests covering content (HTML)
- unit tests covering behavior (JavaScript)
- visual regression tests covering presentation (CSS)

Doing this will allow you to concentrate your manual testing on the aspects of responsive web design that are hard to automate: multi-browser testing, and client-side performance.

No matter how good the dev tools in Chrome become, we will always need to test our code in other browsers. Unfortunately, this is hard to automate. You can always use testing services like BrowserStack[11] but the problem with this is that you're removed from the devices' browsers. It's impossible to test the performance of your site if a browser or device is on the end of an API or only available to you as a screenshot on a website.

Aside: Automating the Testing of the BBC News Quiz Component

The quiz format was originally a one-off interactive that we had made the previous year to cover the Iranian presidential election. We asked our users a number of questions about themselves to see if they would be a valid candidate for president. It was successful so we reused the code for two additional quiz interactives, adding more functionality along the way. When we decided to make the quiz available as a standard component type in our CMS, we formalized the functionality of the quiz by creating a mixture of functional and unit tests to develop against. These tests became the business logic for the quiz.

The functional tests of the quiz format made sure that the title of the quiz and the base element were rendered correctly.

---

11 http://browserstack.com

The functional tests were very high-level, there really just to confirm that our server-side logic (PHP and database) correctly built the HTML that served as the starting point for the quiz. The functional tests made sure that the title of the quiz and the base element where questions would appear in the page were rendered correctly. We also used the functional tests to make sure edge cases worked properly.

For example, as the quiz is rendered using a PHP application, we needed to make sure that the correct error responses were displayed. If the application threw a 500 (problem with the code) or a 404 (quiz not found) error then we'd need to ensure the user received not only the correct error response but also the right caching metadata. (We cache 404 responses the same as 200 responses — for 60 seconds — because that's the expected response when requesting an asset that doesn't exist. We do not cache 500 responses as we never intend for errors to happen, so we do not want that type of response to hang around in our cache.)

Because the quiz is mostly interactive content — a basic HTML form with content that changes when you press a button — most of our testing effort was put into unit testing the JavaScript. We completely refactored the JavaScript and CSS from the original interactive.

The original and subsequent iterations were made to very tight deadlines so the code was rushed and not as good as it could have been. We used TDD (our library of choice was Jasmine[12]) to define how the quiz would work. Once enough JavaScript had been written to pass the unit tests, we could refactor and add additional features to the quiz. As long as the unit tests were passed we would know we had not broken any of the existing functionality, so we could refactor with confidence.

Finally, we used Wraith[13] to visually check for any regressions to the styling of the quiz (Wraith is built and maintained by BBC News). This is an important step as the team responsible for the quiz is a different team than maintains the story pages that the quiz appears in.

---

12   https://github.com/pivotal/jasmine
13   http://bbc-news.github.io/wraith/

This final step ensures that any layout changes caused by updates to the story page or the quiz will be flagged to our testers. Sometimes these changes will be *deliberate* because of a new feature, but sometimes they will be an unintentional regression caused by some of the integration issues.

All three types of testing can be run automatically to check for:

- changes to the HTML output and any errors with the rendering layer (PHP and database)
- changes or errors with the JavaScript
- changes to CSS

Developers and testers in the team run these tests locally. The tests are also run every time a developer makes a new commit to our code repository. We can also run the tests against any of our development environments (integration, test, stage and live).

Doing this will allow you to concentrate your manual testing on the aspects of responsive web design that are hard to automate: multi-browser testing, and client-side performance.

No matter how good the dev tools in Chrome become, we will always need to test our code in other browsers. Unfortunately, this is hard to automate. You can always use testing services like BrowserStack[14] but the problem with this is that you're removed from the devices' browsers.

The extra whitespace created by adding a ghost column increased the legibility of the text.

---

14   http://browserstack.com

It's impossible to test the performance of your site if a browser or device is on the end of an API or only available to you as a screenshot on a website.

Although the change in the design was a great improvement, it caused a problem with the clickable guide component

When Small Changes Go Bad (A War Story from the Trenches)

The BBC News website is made by many designers and developers working in different teams, all with their own areas of responsibility. Among the teams are: the news core team (general ownership of the responsive site, looking after index and story pages); and the visual journalism team (infographics and interactive content, building mostly components to go into pages). In October 2014 the news core team made a change to the story page to improve the reading experience. At viewport sizes of 600px and above (roughly speaking, tablets and desktops), the whitespace on either side of the main body was increased. This extra whitespace increased the legibility of the text.

To increase the horizontal whitespace around the main column, its width had to be decreased. At tablet and desktop widths we apply a 12-column grid to the page. We reduced the size of the main column by one column on either side. Shrinking the main text by two grid columns meant a 624px column would shrink to 493px.

The change in the design tested really well and, when released to production, was a great improvement to the site. Unfortunately, it caused a problem with the clickable guide component (used for displaying contextual information about an image) owned by the visual journalism team.

Why This Happened

There are two reasons why this error occurred. First, the clickable guide component was too coarse. Each version of the clickable guide (976px, 624px and 464px wide) required a minimum amount of width to render. The 624px version, for instance, will render all of its contents as a list up to a 671px breakpoint. At 671px there was enough room in the previous design to change the layout of the content from a list to the interactive infographic. Although we were able to use a media query to correctly work out what the viewport size was, it didn't inform us that the available space in the DOM had shrunk by 16%.

Second, there wasn't enough communication about the change. By the time the news core team had pushed the change to production, there was nothing the visual journalism team could do about it. While both teams did test their changes before each release, they performed their tests in isolation.

How We Solved It

The long-term solution would be to make the clickable guide component's design more robust; to make the interface scalable so it would fit in a greater number of available slot sizes. While this large piece of work will happen in the future, we applied a quick fix to the problem. Clickable guides 976px wide push the secondary column below the central column.

We decided to add a single column mode to the BBC News website, regardless of the available space in the viewport. You can see this in action independent of a clickable guide: go to a story page and add the class name `full-width-mode` to the body element.

For clickable guides 624px wide we made the image break out of the narrower column and fill the whole width of the main column. We also improved our testing to make sure we'd catch this problem before it would make its way to the live site again. Using Wraith we now automatically check the visual rendering of a BBC News story page with a clickable guide in it. Every time one of the teams makes a change to either the clickable guide or the story page, we are alerted to any differences in the way the component renders in the page.

A third, more controversial way of solving this problem was to avoid making clickable guides at 624px resolutions. It sounds bizarre to solve a problem in this way, but when you're working in a business with many teams and people using multiple production tools and ways of working, sometimes avoiding the problem can be the simplest solution.

Future Solutions

A big lesson I learned from this is that when you're contributing code into pages where you have no control of the layout and don't know when or if the layout will change, then you need to make sure what you're putting into the page is flexible enough to render at any width. Don't build the component to a fixed width; make the design scale to fit any available size.

As discussed in the section "Adding Third-Party Code Always Causes Issues" of this chapter, right now my best suggestion would be to use an *iframe*. Unfortunately, if you are building an interface from a collection of independently built components, then a whole page made up of iframes isn't a great solution, so your mileage may vary with this advice. A good rule of thumb is to only use an iframe for content on the page if you are only going to do it once in that page, or if the component is not primary content (that is, it's a part of the page that isn't related to the URL of the page, like a comments system, for example).

Currently, what our industry is missing is a way to apply styles based on the width of the DOM element our component resides in, rather than the viewport width. I hope in 2015 we'll see the first implementation of element media queries. Element media queries look like the final missing part for building components in isolation, especially as another web technology, web components, is now beginning to be supported and will give us an improved packaging solution for third-party code.

320px

chinese   english   diff

2.73 % different

In the example above, the UK and Chinese homepages of Google are compared.

Performance isn't just about total page rendering time. Our users now expect fast, native experiences. We have to deliver delightful, app-like experiences via our webpages. The only way to ensure you are delivering this is to test your code in these devices. You need to make sure pages download fast, but you also need to check that scrolling and interactions are running at a smooth 60 frames per second.

Building up a test suite involving all three types of testing will mean learning how to practice TDD and BDD. If you write a lot of code you should very seriously learn more about these techniques, but if you are more of an HTML and CSS person who likes to write small amounts of JavaScript then you're better off only understanding how these two techniques work, and should concentrate on learning visual regression testing.

USE VISUAL REGRESSION TOOLS TO SPEED UP TESTING RWD WEBSITES

When you deal with large amounts of HTML and CSS it's easy to accidentally make a change that you didn't intend. Sometimes these changes can be obvious, like removing the entire navigation across your website; sometimes they can be subtle, like an increase in whitespace or a change in the order of items in a list. Before I release a website I will visually check the site for these kinds of errors. I'll look at each page, scrolling down to ensure everything is how it should be.

Responsive web design makes this visual inspection process much harder. The inspection of each page is no longer a simple scroll with visual check. Instead, I have to inspect the page multiple times, changing the viewport size of the browser window for each pass. It's now easier than ever to miss a change.

This process gets laborious very quickly — it's not a task a human is particularly good at. Lucky for us there is a solution to automate this process.

Visual regression testing is a process to automate the visual check of your site that a tester would normally do manually. There are many tools that you can download free to perform this for you. The process involves taking an initial screenshot of a webpage and then comparing it against subsequent screenshots every time you make a change. Any differences between the two screenshots will be flagged up. This makes visually checking your site for any changes or regressions very simple. It doesn't do the manual testing for you, but it does tell you where you need to concentrate your efforts. This can be priceless when you have a large amount of testing to do and very little time (or patience).

Visual regression testing is a popular subject and if you were to Google for resources you'd find many options. Choosing the right one for you depends on your circumstances. Here's a few things I think you should consider:

- *Your runtime environment:* Although we should all be aiming to be polyglot programmers (knowing more than one programming language), homogenizing your technology does have its benefits. If all of your code is in Node, for example, then I think it makes sense to choose a visual regression tool that is installable via npm.

- *Type of comparisons made:* Do you want holistic comparisons made across your entire website? Do you only want to test individual components? Do you want to test the same webpage but at multiple viewport sizes or at different points of the user's experience?

- *Fitting into your existing workflow:* A key objective of any testing step in your workflow should be to be as least disruptive as possible. We don't want production to ground to a halt because we have to test. Some visual regression tools are completely standalone processes, while others are testing frameworks in their own right or are extensions of existing testing frameworks. Also, think about how your tests are run: for example, do you need command line integration?

- *Configuration:* Can you configure the page during the test? Can you run the tests across multiple browser rendering engines? Can you define which plugin is used to make the image diff?

Once you have made a list of your testing requirements it's time to choose what visual regression tool you are going to use. There are many options out there, and three really good ones are:

- Wraith[15] by BBC News
- PhantomCSS[16] by Huddle[17]
- dpxdt (pronounced *Depicted*)[18] by Google

Visual Regression Best Practices

Regardless of which one you choose there are a few best practices and gotchas you need to think about when using a visual regression tool.

Be wary of false positives

You need to make sure your tests are as deterministic as possible. A visual regression tool will point out any differences, so if you have a component on your page that always changes (a date, a time) then this will always be different and your test will flag a change.

Make sure you test the same content. This way you are testing the changes to your code as opposed to changes to the content itself.

The time a page takes to render can also falsely flag as a difference; if an element takes too long to load or fails to load then this will signal a change, too. Most tools will give you the option to add additional JavaScript or CSS into the page before testing. Use this feature to hide troublesome elements before capturing screenshots.

---

15 http://bbc-news.github.io/wraith/index.html
16 https://github.com/Huddle/PhantomCSS
17 http://huddle.com
18 https://github.com/bslatkin/dpxdt

Be deliberate in your tests

It's better to test parts of your UI in isolation. Having one single test that can break because of many different things in a page can make it hard to work out what is going wrong. Finer granularity can help with automated test reports, too.

However, this doesn't mean that you should never test complete pages. It's a legitimate way to test, will result in fast tests (as fewer comparisons are being made), and you need to test the complete layout.

Test consistently

Always make sure you test the same content. You don't want to have to manage your tests — if the content changes every week you'll find yourself having to constantly update your tests. If you are testing a web application then expose ways to set content using either mocked or fixed content. This way you are testing the changes to your code as opposed to changes to the content itself.

Don't compare a broken page with another broken page

Visual regression testing compares images. Two screenshots with the same part broken in the same way will pass a regression test. If you find a problem with a page using visual regression testing, either make sure the problem is resolved and retest, or make a note to yourself to manually check this problem next time.

Watch out for common dependencies

If you are comparing the test version of your site against the live version, and they both rely on the same dependency (this could be third-party social media tools or a service you built yourself that is consumed over HTTP), errors caused by the common dependency will be replicated and will not be noticed in the visual comparison. If this error originates with a third party, then it will probably be a low priority for you as you have no control over it. But if you own the dependency, then you will need to conduct additional testing to make sure you don't miss the problem.

Offline versions of the design or site are still important

Even with visual regression testing in place you still need to know how the site is intended to look. Visual regression testing is a tool, not a magic bullet. Testers need to be able to manually test a site without this tool in place, so they need a visual reference.

Phase 3: Expertly Applying Testing To Your Development Workflow

The final testing phase in your IT career is when you work out the best way of implementing testing within your development workflow. This is normally reached when your thirst for testing has gone too far, or the best practices that used to work for the small product in your brand new startup team have now become anti-patterns for the legacy product that is worked on by your now large, established company.

You'll get to a point where you think you've tested enough, or that your entire testing framework needs refactoring. Congratulations! You've reached peak testing. Everything from here on is relative to your own unique development requirements.

Without a constant eye on the big picture, every IT project will eventually go bad. Too much testing or the wrong kind of testing ends up hurting your productivity. You mustn't blame testing for this, though — the technique is not to blame for how it is implemented.

The best piece of advice you can ever give to someone in IT is this (it encapsulates but isn't limited to testing): don't build big IT projects. Big IT is an anti-pattern. You can quote me on that.

> 66 *Big IT is an anti-pattern.*
>
> — Tom Maslen, 2015

A key programming paradigm for any IT project should be *simplicity*. The opposite of simplicity, complexity, destroys IT projects. More requirements, more features, more team members increase the complexity of what you're

trying to achieve. It creates longer release dates, adds more
risk, increases potential failure and requires more testing.

You should be trying to simplify your product
at all its levels. Simplify what browsers have to do,
and keep designs simple so they can be reused in
slightly different configurations. My advice for
testing is the same. Now, don't mistake "simple"
for "easy" — they're two different things. Easy
means the task is going to be done in five minutes,
or that anyone can do it. Simple means splitting
up your problem into many smaller, logical parts,
giving each part a single responsibility. Simple
means clarity, making what each part of what your
codebase does predictable and, ultimately, reliable.

Code as red units; tests as gray units;
changed code as blue units. With a large
monolithic codebase, making a single
change means running all of your tests
and deploying your entire codebase.

Testing is no different. The difference between
moving from a small site to a large site is that
there is more to test. I've learned the hard way that
you simplify testing a large website by breaking up
the site into smaller, self-contained parts. A large
media organization's website doesn't have to be
one product. You could break it up into multiple
products, each product responsible for a different
content page: an index page application, a story
page application.

If you have multiple mini products, then you
can test each one in isolation. Don't get yourself
into a position where making one change to your
codebase means having to test everything before
you can release. Having to test everything before
each release only works for a limited amount of
time. As a product matures and more features are
added, the testing process becomes more complex.

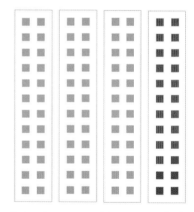

By breaking your codebase into multiple
smaller parts you can make a single
change, run only the relevant tests and
deploy a much smaller section of your
code.

You'll reach a point in your product's life cycle where you will have accrued so much technical debt that you will have to stop delivering features and split up your codebase.

Splitting up your testing into chunks is only possible if you don't have a single, large codebase that can only be shipped in one piece. This means the secret to simplifying your testing process lies in your application architecture.

If the product you are working on has grown organically into a much larger proposition, there is no magic testing bullet. There isn't any methodology you can apply to improve testing. Your only option in staying sane is to refactor and break up your application into smaller pieces. It doesn't matter who you are, how many testers and actual devices you have, or what methodology you use. There are no best practices to making large IT products. If you're testing everything in one go, you're doing it wrong.

IDENTIFYING WHEN TESTING HAS BECOME A PROBLEM

Here are some workflow smells that will tell you if your codebase has become too big:

- Sections of your codebase have had tests run against them more times than they have lines of code.
- Testing takes longer than the development.
- Deployments used to be easy, now they are hard and take longer.
- Team members don't like running the tests.
- Team members start disabling tests to get the build to pass.

If this sounds familiar to you then it's time to break up your product into many smaller pieces. You need to get your project manager to recognize the issue. The longer you leave this, the more features you add, the harder it will be to untangle your codebase and split it into smaller pieces.

COMMON TESTING PROBLEMS AND HOW TO RESOLVE THEM

There are many common pitfalls that all teams get themselves into when testing. Here are a few of them with advice on how to get you out.

Not enough time to test all the browsers

The biggest problem responsive web design presents us with is the increase in what you now need to support. Not only do we have to support many more browsers, we also have to support a crowd of different devices all accessing the internet on a multitude of connection types.

Before the iPhone we had to test across the following variables:

- Browser (Chrome, IE6–IE8, Opera, Safari and Firefox)
- Input type (keyboard and mouse)

After the iPhone we now have to test across the following variables:

- Browser (desktop and mobile Chrome, IE8–IE11, multiple Operas, more than one version of desktop Safari, more than one version of iOS Safari, multiple WebKits, desktop Firefox, mobile Firefox, too many versions of Android, Nokia Ovi, Dolphin and many more I can't think of right now)
- Device size (240px up to greater than 1,000px)
- Input type (touch, keyboard, mouse and D-pad)
- Connection speed (GPRS, 2G, 3G, 4G and broadband)

All of these different variables and their combinations makes testing not only suddenly much more important than before but also much harder. Even companies like the BBC (where I work) struggle with this new paradigm. When your support matrix becomes this complicated, making websites at speed or trying to hit tight deadlines becomes risky. The potential to release bugs into production increases.

You can scale your testing up to meet this demand. You could hire a whole team of testers or try to outsource your testing to India, but this is the most expensive option. A cheaper alternative is to split your testing up into groups, and prioritize what you test. If you tested a select few browsers that you know represent over 50% of your audience, you could then release your latest change and then test the next group of browser/device combos.

This won't work for everyone. If you have a product where the cost of a bug gone live is expensive, then you should be more deliberate and take time with your testing. But if the feature is minor, or the consequences of a bug mean a minor rendering issue then this technique will work for you.

Another alternative is to make your product really simple. Simplify the design, make the JavaScript-driven interface a progressive enhancement of a static webpage, and don't use thousands of lines of CSS or cutting-edge HTML5 capabilities. The simpler a website is, the more likely it is to work across a range of different browser/device combos. You should never underestimate the power of simplicity. Simplicity scales.

Not having enough devices

Lack of devices or not having a large budget to purchase devices is a common problem. Testing responsive web design is expensive: even a minimum rec-ommended group of devices to test (in 2015 this is: non-Samsung Android 4.x, Samsung Android 4.x, iPhone 6, iPhone 5, and your development PC) is going to be expensive.

While testing on real devices is always preferable, sometimes it's not possible and we have to look for alternatives. For desktop browsers it's better that your development machine is a Mac, as you can easily run Windows virtualized via VirtualBox or VMWare to test all versions of Internet Explorer. Microsoft maintains an excellent website, www.modern.ie, that allows you to download virtual machines of their operating system. Testing the other way round, via a PC and using a virtualized version of Mac OS X is problematic.

Google and Apple have IDEs you can download that have built-in emulators for iPhone and Android device testing. Although it's not trivial to get them set up and running, once you have this is a much cheaper alternative to purchasing devices. Your final option should be a service like BrowserStack. Although the barrier to entry of using BrowserStack is much lower than buying devices or setting up emulators, in the long term it is less useful because loading webpages can take a long time.

You can connect your local browser to a browser on a mobile device over WiFi or by USB.

You also lose the immediacy of having an actual device in your hand. Again, BrowserStack lets you test that your layout works and there are no bugs with your JavaScript, but you can't test how the experience feels in the device.

Troubleshooting bugs on mobile devices

The hardest bugs to fix are bugs you can't replicate. You might have a webpage looking really nice in Chrome on your development machine, but then see it rendering incorrectly on your boss's Sony Xperia Tipo. You have a great array of debugging tools on your development machine, but you really need to be able to use them with the browsers on mobile devices. Luckily this problem has been solved with the introduction of remote debugging.

Safari and Chrome both allow you to connect your local browser to a browser on a mobile device. You need to connect the devices either over Wi-Fi or by USB cable (USB is always easier). The syncing can be a bit complicated but once it's done you can then use your local debugging tools on the browser in the phone. When I first saw this demonstrated I wept with joy (I also considered throwing money at the person).

Explaining how this works in a book is useless as the techniques and commands change regularly. I recommend you follow up this technique by visiting the Chrome[19] and Apple[20] online documentation.

19 https://developer.chrome.com/devtools/docs/remote-debugging
20 https://developer.apple.com/safari/tools/

Another pain point with mobile debugging is getting your content viewable in a device. Small teams creating static sites will be able to FTP their content to a publicly viewable space to check on a mobile. But if you are working on a branched version of an application, or the application has a non-trivial back-end that is not easy to deploy, you may want to make your local web server available to view on a device connected directly to the internet.

Services like ProxyLocal[21], once installed on your computer, can make your local web server available on the internet. This allows you to connect any mobile device to your local machine so you don't have to deploy your code to a second location.

Tests take too long, or get in the way of deployment

Tests that take too long to complete can be remedied in a few different ways depending on your situation. The first thing to consider is whether you are testing too much. As outlined above, I strongly recommend that you break up large codebases into smaller fragments; logical divisions of codebases should be tested in isolation. But sometimes this isn't possible.

If this true for you, then here are a few other solutions you can try to improve the time the tests take to run.

Reduce HTTP requests

Look for and remove HTTP requests in the code you are testing. HTTP requests are often performance bottlenecks within web applications. If you are testing a web application that makes its own HTTP requests for data, add a hook into your app so you can set it to use local fixture data instead.

If you are running unit tests for JavaScript that makes AJAX requests, use a library like *Sinon.JS* to mock the AJAX requests. In your tests this is actually preferable to making real AJAX requests as you can control the response. You can deliberately throw 404 and 500 errors and test how your code reacts.

---

21 http://www.proxylocal.com

Speed up your testing

There are many tools and techniques to help you reduce the time it takes to test. *Gremlins.js*[22] is a monkey testing script written in JavaScript for Node and browsers. It tests the robustness of your application by randomly clicking everywhere, entering random strings into web forms and randomly firing events. Leaving Gremlins.js running on your application will also eventually detect memory leaks.

A more deliberate way of testing forms is to prefill your forms with meaningful data. I often find myself filling in a web form quickly, testing something, making a change to the code then refreshing the page, before filling in the web form again. This can be especially tiresome on a mobile device. Chris Coyier's article "Prefill Your Own Forms in Dev"[23] gives a great example of how you can get around this issue.

Testing multiple devices at the same time is also a great way of decreasing the time spent testing. Ghostlab[24] provides a service that lets you synchronize scrolls, clicks, reloads and form inputs across multiple devices. If your JavaScript uses the `setTimeout` method, then your JavaScript unit test will need to wait for the callback to fire, slowing down your tests. Again, Sinon.JS can help as it provides a mocked `setTimeout` method, so you can call a method in your JavaScript, tick the time along and then run our test without having to wait.

Don't run all of your tests all of the time

If you are running 300 tests on each commit, and committing many times a day, you'll spend much of your day waiting for tests to be passed. Much of the time, a good portion of your tests will be checking parts of your codebase that you no longer actively develop. Do these tests really need to be run on every commit? While it's important to make sure all of your codebase does not go stale, you can choose to run parts of your test suite on a daily basis, rather than

---

22 https://github.com/marmelab/gremlins.js
23 http://css-tricks.com/prefill-forms-dev/
24 http://vanamco.com/ghostlab/

on each commit. Running a smaller subset of your entire test suite will speed up your commit workflow.

Run tests in parallel

Modern computers contain multiple processors allowing you to take advantage of serialization, meaning you can run multiple tests at once. You should invest time into seeing if your tests can be run in this way. For example, if you use Cucumber to run BDD tests, you can use the ParallelTests project[25]. If you have JavaScript tests then take advantage of Grunt's concurrent task[26], split your testing into groups and run the groups simultaneously.

Too much is being tested, or testing is duplicated

When using several types of testing it is easy to create duplication in your tests. With BDD tests, you can confirm whether JavaScript is working on a page, but you can also do this with a JavaScript testing framework too. You don't need to test something twice. Unit tests are preferable to functional tests as they generally execute faster owing to the fact that a functional test will need to spin up a web browser and then make HTTP requests.

It's easy to get into the rhythm of continually piling feature upon feature into a codebase. You must not lose focus on the big picture. Continually review your tests. Can two tests now be merged into one? Can we remove certain tests completely? Another problem sometimes is we end up testing too much, especially with BDD.

Because BDD tests are created by listing functionality, it's very easy to map each requirement to a test. While you do want to make sure you capture all of your business logic, you don't want to create too much granularity with a BDD test. Often simply testing to see if a value from the database has been added to the page is enough. Use unit testing to confirm the rest of your business logic.

---

25 https://github.com/grosser/parallel_tests
26 https://github.com/sindresorhus/grunt-concurrent

TESTS BREAK ALL THE TIME, OR THEY ARE TOO FRAGILE

When testing HTML, your tests can become fragile because of the way certain BDD test libraries work. For example, *Jasmine* (a JavaScript framework) allows you to make assertions by searching for elements in the DOM using jQuery:

```
expect($('.pageTitle').html()).toEqual('The end of the world is here!!!');
```

If another developer (let's call him *John*) comes along and decides to refactor all the CSS to use BEM notation, he will change our class name from `pageTitle` to `page__title`. When John runs the Jasmine tests he will get an error: `error: .pageTitle` no longer fetches anything from the DOM.

A better way to write your tests is to use hooks created specifically for tests in your elements. You can do this using data attributes:

```
<h1 class="page__title" data-test-
id="page_title">The end of the world
is here!!!</h1>
```

You can then test for the element's existence using this hook, like so:

```
expect($('[data-test-id=
"page_title"]').html()).toEqual
('The end of the world is here!!!');
```

With this in place, John can refactor the CSS as much as he likes and he won't break our test.

Adding third-party code always causes issues

A common pattern on the web is to include third-party components in your website. From comment plugins to interactive content like maps and charts, to social media buttons, this code written by someone else can cause all kinds of problems. At BBC News this problem also arises between development teams.

We often build responsive infographics and rich, interactive content in isolation from the website. These mini projects are developed by a separate team from the one which develops the website itself. The infographics are static content: once deployed, we never intend to go back and maintain them. However, they reside within a codebase that changes many times a month. If we only had to support Chrome on a desktop computer, much of the complexity of maintaining compatibility between two codebases would disappear.

Unfortunately, this problem is exacerbated by responsive web design because the area in the DOM where the component needs to reside is not one consistent size.

Badly written CSS pollutes the other party's code: CSS's global nature means any CSS can affect any element on the page. If you're lucky then both parties have written their CSS using the BEM methodology. If you've used BEM and the other party has not, then unwanted CSS will be applied to your HTML. Even if there is no pollution, or you've managed to reset all the styles applied to your HTML, then you still have the problem of future CSS selectors and properties that you don't currently know about affecting your page in the future.

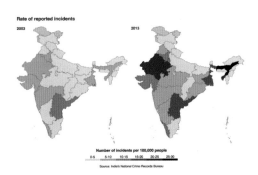

Creating a responsive infographic can be difficult due to the sheer amount of content to display.

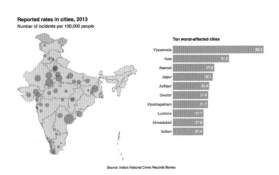

One option to create responsive infographics is by embedding them into a responsive `<iframe>`.

JavaScript has the same concerns, but fortunately a main feature of the language is scope. You'd expect the creator of the third-party HTML not to do something stupid, like define a vague-sounding name (`var i`, for example) in the global scope, which would cause logic between the two parties' codes to leak into one another. A big issue with third-party code is often not the code they write themselves, but the dependencies that come with it.

Another problem is the other code relying on a slightly different version of jQuery that your page does. Double-loading jQuery is an embarrassing performance issue and often causes your code to run in unexpected ways.

Responsive web design makes matching the layout between the two parties' code extremely difficult. If the included code is a very small UI element or something like Google Maps, where the interface basically works at any size or aspect ratio, then you'll get away with this issue. The creator of the plugin needs to make their user interface *very* flexible. Media queries do help with this, but plugin authors can't know what percentage of the width their code will be allowed to expand out into.

It's easy to end up with a very fragile implementation. Fortunately, there is a solution. It involves some JavaScript and an HTML element that belongs to an earlier, more arcane version of the web. An element that's traditionally been very wicked, never positively spoken about, whose only real friends until now have been adverts, and is probably older than you: the iframe.

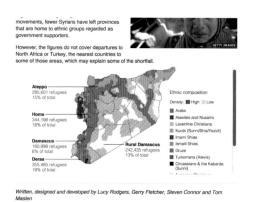

An iframe with an additional scrollbar.

An iframe (inline frame), along with its older brother <frameset>, is an element that allows you to include one HTML document inside another. The very idea of this breaks one of the main concepts of the web: one URL per resource. They act like HTML documents too; you can follow links in them and load another page within the iframe. This action is added to your browser's history, so it can confuse the heck out of users when they press the Back button and the main page doesn't change.

iframes have also traditionally given us accessibility issues, but modern browsers and screen readers are much better at handling them today. The benefit of the iframe is that it's a separate HTML document, so any code you put in it (HTML, JavaScript, CSS, and so on) is completely isolated from the host page. The iframe essentially acts as a sandbox.

The `<iframe>` element is not responsive by default. It acts like a viewport into another document. This means that the height of the iframe element works independently of the height of the iframe's HTML document. Typically, the iframe creates an additional scrollbar in the page allowing users to access content below the fold of the element. Using JavaScript to control the dimensions of the element, you can make any `<iframe>` responsive; see an example online[27].)

As the width of the HTML document changes so too will its height. The variability of the HTML document's width means that we need to set the height of the `<iframe>` element according to the height of the HTML document.

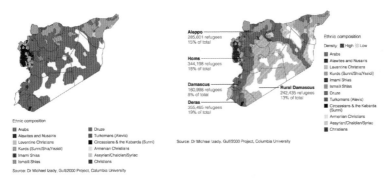

Two images of the same responsive infographic at two different resolutions, showing the variable difference in height and width. The example on the left is rendered in a smaller viewport but requires more height compared with the example on the right.

We can do this dynamically using two snippets of JavaScript. The first, inside the iframe's HTML document, informs the second, in the host page, what the height of the `<iframe>` element needs to be. The source domain of the iframe will often be different from that of the host page, so these two snippets of JavaScript can't talk directly to each other. Standard browser security models will protect your code from malicious third-party attacks by blocking any attempts to interact between scripts that come from different domains. To get around this, our two JavaScript snippets communicate via the browser feature `window.postMessage`. This is an asynchronous communication method in JavaScript.

---

27 http://www.bbc.co.uk/news/world-middle-east-24900116

Here is an example of how it works. First, set up the host page to listen for a sent message:

```
window.addEventListener('message', function (e) {console.log(e.data); //
will output "Hello"
}, false);
```

Then, send a message from the iframe using the postMessage method on the parent's window object:

```
// iframe page
window.parent.postMessage("Hello", "*");
```

Note: this technique can potentially allow any third-party JavaScript to communicate with your code. To find out how to use this feature in a more robust and secure way, read about it on the MDN website[28]. You can download an example of this codebase from Github[29]. Many publishing companies such as the BBC, the Guardian, Telegraph and New York Times use this technique.
The responsive iframe will give you a much more robust way of including third-party code in your page. There are a few gotchas to note, though:

- JavaScript calculates the required height by checking the height of the body in the iframe's HTML document. Any absolutely positioned elements in the document will render separately to the body and so won't be taken into consideration when determining the required height.

- Using position: fixed on an element within the iframed HTML document positions the element relative to the iframe, not the host page. This means the element will not be fixed in the browser.

---

28 https://developer.mozilla.org/en-US/docs/Web/API/Window.postMessage
29 https://github.com/tmaslen/responsive-iframe

- Using any kind of modal state within the iframe will only work within the confines of the iframe itself. If you wanted to use a modal from within the iframe, you need to set the iframe to take up the full viewport of the host page.

- By default, linking to other documents using hyperlinks within the iframe will load the requested page within the iframe. To load a new document into the host page, use the `target` attribute on the hyperlink: `<a href="http://www.google.com" target="_top">Google</a>`.

Ideally, we shouldn't have to use an iframe in this manner to isolate parts of the page from one another. The shadow DOM, which is part of the web components specification, gives us natively sandboxed CSS and JavaScript, as well as a truly responsive element. For now, unfortunately, web components don't have enough browser support to warrant putting this technique into practice, but it does give us a future escape strategy from our current reliance on iframes.

Well-maintained, preprocessed CSS makes debugging CSS really hard

In this chapter I've evangelized breaking up your CSS into multiple Sass files. Sass, like any other preprocessor (LESS, Stylus, etc.), will concatenate all your Sass files into a single CSS file. This is great for performance as the browser will make only one HTTP request for all your styles. Unfortunately, this makes debugging issues harder as the browser's dev tools are not looking at the source files that we edit. When we find a style we wish to change, mapping it to the original source file is not easy.

If you've minified the concatenated output file, the browser dev tools will tell you the style comes from the first line of the CSS file. Not helpful at all.

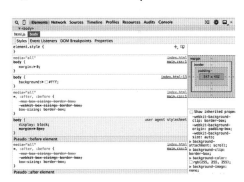

Preprocessed CSS makes debugging really hard because the browser's dev tools are not looking at the source files.

From the very beginning Sass, and LESS helped us by outputting debug comments next to each line of generated CSS. These comments pointed to where in the preprocessor files the styling came from.

```
/* line 76, _normalize.scss */
body {margin: 0;}
```

You can enable CSS source maps in the general settings of Chrome's dev tool.

This is great when you're developing locally but it adds considerable bloat to the file. We wouldn't want to deploy this to our live site as it would increase the rendering time of the page. Once finished working on the page, we'd deploy the CSS without the debugging comments in them. This made investigating CSS issues on the live site hard, as we were once again dealing with minified CSS.

Fortunately, there is a handy feature that helps us with this problem: CSS source maps. Generated by a CSS preprocessor, a source map is an additional file that informs the browser of the origin of each line of CSS in the source files.

To enable CSS source maps you need to:

1. Tell browsers to enable their use. There's typically a setting in the browsers' dev tools. For example, in Chrome 38 it's in the general settings tab of the dev tools.

2. Tell your CSS preprocessor to generate a source map. The preprocessor will append each generated CSS file with a comment informing browsers where to find the map file.

```
main.css
/*# sourceMappingURL=main.css.map */
```

Once these two instructions have been completed, browsers will download and use the CSS source map when the dev tools panel is open. When inspecting a DOM element, each line of styling will point to the original source file instead of the generated CSS output.

You may find setting up your preprocessor to output source maps a little frustrating. I use Grunt for all my front-end dev tasking. Once Grunt runs the Sass task, I instruct it to run `grunt-contrib-cssmin` to minify the generated CSS output.

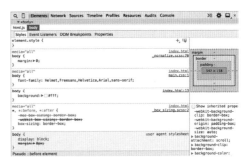

You can now benefit from the concatenation offered by CSS preprocessors without the difficulty a single file presents.

At the time of writing, `grunt-contrib-cssmin` strips out the comment in the CSS that points to the source map. If you are trying to apply source mapping and can't get it to work, check to see if any task downstream of the preprocessing is stripping it out.

Summary

The one theme that I've tried to include throughout the chapter is simplicity. The importance of simplicity would be the one key idea I hope you take from this chapter. Apart from death and taxes, the only other guarantee the future brings is increased complexity. As more people access the web with diverse types of devices, we'll find the best way to tackle this is to make the way we build our products simpler. As developers we now think about performance as a key objective for our codebase (or NFR — non-functional requirement — in product management speak). I'd strongly argue that simplicity should also be a key objective.

Simplicity — and its crime fighting partner, predictability — will persist if you keep doing the following with your codebase:

- Plan the structure of your HTML, CSS and JavaScript — don't make it up as you go along. Modular thinking is key to building maintainable structures of CSS. Always keep in mind the single responsibility principle, not just for splitting content, presentation and interaction into HTML, CSS and JavaScript, but also for breaking up your code into isolated units that are responsible for just one thing.

- When designing and building responsive structures, plan from the content out. Add breakpoints at the point that the design starts to break.

- Start using visual regression testing in your projects today, and start to get a better understanding of other ways of testing as well.

- Be pragmatic. During my career I've swung from one deeply dogmatic way of working (cowboy development) to an opposing and yet still just as dogmatic idealism (testing too much). It's important to understand that delivering on time in a sustainable manner is the preferred way of working.

Hopefully you've enjoyed this chapter as much as I've enjoyed writing it for you. It's taken a long time in my career to get to a point where I can confidently say I'm no longer a terrible web developer.

Cutting The Mustard (continuation of page 368)

Cutting the Mustard is a technique that we've used on the BBC News website to answer the most difficult question responsive web design asks us: how do you support a MacBook Pro with a Retina display and a Nokia C5 with the exact same webpage?

These devices are massively different. Let's take a quick look at them:

Property	15" Macbook Pro (Retina)	Nokia C5
Screen width	15 inches	2.2 inches
Pixel count	2,800×1,800	240×320
CPU	2.8GHz dual-core Intel Core i5	600MHz ARM 11
Memory	16Gb RAM	128Mb RAM
Graphics card	Intel Iris Graphics	n/a
Input	Full keyboard + multi-touch pad	Number pad + D-pad

They are completely different types of device. Their only shared features are:

- a screen
- an internet connection
- a web browser is installed
- a way to input

These devices have as much in common as a luxury yacht and a raft made out of mango trees. To support them both we have to find common ground, somewhere for us to start that we can build on.

The first step of cutting the mustard is to find this common ground: build a basic webpage. This webpage is going to be rendered on a Nokia C5, as well as all the other weird, strange and obscure phones and web browsers out there. This base experience needs to do the following:

- Provide a very basic layout: a single-column design using only HTML4 elements (no fancy stuff!).
- Build this layout using old CSS2 selectors and properties (the only caveat to this is the box model).
- Don't use any JavaScript, or at the very least use only minimal JavaScript (Google Analytics doesn't count in this statement so add that in if you want to).

- If you have content that you want to load in with JavaScript, add a link to the body of your page connecting to another webpage with that content in it (we'll talk about this in a moment).

This webpage is now so basic that anything can render it. The webpage should be able to resolve the needs of your users at the most basic level. If your site is a content-publishing site, then users should be able to read all your content. If your site is an e-commerce site, then your forms should be POST-able, and work without JavaScript. If your site is a web application, then your users should be able to log in without JavaScript and immediately see stuff and potentially interact using POST-able forms.

Supplying a base experience to all users essentially lowers your site's barrier to entry. I like to think of each website I build as a shop. You wouldn't make a shop with a door that is thin, short, shut and takes 30 seconds to open. You'd want the shop door to be as wide and high as possible, open and requiring no effort to walk through. You'd make sure there was nothing stopping people from entering your shop. Yet by making websites that aren't accessible, usable, don't work without JavaScript and are slow to load, you're essentially raising that barrier to entry, making it hard for people to enter your shop.

The next step in the cutting the mustard technique is to add a JavaScript application that improves the base experience. This JavaScript will progressively enhance the base experience, adding more CSS to improve the layout (this is where we can actually implement a responsive layout) and interactive elements into the page (drop-down or slide-out navigation, a dynamic shopping basket or auto save when features are toggled).

Not all browsers get this content, however. The JavaScript application should be conditionally loaded by checking to see how modern the browser is. You can do this with a simple bit of JavaScript feature detection:

```
if (
    "addEventListener" in windows  &&
    "localstorage"     in document &&
    "queryselector"    in document
) {
    // load the premium experience
}
```

If a browser passes this test, we say it cuts the mustard. Can you see what we did with the name?

There is a nice correlation between all browsers that cut the mustard. They are all modern browsers with good HTML5 and CSS3 support. They also have good support for W3C specifications, so you can depend on small, modular JavaScript libraries like Zepto, Ender and jQuery 2. But best of all, problematic browsers that have for years caused us issues — browsers like IE6, 7 and 8 — they don't cut the mustard, so they only get the base experience.

A big criticism of responsive web design is that it doesn't decrease load time and actually makes websites less performant.

This is true of many implementations of responsive web design, but it's not an issue with RWD techniques themselves. You can try to polyfill all the browsers and give them the same experience. You can load hundreds of kilobytes over GPRS connections and force your users to wait until JavaScript is ready before accessing the content. Or you can use the natural ingredients of the web to build an experience that progressively enhances based on the capabilities of the web. Cutting the mustard is an implementation of responsive web design that doesn't try to offer all browsers the same experience, because not all browsers are equal. It's an implementation that recognizes the hostility of the web, and tries to use the way browsers work by default to improve the chances of users getting to the content.

ABOUT THE AUTHOR

Tom gets seriously annoyed when things don't work as expected. He works as a developer within the Visual Journalism team at *BBC News*. When not building responsive infographics, he tends to hunt for Spicy Monster Munch. Tom likes to think that he cuts the mustard every single time he deploys or commits an update, and he still can do the splits (every once and again).

ABOUT THE REVIEWER

Patrick Hamann is a lead client-side engineer at the *Guardian* in London where, amongst other things, he is helping to build the next generation of their web platform. When not speaking or ranting about performance he enjoys spending his spare time discovering new food and craft beer.

RESPONSIVE
EMAIL DESIGN

FABIO CARNEIRO

CHAPTER NINE · BY FABIO CARNEIRO

RESPONSIVE EMAIL DESIGN

EXPLAINING EMAIL DESIGN AND DEVELOPMENT to someone whose primary gig is web design is always an uphill battle, because the majority of web designers already have some sort of idea what it is; many have experience working in the medium, and just about every single one of them I've spoken with *hates* it. To your average web designer, the idea of having to tangle with email design makes them feel very much like the guy in that nice little illustration—stuck on a boat, in a storm, with only a shark for company.

There are some common attitudes web designers have when you ask them about HTML email, and dislike is generally the most common. There's also confusion, and apathy, and — well, you get the picture. They're mostly negative. I've had the conversation about what email design is thousands of times and, almost always, web designers say something I don't believe is true in the least: "Yeah, email design really sucks." That's a tough place to start talking about a particular discipline, regardless of what it might be.

This issue of perception is one of the larger problems in this arena: many web designers think email design is just like web design, but more *wrong*.

More than once, I've heard people say that the practice of designing and developing email essentially consists of throwing modern web design skills and knowledge out the window. But the truth is that designing and developing for email is not about forgetting what you've learned as a web designer; email design is about learning a new set of skills, and working in a medium that shares some commonality with traditional web design, but is altogether *different*.

So, yeah, as a general rule, I don't think email design sucks, but I understand why people think it's some sort of hellish venture. HTML email and a lot of the techniques, technologies, and the industry grown up around it are, in many ways, stuck in the past. For a long time, email was solely the domain of marketers, and things like good design, rewarding user experience, and well-defined content strategy were only considered useful when they were done in service to the almighty principle of ROI. Unfortunately, the perception that commercial email is only about making the largest amount of money with the smallest amount of investment is one that has largely stuck around to this day. It's a state that's analogous to web design back in the mid-2000s, when having a beautiful, usable website was seen more as an isolated, artistic practice. But that was then.

Today, email design is going through an evolution that looks a lot like the one we experienced in modern web design, where design, user experience, content strategy and simple creativity all matter. Also like modern web design, there's a lot of great, forward-looking innovation going on in the email design world.

And that sums up email design as a discipline: a complicated meshing of old and new. It requires the web designer to once again think in `<table>`s versus `<div>`s for layout structure, with all of its limitations and pitfalls, but also involves using modern user experience, content strategy, and design practices to create a great finished product.

If that sounds like a major dichotomy, well, that's because it is. The cool part is that this melding of techniques is absolutely possible. You just need to get the lay of the land before you start.

We've Been Here Before

This is where much of the difficulty inherent in HTML email development starts to become apparent, because the world of email design in 2014 looks a lot like the world of web design did back in the mid-to-late 1990s and early 2000s, when the browser wars were at their peak and web standards was still in its infancy.

Back then, major web browsers like Mosaic, Netscape Navigator, Internet Explorer and Opera (later joined by Firefox, Safari and, finally, Chrome) all allowed users to visit the same World Wide Web, but each worked in a slightly different way and produced a slightly different result in the rendered webpage. Although the HTML 2 spec came on the scene in 1995, followed by 3.2 in January 1997, and 4.0 in December 1997, it took a number of years for web standards to gain any traction, and even longer for the big players in the browser arena to get their products rendering sites according to those newly emerged guidelines. Nowadays, I think it's fair to say that the web design playing field is pretty level; browsers all have good parity with each other and, in cases when they don't, trusty languages like JavaScript are there to bridge any remaining gaps.

None of that ever really happened in the world of email. At least not at the same pace. There are dozens upon dozens of different email clients scattered across multiple platforms — far more than there were browsers — and the rendering engines or code sanitizers of the most popular clients haven't evolved much over time; many are still working the same way they did back when using <marquee> was cool. There's a lot of catching up to do, and there are three major schools of thought around the question of standards for email and how the industry should move forward.

First, there's the old-old-school: that email shouldn't be HTML at all; that an email was never meant to be anything more than a plain text message, and that email, as a whole, isn't a part of the web and shouldn't be treated as such. This argument is made a lot by the extremely security-conscious, but it isn't realistic. That saying that once the genie's out of the bottle, there's no putting it back in is very fitting in this case, and it's abundantly clear that the genie is definitely out of the bottle; a rough estimate via Cisco's Senderbase[1] (which tracks web and email traffic worldwide) shows that there were 432 billion legitimate emails sent worldwide in 2014. That number balloons to 3,034.4 billion if you include spam, which accounts for around 85% of the world's volume of email (spam is, unfortunately, an industry unto itself). Every year, the amount of email sent grows by leaps and bounds; MailChimp, for example, sent 34 billion, 70 billion, and 100.5 billion emails in 2012, 2013 and 2014 respectively. Beyond that, you can look to the massive industry that's grown up around creating and sending email, and at the largest email senders like Amazon and Google, to understand that HTML email isn't going anywhere.

The second school of thought has been around since as recently as late 2014, and is centered around the idea that email should have its very own standard, distinct from web standards, and complete (some argue) with its own markup language, scripting libraries, the works. The thinking here is that the creation of email standards and a dedicated email markup language will formalize email, push the companies behind email clients to modernize and maintain a healthy ecosystem for email, and move the industry forward. But there isn't particularly strong support for this idea, and making it happen would require a concerted effort by a staggering number of companies and people. Given how slowly standards bodies tend to move, it would take at least a decade before anything concrete would present itself. Maybe someday, but, in my opinion, this is one of those "don't hold your breath" sort of things.

Finally, the third view, and the one that I and most others in the email design world find the most realistic: that the standards already exist in the form of web standards that have been set forth by the W3C, and that the catching-up must be done by the companies responsible for the most popular email clients. If that sounds like a familiar situation, that's because it is; web browsers went through the same evolution years ago. Despite the fact that it's certainly not perfect (there would be very little improvement in security, for instance), I think this plan is the most workable in the industry right now, because it's the path of least resistance. The sticking point lies in the fact that the way forward is essentially in the

---

[1] https://www.senderbase.org/static/email/

hands of Google and Microsoft, because their email clients, Gmail and Outlook Desktop, are two of the most popular in the world — yet also among the most outdated. Unfortunately, although both companies have expressed interest in moving forward, neither has yet taken action.

Whatever anyone thinks makes the most sense, email design in the present day is still a discipline centered around the HTML4 and XHTML markup languages, along with CSS2 for styling. And using programming languages like JavaScript to help fix the quirks across email clients? That's a pipe dream, as most email service and email client providers strip out scripting because of security concerns. The email developer is left with two major tools at their disposal: the markup and their wits. Email development has a steep learning curve that's daunting to conquer, in large part because the host of issues inherent to the discipline are:

1. *Obscure*: because there isn't a master list out there that details the problems you can encounter;
2. *Bizarre*: due to inconsistencies between email client rendering engines that multiply across platforms;
3. *Immutable*: because solutions to these problems aren't in the hands of email developers.

Despite these issues, you can still take comfort in the fact that, as a web designer, you already have the lion's share of the knowledge you'll need to develop email. At the end of the day, email is just HTML and CSS, and if you can get a webpage put together, you can do the same with an email. You just have to get used to the fact that, especially at first, it's not an *easy* job to do.

The Email Development Landscape

Good development requires that you know as much as possible about the environment you're working in. In email development, that can be a daunting prospect because of the large number of email clients, including some that have been around for at least a decade. Each client tends to work differently from another depending on their platform or OS, which can make it even more difficult to achieve consistent rendering for a single email.

WRITING HTML FOR EMAIL

Knowing how to write HTML for email is one of the first stumbling blocks that any newcomer to email development will encounter. In essence, there's one major, giant, unmissable difference between building an email and building a website.

You know those `<div>` elements you like so much? Yeah. Ain't gonna happen. Sorry. Building emails requires you to take a trip down memory lane, and build your layouts using `<table>` elements instead.

There are a few reasons for this difference, though it stems primarily from the fact that many email clients don't fully adhere to web standards established by the W3C, and thus don't have equal support for HTML elements and CSS properties among them. Setting two `<div>`s side by side, for instance, is impossible in a number of major webmail and desktop clients, because they don't support the `float` property, meaning that the creation of a two-column layout depends on a table built with two `<td>` elements.

There are a few reasons why clients behave this way, but the particulars aren't especially important. It all boils down to the fact that to get the most consistent layout rendering between clients, you *must* use tables in your build — especially for multi-column layouts.

Beyond this significant difference, the HTML written for email works in much the same way as that for websites. CSS, however, is a different story.

CSS IN EMAIL

While the CSS you'll use in email tends to be pretty straightforward and familiar, there are notable differences that can run counter to established practices and wisdom present in modern web design.

These differences aren't just limited to which CSS properties are or aren't supported. One of the most notable contradictions to modern web design practice involves *where* the CSS goes. While the external style sheet is the most used way to serve the styles of a site, in email linking an external style sheet is a point of failure, since some email clients strip `<link>` elements from the markup. And even if a client leaves `<link>` alone, there's no guarantee that your style sheet will be pulled in and rendered correctly. There are email clients that strip either the `<head>` or `<style>` elements when an email's markup is rendered, leaving the entire thing unstyled — of these, Gmail is the most notable. This means the only way to write CSS and have it affect the markup properly is to write it inline.

Thankfully, this incredibly tedious task isn't something you have to handle yourself, since some email service providers (ESPs) will

HTML goes in; email comes out. You can't explain that.

automatically handle CSS inlining for you as long as an external style sheet exists or CSS is written in a `<style>` element. Unfortunately, you can't always rely on an ESP to do this work, so that's where CSS inliners[2] come in.

All they require is for you to paste your markup, with CSS attached via `<link>` or placed in `<style>`, and the inlining is done for you, sparing you the nasty job of having to do it all by hand.

If you prefer to write all of the CSS yourself, however, you need to keep a few things in mind regarding syntax. Because some clients don't parse them correctly, it's a good idea to avoid shorthand in the CSS you write. For hex color declarations, use `#EEEEEE` in favor of `#EEE`, and don't use shorthand properties like `font` or `background`; stick with writing out each individual property (i.e. `font-family` and `background-color`) instead.

---

2 http://templates.mailchimp.com/resources/inline-css/

Now that you know where to put your CSS, you can go to town, right? Not exactly. CSS support in email is a huge point of frustration for developers because of how wildly different its handling can be from client to client. Properties that any one client might support can vary depending on the rendering engine of the client, or, in the case of webmail clients, their code sanitizers. There are also differences in style rendering based on the HTML element a particular CSS property is used on; padding, for instance, is supported on a `<td>` in Outlook 2013, but not on an `<h1>`.

Some email clients, and web clients in particular, add their own styles to markup elements, with some going far enough to force style overrides that can't be overcome even by the mighty `!important`. These issues can sometimes be compounded by the browser itself; you're forced to account for how the email client renders HTML and CSS, and also how the browser that client is viewed in renders HTML and CSS. An email viewed in Gmail in Firefox, for example, can look different from one in Gmail in Internet Explorer 10.

All that being said, the CSS2.1 specification is going to provide you with the most stability and rendering consistency, as that was the most current version at the time many email clients were built and released to the public. As a general rule, it offers the best foundation for styling in an email. Even then, there are some email clients that don't fully support this older spec — Lotus/IBM Notes, for instance — and that means you could be doing a lot of attribute-based styling if you're required to support these older clients, which many large and slow-to-update corporations still rely on; outdated desktop clients like Lotus Notes or Outlook 2000 are still prevalent across many email lists.

Email Clients

Saying that there are a lot of email clients out there is an understatement verging on the absurd. At the time of writing, and just across MailChimp's user base of more than 7 million users, there are *63 active email clients*.

The majority of that user base is spread across North and South America and Europe. If you pull the view back to the entire world, the number of active email clients is over 100.

If you're new to email design, this fact is sure to give you pause, if not heart palpitations.

But you can rest easy because, thankfully, there's no need to account for every single email client out there. While diversity and competition are normally good things, the market belongs to only a handful of powerful players, which makes the task of developing robust emails significantly easier.

We only need to take a look at these major clients and identify the biggest pitfalls and quirks to look out for. There are three major types of email client to consider when designing and developing an email:

- *Desktop clients*, like Microsoft Outlook, Apple Mail and Mozilla Thunderbird;
- *Webmail clients*, like Gmail, Yahoo Mail and Outlook.com;
- *Mobile clients*, like iOS Mail, Gmail, Inbox, Mailbox, and on and on…

Let's begin with a look at the most popular desktop clients, starting with one that's been the bane of the email developer for a long time.

MICROSOFT OUTLOOK

In your average office environment, the desktop mail client is ubiquitous. Even in this era of mobile-everything, they remain the most common way to check, read and send emails. Of all these desktop clients, Microsoft Outlook is king, reigning supreme as the market share champion across the planet due to its inclusion in the Office software suite. On Windows machines, Outlook comes in two flavors: pre- and post-2007.

Why 2007? Because that marks the year when Outlook's HTML rendering engine shifted from the one used in Internet Explorer 6 to the one used in Microsoft Word. Usually, this bit throws people for a loop, so I'll give you a moment to read that sentence again.

This move made sense to Microsoft for the consumer's sake, since users of Office could put an email together in Word, then send it via Outlook to other people who'd then view that email in Outlook; Microsoft was building

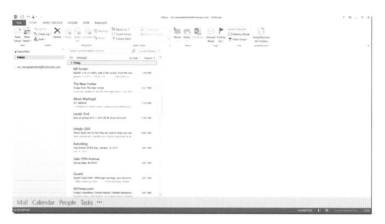

This bit of software is why email developers seem so cranky all of the time.

for a closed environment. Sadly, the introduction of Outlook 2007 and its use of a word processor's rendering engine was a huge step backward for email development, since the Word engine's support for HTML and CSS is atrocious at best. Even the newest version of Outlook, bundled in Office 2016, uses the same engine.

The MSDN is a must-have resource for email developers, even if the content is a little soul-crushing.

Say what you want about IE6, but it at least supported a fairly full array of the HTML and CSS that was more or less modern at the time of its release; from the outset, it was actually built to render that HTML and CSS. Unlike, y'know, a word processor. Almost unbelievably, there's a bright side to this: Outlook might be a terrible email client, but it's been consistently terrible over a *near decade-long arc.* Though it's not an ideal environment to have to account for, Outlook's consistent terribleness makes it predictable and tameable with a couple of resources[3].

---

3 https://msdn.microsoft.com/en-us/library/aa338201.aspx

The first is documentation on the Microsoft Developer Network (MSDN) devoted to the HTML and CSS rendering capabilities of the Word engine (see above). It's a thorough overview of all the HTML elements and CSS properties that enjoy full, partial, or no support in the Word engine, and covers every version of Outlook for Windows from 2007 on. The second resource is one that web designers who've had to optimize sites for older versions of Internet Explorer will be familiar with, the conditional comment[4]:

```
<!--[if gte mso 9]>
    /* Your Outlook-specific markup or CSS goes here. */
<![endif]-->
```

It's the same thing you could use to target older versions of Internet Explorer when building a website, except it targets Microsoft Office, or mso. In the example above, gte is added to have the comment apply only to versions of Microsoft Office *greater than or equal to 9*. You can also target earlier versions by using lt. Using gt and lte will target versions greater than, or less than or equal to, respectively. The Microsoft Office version number that follows allows you to target specific Outlook clients. In the example above,

Outlook 2000	Version 9
Outlook 2002	Version 10
Outlook 2003	Version 11
Outlook 2007	Version 12
Outlook 2010	Version 14
Outlook 2013	Version 15
Outlook 2016	Version 16

mso 9 is Office 2000, which means you're targeting Outlook 2000. Other version numbers allow you to target other clients (see the image on the right side).

Conditional commenting is an invaluable resource, as you'll see later in this chapter. With the weird rendering issues Outlook's engine introduces into emails, the ability to provide Outlook-specific code can usually provide a pretty low-impact, but high-grade solution, allowing you to include HTML or even a CSS style sheet specifically intended to counter the client's long list of quirks.

---

4 https://msdn.microsoft.com/en-us/library/ms537512.aspx

WINDOWS LIVE MAIL

Microsoft has a second offering for Windows in the form of Live Mail, a free desktop client that's bundled inside the Windows Essentials software suite[5].

Given Microsoft's track record with email clients, Live Mail is surprisingly good, boasting pretty broad support for modern HTML and CSS. Even though its rendering engine is leagues better than Outlook's, Live Mail's user base is microscopically small compared to its big brother, not to mention the other clients floating around out there.

Look at it, blissfully unaware of the Word engine.

APPLE MAIL

On the other side of the PC divide stands Apple and its Mail app for Mac OS X, which is mostly flawless as an email client.

Its rendering engine is WebKit, which powers browsers like Safari and Chrome (Chrome uses a fork of WebKit's WebCore component, named Blink), and even that of the PlayStation 4. CSS support is state-of-the-art, and includes CSS3, media query and web font support.

MOZILLA THUNDERBIRD

The email client from the same company responsible for Firefox is, as you'd probably expect, a good solid email client. Unfortunately, its user base is pretty small among other desktop email clients.

Thunderbird is a cross-platform client, available on both Windows and Mac OS X machines, and it works much the same way on both because of a rendering engine that's shared with Firefox.

---

5   http://windows.microsoft.com/en-us/windows-live/essentials-other#essentials=overviewother

Webmail Clients

Webmail is how the world receives its email, even though its popularity has been sinking year after year owing to the rise of mobile readership. It wasn't always like this; back in the mid-1990s, webmail began its meteoric rise with the release of HoTMaiL, one of the first free email services available on the web.

OUTLOOK.COM

Microsoft's Outlook.com is the current evolution of that client. It's easy to take pot shots at Microsoft and some of its products, but Outlook.com ranks as one of the best webmail clients available today.

Its support for HTML and CSS is very robust, though it isn't perfect: web fonts aren't supported, and neither are more advanced CSS3 properties like `animation`. It also has some pesky CSS quirks that are known to cause frustration, like the lack of support for the `margin` property, and finicky handling of `line-height`. Thankfully, these issues are fairly minor and easy to work around.

YAHOO MAIL

Another email client with a long history, Yahoo Mail, launched in 1997 during the free webmail boom. Today, it's the third most popular webmail service after Gmail and Outlook.com.

Like Outlook.com, Yahoo Mail has come a long way over the years, and boasts fairly comprehensive support for HTML and CSS. It does, however, fall short on support for CSS3 properties like `border-radius`, and doesn't support web fonts.

GMAIL

Of the major webmail services, Gmail is the youngest, only becoming available to the general public in 2007.

In the relatively short amount of time it has been around, Gmail's user base growth has been nothing short of explosive, owing to the proliferation of Android devices worldwide. Ironically, despite its newness, Gmail's email rendering capability is closer to desktop Outlook than Outlook.com. That's primarily due to the fact that Gmail's code sanitizer strips `<head>` and `<style>` elements, meaning all CSS in an email needs to be inlined in order to work, which makes responsive email impossible.

AOL MAIL

Finally, there's AOL Mail, and it's one of the better webmail clients out there. No, seriously. Its rendering engine is better than those you find driving some other webmail services.

It has its share of problems, however. Like Gmail, CSS needs to be inlined for styling to render because `<head>` and `<style>` are both stripped from the email's HTML. This also means that media queries aren't supported, despite the fact that the client itself is adaptive on smaller displays. Additionally, there's a lack of support for some CSS3 properties.

Mobile Clients

Mobile clients have taken a huge chunk of the email client market in the last three years, and now account for over half of all email opens worldwide. That shouldn't be terribly surprising; both email and mobile phones (and, to a lesser extent, tablets) are very personal, vital parts of modern life. Our devices are always with us, and, by extension, so is email. A mobile-centric web ecosystem isn't the future; really, it's the *now*. But that doesn't mean email on mobile doesn't suffer any of the problems of the past.

GMAIL

Gmail on Android and iOS is a prime example. Both mobile versions of the client share a host of problems with their webmail counterpart.

That means you'll run into the same issues raised by Gmail's lack of support for non-inlined CSS. This includes Gmail's nonexistent media query support, which means that true responsive email isn't possible in Gmail on mobile devices. Google's new Inbox app is exactly the same, sadly.

IOS MAIL

If Gmail represents the bad end of the mobile client spectrum, then iOS Mail is undoubtedly on the good end.

Much like its desktop Mac OS X-based cousin, iOS's version of Mail is almost entirely without fault. CSS3, media queries, web fonts — support for all of it's there. It has the rendering engine that lesser apps aspire to have.

OUTLOOK.COM

If you're not a big fan of either Gmail or iOS Mail, there's a great third option. The Outlook.com app, which is available on Android or iOS, is fantastic.

Email rendering is just about perfect, with robust support for CSS3, media queries, web fonts, and just about anything else you want to throw at it.

The Question Of Market Share

Whether you're developing emails for yourself or someone else, knowing the distribution of these email clients across the list you're sending to is an invaluable bit of information that can allow you to fine-tune your code to offer better experiences for readers.

Many ESPs will provide that data for you, but if you're in a corporate or agency setting, you may not have access. If you can't currently get that sort of data, you should fight tooth and nail for it, because developing without the knowledge of whether or not you have to support a particularly bad client is a massive handicap.

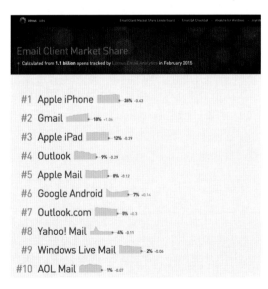

Although emailclientmarketshare.com is a mouthful for a URL, it's a wonderfully helpful page.

iOS	45%	ANDROID BROWSER	5%
GMAIL	10%	OUTLOOK 2007	4%
OUTLOOK.COM	8%	YAHOO! MAIL	3%
APPLE MAIL	8%	ANDROID MAIL	3%
OUTLOOK 2010	6%	WINDOWS LIVE MAIL	2%

The top ten clients used by subscribers across MailChimp's entire user base.

If you still don't have access, you can find more generalized market share numbers on the web, though it might take a little bit of hunting. Litmus, helpfully, has done some of the footwork here.

Though its numbers are calculated from a relatively small portion of email opens, the snapshot of market share that Litmus presents is accurate, and they end up being fairly similar to the top ten clients used by subscribers across the lists of MailChimp's entire user base (see the image above).

In the end, all the work of knowing what CSS is supported where, and which clients are the most popular in the world, or a particular country, or on an email list, is foundational. It's not the end point of great email design and development, it's where you *start*.

Armed with the knowledge of what can and can't be done in email because of the constraints put in place by email clients, it should be plain to see that designing for email isn't exceptionally different from designing for the web — there are simply more limitations to work around.

Emails Aren't Websites

For anyone new to email design, thinking of emails as single-serving websites isn't a bad parallel to draw, but it's important to keep in mind that a lot of the concepts that may be familiar on a website don't completely translate to email, if at all.

That being said, it doesn't mean you should throw out the window every principle of good design or development you've ever learned. Many of the same concepts translate from web design to email design; they just need a bit of adjustment to work effectively in this new medium.

"ALMOST" IS GOOD ENOUGH

Avoiding slavish adherence to a design is the most important principle to keep in mind when designing and developing email. In this discipline, the mantra that will preserve your sanity is a simple one: *pixel-perfect design is a fool's game.*

Because of the differences between how email clients render styles, combined with the sheer number of active email clients out there, exactness of design just isn't a viable goal. More often than not, trying to get an email to look the same across a variety of clients and platforms only guarantees that you'll have wasted a vast amount of time. Seriously. Don't bother. It's not worth it.

Even something as fundamental as the box model isn't rendered or handled consistently across email clients. To a web designer, the basic diagram of the box model should look pretty familiar:

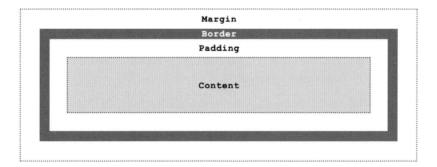

The box model is a foundational standard of the web, so of course it's totally wonky in email. #yolo

Email designers can't take box model rendering for granted, however, because some major clients don't have full support for even the more basic box model properties. Notable examples include Outlook.com, which has no support for margin, and its desktop sibling Outlook 2007 (and newer), which has no support for `height`, `max-width`, or `min-width`, and inconsistent support for `padding` and `width`, depending on the element. On top of all of that, desktop Outlook also plays it fast and loose with its dpi scaling[6], which can cause your email to look quite odd.

All this being said, it doesn't mean you can't get close to pixel-perfect design in your emails, or that you shouldn't bother trying to normalize styles across clients, but it's important to remember that email design is less about remaining perfectly true to some PSD you've got, and more about building the best version of that PSD across different clients. Email design is the exact science of inexactness. As Bruce Lee once said, "...be water, my friend."

AUDIENCE DETERMINES EVERYTHING

Good email design, like web design, requires context. Knowing *how* to design an email so that it holds up across multiple clients — and avoiding pixel-perfection when you do — is only the first step of the entire design process. Think of it as the mechanical part of the task.

Knowing *who* you're designing for, then what you're designing for them is what actually creates context; it's the organic bit. Context in email is different from context on the web, however. Websites are generally made to cater to everyone, because there's a whole planet of people out there who can end up visiting the site. Because of that, design and top-level site content tend to be geared towards a fairly wide audience, and more narrowly focused subjects get relegated to deeper parts of a site. One of the chief strengths of email is that it allows you a much greater degree of focus and clarity. This is because email is

Finding reviews for a specific platform, like Playstation 4,
requires drilling down Polygon's navigation.

---

6   http://blog.jmwhite.co.uk/2014/03/28/solving-dpi-scaling-issues-with-html-email-in-outlook/

based on interest and participation; much more than any website or social media service, email can have an incredible degree of relevance because you can cater to very specific groups of people. Because the user comes to you and signs up for an email (or purchases a product), you have some information to start with, and a purpose to design to. There's more context because you can ask for it.

A sign-up form is the most basic way to glean a bit of hard information about who your audience is. Having that information is immensely powerful, because it allows you to tailor the design, development and content of your emails to better serve relevant and useful content.

You can focus enough to give that one person — or a group of people who think in similar ways — what they want because email is a much more iterative medium than a website is; it's possible to test, tweak and tune your message so that you zero in closer and closer to something people value, since feedback is on a quicker timeline.

The sign-up form for MailChimp's UX newsletter allows recipients to choose an area of interest.

PURPOSEFUL DESIGN

Another way to achieve that focus is to design an email to have one purpose and to meet a particular goal. The aim of all email falls into four broad categories, which is a good place to start:

1. "Read Me" emails, also known as newsletters
2. "Buy Me", or e-commerce emails
3. "Join Me" emails, which serve as singular calls to action
4. Transactional emails, built to deliver information

The first three categories of email are known as one-to-many messages: sent from one point and delivered to several, via a list of subscriber emails. They're so prevalent in our inboxes that clients like Gmail and Outlook.com have entire feature sets dedicated to sorting and categorizing them.

The first category, *Read Me*, covers emails that are generally centered around the purposes of cultivating relationships and spreading ideas, like MailChimp's UX newsletter.

Built for the consumption of content, these emails depend on nicely thought out typography and, most importantly, strong writing. They're also the only type of email that can work well while ignoring the 'shorter is better' rule of thumb for email.

The second category, *Buy Me*, covers retail emails. The best-designed emails in this group focus on a single goal, the creation of enticement in a recipient to spend money.

A good e-commerce email relies on the use of compelling imagery, clear calls to action and concise copy to focus the recipient's attention on the act of clicking the 'Shop Now' button and spending some money.

The third category of emails, *Join Me*, are also built around the idea of persuading a recipient to take action, though not necessarily in service to making a buck (see example on the next page).

Issue 27 // Concepts and Code

As UX designers, developers, and researchers, our objective is to create experiences that are straightforward, positive, and satisfying—but this isn't easy to accomplish! Creating a good user experience is the result of careful consideration, constant tweaking, and lots of feedback. A typical project involves our UX designers working through and prototyping an idea, followed by our UX developers stepping in to begin building it. But then we're faced with yet another challenge: the intense process of actually creating something that achieves the look and feel that we originally envisioned and intended.

A long-form email covering a variety of subjects, the UX newsletter goes out to over 22,000 subscribers.

The simplicity of design in Everlane's emails ensures that the product takes center stage.

The clear, interesting presentation of important details make Brother Moto's email a very effective one.

Transactional emails work best with simplified, easy to understand layout and content.

Join Me emails range from event notices to invitations, party announcements to survey requests. In these emails, information hierarchy is the key to their usefulness; it's best that important details such as date and time be clearly defined and obvious, and calls to action should be bold.

In the final category, *Transactional*, emails are made to convey information in a straightforward and comprehensive way. Transactional emails differ from the other three types in that they're one-to-one messages, and are triggered by — you guessed it — a transaction.

A fairly wide variety of emails falls into this category, including receipts, order summaries, and security and delivery notifications. Despite this broad range, they all share a single important feature: clarity of information. Well-designed transactional emails should be focused, practical, and free from as much distraction as possible.

Giving your emails one of these specific purposes and designing with the aim of fulfilling that purpose makes the task of sending more useful and relevant email much simpler, and it's one of the best things you can do to home in on a better experience for recipients.

TYPOGRAPHY MAKETH THE EMAIL

If there's one constant that's threaded across each of these categories of email, it's type. It's difficult to overstate how massively important textual content and, in turn, typography is to email, but its significance is easy to grasp: unlike any other sort of content you can drop in an email, it's the one thing that is consistently rendered across different clients.

In many emails — most of them, I'd venture to say — typography doesn't get the attention it deserves. Not by a long shot. In emails from retailers especially, real text is often completely ignored in favor of in-image text.

The trouble is that desktop clients like Outlook 2013 and Thunderbird block images by default, and webmail clients like AOL Mail block images from first-time senders. And `alt` text? It isn't guaranteed to show, meaning that emails that rely on images for all of their content can end up being entirely meaningless.

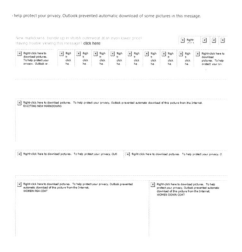

Not even Professor X could tell you what this email is for. Thanks, Outlook 2013

Ideally, your message should still come across without images, because email recipients will almost always see the text of an email before they see anything else. That makes typography your email's most important design asset.

Certainly, there are differences between how typography is handled in email and how it's handled on the web. For starters, there's a wide amount of variability between the possible units of measurement. The em and rem familiar to web designers all get rendered differently across email clients, if they're rendered at all — most of the time, measurement units are converted into the kind that the email client prefers. Even if you luck out with unit rendering, some clients may override any styles you provide. Line height is particularly troublesome; there are varied baselines in Gmail (13px), Outlook.com (15px) and Apple Mail (12px), for example. Consequently, they wreak havoc with type that's sized with the more malleable em or rem.

Which unit is rendered most consistently and explicitly? The almighty pixel. 16px is 16px across most email clients, meaning px should be how you define text sizes and line heights across emails. That doesn't mean you should rush to set up a perfect typographic baseline for your entire email; pixels may render consistently, but some clients (desktop Outlook, in particular) force a conversion to points, and other clients may force spacing overrides that ignore the styles you set.

Semantically structured content also plays an important role, though this is a point of contention in the email design community. The argument against using semantically meaningful elements like <p> and <h1> in email stems largely from the fact that some email clients have built-in CSS overrides for some elements that make semantically marked-up content more difficult for a developer to style. Older clients can also present problems for semantic markup, as some require the use of the <font> element for any sort of text styling.

Though the line between semantic and non-semantic markup is blurrier in email than it is on the web, ultimately there's enough consistent support across email clients to stick with the practice — even if it means compromising on some parts of an email's design. That's because of one significant reason: semantic markup is hugely important for accessibility. As far as many assistive technologies like screen readers are concerned, an <h1> has a higher semantic importance than an <h2>, which has a higher semantic importance than a <p>, even if it's in email. I believe this fact trumps the arguments I've heard purporting that semantic markup makes email development more difficult.

My view essentially comes down to this: do as much as you can get away with. It doesn't always work out perfectly, of course; in older desktop clients especially, there's no appreciable difference between <b> and <strong> and font-weight: bold;, but making your email more accessible is still worth the effort. An email that ends up with a slightly different line height than you intended in one or two clients is a fair trade for it being more easily understood by someone using a screen reader.

You also need to keep track of widely supported cross-platform fonts, and include them in your font stacks after more exotic choices. It's worth the effort to provide comprehensive font stacks, since it's relatively little work to ensure wider design fidelity across clients:

```
.bodyContent {
    font-family: 'Open Sans', 'Helvetica Neue', Helvetica, Arial,
sans-serif
}
```

You can most reliably count on quite a few of them, all oldies-but-goodies, to supplement typefaces that more appropriately fit your design:

Sans-serif

Arial		Arial Black		Arial Narrow	
Win: 99.84%	Mac: 98.74%	Win: 98.08%	Mac: 96.22%	Win: 88.39%	Mac: 94.77%
Arial Rounded MT Bold		Avant Garde		Calibri	
Win: 59.53%	Mac: 95.14%	Win: 0%	Mac: 1.08%	Win: 83.41%	Mac: 38.74%
Candara		Century Gothic		Franklin Gothic Medium	
Win: 83.08%	Mac: 34.41%	Win: 87.62%	Mac: 53.15%	Win: 99.18%	Mac: 2.1%
Futura		Geneva		Gill Sans	
Win: 1.26%	Mac: 94.41%	Win: 2.08%	Mac: 99.64%	Win: 58.54%	Mac: 95.5%
Helvetica		Impact		Lucida Grande	
Win: 7.34%	Mac: 100%	Win: 0%	Mac: 95.14%	Win: 0%	Mac: 100%
Optima		Segoe UI		Tahoma	
Win: 2.52%	Mac: 93.89%	Win: 75.36%	Mac: 0%	Win: 99.95%	Mac: 91.71%
Trebuchet MS		Verdana			
Win: 99.67%	Mac: 97.12%	Win: 99.84%	Mac: 99.1%		

Finding the safest fonts is simple at sites like cssfontstack.com.

I'll grant that the list of typefaces displayed here is pretty damned boring, and I can understand why, from the marketer's and designer's perspectives, image-based type is so often preferred. That's where web fonts can be useful, allowing you more type options without having to resort to image-based text.

WEB FONTS

Web fonts are now a common sight in modern web design, gracing just about every well-designed page you can lay your eyes on. While there isn't support across the board for web fonts in email clients, you absolutely can use them in your designs — so long as you clear two hurdles.

The first hurdle is serving web fonts without JavaScript[7]. The two most popular options here are to host the fonts yourself, or to use a service that allows fonts to be served externally via CSS. If you plan to host the fonts, be sure to keep the size of your email list in mind; using a CDN might save your servers from meltdown. Going with a service might be the better option, however. Google Fonts is the most popular, given it costs nothing while still providing a reasonable variety of well-crafted fonts, but other services like Monotype or MyFonts also work very well and tend to have higher quality fonts to choose from.

Web clients:	EOT in head	TTF in head	WOFF2 in head	WOFF in head	All in head[1]	@import	\<link\>
AOL IE11	No	No	No	Yes	Yes	No	No
Desktop:	EOT in head	TTF in head	WOFF2 in head	WOFF in head	All in head[1]	@import	\<link\>
Outlook Express 6	Yes	No	No	No	Yes	Yes	Yes
Outlook 2000	Yes	No	No	No	Yes	Yes	Yes
Outlook 2002	Yes	No	No	No	Yes	Yes	Yes
Outlook 2011 (Mac)	No	Yes	No	Yes	Yes	Yes	Yes
Outlook 2015	No	Yes	No	Yes	Yes	Yes	Yes
Apple Mail 6	No	Yes	No	Yes	Yes	Yes	Yes
Apple Mail 7	No	Yes	No	Yes	Yes	Yes	Yes
Apple Mail 8	No	Yes	No	Yes	Yes	Yes	Yes
Lotus Notes 8	Yes	No	No	No	Yes	Yes	Yes
Thunderbird	No	Yes	No	Yes	Yes	Yes	Yes

This small portion of StyleCampaign's web font support matrix doesn't do its thoroughness any justice.

7 http://stylecampaign.com/blog/2015/02/web-font-services-for-email/

The second hurdle arises from email clients themselves. Whether or not a particular client supports web fonts is entirely dependent on whether or not it allows external linking. Web-based clients like Gmail and Outlook prevent the import of any sort of external information owing to security considerations, meaning support for web fonts is nonexistent.

It's not all bad, though. Many desktop and mobile clients do allow external linking via the use of `<link>`, `@import`, or `@font-face`; there's a surprisingly broad selection of clients that import and render web fonts with no problems at all, as evidenced by StyleCampaign's comprehensive write-up on the subject[8].

Testing seven linking methods across more than 30 desktop, web-based and mobile email clients, StyleCampaign has created what's very likely the most exhaustive look at web font support in email ever done, reaching the conclusion that `<link>` provides the greatest possible coverage, with `@font-face` coming a close second, and `@import` third.

Importing and using web fonts is straightforward, employing standard HTML and CSS syntaxes that most web designers are used to seeing. The choice with the most robust support, `<link>`, is HTML:

```
<link href="http://fonts.googleapis.com/css?family=Open+Sans"
rel="stylesheet" type="text/css">
```

The first CSS-based method of importing fonts, `@font-face`, includes exactly what you'd see on visiting the URL in the `<link>` example above:

```
<style="text/css">
    @font-face {
        font-family:'Open Sans';
        font-style:normal;
        font-weight:400;
        src:local('Open Sans'),local('OpenSans'),url('http://fonts.gstat
ic.com/s/opensans/v10/cJZKeOuBrn4kERxqtaUH3bO3LdcAZYWl9Si6vvxL-qU.woff')
format('woff');
        }
</style>
```

---

8 http://stylecampaign.com/blog/2015/02/webfont-support-in-email/

The second method, @import, is the cleanest of the CSS-based ones, requiring only the URL to be provided:

```
<style="text/css">
    @import url('http://fonts.googleapis.com/css?family=Open+Sans');
</style>
```

Regardless of the method you choose, after the import is complete you can set the font-family value as you normally would:

```
<style="text/css">
    .emailContent{
        font-family:'Open Sans', 'Helvetica Neue', Helvetica, Arial,
sans-serif;
    }
</style>
```

It's worth noting that each of these methods, along with the use of web fonts in email in general, requires you to consider the performance of an email just as you would for a website.

Keep in mind, too, that depending on the email client, an email may not render fully until the web font is downloaded, and that the number of web font requests adds to the total data load size.

IMAGE FALLBACKS

Sometimes, though, there's no winning, and you have to resort to setting type in images because design guidelines may demand it. In those cases where staying on brand is mission number one, Arial, Georgia, and even web font choices can leave a little something to be desired when you need a design to wow a recipient, and you may be forced to use image-based type.

Even then, providing a fallback is important. Your first option for doing so, and also the simplest method, is styling an image's alt text. This is easily done, requiring only that you add text styles to the <img> element:

459

```
<a href="..." target="_blank"><img src="..." alt="MANDRILL" height="36"
width="140" style="border:0;color:#E5E5E5;display:block;font-family:'Hel-
vetica Neue', Arial, Helvetica, sans-serif; font-size:13px; font-
weight:bold;letter-spacing:2px;outline:none;text-decoration:none;"></a>
```

Using this technique, you ensure that important content like brand names or headings aren't lost when images aren't loaded:

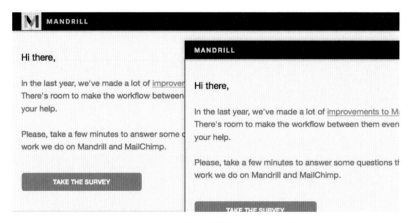

alt text styling means Mandrill's image-based logo fails
from Freight Sans to a similar Helvetica.

Of course, it doesn't always make sense to provide alt text, styled or unstyled, for your images, because there are times when a text backup doesn't do enough to convey the same message.

In those cases, there's a pretty incredible technique you can use to create a unique fallback for an email's hero image. By slicing an image in such a way that allows its containing table cells to be colored as fallback content, you can mimic an image or provide an analog.

This technique is one that's becoming quite popular in email design, but it does present a couple of issues that developers should be mindful of. First, it can greatly increase design and development time on an email, and, depending on the design, may not work particularly well in a responsive context.

Second, there's the matter of the lengthened loading time that the email's recipient will be forced to wait through; each image has to load sequentially, which could take a while on slower mobile connections. Still, despite these drawbacks, it's a neat practice and one hell of a delighter.

CODE-BASED BUTTONS

It's common to see image-based buttons in emails as well. Unfortunately, these suffer from the same problems as other image-based bits of content, failing completely in clients that block images and becoming victim to server issues where the image's load time could be affected.

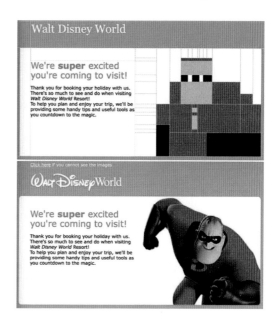

Yep. I made a pun. Forward all groans of disapproval via Twitter or email.

Because button-based calls to action tend to have meaningful actions attached to them, like purchasing a product or responding to an invitation, an image-based button provides less than ideal coverage across email clients for a crucial user pathway.

The best, most stable solution is a button built with HTML and CSS, commonly known in the email design world as the bulletproof button. In web design, code-based buttons are a pretty simple affair, generally consisting only of a styled <a> element:

```
<style type="text/css">
    .buyButton {
        background: #E85C41;
        border-radius: 4px;
        color: #FFFFFF;
        font-family: Helvetica, sans-serif;
        font-size: 14px;
        line-height: 16px;
```

```
    padding: 15px 25px;
    text-decoration: none;
  }
</style>

<a href="..." class="buyButton">Buy Now</a>
```

In email, of course, it has to be done a little differently, because some email clients (most notably desktop Outlook) don't render padding on anchors, meaning buttons end up not quite looking like, you know, buttons.

Spruce is proud to present the **Cities Collection**, featuring beautiful pieces of furniture and artwork inspired and created by the world's most noteworthy artists of the modern era.

Buy Now

If it's not abundantly clear yet, no, Outlook can't do anything right.

The most popular method for creating reliable, code-based buttons in email involves using a single-row, single-cell table for the button structure, and a link within that single cell for the button text:

```
<table border="0" cellpadding="0" cellspacing="0" style="back
ground:#E85C41; border-radius:4px;">
    <tr>
        <td align="center" valign="middle" style="padding-top:15px;
padding-right:25px; padding-bottom:15px; padding-left:25px;">
            <a href="..." style="color:#FFFFFF; font-size:14px; line-
height:16px; text-decoration:none;">Buy Now</a>
        </td>
    </tr>
</table>
```

This type of button provides the most consistent rendering across email clients, as the majority support the use of padding on table cells, though it does have two drawbacks.

The first is fairly obvious: what takes a single line of HTML to do on a website takes seven lines in an email. The second is that only the link text is clickable, and not the entire button itself. The additional code weight isn't a major issue, as the difference in actual file size is negligible, but a lot of designers and developers have a problem with the entire button not being an actionable area.

If you're the sort to find that problematic, there's another method for creating a code-based button that's fully clickable and renders fairly consistently across clients. Additionally, it requires less code:

```
<a href="..." style="background:#E85C41; border-top:15px solid #E85C41;
border-right:25px solid #E85C41; border-bottom:15px solid #E85C41;
border-left:25px solid #E85C41; border-radius:4px; color:#FFFFFF; font-
size:14px; line-height:16px; text-decoration:none;">Buy Now</a>
```

This biggest advantage of using this border-based button is the fact that its entire area is actionable, meaning a little less precision in clicking or tapping is required of the user. Despite its benefits, however, this type of button doesn't come without its own drawbacks. Because of how it's built, it's fairly inflexible in design, so things like background images and gradients could be troublesome or impossible to include.

Additionally, desktop Outlook also has some problems rendering the borders as specified, reducing their size and making the button appear smaller than intended:

The exact same code, with Apple Mail's rendering on the left, and Outlook 2013's on the right.

Still, the benefits of the border button method outweigh its downsides, and this type of button is the one I use most in my own work.

These aren't the only two methods for creating code-based, email-friend-ly buttons, but they're the simplest and most reliable, and can prevent a fair amount of hassle in putting an email together; not to mention that they're not susceptible to the same problems that image-based buttons often suffer, meaning recipients will see that nice, important call to action without having to rely on image loading or well-behaved email clients.

NAVIGATION IN EMAIL

One of the web's most common sights, the navigation bar, also requires a different treatment when it's used in email. Navigation is very often found in emails from retailers, and is generally used to convey the existence of different categories of items that shoppers have to choose from:

If you're thinking eight nav items is too many for an email, you're right.

Despite their prevalence in e-commerce emails, not everyone agrees that the use of a navigation bar makes sense; there's a fairly clear divide on the topic, between those for it and against it.

On one side of the debate are those who swear by navigation bars and tout their necessity in making it clear to potential shoppers the different product options available. The opposite side — and the camp I'm in — is that conventional navigation doesn't make much sense in the case of email, and that there are better methods for revealing the same sort of information.

Navigation is meaningful on websites because every page is linked together into what can be considered a single thread, but an email is a siloed instance of HTML; page-to-page navigation doesn't (yet) exist, so document traversal is limited to local page anchors, or linking to external sites.

Though there's obviously a valid case for including external links to other product categories, I feel that there are better solutions than using the navigation bars we are used to seeing — especially since their use seems to be based on the comfort of the familiar, rather than them being more effective than other methods. A good solution for replacing navigation in an email recalls the old adage of show, don't tell, and involves using images and text in the form of call-out-style navigation blocks.

Of course, you may not always have a say or choice in whether or not a navigation bar is included in an email.

In those cases where you must use navigation, be mindful of available space, especially on small displays. If you can, reducing the navigation bar's size and limiting the number of options could help simplify the email and focus its message. A small number of retailers, including Banana Republic, take this approach in their emails, including abridged navigation bars, as you can see in the image above.

BANANA REPUBLIC

| MEN | WOMEN | PETITES |

When navigation is necessary, a pared-down version like Banana Republic's is a good compromise.

Another good option for dealing with navigation, given the limited real estate on small displays, is to move it from the top of the email to the bottom.

Saks Fifth Avenue uses this technique to good effect, providing a slightly different navigation structure that stays hidden in the footer of emails and shows on small displays in clients that support media queries.

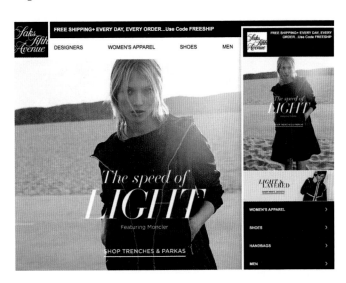

Though Saks Fifth Avenue uses navigation in email, they're mindful of its purpose and position.

Moving the navigation structure to the bottom of the email means that Saks keeps the most important stuff in their message — the content about their products — up top and free of potential distractions.

MAKING EMAIL MOVE

Animation in email has experienced a surge in popularity in the last couple of years, giving designers another way to add personality and visual interest to messages. There are a few different ways to bring animation to email, though three in particular stand out above the rest, each with their pros and cons.

By far, the most commonly used method for adding motion to an email is the venerable animated GIF. Because of how easy they are to create, and because email client support is incredibly broad, GIFs are the simplest and way to bring animation to your email.

The only real downsides to using GIFs are their generally poor image quality and poten-tially large file sizes, though both of these issues can be mitigated with the use of desktop and mobile apps[9], or video-to-GIF conversion sites like Imgur's[10]. There's one more issue to be aware of as far as GIFs are concerned —they can fail to render or animate in older email clients. Desktop Outlook is the most notable of these; there's no support for animation, though the first frame of the GIF is rendered as a fallback.

If you stare at this, wiggle the page, and shake your head really fast, it'll move. Get a friend to help.

---

9   http://www.cockos.com/licecap/
10 http://imgur.com/vidgif

CSS animation[11] provides another option for bringing motion to email, though support for the method is much weaker across clients. CSS animation works the same in email as it does on the web, based on the @keyframes rule and related properties:

```
@keyframes fadeOut {
    0% {opacity:1;}
    25% {opacity:.75;}
    50% {opacity:.5;}
    75% {opacity:.25;}
    100% {opacity:0;}
}

.vanishingTable {
    animation-name: fadeOut;
    animation-duration: 10s;
    animation-iteration-count: infinite;
}
```

Support for animation is closely related to support for media queries in general, though there are some clients that support media queries but not animation. In addition, CSS animations are a little time-consuming to build, and truly complex, video-like movement is difficult to achieve.

The upshot is that despite the lack of full support you're still dealing with HTML and CSS, meaning you can easily provide fallbacks in clients where animation isn't supported. Another benefit is that CSS animation is incredibly lightweight, meaning it reduces the data burden that a recipient has to shoulder.

Finally, there's HTML5 video. To be honest, I was conflicted on whether or not to even say anything about it, because there are more reasons to warn against its use than there are to recommend it. For starters, support is limited almost exclusively to Apple Mail, iOS Mail (iOS 6 and 7, but not iOS 8), Mozilla Thunderbird and Outlook.com. If that narrow amount of coverage isn't enough to dissuade you from using HTML5 video in an email, there's the additional

11   https://css-tricks.com/snippets/css/keyframe-animation-syntax/,
     https://developer.mozilla.org/en-US/docs/Web/Guide/CSS/Using_CSS_animations

issue of file size; video is *heavy*, especially where a recipient's mobile data plan is concerned. With all of my "please don't do this" pleading out of the way, adding HTML5 video to an email is a relatively simple affair:

```
<table border="0" cellpadding="0" cellspacing="0" width="600">
    <tr>
        <td align="center" valign="top">
            <video height="400" width="600" controls>
                <source src="..." type="video/mp4">
                    <a href="..." ><img src="fallback.jpg" /></a>
            </video>
        </td>
    </tr>
</table>
```

If you do choose to include video in your email, remember that you're potentially giving up the opportunity to drive recipient traffic from your email to a landing page where you can extend the video's usefulness by providing more content and a richer experience for the user, a tactic that many, including Wistia[12], feel is more impactful than allowing a video to be watched in an email.

Email Development Basics

With a good idea of the pitfalls you'll face in email development, and some basic design principles in place, we can get into actually writing code. Development of an HTML email is simple enough to be done in only 15 lines of code:

```
<!doctype html>
<html lang="en">
    <head>
        <meta charset="UTF-8">
    </head>
    <body>
        <center>
            <table border="0" cellpadding="0" cellspacing="0" width="600">
                <tr>
```

---

12 http://wistia.com/blog/embedding-video-in-email

```
            <td align="left" valign="top">
                Hi mom &amp; dad,
                <br />
                <br />
                Sorry I don't write more often.
            </td>
        </tr>
    </table>
</center>
</body>
</html>
```

That's all it takes to build an HTML email, really.

So… the chapter's over — thanks for reading!

Mom? Dad? Did you unsubscribe from my email list?

Actually, we've not reached the nitty-gritty yet, but you can plop that little bit of code in your delivery system of choice and just about every email client on the planet will render the message.

It's a pretty simple chunk of code. It opens with the HTML5 doctype and the UTF-8 character set `<meta>` tag. In the `<body>` we have our first bit of deprecated code, `<center>`, which is used to align the email container. The use of this element is based on personal choice and necessity; I use it to provide an old-school fallback, in case the email ends up in a dinosaur of a client.

Following `<center>`, a standard single-cell `<table>` is used to hold content. When building an email, it's important to include and set the values of attributes on `<table>` and `<td>` elements; some clients, like desktop Outlook, don't assume that no attribute or value equals zero, so if `cellpadding` or `cellspacing` are left out, you can run into a variety of spacing issues.

RESET AND CLIENT-SPECIFIC CSS

That's just the bare minimum necessary for an HTML email. From here, we can get a little more complex and start refining the code to create a more robust foundation for our email. Like in web design, it's helpful to include some CSS styles in an attempt to reset and normalize rendering across clients. All of this

CSS gets placed in a `<style>` element in the email's `<head>`, in anticipation of running the whole thing through an inliner later. I always include a number of basic reset styles:

```
<style type="text/css">
    /* RESET STYLES */
    p{margin:1em 0;}
    a{word-wrap:break-word;}
    table{border-collapse:collapse;}
    img, a img{border:0; height:auto; outline:none; text-decoration:
none;}
    body, #bodyTable{height:100% !important; margin:0; padding:0;
width:100% !important;}
    ...
```

The most notable style declaration here is `border-collapse:collapse;`, which is used to ensure that our email's tables don't inherit any spacing from email client default styles, which is a must when nesting tables in an email.

Our next addition is a group of client-specific styles, which get a bit more complex. Each requires a bit of explanation, so let's look at them line by line:

```
    ...
    /* CLIENT-SPECIFIC STYLES */
    #outlook a{padding:0;}
```

This first rule set is pretty straightforward in its effect, triggering the UI in desktop versions of Outlook to provide a "view in browser" message for the email. Since we know that Outlook renders emails pretty poorly, this gives readers a way to view emails closer to what's originally intended, thanks to the better HTML rendering available in the browser. Outlook users end up seeing this message at the top of the viewing pane:

The next rule set targets all images, and includes the proprietary Microsoft property `-ms-interpolation-mode`. This property is used to set the method used by IE to resample images that get resized via CSS or HTML attributes:

```
    img{-ms-interpolation-mode:bicubic;}
```

Simply put, it makes images look a little better when they're sized differently from their native sizes, which is useful in mobile-friendly development. The value, `bicubic`, is for the best-quality interpolation method. This property was deprecated in IE9, but still works in the case of email.

The next rule set includes more Outlook-specific fun. We trot out more proprietary properties, this time to act a bit like the `border-collapse` reset style declared earlier:

```
table{mso-table-lspace:0pt; mso-table-rspace:0pt;}
```

These Microsoft Office properties set the spacing on the left and right side of a `<table>` to zero points in Outlook 2007 and beyond. We can also tell Outlook to render line heights as they're originally set:

```
p, a, li, td, blockquote{mso-line-height-rule:exactly;}
```

Next, because a lot of email and browser apps on mobile devices run some sort of autodetection on phone numbers and turn them into links, we need to set up a style to force proper inheritance of link colors. Unless you're a fan of that ol' HTML blue, it's a good idea to specify that these links take on the colors you define elsewhere in your CSS:

```
a[href^="tel"], a[href^="sms"]{color:inherit; cursor:default;
text-decoration:inherit;}
```

This reset isn't a silver bullet, unfortunately; there are times when mobile devices will still force link styles on certain bits of content. In those cases, it's best to wrap the content in a `<span>`, then specify a CSS `color` to attempt an override.

While we're on a mobile-targeting kick, we can tell Windows- and Web-Kit-based rendering engines to leave specified text sizes alone, instead of trying to accommodate for small displays on their own:

```
p, a, li, td, body, table, blockquote{-ms-text-size-adjust:100%;
-webkit-text-size-adjust:100%;}
```

And, finally, another style override for a style override that's commonly seen in iOS and Mac OS X:

```
a[x-apple-data-detectors]{color:inherit !important; text-decoration:
none !important; font-size:inherit !important; font-family:inherit !im
portant; font-weight:inherit !important; line-height:inherit !important;}
```

This applies to bits of content that the platforms use to build triggers to open other apps and so receive the `x-apple-data-detectors` attribute — dates, addresses and phone numbers, to name a few. Similar to the phone number style override covered above, this rule set is included to ensure that the dreaded blue link doesn't rear its ugly head, and the styles you set take precedence. All told, we end up with the following reset and client-specific styles at the top of the email:

```
<style type="text/css">
    /* RESET STYLES */
    p{margin:1em 0;}
    table{border-collapse:collapse;}
    img, a img{border:0; height:auto; outline:none; text-decoration:
none;}
    body, #bodyTable, #bodyCell{height:100% !important; margin:0;
    padding:0; width:100% !important;}

    /* CLIENT-SPECIFIC STYLES */
    #outlook a{padding:0;}
    img{-ms-interpolation-mode:bicubic;}
    table{mso-table-lspace:0pt; mso-table-rspace:0pt;}
    p, a, li, td, blockquote{mso-line-height-rule:exactly;}
    a[href^="tel"], a[href^="sms"]{color:inherit; cursor:default;
text-decoration:inherit;}
    p, a, li, td, body, table, blockquote{-ms-text-size-adjust:100%;
-webkit-text-size-adjust:100%;}
    a[x-apple-data-detectors]{color:inherit !important; text-decoration:
none !important; font-size:inherit !important; font-family:inherit !im
portant; font-weight:inherit !important; line-height:inherit !important;}
</style>
```

FOUNDATIONAL MARKUP

With those reset and client-specific CSS styles out of the way, we can turn back to the email's markup. The opening sample was a pretty simplistic one and lacked a few important bits, so let's take a look at a more comprehensive version and break down the differences between that bare minimum example and this one:

```html
<!doctype html>
<html lang="en">
    <head>
        <meta charset="UTF-8">
        <meta http-equiv="X-UA-Compatible" content="IE=edge">
        <meta name="viewport" content="width=device-width,
        initial-scale=1">
        <title>Smashing Book 5: The Email!</title>
        <style type="text/css">
            (All that stuff covered above.)
        </style>
    </head>
    <body>
        <center>
            <table align="center" border="0" cellpadding="0"
            cellspacing="0" height="100%" width="100%" id="bodyTable">
                <tr>
                    <td align="center" valign="top">
                        ...
                    </td>
                </tr>
            </table>
        </center>
    </body>
</html>
```

First, at the top alongside the UTF-8 `<meta>` tag, there's an Internet Explorer compatibility declaration, used to specify a document mode for the browser[13]:

```html
<meta http-equiv="X-UA-Compatible" content="IE=edge">
```

---

13 http://msdn.microsoft.com/en-us/library/ie/ms533876%28v=vs.85%29.aspx

In this case, the value `IE=edge` tells IE to use the newest available rendering engine which, one would hope, provides the best HTML and CSS support. After that, there's the familiar viewport declaration, with `width=device-width` and `initial-scale=1` being set for mobile devices:

```
<meta name="viewport" content="width=device-width, initial-scale=1">
```

The `<title>` element also gets included, since some email clients actually display it in their preview panes. In the `<body>`, the `<center>` element is still included, but what follows is a little different. The initial `<table>` included in the earlier example is modified to mimic the `<body>` element, with `align="center"` being added, along with `height="100%"`, `width="100%"`, and an `id="bodyTable"`:

```
<table align="center" border="0" cellpadding="0" cellspacing="0"
height="100%" width="100%" id="bodyTable">
    <tr>
        <td align="center" valign="top">
            ...
        </td>
    </tr>
</table>
```

This step is an absolute *must* in every email you build because a handful of clients actually strip out the `<body>` element when the email's code is sanitized for the inbox. Though Gmail is the most notable of these clients, other webmail clients are also guilty, which means adding a body table with a single row and cell is a necessity. From this point, all additional structural `<table>` elements added to the email will be nested inside `bodyTable` to build the full email.

Nesting tables is a vitally important practice in email development. Though the technique may sound a little messy, and may bloat the code a bit, nesting these elements affords you the greatest amount of control over layout, because all structural spacing can be done using CSS `padding` on the `<td>` elements of the email. Relying on `padding` is preferable to trying to use `margin` because, as mentioned earlier during all of that box model talk, `padding` is more widely supported across clients, and you can resort to using `cellpadding` in a pinch if you need to.

We end up with a template that combines reset and client-specific CSS styles along with some fairly basic markup to form a good foundation for responsive email.

The Principles Of Responsive Email Development

Building responsive emails is easier said than done, of course, because it isn't a matter of simply working *only* with media queries to override CSS styles dependent on device width.

When developing responsive email, it's best to aim for the broadest possible coverage across clients, and to try to write code in a robust yet flexible manner, because the variance between email clients is fairly large, and isn't getting smaller. Actually putting all of that into practice requires the combination of different techniques into a development method that's centered around the use of:

1. **Spongy development**, for layout flexibility
2. **Pattern-based design**, for modular content structures
3. **Media queries**, for progressive enhancement

This layered approach works really well in email because the capabilities of the major email clients are fairly stratified, meaning that once you have the base experience settled, you can heap on more advanced CSS without worrying that it will negatively affect older clients.

Both spongy development and pattern-based design are focused primarily on the markup used in an email; they work together to create a robust foundation of code that's flexible enough to adapt to email clients new and old based on how the HTML is written and not necessarily on how it's styled.

The use of media queries carries forward from there, allowing for styling enhancements to take advantage of more modern and capable clients, and providing a recipient with a more full and website-like experience.

SPONGY DEVELOPMENT

Let me explain the funny name and it'll start to make sense. At MailChimp, in late 2012, I needed to develop a solution to the problem of providing users with email templates that were flexible for any use, but robust enough to render properly on as wide a variety of email clients as possible. In particular, the emails needed to work as well as possible in the two most used yet most troublesome clients around: desktop Outlook and the Gmail mobile app.

To that end, the templates needed to have explicitly defined layout structures — because of Outlook's poor rendering — and common content blocks (like an image with caption) that could adapt nicely into mobile-friendly configurations *without* using media queries to drive those layout changes — because of Gmail's lack of media query support.

I called the method "spongy development" because the resulting templates were malleable enough to fit different containers (or, in this case, email clients or display sizes), but weren't fully fluid — much like a sponge can fit a glass or a bowl but still retain a structure. Since then, the technique has also become known as hybrid coding[14] in the email design world, a name coined by Mike Ragan[15], a developer at the agency Action Rocket who has done a lot of impressive work in extending the method's concepts and expanding further on the idea.

Whichever name you prefer, the result is much the same, and the chief benefit of the method is that with a bit of forethought an email could be built to adapt to multiple display sizes without single a line of media query CSS.

This flexibility is dependent on two bits of markup, working in conjunction with each other: the `align` attribute; and pixel- and percentage-based values in the `width` attribute; all of which is defined on an email's structural tables. In a two-column layout, for example, the left and right column tables are given specific widths and placed inside a fluid container. Additionally, each of those column tables is aligned, allowing them to wrap naturally as the fluid container sheds width.

---

14 http://labs.actionrocket.co/the-hybrid-coding-approach
15 https://twitter.com/Mike_Raganlabs.actionrocket.co

The use of the `align` attribute is absolutely crucial to multi-column email layouts stacking vertically without the use of media queries, because it acts almost exactly like the CSS `float` property when placed on a `table` element.

Why isn't float used to shift a layout's tables? Primarily because Outlook.com — a very widely used client — doesn't support the property, meaning the tables stack vertically regardless of available space. The `align` attribute works just fine, however; it's the `float` property's granddaddy, and support for it is broad because it's from the older HTML 4.01 specification, meaning it's been baked into the rendering engines of every email client.

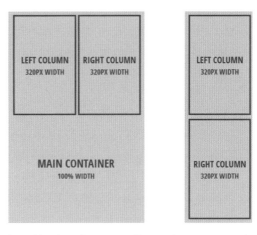

In multi-column layouts, stacking can happen automatically on small displays using widths and alignment.

Unfortunately, *desktop* Outlook struggles with `align`. Though that's primarily because of its wonky box model rendering, layouts based on aligned tables also suffer because Outlook 2007 and 2010 automatically insert a page break when a document reaches a length of 22 inches, or roughly 1,800 pixels. This oh-so-helpful feature is a direct result of Outlook's Word-based rendering engine, and it causes aligned tables to wrap.

Without conditionally served markup, Outlook wreaks havoc with free-floating layouts.

Fortunately, there's a fix for this issue: using Microsoft conditional comments to include additional Outlook-specific tables. This additional markup is used to corral an email's floated layout structures, keeping them in place by compensating for desktop Outlook's lack of `max-width` support, preventing aligned tables from wrapping unintentionally, and keeping the page-break bug from causing too much damage to a layout — all at a single stroke.

Mash the `align` attribute, fixed and fluid widths, and conditional comments together, and you get spongy development; your emails work across various screen sizes, all without relying on media queries, and even if they exhibit more complicated multi-column layouts.

PATTERN-BASED DESIGN

Achieving that kind of mobile-friendliness without using media queries requires a fair amount of careful planning, and not just with the overall layout structures of an email. To maintain layout and the flexibility established by the spongy development method, while still avoiding having to rely on media queries, we need to turn to the second major principle of robust responsive email: pattern-based design.

Involving the creation of discrete, modular blocks that can be shuffled around the same way the layout structures are, this principle allows for a great degree of flexibility while still retaining the semantically meaningful forms and orders that are critical to content.

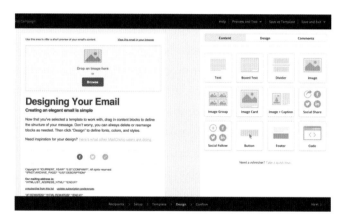

The idea of pattern-based design drives MailChimp's drag-and-drop email editor.

These blocks are built in mostly the same way as the spongy layouts are, though they can be considered more micro in scale, as they're meant to be nested inside broader structures.

Putting together a good pattern library requires a fair amount of work on the front end, but also frees you from having to build an email from scratch for every single project — a prospect that can easily become untenable. Additionally, because of email development's inherent difficulty and the large amount of time that can be spent troubleshooting issues across multiple email clients, using a pattern library vastly reduces the amount of effort required to build an email that works well.

Even if it does make it much easier to quickly build emails later on, the scale of your project should be one of the deciding factors that affect whether or not pattern-based development is a worthwhile investment of your time.

Are you building email infrequently and sending sporadically? Then it might not be worth the effort required to build and maintain a pattern library. If you're in a situation where sending frequency is high, however, and you're required to spin up a lot of different emails quickly, then pattern-based design becomes a really attractive option.

Responsive Email Patterns provides a large number of commonly used, pre-built email patterns.

Pattern-based design lends itself especially well to an automated building process. On this front, DEG's Brian Graves[16] and Code School's Dan Denney[17] have both done a lot of great work.

Brian's approach, described in the Smashing Magazine article "Improve Your Email Workflow With Modular Design"[18], details the creation of a modular framework of email-ready components, design and all, atop a static site generator; in this case, that generator is the popular *Middleman*, which also has Sass integrated for CSS.

Dan's method, dubbed *Emayll*[19], is similar in purpose, though maybe a little simpler in execution. Using a combination of Jekyll, Haml and YAML, Emayll

---

16 twitter.com/briangraves
17 twitter.com/dandenney
18 http://www.smashingmagazine.com/2014/08/04/improve-your-email-workflow-with-modular-design/
19 https://github.com/dandenney/emayll

allows the automated creation of email templates in a markup format that's a little cleaner than straight HTML.

Regardless of which approach you choose, the creation of a pattern library for email means defining, designing and building patterns using a practical methodology. In figuring out how pattern-based emails would work in MailChimp's email designer, I worked through a process of:

1. *Anticipating* common use cases
2. *Determining* patterns for those use cases
3. *Creating* modular HTML structures based on those patterns

By anticipating common use cases, you establish rough ideas of just what sorts of content structures you'll need to develop for your particular requirements. The idea of purposeful design plays a significant role here, because those email types discussed earlier lay much of the necessary groundwork in working out an email's primary use case.

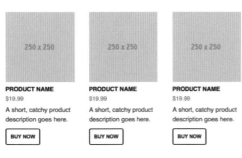

An image, name, price, description and call to action: a commonly seen retail pattern.

Take the *Buy Me* email as an example; because we know that they're built around the enticement to spend money, we can determine a pattern within that use case, the product block. Once you know that pattern will be useful in a library, creating a modular HTML structure based on that pattern is the next step. Here, it pays to take time to think on different iterations of the pattern, then build them as well.

Regardless of use case, and despite how different one email might be from the next, they all share common components. Buttons, product blocks, captioned images, callouts, and much more — by examining these common threads between the types of email, some shared design patterns begin to emerge, and you can then compile a list of content blocks your pattern library needs.

MEDIA QUERIES

At their cores, both spongy development and pattern-based design are used as methods to overcome the more significant issues caused by the poor rendering capabilities of desktop Outlook and Gmail mobile clients.

Essentially, each of the methods is focused on the graceful degradation side of the email design equation, and allows an email developer to concentrate on simplicity and stability in an email's markup, having only to rely on more well-supported HTML elements and CSS2 properties.

But Outlook and Gmail aren't the only email clients out there, they're just the worst, and good design and development never serve *just* the lowest common denominator. You can push an email beyond the basics, to include more sophisticated styling, because the principle of progressive enhancement holds as true in email design as it does in web design.

While it's true that the media query has varying levels of support across email clients, that support isn't as weak as you'd expect, especially given the dominance of mobile email; over 50% of all email opens happen on mobile devices, meaning you can take advantage of clients that generally have more competent rendering engines than those found in desktop and webmail clients, and make use of them to enhance the experience of an email as a whole.

The good stuff's not only happening on mobile, however; many webmail clients have made great strides to further increase support for more advanced CSS in the last couple of years, including media queries. Outlook.com, Yahoo Mail and AOL all support the use of media queries, while Gmail does not. On the desktop client front, Apple Mail, Mozilla Thunderbird, and Windows Live Mail also have media query support. That's not a bad collection of email clients, truth be told.

Using them in email is virtually no different from doing so on a website; the same syntax applies and the same media features can be used.:

```
@media only screen and (max-width:480px) {
    #emailContainer{width:480px !important;}
    p{font-size:18px !important;}
}
```

The only significant difference between media queries for email and media queries for websites is a more liberal use of !important. This is necessary because all CSS in an email must be inlined, meaning those inlined properties have a level of specificity that can only be overridden by the !important declaration.

Combining spongy development with pattern-based design, and using media queries to smooth out the rough edges of both, then going further to provide more advanced styling means you end up with an email that performs well regardless of the email client or display size it's viewed in.

Principle Into Practice

Let's take a closer look at how to build such an email, by going through a few chunks of code that will illustrate each of the three principles. I'll start with the broadest bit first, the outer scaffolding that forms the layout of the email.

BUILDING FLUID STRUCTURES

In all of the responsive emails I've built, the container table that forms the email's outermost structure is always fluid, having its width set to 100%. Let's pick up our email code where we left off, and add that fluid table inside bodyTable:

```
<table align="center" border="0" cellpadding="0" cellspacing="0"
height="100%" width="100%" id="bodyTable">
    <tr>
        <td align="center" valign="top">
            <table align="center" border="0" cellpadding="0"
            cellspacing="0" width="100%" class="flexibleContainer">
                <tr>
                    <td valign="top">
                        . . .
                    </td>
                </tr>
            </table>
        </td>
    </tr>
</table>
```

The table receives a generic class, `flexibleContainer`, which is used to control the email's width across various platforms. All that's set initially is an upper width limit, which is set via the `max-width` property:

```
/* STRUCTURAL STYLES */
.flexibleContainer{max-width:640px;}
```

Unfortunately we can't just stop there because desktop Outlook doesn't support the `max-width` property, which is currently the only thing that gives our fluidly built email its main structural limit. This is where Microsoft's conditional comments come in handy. They can be used as wrappers placed around the opening and closing sections of the table that, in this case, performs one function — providing a set width around the entire email in Outlook:

```
<table align="center" border="0" cellpadding="0" cellspacing="0"
height="100%" width="100%" id="bodyTable">
    <tr>
        <td align="center" valign="top">
            <!--[if gte mso 9]>
            <table align="center" border="0" cellpadding="0"
            cellspacing="0" width="640">
            <tr>
            <td align="center" valign="top">
            <![endif]-->
            <table align="center" border="0" cellpadding="0"
            cellspacing="0" width="100%" class="flexibleContainer">
                <tr>
                    <td valign="top">
                        . . .
                    </td>
                </tr>
            </table>
            <!--[if gte mso 9]>
            </td>
            </tr>
            </table>
            <![endif]-->
        </td>
    </tr>
</table>
```

With this structural limit in place, we can continue to add more elaborate structures to the flexibleContainer table.

MULTI-COLUMN LAYOUTS

A basic two-column structure, a layout commonly found in email, is a good place to start, and this is where that important second bit of spongy develop-ment markup comes in, the almighty align[20] attribute. We'll add another row to the flexibleContainer table, then two tables inside of that, each aligned left and classed as leftColumn and rightColumn, respectively:

```
<table align="center" border="0" cellpadding="0" cellspacing="0"
width="100%" class="flexibleContainer">
    <tr>
        <td valign="top">
            ...
        </td>
    </tr>
    <tr>
        <td valign="top">
            <table align="left" border="0" cellpadding="0"
            cellspacing="0" width="100%" class="leftColumn">
                <tr>
                    <td align="left" valign="top">
                        <p>This is the left column.</p>
                    </td>
                </tr>
            </table>
            <table align="left" border="0" cellpadding="0"
            cellspacing="0" width="100%" class="rightColumn">
                <tr>
                    <td align="left" valign="top">
                        <p>This is the right column.</p>
                    </td>
                </tr>
            </table>
        </td>
    </tr>
</table>
```

---

20 http://www.w3.org/TR/html401/present/graphics.html#h-15.1.3

With the markup added, the only thing that needs to be done to each column is the addition of an upper width limit:

```
/* STRUCTURAL STYLES */
.flexibleContainer{max-width:640px;}
.leftColumn, .rightColumn{max-width:320px;}
```

Next, we need to resolve desktop Outlook's problems with the `align` attribute. This is where the next bit of Outlook-specific markup gets added; another table, but this time containing two cells:

```
<table align="center" border="0" cellpadding="0" cellspacing="0"
width="100%" class="flexibleContainer">
    <tr>
        <td valign="top">
            ...
        </td>
    </tr>
    <tr>
        <td valign="top">
            <!--[if gte mso 9]>
            <table align="center" border="0" cellpadding="0"
            cellspacing="0" width="640">
            <tr>
            <td align="center" valign="top" width="320">
            <![endif]-->
            <table align="left" border="0" cellpadding="0"
            cellspacing="0" width="100%" class="leftColumn">
                <tr>
                    <td align="left" valign="top">
                        <p>This is the left column.</p>
                    </td>
                </tr>
            </table>
            <!--[if gte mso 9]>
            </td>
            <td align="center" valign="top" width="320">
            <![endif]-->
            <table align="left" border="0" cellpadding="0"
            cellspacing="0" width="100%" class="rightColumn">
```

```
        <tr>
            <td align="left" valign="top">
                <p>This is the right column.</p>
            </td>
        </tr>
    </table>
    <!--[if gte mso 9]>
    </td>
    </tr>
    </table>
    <![endif]-->
        </td>
    </tr>
</table>
```

With that done, the columns don't blow out in Outlook, and with the CSS limits in place they stack neatly on small displays. The same method can be used for three- and four-column layouts as well; creating them is just a matter of adding more aligned tables and Outlook-specific structures to support them.

SEMANTIC ORDERING

A two-column layout with equal-width column structures is pretty easy to deal with, so let's throw a couple more challenges in the mix with the addition of another two-column layout, this time consisting of a left-hand sidebar and right-hand main content area.

The biggest difference, other than the column widths, is a semantic one; by introducing a sidebar, we introduce secondary content, which means that, ideally, the sidebar should slip under the main content so that the order of importance between the two is preserved when the email stacks vertically.

The content's semantic order is established In the markup, with the main content table written first, and the sidebar table second. Reversing each table's visual order is then just a matter of setting their align directions:

```
<tr>
    <td valign="top">
        <table align="right" border="0" cellpadding="0" cellspacing="0"
```

```
        width="100%" class="mainContent">
            <tr>
                <td align="left" valign="top">
                    <p>This is the main content.</p>
                </td>
            </tr>
        </table>
        <table align="left" border="0" cellpadding="0" cellspacing="0"
        width="100%" class="sidebarContent">
            <tr>
                <td align="left" valign="top">
                    <p>This is the sidebar.</p>
                </td>
            </tr>
        </table>
    </td>
</tr>
```

With the `mainContent` table aligned right and the `sidebarContent` table aligned to the left, we get the visual order we want. Next, the width limits get added to each:

```
/* STRUCTURAL STYLES */
.flexibleContainer{max-width:640px;}
.leftColumn, .rightColumn{max-width:320px;}
.mainContent{max-width:440px;}
.sidebarContent{max-width:200px;}
```

Again, much like the previous two-column structure, this one requires Outlook-specific markup to make the aligned tables play nice:

```
<tr>
    <td valign="top">
        <!--[if gte mso 9]>
        <table align="center" border="0" cellspacing="0" cellpadding="0"
        width="640">
        <tr>
        <td align="center" valign="top" width="440">
        <![endif]-->
```

```
<table align="right" border="0" cellpadding="0" cellspacing="0"
width="100%" class="mainContent">
    <tr>
        <td align="left" valign="top">
            <p>This is the main content.</p>
        </td>
    </tr>
</table>
<!--[if gte mso 9]>
</td>
<td align="center" valign="top" width="200">
<![endif]-->
<table align="left" border="0" cellpadding="0" cellspacing="0"
width="100%" class="sidebarContent">
    <tr>
        <td align="left" valign="top">
            <p>This is the sidebar.</p>
        </td>
    </tr>
</table>
<!--[if gte mso 9]>
</td>
</tr>
</table>
<![endif]-->
        </td>
    </tr>
```

But wait, there's more! This section's not quite finished, because the semantic order of the main content and sidebar tables presents an issue for the Outlook-specific table; its individual cells for the main content and sidebar tables reverses the visual order of those two content areas.

The sidebar ends up on the right, since it's second in the markup and sits inside the second table cell. Luckily, the workaround is a simple one. By using the dir attribute, along with the rtl value on the Outlook table, we can reverse the visual order of the two content sections for desktop Outlook clients:

```
<tr>
    <td valign="top">
        <!--[if gte mso 9]>
```

```
<table align="center" border="0" cellspacing="0" cellpadding="0"
dir="rtl" width="640">
<tr>
<td align="center" valign="top" width="440">
<![endif]-->
...
```

Now, when the Outlook-specific markup is rendered, the table's cells will have their orders reversed owing to the use of the `dir` attribute, and the visual order of the sidebar and main content areas is restored.

All of these techniques can be used over and over again to create different layouts that remain flexible enough to adapt to a wide range of email clients, and they can also be applied to the content structures inside.

SPONGY PATTERNS

Let's take a quick look at how the product block mentioned earlier would be put together using these same methods.

The significant bits of content in this block are the product title, image, and summary (which includes the price, a description of the product, and a button). By separating each of these three items into aligned tables, we can set it up to have a different layout on small displays. We'll add it to the first cell of the `mainContent` table, since its narrower width works well for this kind of block:

```
<table align="center" border="0" cellpadding="0" cellspacing="0"
width="100%" class="productBlock">
    <tr>
        <td valign="top">
            <table align="right" border="0" cellpadding="0" cellspacing="0"
            width="100%" class="productTitle" style="max-width:270px;">
                <tr>
                    <td align="left" valign="top">
                        <h4>Product Title</h4>
                    </td>
                </tr>
            </table>
            <table align="left" border="0" cellpadding="0" cellspacing="0"
            width="100%" class="productImage" style="max-width:150px;">
```

```
        <tr>
            <td align="left" valign="top">
                <img src="http://placehold.it/150x150"
                height="150" width="150">
            </td>
        </tr>
    </table>
    <table align="right" border="0" cellpadding="0" cellspacing="0"
    class="productSummary" style="max-width:270px;">
        <tr>
            <td align="left" valign="top">
                <p>$19.99</p>
                <p>A catchy product description goes here.</p>
                <a href="...">BUY NOW</a>
            </td>
        </tr>
    </table>
    </td>
    </tr>
</table>
```

The `productTitle` table is first in the markup, then aligned right; then the `productImage` table follows and is aligned left; and finally comes the `productSummary` table, aligned right again. Each table then has a width limit set:

```
/* STRUCTURAL STYLES */
.flexibleContainer{max-width:640px;}
.leftColumn, .rightColumn{max-width:320px;}
.mainContent{max-width:440px;}
.sidebarContent{max-width:200px;}
.productTitle, .productSummary{max-width:270px;}
.productImage{max-width:150px;}
```

With all that done, each item stacks in an order that makes semantic and visual sense, simply because of how the specific sections of the product block were put together.

Now we can start pouring on the media query styles, to ensure our email's layout holds together a little better and to provide a few more styling bells and whistles to clients that can support them.

REINFORCING AND ENHANCING

So far, the table structures that have been built are all given width limits via max-width, which works all right as a baseline, but doesn't look that great in competent email clients that support modern CSS.

We're also not accounting for occasions where max-width isn't supported but media queries are. That sounds ludicrous, but it does happen — this is email we're talking about. In such cases, you have to set an explicit width on each container, so that the content within still retains the layout you plan for. That means writing some simple media query rule sets to apply those widths:

```
@media screen and (min-width:768px){
    /* STRUCTURAL STYLES */
    .flexibleContainer{width:640px !important;}
    .leftColumn, .rightColumn{width:320px !important;}
    .mainContent{width:440px !important;}
    .sidebarContent{width:200px !important;}
    .productTitle, .productSummary{width:270px !important;}
    .productImage{width:150px !important;}
}
@media screen and (max-width:480px){
    /* STRUCTURAL STYLES */
    .flexibleContainer,
    .leftColumn,
    .rightColumn,
    .mainContent,
    .sidebarContent,
    .productTitle,
    .productSummary,
    .productImage{width:100% !important;}
}
```

Obviously, there are more nuanced ways to do all of this, and we can provide more styles for tablets and all, but this bit doesn't require anything fancy, so don't worry about how primitive these look; they're simply illustrative of the concept.

By triggering one @media at min-width:768px, the email's structures get width limits set at desktop sizes and up. Additionally, for small display sizes, widths are changed to 100%, so everything stacks nicely.

In Summary

That's modern email design, a discipline that — for better or worse — lives in both the past and the present of the web.

While I can't imagine that after reading all of this you'll suddenly jump to your feet and say, "Holy crap! I *love* email design!", if you happen to, you'll be in good company; the email design world is inhabited by some of the most passionate, bright and skilled professionals I've ever known, all working with the same limited set of tools to produce some incredible work.

Even if it doesn't make you jump for joy, my hope is that the next time you're faced with the prospect of designing or developing an email, the whole process is a little... if not easier, then at least clearer. Email development is a pretty dense subject, however. There are so many techniques and so much information to keep track of that a single chapter only allows me to cover the proverbial tip of the iceberg. Don't worry, though; I won't let you leave empty-handed.

THE EMAIL

The latter part of this chapter is pretty dang code-heavy, and explaining code on paper just doesn't work as well as letting someone loose in an actual code sample, to tinker and play and understand. To that end, I've put together a few email templates that encompass all of the lessons in this chapter and are more fully fleshed out. You'll find them at http://smashed.by/email-template.

Like other templates I've released in the past, they're licensed under Creative Commons and you're welcome to use it for whatever you'd like. I've commented the code where I felt necessary and have included styled and unstyled versions.

RESOURCES

When I began my career as an email developer six years ago, one of the more frustrating problems I experienced was an almost complete lack of places to turn when I ran into trouble. Any information that shed light on why things worked the way they did was really hard to come by and I, like pretty much everyone else, was left to figure things out on my own.

Fortunately, the obscurity of the problems people commonly run across when developing email is something that's being remedied by a lot of great resources. Here's a list of my personal favorites, abridged to only five links per section because, c'mon, I have to stop somewhere.

BLOGS

- MailChimp Blog: http://blog.mailchimp.com
- STYLECampaign: http://stylecampaign.com/blog/
- Litmus Blog: https://litmus.com/blog/
- Email Design Review: http://www.emaildesignreview.com
- Display Block: https://www.displayblock.com/blog/

NEWSLETTERS

- The UX Newsletter: http://www.theuxnewsletter.com
- Email Weekly: http://emailweekly.co
- Email Design Monthly: https://litmus.com/email-design-newsletter

REFERENCE AND DISCUSSION

- The Email Design Reference: http://emaildesign.com
- The Litmus Community: http://litmus.com/community
- Action Rocket Labs: http://labs.actionrocket.co

TEMPLATES AND FRAMEWORKS

- MailChimp Blueprints: https://github.com/mailchimp/Email-Blueprints
- Cerberus: https://github.com/TedGoas/Cerberus
- Emayll: https://github.com/dandenney/emayll
- Middlemail: https://github.com/degdigital/MiddleMail
- Zenith: https://github.com/Omgitsonlyalex/ZenithFramework

All of these resources have been contributed to or created by a huge number of amazingly talented folks. This list goes to 11.

- Justine Jordan (Litmus): @meladorri
- Elliot Ross (Action Rocket): @iamelliot
- Jason Rodriguez (Litmus): @rodriguezcommaj
- Mike Ragan (Action Rocket): @mike_ragan
- Anna Yeaman (STYLECampaign): @stylecampaign
- Alex Ilhan (Display Block): @omgitsonlyalex
- Mark Robbins (RebelMail): @m_j_robbins
- Matt Byrd (Uber): @mparkerbyrd
- Ted Goas (Canfield Scientific): @tedgoas
- Kevin Mandeville (Litmus): @kevinmanderville
- Paul Airy (Beyond The Envelope): @paul_airy

ABOUT THE AUTHOR

Fabio has been crafting responsive emails for quite some time. As an email and UX designer at *Mailchimp* in Atlanta, GA, he spends his days neck-deep in HTML email, designing and developing versatile, responsive templates for million of users. Sometimes he pretends to be an astrophysicist, is a long-time car enthusiast and really likes cats, among other things.

BEYOND RESPONSIVE: OPTIMIZING FOR OFFLINE

BY JOHN ALLSOPP AND MATT GAUNT

CHAPTER TEN · BY JOHN ALLSOPP AND MATT GAUNT

BEYOND RESPONSIVE:
OPTIMIZING FOR OFFLINE

W E SPEND A LOT OF TIME DISCUSSING LAYOUTS and breakpoints and media queries and adjustments between various form factors, but perhaps there is one aspect of responsiveness that we tend to not spend enough time talking about. What if we think a bit beyond all those familiar aspects, and consider how responsive a website or an application should be when the user isn't online? What if we told you that as a user, you don't have to be online to use the web, and a website or a web application would respond to this accordingly?

There's a general (and understandable) belief held by many developers, not to mention most users, that websites and web applications have a very serious limitation — they can only be used when the browser has a web connection. Indeed, this is routinely cited as one of the real advantages of so-called "native apps" over the web. Typically, when a user was offline, if they tried visiting a URL, even one they'd recently visited, the browser just wouldn't load the page. The rise of mobile, portable computing didn't make the situation easier: these days users are less likely to have guaranteed high-bandwidth connectivity and more likely to be connected via slower cellular networks.

Because users are on the go, often being online isn't even a matter of good coverage, but rather a matter of difficult locations which don't have a reliable connectivity — trains, tunnels, remote locations, disconnected environments.

As counter-intuitive as it sounds, in almost every modern browser on any device (including Internet Explorer from version 10), it's no longer the case that users need to be connected to the web to use our websites and applications, provided we do a little extra work to make our site or application persist when a browser is offline.

This opens up a whole range of opportunities, leveling the field with native apps that can be installed on the user's phone, tablet, laptop or desktop computer, or indeed any other device capable of running apps. But there are many more benefits to offline technologies than simply allowing websites and apps to work offline, as we'll soon discover.

As the team behind the Hoodie[1] framework wrote on their "Initiatives" page[2], even in the developed world, mobile bandwidth and connectivity, increasingly the primary way in which people connect to the Web, are not always guaranteed to be there, or be reliable. They state:

> "We can't keep building apps with the desktop mindset of permanent, fast connec-
> tivity in mind, where a temporary disconnection or slow service is regarded as a
> problem and communicated to the user as an error."

And when we think of offline and online, we typically only focus on the client; but servers go offline as well, for routine maintenance, or in times of crisis, or under heavy stress. What if your user could continue to use all, or the core, of your site's functionality even when your site is offline?

In this chapter, we'll cover a few technologies and practices that you'll need to use to make your apps work as well offline as they do online. We'll discuss how to detect if we are online or not, HTML5 Application Cache, Web Storage, offline events, and emerging standards such as service workers. Let's dig into it.

---

1   http://hood.ie/
2   http://hood.ie/blog/say-hello-to-offline-first.html

Are We Online Yet?

When we develop a website or app that might be used online or offline, it's useful to know whether the browser is currently connected. We might enable or disable upload or submit buttons as appropriate, or otherwise adapt a user interface or other functionality based on the current connection state.

You might have thought it was straightforward for a browser to know whether it is online or not, and then to let us know. Sadly, this isn't the case.

HTML5 gives us two ways we can try to determine the current online status of the browser. We can check the onLine attribute of the navigator object, or we can listen for online and offline events. We can also use the (currently still in draft) Network Information API standard supported in some browsers. Additionally, there are some other hacks for trying to determine whether the user is connected. We'll cover them below.

NAVIGATOR.ONLINE

The navigator object is part of the DOM (or more accurately the BOM or browser object model) that represents the browser itself. It's traditionally most commonly used to access information about the browser version, but increasingly we're seeing device-level APIs like DeviceMotion associated with the navigator object. One of the properties of the navigator object is onLine, which is true if the browser is online and false if offline.

But navigator.onLine will be false if the browser is definitely not connected to a network. However, it's true if it is connected to a network, even if that network is not connected to the internet. So, while a value of false indicates we're definitely offline, a value of true does not necessarily mean we will be able to connect to a web server.

There's an added complication in Firefox and Internet Explorer. These browsers have an offline mode that allows the user to disconnect the browser from the internet, even while the system they're running on is connected. In Firefox and Internet Explorer 8+ navigator.onLine means both that the local system is connected to a network (as described above) and the browser is not in this offline mode.

In Internet Explorer 7, a value of `false` indicated solely that the user was in offline mode while a value of true indicates nothing about whether the system itself was connected to a network.

In summary, the value of `navigator.onLine` is of limited value. We can use it to determine (in all browsers from Internet Explorer 8+) that the browser is definitely offline, but not to determine that the browser definitely has a `connection` to the internet. We'll see shortly that this still has some benefits.

Online and Offline Events

While it's good to be able to check whether the user is (probably? possibly?) online or offline, it would be nice to not have to constantly ask the navigator object whether the user is connected or not, but receive a notification when the user goes online or offline. We can do this by providing an event handler for two different events, `offline` and `online`. In theory, we can attach this handler to the `window`, document or even body objects. But in practice, the only way to attach an event handler that works across all modern browsers which support online events is to attach it to the `window`, using `addEventListener` (but we can't use `window.online = function reference`). So, we'd ask the `window` to call the function `updateUI()` when the user goes offline like this:

```
window.addEventListener("offline", updateUI);
```

Again, as with `navigator.offLine`, with WebKit browsers the events are fired when the user connects to, or loses connection to, a local area network (for example by turning off Wi-Fi or unplugging from ethernet) or, with Firefox and Internet Explorer 8+, also when the user goes into or out of offline mode.

How might we use these events or the `navigator.onLine` property?

A simple way to improve our application or page user experience would be to disable options that require the user to be online (for example, a submit button for a form) and to inform the user somehow why this is disabled.

For operations which happen without user intervention between browser and server (for example, synchronizing data using `XMLHttpRequest`), rather than attempting the operation and waiting for a timeout, we could determine whether the user is definitely offline or not, and if offline, save the data to synchronize in localStorage, then try the operation once the browser receives an online event.

W3C Network Information API

Clearly, as web applications become more sophisticated we'd like to know more than whether the browser *might* be connected to the web. To this end, the W3C is currently developing the Network Information API, which provides information about the current network bandwidth availability.

NAVIGATOR.CONNECTION

The Network Information API adds a connection object to the navigator. The connection object has two properties:

- bandwidth is a number that represents the current *download* bandwidth. If the browser is offline, this is 0. If the bandwidth is unknown, the value is infinity.
- metered is true if the connection is metered (the user is currently paying for their bandwidth).

The connection object also receives a change event when the connection changes. This could be because the user has moved from a metered to a non-metered connection or because the network speed has changed. If a change occurs, we could determine whether the current bandwidth is zero and, if so, we know the browser has now gone offline. For subsequent change events, we could check to see whether this value is no longer zero, in which case the browser will now be online.

Currently, the Network Information API is still a draft specification, though it is supported in Firefox and Android. Why mention it? Well, as we saw, navigator.onLine and the online and offline events only really tell us whether a browser is definitely offline or possibly online.

But because Mozilla-based browsers support a draft version of the Network API, we can use this API to determine whether Firefox is *really* online.

```
navigator.connection.addEventListener('change', connectionChanged,
false);
//Add the change event listener

function connectionChanged(event){
        if(navigator.connection.bandwidth !== 0) {
                // We're online
        }

        else {
                // We're offline
        }
}
```

Other Ways of Determining Whether We're Offline or Online

Because of the shortcomings of onLine and of the offline and online events, as well as lack of widespread support for the Network Information API, several developers, including Remy Sharp and Paul Kinlan, have come up with a number of clever ways to try to detect whether a browser is online or offline. These include using the AppCache errors and XMLHttpRequest. Here's a quick overview of these techniques.

USING THE APPCACHE ERROR EVENT

If we request an update to the AppCache and something goes wrong, we receive an error. Now it could be that the manifest file or one of the resources in the manifest are missing, but if we know they aren't, we might reasonably guess that the user, our server or both are offline, which for the purposes of our site is largely the same thing most of the time.

Let's add an event handler for the error event to the AppCache so that when the AppCache is updated we record the current status.

```
window.applicationCache.addEventListener("error", onlineStatus, false);

function onlineStatus(event) {
  //We're probably offline as we got an AppCache error
}
```

One downside to this is we'll only check the online status when the page originally loads, so if the user comes online we'll have to manually trigger an AppCache update.

```
function checkOnline() {
  //Try to update the appcache. If that throws an error, it will call
onlineStatus
  window.applicationCache.update();
}
```

USING XMLHTTPREQUEST

One of the more traditional ways of determining whether a browser is online is to make an XMLHttpRequest (XHR) for a resource on a server. The idea is quite straightforward, though the code involved is somewhat convoluted; you can grab Remy Sharp's polyfill using XHR[3] and Paul Kinlan's detailed HTML5 Rocks article[4] which has a fully working example of the XHR approach (along with the AppCache approach).

Reliably detecting whether a browser is online is still far from straightforward, particularly doing so across several browsers; certainly, there's no reliable standards-based way. There are, however, techniques you can use that will help you determine this with some confidence, should it be something vital you need to know about.

---

3 https://github.com/remy/polyfills/blob/master/offline-events.js
4 http://www.html5rocks.com/en/mobile/workingoffthegrid/

Service Workers

We can figure out when a user is definitely offline. What now? Well, we can design the experience for the case when online isn't available. There are a number of ways to do that. We are pretty familiar with the good ol' HTTP Cache, yet its major limitation is that it wasn't designed to allow sites to work while a browser wasn't connected to the network. Service workers were designed to solve just this issue. As a successor of AppCache, service workers resolve quite a number of its shortcomings, and when used properly they can do the job well.

We can't cover AppCache in full detail in this chapter, but it's important to understand that with AppCache we basically tell browsers what we want cached and let them work out how to do the caching, routing and updating; this hands-off approach is declarative. The service worker approach requires us to use code to control how and when resources are cached. This means we have to write a little more code, but we can create experiences that are simply impossible with a declarative approach. Service workers, like web manifests, are very much in a state of development. But even more than web manifests, they are supported by multiple browsers (including Chrome and Firefox) and will be the future of how web applications work offline.

WHAT IS A SERVICE WORKER?

The best way to think of a service worker is as a special background process running JavaScript that the browser can treat as a proxy server on a user's device. A web-based application can register a service worker, which will then intercept all network traffic between your application and the outside world.

Once a service worker is registered and installed for a site (in essence, for a domain or path within a domain, called the *scope*), the next time the user attempts to navigate to that domain, whether by a bookmark, link, entering a URL in the browser or any other way, the browser's first step will be to start up the service worker — which will be installed locally and be available offline — and dispatch an event to the service worker for each network request.

For instance, if we have a service worker installed for *https://gauntface.com* and the browser receives a request for any page on this domain, the request will be sent to the service worker, as will any request made by these pages. The service worker can then do whatever it wants: modify the request to retrieve something different; simply respond with some text without passing that request on to the network; or just leave the request alone and let the browser do what it normally would. The key thing to realize is that for the first time, you can sit between your webpage and the internet to decide how to handle network requests.

In case you were wondering how this would affect load time performance, it takes negligible time to start a service worker and handle requests. Once set up, you'll be caching assets, which prevents a network trip and download so you'll quickly improve the load time of your page. As for runtime performance, it's not affected since service workers are a special kind of JavaScript worker, which run in the background on a different thread and have no direct access to the DOM.

WHY ADD A SERVICE WORKER?

There are a few reasons you should consider adding a service worker.

- Caching for an entirely offline experience.
- Improving the speed of your site by caching key resources.
- Ability to have greater control of network requests and failures.

The one use case you'll hear over and over again is that you can make your web app work offline — and you totally can. If you have a simple single-page web app or static site, offline support is trivial: you just need to know what files to cache in your service worker. If you have a large dynamic site (think e-commerce) then it doesn't make sense to cache everything. Instead, you should cache certain key pages or assets of your web app.

But there are other use cases and you could argue they are a little easier to stomach than full offline support when you first start using service workers. Many sites will have certain files that won't change that frequently, particularly JavaScript, CSS or font files, for example. These assets would be prime candidates for caching with a service worker since it will improve the load time performance of your site by skipping the network request. You can then decide when and how to update the cached version of those files.

The great thing with service workers is that they can be treated as a progressive enhancement. Since service workers intercept network requests and run outside of the page, you don't have to code your site any differently to take advantage of these features. Should there be any kind of problem loading the service worker script, or if the browser doesn't support service workers at all, then it will fail to register and the browser will simply carry on as normal, making it easy to treat as an enhancement to your app.

Finally, one big concern developers had with AppCache is that if something went wrong, you could get into a scenario where you couldn't update the cached version of your site on a user's device: the user would have to know how to clear the cache manually. When the browser requests a service worker script, a Cache-Control header is used to determine how long it should be cached for; but the browser will cap the cache to 24 hours, which means that it will always try to get a new version of the service worker script at least once every 24 hours. This allows you to avoid the scenario where you can't gain control of your site.

CACHING WITH SERVICE WORKERS

One of the most important capabilities we need for offline web content is the ability to cache resources. Service workers allow us to do this using the Cache API, which gives us cache objects (a service worker may have any number of caches).

Compared with AppCache, you are swapping the AppCache manifest file for JavaScript. The code is relatively simple and you'll save a great deal of time not having to cope with AppCache's rather complex and frustrating rules of caching. Service workers allow you to decide when resources should be cached, fetched or refreshed, putting you in full control of the user experience.

Generally you'll have two ways to cache files: `cache.addAll()`, which takes a list of asset URLs you want to cache; or `cache.put()`, which takes a request and response object pair. The response object is obtained by requesting an asset from the network using the new `fetch()` API, making it a pretty vital API for service workers. Before we look at the Fetch API, we need to look at JavaScript promises first, which play an important role in Fetch and service workers.

PROMISES

Promises are a simple way to work with asynchronous events and have the added benefit that they can be chained together, so you only have to care about success or failure. I'm only going to give you a brief overview of how promises work; Jake Archibald has written up a great blog post on JavaScript promises6 which I strongly urge you to check out — and yes, some of this is shamefully lifted from that post (it's just too good not to).

A promise has a few specific states: it can be *pending* or *settled*. If the promise is pending, it means it hasn't completed its task; if a promise is settled, then it has completed its intended action and has either been *resolved* or *rejected*. Resolved means that the promise completed its work successfully, without errors. If a promise is rejected, then either its task could not be completed or an error was thrown unexpectedly.

How does this help us? Well, whenever we need to handle an asynchronous task, we add two callbacks, `then()` and `catch()` which relate to resolved and rejected, which you can see below.

```
somePromise.then(function(arg) {
  // The promise resolved successfully
  console.log("Success", arg);
}).catch(function(error) {
  // The promise rejected
  console.error("Failure", error);
});
```

The advantage of this is that it simplifies code when you compare it to event callbacks, especially when you chain promises together.

Let's imagine we want to get some JSON from a server and, once we've got it, we want parse it and make a second request with an ID from the first response; then, finally, from this second response we do something fancy. We can do this by chaining the promises like so:

```
fetch('something.json').then(function(response) {
  // Step 1
  return JSON.parse(response);
}).then(function(parsedJson) {
  // Step 2
  return get('somethingelse.json?id=' + parsedJson.id);
}).then(function(response) {
  // Step 3
  console.log('Woop Woop. We have our second bit of data', response);
}).catch(function(err) {
  console.error('Oops. Something went bad.', err);
});
```

Essentially, we wait for the first call to get('something.json') to succeed, we return the parsed JSON in the first callback, which passes it into the second step of the chain, and note that the value passed in, parsedJson, is the return of JSON.parse. In the second chain we return get('somethingelse.json?id=' + data.id), which for the sake of this example returns a promise. Because we return a promise in this second step, the chain will wait for the returned promise to settle (reject or resolve) before it calls the next step in the chain (in this case, step 3). This is why we can return a promise from get() and in the following then() callback, the response from get('somethingelse.json?id=' + data.id) is passed in.

This looks pretty complex and takes a little getting used to, but once you start following this pattern and become familiar with the Promise API, it makes handling asynchronous code much easier than using event listeners. (At this point, I really *do* urge you to read Jake Archibald's article on promises[5]. I've only covered enough so that we can jump into Fetch and service workers.)

We briefly mentioned that a common way to cache resources is to make a request using the fetch() method and caching the response, so let's look at a real example.

---

5 http://www.html5rocks.com/en/tutorials/es6/promises/

Fetch

You can think of Fetch as an API which allows you to make network requests similar to XHR. The key differences are that it has an easier API, uses promises, and it allows you to make cross-origin requests regardless of the CORS headers — something XHR is unable to do. Let's look at a typical fetch() request.

```
fetch('api/some.json')
  .then(function(response) {
    // Read the response as text
    return response.text();
  })
  .then(function(text) {
    // Print out the responses text
    console.log(text);
  })
  .catch(function(err) {
    console.error('Fetch Error :-S', err);
  });
```

We simply pass in a URL to our fetch() call, which returns a promise and we handle the resolve and rejection. If the request is successful, the promise will resolve calling the first step in our chain with a response object. If there is an error, the promise will reject and call the catch() function in our chain.

The *response body* is a *stream*. This means that the response may still be in progress while we decide how to consume it. When we call response.text(), a promise is returned to take care of the asynchronous retrieval of the stream and, as we learned before, only after this promise is complete will the next step in the promise chain be called, where we log the response text to the console.

If we wanted to make a request for an asset that doesn't support CORS headers on a different origin, we can do that by defining the mode of the fetch() request.

```
fetch(url, {'mode': 'no-cors'}).then(function(response) {
    if (response.type === 'opaque') {
      console.log("The Response is opaque so we can't examine
it");
```

```
    // Do something with the response (i.e. cache it for offline
support)
      return;
    }
    if (response.status !== 200) {
      console.log('Looks like there was a problem. Status Code: ' + re
sponse.status);
      throw new Error('Bad status code');
    }

    // Examine the text in the response
    return response.text()
.then(function(responseText) {
      console.log(responseText);
    });
  }).catch(function(err) {
    console.error('Fetch Error :-S', err);
  });
```

With this call, we've passed in a URL and an object with a mode parameter of no-cors. Without the no-cors mode parameter, fetch() will fail when you try to get a resource on a different origin without the CORS headers.

This object can contain other options to alter the kind of request which is made, like making a POST request instead of GET.

There is one caveat with no-cors requests. If you make a request to another origin and it doesn't have CORS, you'll get a response, but you won't be able to examine the contents of the response or see what the status code is. You can still cache and use the response, but there is no certainty that the request was successful. These restrictions are in place for security reasons while allowing you to cache these resources and serve them up from a service worker.

In our example above, we handle no-cors responses differently by checking the response type to see if it's opaque. We know we can't read the response's status or data if the type is opaque. If it's not opaque, we know the request type is either cors or basic and we can examine the status and response.

The main difference between a basic and cors response is that a CORS request restricts which headers you can read.

I've written an article on HTML5Rocks[6] which covers a few more examples of the Fetch API including how to send credentials and make POST requests.

Adding a Service Worker to Your Site

We've looked at promises and `fetch()`, which are building blocks we'll use in our service worker, but before we jump into the code, let's quickly go over the life cycle of a service worker so that as we introduce each bit of code you'll know how it fits into the bigger picture of a service worker.

LIFE CYCLE OF A SERVICE WORKER

A simplified view of the service worker life cycle has three main states.

1. Installing
1. Activating
2. Idle or Terminated

A service worker *install* event is dispatched when a new service worker is registered for a page, before it controls any pages.

The *activate* event is dispatched when a new service worker takes control of an origin (you can think of an origin as a domain with protocol and port number). This is a good time to clean up your cache or anything else if needed.

Between these and other events, the service worker can be idle, in which case the browser is keeping your service worker alive in the background in case it's needed; otherwise the browser can terminate your service worker to save resources. Let's take a look at adding a service worker to a site and how we use these life cycle events.

Register Your Service Worker

The first step to adding a service worker to your app is to tell the browser about your service worker script, which you do by registering it inside your web app.

---

6 http://updates.html5rocks.com/2015/03/introduction-to-fetch

```
if ('serviceWorker' in navigator) {
    navigator.serviceWorker.register('/serviceworker.js')
        .then(function(registration) {
            // Registration was successful :)
            console.log('ServiceWorker registration successful');
        })
        .catch(function(err) {
            // Registration failed :(
            console.log('ServiceWorker registration failed: ', err);
        });
}
```

In our web application, a user will visit our webpage and this bit of code checks if the Service Worker API exists. If it does, we register our service worker file, in this case called *serviceworker.js*. This is the clear-cut progressive enhancement step where browsers without service worker support will skip over everything and carry on as normal.

You can call `register()` as many times as you want and the browser will figure out that it's the same service worker.

There is one subtlety to the `register()` method and that comes down to the location of the service worker file on your server. In the example above, the *serviceworker.js* file is at the root of the domain, which means the service worker can intercept requests for the entire origin. However, if we placed the service worker file under */blog/serviceworker.js*, then the service worker would only be able to control pages starting with */blog* (e.g. */blog/index.html*, */blog/foo/bar/index. html* etc.). This is referred to as the *scope* of the service worker.

The original code example could be written to specify the scope:

```
if ('serviceWorker' in navigator) {
    navigator.serviceWorker.register('/serviceworker.js', {scope: './'})
        .then(function(registration) {
            // Registration was successful :)
            console.log('ServiceWorker registration successful');
        })
        .catch(function(err) {
            // Registration failed :(
```

```
            console.log('ServiceWorker registration failed: ', err);
        });
}
```

Here, the {scope: './'} is relative to the location of the current page. Using the scope parameter, you could reduce the scope while keeping the service worker at the root of your domain. For the blog example, we can reduce the scope to just *blog** URLs by doing either of the following: register('/ser-viceworker.js', {scope: './blog/'}); or moving the position of the file to register('/blog/serviceworker.js').

INSTALL STEP

After you've registered a service worker from your webpage, the browser will download your service worker file in the background before dispatching an install event.

The install event is the perfect time to cache any files that the majority of your users will need or are vital for your site to work offline.

Generally, in the install event you'll do the following:

1. Open a cache
2. Cache a set of files you know you'll need

Which you do like so:

```
var CACHE_NAME = 'my-site-cache-v1';
var urlsToCache = [
    '/index.html',
    '/styles/main.css',
    '/script/main.js'
];

self.addEventListener('install', function(event) {
    event.waitUntil(
        caches.open(CACHE_NAME)
            .then(function(cache) {
                console.log('Opened cache');
```

```
            return cache.addAll(urlsToCache);
        })
    );
});
```

What we are doing is adding an event listener for the install event, then when it's called we open a cache, giving it a name (in this case my-site-cache-v1 through CACHE_NAME) and finally call cache.addAll(urlsToCache), which requests all of the URLs in the urlsToCache array and stores them.

cache.addAll() is in the specification but is not currently implemented in Chrome at the time of writing, so to make it work you can grab the Cache polyfill[7] from GitHub.

This was my first time playing around with promises, and if you are the same you might be curious about the event.waitUntil() method. event. waitUntil takes a promise and ensures the service worker waits for the event to settle, meaning the service worker stays alive. Once the install event is complete, the service worker will start to control any pages with this origin when the user next returns to your page (either navigating to a new page or refreshing the page).

The important thing with the install event is that if the promise you return to event.waitUntil() rejects, the entire installation of the service worker will fail and it won't control your pages. Why? Well, if the caching failed for some reason (e.g. network failure for one of the assets) it could leave your pages without a file they absolutely need. But since the the cache.addAll() promise rejects on a failure, it results in the install step failing and prevents the service worker from controlling the page. The flip side of this is that *you should only cache what you really need* in the install step. More files increases the risk that one might fail and prevent your service worker from installing.

If you wanted to simply try to cache some assets, but still install regardless of whether the caching is successful or not, then you can catch the rejection, preventing event.waitUntil() from catching it.

---

7 https://github.com/coonsta/cache-polyfill

```
self.addEventListener('install', function(event) {
    // Perform install steps
        event.waitUntil(
            caches.open(CACHE_NAME)
                .then(function(cache) {
                console.log('Opened cache');
                return cache.addAll(urlsToCache);
            })
            .catch(function(err) {
                // Catch any errors so our SW will still install
                console.log('Error occured while caching install assets');
            });
        );
});
```

It's worth pointing out that the Cache API is completely separate from the HTTP cache. The Cache API is used to programmatically store request/response pairs which you manage. The HTTP cache will only be used when you make a fetch() request, which we'll look at in the next section.

The self variable is similar to window in pages. It can be used to reference the global scope of a JavaScript worker.

ACTIVATE STEP

After the service worker has successfully installed it will dispatch an activate event. This event has little use the first time it's run after a service worker is installed, but whenever you update your service worker, it's the perfect point to clean up any cached assets you no longer need.

Sooner or later you'll need to update your service worker and when you do, these are the steps that'll occur behind the scenes:

1. You publish a new version of your service worker script.
2. A user will visit your page.
3. The browser downloads your new service worker file in the background and determines it's different from the previous one.

4. Once downloaded, the install event will be dispatched in your new service worker. Meanwhile your old service worker will continue controlling your pages.

5. After the install event is complete, your new service worker will enter a waiting state.

6. When the currently open pages of your site are closed, the old service worker will be killed and the new service worker will take control of pages opened in future.

7. The new service worker will dispatch an *activate* event.

The activate event is the perfect point to manage your cache, because if you were to delete any existing caches in the install step, the previous service worker (which will still be controlling any open pages) will no longer be able to make use of that cache.

Imagine we started off with one cache, *my-site-cache-v1,* to store all of our responses, but later we decide that splitting the cached responses into *pages-cache-v1* and *blog-posts-cache-v1* to separate static pages and blog posts was a good idea. This would be the ideal scenario to clean up the old cache in the activate step.

```
self.addEventListener('activate', function(event) {

    var cacheWhitelist = ['pages-cache-v1', 'blog-posts-cache-v1'];

      event.waitUntil(
        caches.keys().then(function(cacheNames) {
          return Promise.all(
            cacheNames.map(function(cacheName) {
              if (cacheWhitelist.indexOf(cacheName) === -1) {
                return caches.delete(cacheName);
              }
            })
          );
        })
      );
});
```

The above code gets all the cache names (or keys) and iterates over them, deleting any cache that isn't in the cacheWhitelist array.

Now that we've covered the life cycle events and installed a service worker, it's time to make use of our well-managed caches.

FETCH EVENTS

The fetch event is the where everything starts to come together. The fetch event is dispatched whenever a request is made from a page controlled by your service worker.

The most basic fetch event logic you could use is to check if the requested resource is in the cache, and if so return the cached response, or otherwise fetch it from the network.

```
self.addEventListener('fetch', function(event) {
    event.respondWith(
        caches.match(event.request)
            .then(function(response) {
                // Cache hit - return response
                if (response) {
                    return response;
                }

                return fetch(event.request);
            }
        );
    );
});
```

In this very simple example, we add a fetch event listener and when it gets called we check if we have a cached response by calling caches.match(), passing in the request object. When that resolves we check to see if we have a cached response. If we do, we return this cached response to the browser; otherwise we return the promise from a fetch request which will attempt to get the resource from the network.

Once again, promises are used to determine when the event has been handled. In this case we pass a promise into event.respondWith() which will wait for the promise to resolve before returning a response to the browser.

This is a basic use case of the fetch event. It assumes we've cached some assets during the install event and either used the fetch event to return these cached assets, or got the resource from the network.

One subtlety that isn't clear from the above code is that both the event. request and response objects are streams; once you've read part of a stream, you can't read that part a second time. A common pitfall, as you'll see in the next example, is that when returning the request and response objects from a method, you can't easily tell when or if they'll be consumed. You can easily create a clone of a stream and pass the two objects as necessary to avoid the scenario of a single stream being read more than once.

To show you a slightly more complex example and illustrate this stream issue, let's cache pages as our users visit them.

```
self.addEventListener('fetch', function(event) {
  event.respondWith(
    caches.match(event.request).then(function(response) {
      // Cache hit - return response.
      if (response) {
        return response;
      };

      return fetch(event.request).then(
        function(response) {
          // Check if we received a valid response.

          if (response.type !== 'basic' || response.status !== 200) {
            return response;
          }

          // IMPORTANT: Clone the response. A response is a stream
          // and because we want the browser to consume the response
          // as well as the cache, we need to clone it so we have two streams.

          var responseToCache = response.clone();
          caches.open(CACHE_NAME).then(function(cache) {
              cache.put(event.request, responseToCache);
            });
```

```
            return response;
          }
        );
      })
    );
});
```

Let's break up each part of this. First, we check if the resource is already cached and if it is we return it, which we've seen before.

```
caches.match(event.request)
      .then(function(response) {
        // Cache hit - return response
        if (response) {
          return response;
        }
```

If we don't have the request cached, we call fetch() to get it from the network.

```
return fetch(event.request).then(
    function(response) {
        // Check if we received a valid response.
        if(response.type === 'opaque' || response.status !== 200) {
          return response;
        }

        // IMPORTANT: Clone the response. A response is a stream
        // and because we want the browser to consume the response
        // as well as the cache consuming the response, we need
        // to clone it so we have two streams.
        var responseToCache = response.clone();

        caches.open(CACHE_NAME)
          .then(function(cache) {
            cache.put(event.request, responseToCache);
          });

        return response;
    }
);
```

When a response is returned by `fetch()`, the first thing we do is check the type and status. We check for an opaque type or a non-200 status and treat these as assets we don't want to cache and return them to the browser.

If we want to cache the response, we clone it. This is because we're going to pass one response stream to the cache, and we return the original response at the end of the function. This results in `event.respondWith()` passing it to the browser to consume the stream.

Before returning the response from `fetch()`, we open our cache and put our request and response into the cache.

This is a common pattern to get you to think about the best way to implement caching for your site or web app. The world is your oyster with the fetch event. You might decide to only use the cache as a last resort when the network fails, or perhaps you want to cache specific pages you think your users are going to visit ahead of time.

Key things you need to be mindful of are how to handle slow internet connections and how to handle no internet while the device thinks it's connected. A service worker does not take into account the state of the internet `connection`, so you decide how to use the cache and network. Using the cache for every request might result in the user receiving stale information, but getting it very quickly. Serving from the network may lead to really slow responses that fail and result in the use of the cache anyway.

If you aren't sure of the best use of the network and cache for your use case and want some ideas or code examples, Jake Archibald has a fantastic blog post called "The offline cookbook"[8] which covers a range of options and is definitely worth a read if you need inspiration.

---

8 http://jakearchibald.com/2014/offline-cookbook/

Tips and Tricks

This is pretty much everything you need to know to get going with service workers. Just in case you are just starting out using service workers, this might be a good spot to give you some tips and tricks learned along the way.

CACHE CAREFULLY

Given the choice of caching everything or just specific things, always go for the specific things. It may seem like a great idea to cache anything and everything you can, but there are scenarios where this is inappropriate. Think of pages requiring sign in, or calls to RESTful APIs: do you *really* want to serve up cached versions? There are plenty of cases where caching is useful for these scenarios, but make sure you test and handle any specific needs.

It's easier to cache a few specific assets up-front and add extra non-essential things later.

CTRL + SHIFT + R

When you're developing in Chrome (and hopefully other browsers), you can force a hard refresh (*Ctrl + Shift + R* on Windows and Linux; *Cmd + Shift + R* on Mac OS X) to prevent the browser from using the HTTP cache or service worker. This allows you to test the registration of your service worker, allow a new service worker to take control of a page, or force new HTML content and assets to be pulled from the network to see if the cached version is working or not.

IMPORTSCRIPTS()

If you need to pull any JavaScript files into your service worker you can do so with `importScripts('./js/script-to-import.js')`. This works in a similar way to `<script>` elements in HTML: the included JavaScript becomes available in the global scope. Browsers will automatically cache these files for you and make them available in your service worker.

This can be a great way to split up your code into logical JavaScript files, helping to organize your code.

Constraints and Restrictions of Service Workers

One requirement of service workers is HTTPS, and there is one clear reason for this. You've probably noticed that any time you use almost any major web application (mail, social media and so on) HTTPS is used. This is because with simple HTTP it's trivially easy to intercept traffic, and inspect and even change the communication between the browser and server. Since service workers persist on a device once they've been installed, they are particularly vulnerable, even after you've left a Wi-Fi network which has been intercepting your traffic. A service worker installed or altered while using a compromised network will continue to persist on the user's device.

To use service workers, then, you'll need to serve content over HTTPS. Fortunately, this is becoming fairly straightforward. It's increasingly clear that Google is encouraging the use of HTTPS (calling for "HTTPS Everywhere"[9] at Google I/O 2014, and announcing that HTTPS will be regarded as a signal of quality in search results[10]).

The major obstacle to HTTPS for many sites is that third parties use HTTP and including these resources in a secure page will result in a mixed content warning, with browsers likely to block that content. In many cases the third party service will offer an HTTPS version; if they don't, however, you'll have to consider your strategy for when and how to move to HTTPS before implementing service workers.

Current Support

Service workers are still in an early stage of development, but Chrome has support for everything discussed in this chapter. Nightly builds of Firefox have implemented aspects of the service worker specification, and other browsers will hopefully start working on it soon. Owing to the way service workers operate outside the page, you can treat them as a progressive enhancement and start using them in your web apps today.

---

9   https://www.youtube.com/watch?v=cBhZ6S0PFCY
10   http://googleonlinesecurity.blogspot.de/2014/08/https-as-ranking-signal_6.html

Future of Service Workers

While the service worker specification is still being developed, part of its purpose is to cater for new use cases and answer developer feedback. The core of the API which we've looked at in this chapter is unlikely to change.

Instead, new methods are being added to provide extra functionality and behaviors to service workers, which I'm sure we'll all learn more about as they become available.

While we've focused on offline support, it's worth highlighting that service workers are required for a range of new features that will be coming to the web soon, including push notifications[11], background sync and geofencing.

Beyond Service Workers: Web Storage

Service workers are very powerful, yet it might not be the right tool for every single offline use case. Until recently, the only way to maintain a user's data between visits to your site has been to store it on the server or use cookies in the browser. With Web Storage — a simple, in-browser database — we can get rid of much of the need for cookies and dramatically reduce the need for server-side functionality. Google Search, Bing and other high-traffic sites also use it for caching on the client.

SERVER-SIDE DATA

Storing data on the server requires the creation and management of user accounts, sanitizing data sent to the server, worrying about server-side security risks and about security in the transmission of data between the client and the server. For many applications, storing data on the server is required, but in many other cases simply keeping data for the client locally during a session or between sessions, without the need to send it back and forward to the server, means a lot less development work and potentially fewer vectors for security breaches. On top of that, even when we need to send data to the server, if the client is offline or the server is down, we can store this locally and then synchronize once the client reconnects or the server comes back online.

---

11   http://updates.html5rocks.com/2015/03/push-notificatons-on-the-open-web

What about Cookies?

Cookies, while long used to keep data on the client during and between sessions, were actually designed for communication between browser and server that persists between sessions, so that the server could keep track of the state of previous interactions with this client (technically, they're called HTTP cookies). They're typically used for identifying a user on return visits and storing details about that user (such as if they're still logged in). Cookies are sent between the browser and server in *unencrypted plain text* each time the user opens a page. Unless an application encrypts cookie contents it's quite trivial to read them, particularly on public Wi-Fi networks when used over standard HTTP (though much less easily over encrypted HTTPS).

Storing all client data on the server creates usability issues as well, as users need to be logged in each time they use that site. The heavy lifting of ensuring data is secure during transmission and on the server is left to you as the developer. The round-trip between browser and server will affect the performance of your site or application, and it's rather tricky to build apps which work when the user is offline if the user's data is all stored on the server.

For all these reasons, as web applications become increasingly sophisticated developers need ways to keep data around in the browser (particularly if we want our applications to work when the user is offline). And we want this data to be secure.

Two closely related technologies exist to help keep track of information entirely in the browser. Together known as *Web Storage*, they allow us to store far more structured data than cookies, are much easier to develop with than cookies, and the information stored can only be transmitted to a server explicitly by the application.

- *sessionStorage* stores data during a session and is deleted by the browser once a session is finished.
- *localStorage* is almost identical, but the data stored persists indefinitely, until removed by the application.

Let's start with `sessionStorage`, keeping in mind that we use `localStorage` almost identically.

SESSION STORAGE

The key feature of `sessionStorage` is that data only persists for a session. But just what is a session? HTML5 has the concept of a top-level browsing context; this is, in essence, a browser window or tab. A session lasts for that top-level browsing context while it is open and while that top-level browsing context is pointed at the same fully qualified[12] domain (or, strictly speaking, the same origin). The user can visit different URLs within the same the domain, visit a different domain and then return to the original domain, and they would still be in the same session.

During the session, a user may visit other pages of the same domain or other sites entirely, then return to the original domain. Any data saved in sessionStorage during that session will remain available, but only to pages in the original domain, and only until the tab or `window` is closed.

If the user opens a link to your site in another tab or `window`, then the new tab or `window` has no access to this `sessionStorage`, since this new tab or `window` is a new session. That `window` will have its own, entirely separate `session-Storage` for the particular domain. It's worth noting that sessionStorage is also shared with webpages inside subframes in the same domain as the top-level `document` in the `window`. So, just to clarify, if we:

* visit *http://webdirections.org* in a tab and save data to sessionStorage
* then follow a link to *http://westciv.com* in this same tab
* and then come back to *http://webdirections.org* still in the same tab,

we return to the same session for *http://webdirections.org*, and the data in the original `sessionStorage` will still be available.

---

12 A fully qualified domain as we saw earlier means the protocol, domain, and subdomain combined. So https://webdirections.org and http: //webdirections.org are different fully qualified domains, as are tools.webdirections.org and www.webdirections.org.

However, if we:

- visit *http://webdirections.org* in a tab and save data to sessionStorage
- then follow a link to *http://webdirections.org* in a new tab or window,

the data in the original sessionStorage will not available to this new tab.

The one exception to this is when a browser crashes and is restarted. Typically in this case, browsers will reopen all the windows that were open when the browser crashed. In this situation, the specification allows session-Storage to persist for reopened windows from before the crash (Safari, Blink, Chrome, Firefox and Opera browsers support this; IE8 does not, though IE9 and up do).

Which may sound like a great boon for the user, but as an application developer you might wish to consider whether you want session data to persist after a crash. A user might assume their login details were purged when their browser crashed while using a service like webmail or online banking at an internet café or another public computer; but if they were stored in session-Storage then the next user to launch the browser will resume the session that was current when the browser crashed. Ruh-roh.

What could we do about this?

Well, when a document loads we get a load event. Why not have an event handler that deletes the current sessionStorage when this event fires?

```
window.addEventListener("load", clearSessionStorage, false);

function clearSessionStorage() {
    window.sessionStorage.clear();
}
```

We'll look more at the clear method of sessionStorage shortly.

WHAT GOOD IS SESSIONSTORAGE?

One very useful application would be to maintain sensitive information during a transaction, sign-up, sign-in and so on, which will be purged as soon as the user closes the window or tab. It can be used to create a multi-page form or application, where the information in each page can persist and then be sent to the server all at once when the transaction is complete. It also moves some of the heavy lifting for protecting sensitive data away from application developers to the browser developer.

Applications, like an email reader, could use it to keep local copies of emails, which will be automatically purged as soon as the user closes the window or tab.

USING SESSIONSTORAGE

sessionStorage is a property of the window object in the DOM. Because it is not universally supported, we need to check that this property exists before using it:

```
if('sessionStorage' in window) {
   // We use sessionStorage
}

else {
   // We do something else, perhaps use cookies, or another fallback
}
```

Right, now we have our sessionStorage object, how do we use it?

KEY-VALUE PAIRS

sessionStorage stores key–value pairs. Each pair is a piece of information (the *value*) identified by a unique identifier (the *key*). Both the key and the value are strings (more on the implications of this in a moment). We use the setItem method of the sessionStorage object to store data like so:

```
// Get the value of the input with id="name"
var name = document.querySelector('#name').value;

// Store this value with the key "name"
window.sessionStorage.setItem('name', name);
```

Now we've stored the value of the input "name" in an item of the session-Storage object also called 'name'. It will remain there until this window or tab is closed and it will then automatically be purged by the browser when the user closes that window or tab[13].

Notice that we haven't had to create a sessionStorage object, initialize it, or even create an item. Where supported, sessionStorage is waiting there, ready for us to use. And simply setting an item using setItem creates that item if it doesn't exist.

READING FROM SESSIONSTORAGE

There's not much point in storing these details if we can't get them back at some point. We do this by using the function getItem of the sessionStorage object, using a single parameter, the key we used to set the item.

So, to get the value of the item with the key "name", we'd use:

```
var name = window.sessionStorage.getItem('name');
Nonexistent Items
```

Now, what happens if for some reason there's no item in sessionStorage with the key we are trying to access? In place of a string value, it returns null, not the empty string. So, it's worthwhile testing whether the result returned is not null before using it:

```
var savedEmail = window.sessionStorage.getItem('email');
if (savedEmail !== null) {
    document.querySelector('#email').value = savedEmail;
}
```

---

13 By using Chrome's "Reopen Last Closed Tab", the sessionStorage is restored from before a tab was closed.

Saving Data Between Sessions

When information is less sensitive, it often makes sense to store it between sessions. Particularly as websites become more application-like and can increasingly work offline, saving preferences or the state of a document can make for much better usability. For these situations we have localStorage. In almost every way identical to sessionStorage, the key differences are that:

- where the contents of a particular sessionStorage are only available to the window or tab in which they were saved — and only for the fully qualified domain in which they were saved — with localStorage, any window or tab at the same fully qualified domain can access the localStorage for that domain.
- the data stored in localStorage persists between sessions

Best of all, using localStorage for persistence between sessions is almost identical to using sessionStorage.

USING LOCALSTORAGE

As we've mentioned, all the methods of localStorage are the same as the methods of sessionStorage:

- we set items with setItem
- we get items with getItem

Let's look at some further features of sessionStorage and localStorage.

localStorage.removeItem()

Because items in localStorage will otherwise persist forever, there are times we may want to delete them. We can do this with localStorage.removeItem(key), using the key for the item we want to remove. We can also use this with sessionStorage, but since that is purged completely when the user closes the window or tab, we're less likely to want to do that.

localStorage.clear()

If we want to delete the entire `localStorage`, we can use `localStorage.clear()`. But be warned: anything your app has saved to `localStorage` for this user is gone for good. We saw a little earlier that `sessionStorage` too has a clear method, which we used on page load to ensure that if the browser has crashed, the `sessionStorage` isn't restored. We won't necessarily want to do that, but if there's sensitive information the user might assume is deleted when the browser crashes, you may want to do this.

localStorage.key()

As we saw, we access `localStorage` and `sessionStorage` with keys, which are strings. Web Storage provides a way of getting the keys, using the `key()` method. This takes an integer argument and returns the associated key value. For example, let's suppose we did this:

```
window.localStorage.setItem("title", "Mr");
window.localStorage.setItem("name", "John");
window.localStorage.setItem("familyName", "Allsopp");
```

Then we ask for the `window.localStorage.key(2)`, we'll get "familyName" (remember, indexes to arrays in JavaScript are zero-based). What good is this? Well, combined with the length property, which we'll see just below, we can now iterate over all the items in `localStorage` or `sessionStorage`.

localStorage.length()

We can determine how many items `sessionStorage` or `localStorage` is currently storing using the length property. We could then use this, along with the key method, to iterate over the items in the storage. Here, we'll get every item in the `localStorage` and add it to an array. I'm not saying you're going to need to do this very often, though `localStorage` and `sessionStorage` are synchronous, and we can't be sure some or all of the items aren't stored on disk, so working with them may be slow. This is one way of moving them into memory before working on them.

```
var currentKey;
var currentItem;
var allItems = [];
for (var i=0; i < window.localStorage.length; i++) {
    currentKey = window.localStorage.key(i);
    currentItem = window.localStorage.getItem(currentKey);
    allItems.push({key: currentKey, item: currentItem});
};
```

Gotchas, Tips And Tricks

While Web Storage is not too burdened with gotchas, there are a number of quirks and issues you'll need to be aware of to work most effectively with it.

SESSIONSTORAGE AND LOCALSTORAGE STORE ALL DATA AS STRINGS

As mentioned earlier, the values stored in localStorage and sessionStorage are strings, which has some of implications for developers.

Among other things, when we store Boolean values, integers, floating point numbers, dates, objects and other non-string values, we need to convert to and from a string when writing to and reading from storage. Perhaps the most effective way of doing this is to use the JSON format.

JSON AND LOCALSTORAGE

As we've just seen, when working with non-string values, we'll need to convert them to strings if we want to store them in localStorage or sessionStorage; we'll need to convert them back from strings to their original format when we get them out of storage. The most straightforward way to do this is to use JavaScript's JSON object to convert to and from a string value.

If you're not familiar with it, JSON (JavaScript Object Notation) is a format for representing JavaScript values (numbers, booleans, arrays and objects) as strings. The standard JavaScript JSON object can convert to and from JSON strings and JavaScript values.

The JSON object has two methods:

- JSON.stringify(), which converts a JavaScript value to a JSON formatted string. You may be wondering why it's not JSON.toString. In JavaScript, all objects have a toString method which returns the string representation of the object itself. In this case, we don't want the string representation of the JSON object, which is what JSON.toString would give us. JSON.parse(), which takes a string and recreates the object, array or other value that this string represents (provided the string is valid JSON).

When saving any non-string value to localStorage, we'll need to convert it to JSON; and when reading from localStorage, we'll need to parse it back from the JSON-formatted string. Something like this:

```
var person = JSON.parse(window.localStorage.getItem("john"));
window.localStorage.setItem("john", JSON.stringify(person));
```

There's also a more subtle side effect of storing values as strings. JavaScript strings are 16-bit, so each character, even an ASCII character, is two bytes (in UTF-8, characters are one byte). This effectively halves the available storage space.

LOCALSTORAGE AND PRIVACY SETTINGS

While we know localStorage is a different technology from cookies, browsers largely treat them as the same from a user's privacy perspective. Where a user chooses to prevent a site from storing cookies, attempts to access localStorage for that site (both writing and reading previously saved data) will report a security error.

Even if the user has a privacy setting that blocks the use of localStorage, the window.localStorage will still exist, and there's no method or property of the localStorage object that allows us to determine whether this is the case. But we can test for whether localStorage is available by attempting to set an item, and catching any exceptions:

```
function storageEnabled(){
  //  Are cookies enabled? try setting an item to see if we get an error

    try {
        window.localStorage.setItem("test", "t");
        return true
    }
    catch (exception) {
        // It's possible we're out of space, but it's only 1 byte,
        // So much more likely it's a security error
        // Most browsers report an error of 18, if you want to check
        return false

    }
}
```

If the European Cookies Law (the EU e-Privacy Directive) applies to sites you build, be mindful that the law also applies to HTML5 Web Storage[14].

Private Browsing

Many browsers now have *private* (or *incognito*) browsing modes, where no history or other details are stored between sessions. In this situation, what happens with sessionStorage and localStorage varies widely by browser.

- Safari returns null for any item set using localStorage.setItem either before or during the private browsing session. In essence, neither sessionStorage nor localStorage are available in private browsing mode. Safari throws the same error it gives when it exceeds the limit for a domain — QUOTA_EXCEEDED_ERR (more on this below) — rather than a security error, as it does when cookies are disabled.
- Chrome and Opera return items set prior to the start of private browsing, but once private browsing begins they treat localStorage like sessionStorage: only items set on the localStorage by that session will be returned; and like localStorage for other private windows and tabs.

---

14 http://www.theeucookielaw.com

• Firefox, like Chrome, will not retrieve items set on localStorage prior to a private session starting; but in private browsing treats localStorage like sessionStorage for non-private windows and tabs, and like localStorage for other private windows and tabs.

Getters and Setters

In addition to using getItem and setItem, we can use a key directly to get and set an item in sessionStorage and localStorage, like so (where the key here is "familyName"):

```
var itemValue = window.localStorage.familyName;
window.localStorage.familyName = itemValue;
```

If we want to set or get an item using a key value calculated within the program itself, we can do so using array notation and the key name. The equivalent to the example above would be:

```
var keyname = "familyName"
var itemValue = window.localStorage[keyname];
window.localStorage[keyname] = itemValue;
```

LocalStorage and SessionStorage Limits

The Web Storage specification recommends browsers implement a limit on the amount of data localStorage or sessionStorage can save for a given domain. If you try to exceed the limit that various browsers have in place (for some browsers, users can change this allowance), setItem throws an error. There's no way of asking localStorage for the amount of space remaining, so it's best to set item values within a try and catch for any error:

```
try {
    window.localStorage.setItem(key, value);
}
catch (exception) {
    // Test if this is a QUOTA_EXCEEDED_ERR
}
```

If the available space for this localStorage is exceeded, the exception object will have the name QUOTA_EXCEEDED_ERR and an error code of 22.

As mentioned, strings are 16-bit in JavaScript, which means that each and every one-byte character is two bytes. On the web we typically use UTF-8 encoding, a one-byte encoding; when saving the string "John" (four bytes in UTF-8), we are actually storing eight bytes. This effectively halves the available storage space.

Currently, major browsers have the following limits per domain[15] on Web Storage. Note that these are the sizes in bytes, and so the numbers of characters you can store uncompressed are half these:

- Chrome: 5MB
- Firefox: localStorage 5MB; sessionStorage unlimited
- Opera: 5MB
- Safari iOS: 5MB
- Internet Explorer: 10MB
- Android: localStorage 5MB; sessionStorage unlimited
- Safari: localStorage 5MB; sessionStorage unlimited

If the storage needs of your application are likely to exceed 5MB, then web databases are likely a better solution. However, the situation with web databases is complicated, with two different standards. One, Web SQL, is widely supported but deprecated; the other, IndexedDB, is currently supported in Firefox, Chrome, Opera, Android 4.4+ and IE10. When iOS8 and Safari 8 for Mac OS X are released, IndexedDB will be supported in all major browsers and on all major platforms.

---

15 http://dev-test.nemikor.com/web-storage/support-test/

Storage Events

One of the features of `localStorage` is that the same database can be shared between multiple open tabs or windows; which also raises the issue of how these different top-level browsing contexts (the technical term for a window or tab in HTML5) can keep data synchronized. Here's where storage events come into play. When `localStorage` changes, a `storageChanged` event is sent to the *other* windows and tabs open for that domain (there's a reason for the emphasis).

We can create an event handler, so that when a storage object has been changed we can be notified and respond to those changes.

```
window.addEventListener('storage', storageChanged, false);
```

Now, when `localStorage` is changed (by setting a new item, deleting an item or changing an existing item) our function `storageChanged(event)` will be called. The event passed as a parameter to this function has a property, `storageArea`, which is the window's `localStorage` object. (Note this doesn't work for `sessionStorage` because `sessionStorage` is restricted to a single window or tab.) What other information do we get in our event handler? The event has these storage-specific properties:

- `key`: the key of the item changed
- `oldValue`: the value changed from
- `newValue`: the value changed to
- `url`: the URL of the page whose `localStorage` was changed

There are two things to be aware of with storage events.

- The event only fires if the storage is changed, not if it is simply accessed and not if we set an item to the same value that it currently has.

• In the specification, the event is not received in the window or tab where the change occurred, only in other open windows and tabs that have access to this localStorage. Some browsers have implemented storage events in such a way that the event is also received by the window or tab that causes the change, but you shouldn't rely on this.

While it may be useful to know a stored value has been changed if the user has two or more tabs or windows open for your site or app, storage events can be more useful than that. We can use them to very simply pass messages between different open windows that are pointed to the same domain. Now, you might be thinking that we already have postMessage for this very purpose, but here we can kill two birds with one stone — persist the state of an application in localStorage, as well as pass a message to other windows open at the domain about the state change. Another reason this is superior to postMessage is that unlike with postMessage we don't have to know about the existence of other windows to send them messages.

How might we use storage events? Well, suppose the user logs out of our app in one window, but has other windows open for the app. We could listen for changes to localStorage and then log the user out in all open windows of the app. Here's how we might listen to whether the user is signed in or out of our service in our storage event handler. We'll use an item with the key "status" to save the current status. To make things simpler (so we don't need to convert to and from a Boolean value), we'll use a string value ("signed in") when the user is signed in.

```
function storageChanged(storageEvent) {
  if(storageEvent.key === "status"&& storageEvent.newValue === "signed in")

  {
    // The user just signed in
  }

  else if (storageEvent.key === "status") {
    // The user just signed out
  }
}
```

WEB STORAGE PERFORMANCE CONCERNS

Quite often developers tend to avoid localStorage because of its performance shortcomings. The key criticism relates to the fact that Web Storage is synchronous. This means a script using sessionStorage or localStorage waits while getItem, setItem and other methods are invoked. In theory, this can affect both the browser's response to user input and execution of JavaScript in a page. In practice, I'd argue that this is not likely to be a significant problem in most cases.

To consider these concerns, John conducted tests across a number of devices and browsers which demonstrate that even for poorly implemented code that performs a very significant number of getItem and setItem operations, the performance of Web Storage is unlikely to have a significant impact. Yes, if you are writing hundreds of large (10s or 100s of KB of data per access) to localStorage frequently, it may not be the ideal solution. But in most situations for which Web Storage was designed, it's going to be adequate.

Origin Restrictions

We said earlier that that sessionStorage and localStorage are restricted to windows or tabs in the same domain, but in fact, the restriction is tighter than simply the top-level domain (such as *webdirections.org*).

To have access to one another's Web Storage, tabs or windows must have the same fully qualified domain; that is, top-level domains (for example *webdirections.org*), subdomains (for example *test.webdirections.org*); and protocol (*https:// webdirections.org* has a different localStorage from *http://webdirections.org*). At first glance this might seem overly restrictive but imagine *john.wordpress.org* having access to the localStorage of *james.wordpress.org*?

BROWSER SUPPORT

Web Storage is supported in all versions of Internet Explorer since IE8, as well as Firefox, Chrome and Safari for many versions, and on Safari for iOS and the stock Android browser for many versions as well. The challenge for backwards compatibility is essentially limited to IE7 and earlier.

For browsers that don't support Web Storage there are several polyfills[16], that provide support for the localStorage API in these browsers.

JSON is supported natively in all browsers which support `localStorage`.

Web Storage solves a long-standing challenge for web developers: reliably and more securely storing data between sessions entirely on the client-side. While there are assertions that performance limitations make `localStorage` harmful, in the real world, services like Google and Bing are using `localStorage`, and performance experts like Steve Souders and Nicholas Zakas defend and advocate their use. That's not to say Web Storage is perfect or ideal in all situations. The synchronous nature of the API and potential limits per origin do mean that in certain circumstances an alternative may be required. Web Storage is, however, eminently usable for a great many client side data storage needs.

> While Web Storage is a good solution for storing a relatively small amount of simple data, for more complex situations it's not ideal. When a more sophisticated database solution is required, we can use IndexedDB and Web SQL, but an introduction to them is beyond the scope of this chapter.

AN OFFLINE-FRIENDLY WEB

The capabilities to build websites and apps which work when the user isn't connected have long been at hand. It's less the technical capabilities of the Web platform than that the user experience has been holding back a more offline-capable web.

Web-friendly, even web-native platforms like Firefox OS and Chrome OS are on the rise; the capabilities of Android and iOS browsers are moving toward parity with native apps. I'm confident the current period of the web being a second-class citizen on these (indeed, on all) platforms, will be seen increasingly as a distant memory.

---

16 https://github.com/Modernizr/Modernizr/wiki/HTML5-Cross-Browser-Polyfills#web-storage-lo-calstorage-and-sessionstorage

Are we entirely there yet? Not quite. But in many ways that's all the more reason to adopt these technologies. Their day is coming and early adopters are always best placed to really benefit when those technologies are ready for prime time.

ABOUT THE AUTHOR

John invented the foundation of responsive design way ahead of its time. With his article *Dao of Flexibility*, he prompted designers and developers to embrace the fluidity and flexibility of the web, not decry them as bugs. Residing in Sydney, Australia, he spends a lot of time writing, coding and running conferences, recently focusing his research on offline technologies. He is very friendly, knowing a thing or two about good food, with a particular passion for sushi.

ABOUT THE AUTHOR

With a background in mobile software engineering, Matt now spends most of his time working on everything related to the open web. He is a senior developer advocate at *Google*, caring about Service Workers, amongst other things. He also loves playing the guitar and enjoys hardware hacking, although he's new to it.

ABOUT THE REVIEWER

Jake Archibald works in Google Chrome's developer relations team, working on specs, testing implementations, and ensuring developers have tools to make their jobs less painful. He's a big fan of time-to-render optimizations, progressive enhancement, and all of that responsive stuff.

COUNTING STARS: CREATIVITY OVER PREDICTABILITY

ANDREW CLARKE

CHAPTER ELEVEN · BY ANDREW CLARKE

COUNTING STARS:
CREAVITY OVER PREDICTABILITY

P EOPLE HAVE CALLED ME A LOT OF THINGS since I started working on the web. I try to forget some of them, but Jeffrey Zeldman — without whom most of us wouldn't be working in this industry — once called me a "triple-talented bastard." If you know how much I admire Jeffrey, you'll also know how much that meant.

My background's in fine art, rather than in graphic design or technology, and for the last sixteen years, I've worked as an art director and designer in a small creative studio called Stuff and Nonsense[1]. We spend our time designing for clients and for screens. As my friend Brendan Dawes once said (of himself), we "make fillings for rectangles."

---

1   http://stuffandnonsense.co.uk

I've been designing for the web for most of my working life, and so it feels like I know the medium pretty well. I've seen it change in ways that go far beyond what we see on screen. Beyond the emergence of the web standards technologies that Jeffrey Zeldman championed. Beyond the rise of mobile and the challenges of responsive web design.

At the same time, I'm watching our industry mature into something that's very different from the almost joyfully naive, creative designer's playground it was when I started. It's now a place where designers rub shoulders with developers, researchers, scientists and user experience professionals.

Much of what has changed has been for the better; our combined knowledge and experience, plus the growing maturity of the ways we approach our work, have led, in many ways, to a better web. We've made a web that's more accessible, flexible and responsive to users' needs as well as to devices of all kinds.

Yet, as proud as I am with what we've achieved, I look at today's web design with a growing sense of dissatisfaction, almost melancholy, because for everything we've gained, I fear there's something that we're losing.

While we focus our thoughts on processes, methods and mechanics for making the web more responsive, instead of on ideas, we're losing the creative *soul* of our work. Soul that embodies individuality, personality, originality, and opinion. Soul that connects people with ideas. Soul that makes ideas memorable. Soul that makes what we do matter.

I fear that our designs lack energy and spontaneity because we're thinking too early and then too often about the consequences of failure. I fear that we're creating a web that's full of safe designs because we're driven by the need in some of us for predictability, reliability and repeatability. We're creating a web where design rarely dares to stray beyond the boundaries of established conventions.

The modern web demands to be responsive and this is a creative challenge that we should relish. Multiscreen design represents an incredible opportunity to be creative, but so many of our designs follow same responsive formulas.

I don't fear that all hope is lost and I know that we can recover our ability to make memorable creative work for the web. I hope that this soulless period will pass like so many phases before it. I'm hopeful that we're still capable of making work that, as Jony Ive said when he spoke about Steve Jobs in an interview for Time magazine, can "suck the air from the room."[2]

Giving our work soul, making space and time for creativity, experimentation and, above all, ideas — that's the subject of this chapter. I've taken its title from a quote from Mad Men's Don Draper. It's from an episode called 'The Monolith' in season seven, set in 1968. Don was told that "the IBM 360 (computer) can count more stars in a day than we can in a lifetime," and he replied, "But what man laid on his back counting stars and thought about a number?"

The advertising world that Don inhabits is going to be the backdrop to this chapter because I believe that advertising is one place where we can look for the soul we're missing. It's also where we can learn as much about clear and concise communication, reduction and simplification as we can in what many now call user experience. I find advertising fascinating, but I know that not everyone shares my enthusiasm.

Our Responsive Designs Lack Soul

As someone who studied fine art, I believe that the job of solving our biggest problems should be for artists as well as for designers or engineers. I'm also as much of a sucker for an artist's quote as I am for advertising. However, the artist Banksy doesn't share my fondness for advertising, and he wrote:

> ❝ *People are taking the piss out of you every day. They butt into your life, take a cheap shot at you and then disappear. They leer at you from tall buildings and make you feel small. They make flippant comments from buses that imply you're not sexy enough and that all the fun is happening somewhere else. They are on TV making your girlfriend feel inadequate. They have access to the most sophisticated technology the world has ever seen and they bully you with it. They are The Advertisers and they are laughing at you.*"[3]

2 http://time.com/jonathan-ive-apple-interview/
3 http://lit.genius.com/Banksy-letter-on-advertising-annotated

There's a common perception that advertising is an industry that routinely interrupts you when you least want interrupting, regularly attempts to sell you products you neither want nor need, and lies to you as it sells.

Writer and humorist Stephen Leacock once wrote:

> 66 *Advertising may be described as the science of arresting the human intelligence long enough to get money from it."*[4]

Ouch. For some, "advertising" has become a dirty word.

So how can advertising — an industry that some might argue is outdated and irrelevant — teach us anything about the very different industry that we work in today? In his book *Purple Cow*, Seth Godin wants us to:

> 66 *Stop advertising and start innovating [...] because as consumers we're too busy to pay attention to advertising."*[5]

Yet he acknowledges that it's probably impossible to read through a list of successful brands without either picturing one of their commercials, remembering their taglines or hearing their jingles ringing in our ears. Advertising has given us some of the strongest and most memorable creative work in decades, and the mark of great advertising is that it stays with us long after a campaign is over.

IT'S THE TASTE

I guess that every generation remembers particular advertising. For me, it's DDB's chimpanzee campaign for PG Tips tea — "It's the tea you can really taste." The campaign began in 1956 with a black-and-white commercial and a voiceover by none other than Peter Sellers. The chimpanzees, often voiced by famous actors and comedians, parodied popular culture, politics, sports, and television for the next three decades. In 1971, "Avez vous un cuppa?" and "Cooey,

---

4   http://simple.wikiquote.org/wiki/Stephen_Leacock
5   http://www.sethgodin.com/purple/

Mister Shifter" became catchphrases that were as memorable as the campaign's taglines, "There's no other tea to beat PG" and "It's the tea you can really taste."

In the first two years of the chimpanzee campaign and off the back of its advertising, PG Tips went from fourth position to number one, and they maintained the top spot for the next 32 years, largely owing to their creative advertising. The campaign was more than clever copywriting and well-trained chimpanzees, and it succeeded because the combination of advertising and entertainment made the pleasure of watching the commercials synonymous with drinking PG Tips tea.

Mister Shifter, one of the most fondly remembered PG Tips commercials from the 1970s.

I could write an entire book about PG Tips and the chimpanzee advertising — and maybe one day I will — or about Leonard Rossiter and Joan Collins' commercials for Cinzano. Please don't get me started on Cadbury's Smash instant mashed potato; or 1970s Texan bars, a toffee chocolate bar whose commercials featured a cartoon cowboy and possibly the best/worst cowboy tagline, "A man's gotta chew what a man's gotta chew." Texan bars sure were "a mighty chew."

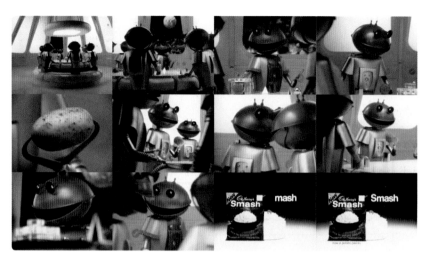

Advertising agency Boase Massimi Pollitt and the Smash Martians helped to make Smash popular in 1974.

Today's equivalent might be Wieden+Kennedy's campaign for Old Spice's "The Man Your Man Could Smell Like": a series of commercials that cleverly targeted a male body wash product at female buyers who imagined their man smelling like the man in the commercials.

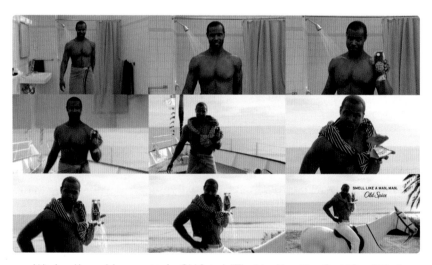

Wieden+Kennedy's campaign for Old Spice's "The Man Your Man Could Smell Like."

THE SMELL OF A NEW CAR

Some people confuse advertising with misleading people about a product. However, successful and effective advertising, through a process of reduction, of removing messages that may cloud communication, aims to communicate and emphasize a truth about a product or a service or brand.

DDB's famous campaign for the VW Beetle — the campaign that invented the modern advertising industry — wasn't just memorable for its clever copywriting and distinctive art direction, but because it told the truth about Volkswagen's product. The Beetle was noisy and small but it was also well built and reliable. That was the truth. DDB's advertising didn't hide it and customers responded to that and the messages the advertising conveyed.

It still being the post-war period, consumers also responded to Volkswagen's carefully constructed messages about the Beetle's size and economy. A Beetle was a smart choice and people aspired to feel smart about choosing one. In many ways the ads said, "this car is smart and individual, like you."

Successful advertising always provokes an emotional response in us as consumers; and as Don Draper said in the first ever episode of Mad Men:

> 66 *Advertising is based on one thing: happiness. And you know what happiness is? Happiness is the smell of a new car. It's freedom from fear. It's a billboard on the side of the road that screams reassurance that whatever you are doing is okay. You are okay."*[6]

Old Spice's "The Man Your Man Could Smell Like" commercials say nothing about the product itself apart from the fact that it doesn't smell "lady-scented." They also knowingly play on the fact that the advertisers and the audience know that the product won't turn men into Isaiah Mustafa.

I would argue that Old Spice also told the truth about what it thinks many women consumers were thinking. They wanted their man to smell (and look) like Isaiah. Leonard Rossiter, Joan Collins and the Cinzano advertisers told the truth too. Just like Rossiter's character, Cinzano was pretending to belong to a

---

6   http://en.wikiquote.org/wiki/Mad_Men#Smoke_Gets_in_Your_Eyes_.5B1.01.5D

higher social class. For thirty years, PG Tips owned the truth about tea. Drinking a cup of PG Tips makes people happy.

All these campaigns conveyed messages about the products they advertised and they did it with the charm, personality and wit that's so vital in making creative work memorable.

While we can all probably point to a memorable commercial (PG Tips), poster campaign (United Colors of Benetton), or magazine ad (Levi's 501 black,) can you point to as memorable a website from recent times?

I can think of many websites that are well presented, easy to use, triumphs of user experience and technically competent, but few that might be remembered for years to come. Why do you think this is? Why are so few websites memorable? Why do so few bare their souls? What could be the reasons?

Could the design processes we've come to rely on, particularly in relation to responsive design, have hindered our creativity? Our modern web design magazines are full of advice about process, techniques and tools, but little about creativity, about humanity, or about ideas.

Can our emphasis on human–computer interaction mean that we forget the importance of human–human communication?

Does our reliance on research and testing mean that we're simply delegating decision-making and abdicating responsibility for our designs?

Has our current preoccupation with user experience methodologies meant that we're less willing to take risks? Have we become so fixated with designing digital products that we've forgotten that the web is a medium for communication outside of applications? Much of what I read today amplifies the voices of data-driven design over ideas-led design. Irene Au is the former head of design at Google and Yahoo and she explains user experience like this:

> ❝ User experience design is a multidisciplinary field. A well-designed product
> must be visually appealing and simple, and easy to understand, learn, and use.
> Creating a well-designed product is an endeavor that requires technical skills—an
> understanding of computer science, human computer interaction, and visual
> perception and cognition—and tremendous creativity."[7]

---

7   https://medium.com/@ireneau/understanding-ux-skills-21ad9c22f0bf

I believe that all these factors have combined to create an environment that produces work that, while aesthetically appealing, well-considered and technically accomplished, still somehow lacks the emotional appeal that's as important as functional abilities.

LETTERS TO A JUNIOR DESIGNER

In April 2014, A List Apart magazine published a "Letter to a Junior Designer"[8] by columnist, product designer at Twitter, and author of *Undercover User Experience Design* Cennydd Bowles. In it he made his case for young or new designers to "slow down," "think it through," and "temper their passion."

"*Slow down,*" he wrote. "You pluck an idea from the branch and throw it onto the plate before it has time to ripen." He went on:

> 66 *Perhaps your teachers exalted The Idea as the gem of creative work; taught you The Idea is the hard part. I disagree. Ideas aren't to be trusted. They need to be wrung dry, ripped apart.*"

When I read his words and I thought about the junior designers Cennydd was writing to, I imagined design as it might be in a dystopian future where there's little time for an idea to blossom before it's crushed under the boot of user experience.

When Cennydd wrote:

> 66 *In time, the distinction between idea and iteration will blur. Eventually, the two become one.*"

I heard the words of George Orwell:

> 66 *Power is in tearing human minds to pieces and putting them together again in new shapes of your own choosing.*"[9]

---

8 http://alistapart.com/column/letter-to-a-junior-designer
9 http://en.wikiquote.org/wiki/Nineteen_Eighty-Four#Chapter_3_3

Like Winston Smith's character at the end of 1984, I imagined the junior designers Cennydd was writing to as disheartened and demoralized, yet somehow accepting their fate.

I felt compelled to respond, so I wrote "A Different Letter to a Junior Designer."[10] One that I hoped would inspire rather than depress those same junior designers.

I wanted to tell them that there can be a future where their energy and enthusiasm will make a difference. That they must never forget that it's ideas that matter most, that without them there would be nothing. That you can't turn a poor idea into a brilliant one by iterating. That instead of having fewer ideas, we must make more.

"Don't slow down," as Cennydd suggested. *"Speed up."* I wrote:

❝ *Your mind is a muscle, just like any other: you need to use it to keep it in top condition. To keep making ideas happen, make more of them, more often. Feed your mind with inspiration wherever you can find it. Exercise it with play. Make idea after idea until making them becomes a reflex."*

The truth is, we don't always need to think things through, at least not right away. We can't ever predict the path our ideas will take. We can't know the restrictions they'll face nor the limitations that will be put on them. My advice is not to try.

Too often I see brilliant ideas extinguished because people think about practicalities too early. How will this be built? How can we make it responsive? How will someone use it? These are important questions, at the right time. Naturally, some ideas will fade, but others will dazzle. Before we pinch out the flickering flame of a new idea, let it burn brightly for a while longer, unhindered by practicalities.

---

10 http://alistapart.com/blog/post/a-different-letter-to-a-junior-designer

CREATIVE HIJINKS

A tension between approaches to design — between data- and implementation-led digital product design and ideas-driven web design, as starkly illustrated by Cennydd's and my respective letters to junior designers — certainly isn't a new phenomenon.

Towards the end of the 1960s, technology had begun to creep into advertising and in 1968, Mad Men's Sterling Cooper & Partners agency installed their first computer, the room-filling, low-humming IBM System/360 that I mentioned earlier. Of course, this being Mad Men, nothing's ever as straightforward as installing a computer.

Practically, entering the future means installing that computer on the site of the agency's creative lounge, a space where art directors and copywriters meet to collaborate. Without a central space to share, the creatives are forced back into their separate offices, afraid that the computer will replace them. Don Draper's only half joking when he asks the engineer who's installing the computer: "Who's winning? Who's replacing more humans?"

New partner Jim Cutler's vision for SC&P is in stark contrast to Don's when he says:

> 66 *I know what this company should look like. Computer services."*

and:

> 66 *This agency is too dependent on creative personalities. We need to tell our clients we're thinking about the future, not creative hijinks."*[11]

It might seem at first that Cennydd's data-led digital product design and my ideas-driven web design are at opposite ends of a spectrum of design styles, but ideas aren't at odds with user experience — they are a fundamental part of it. The mixing of the two is a wonderful creative challenge. There is common ground that gives me hope. Cennydd wrote in his letter to a junior designer:

---

11 http://www.reddit.com/r/madmen/comments/24f5qh/quotes_from_duck_phillips_and_jim_cutler/

66 *We'd love to believe design speaks for itself, but a large part of the job is helping others hear its voice."*

I agree, because when our work has a voice, it means that it stands for something.

ALLERGIC TO RESEARCH

Sir John Hegarty is a co-founder of advertising agency Bartle Bogle Hegarty, BBH. He's written about advertising in his book *Hegarty On Advertising: Turning Intelligence Into Magic* and most recently about creativity in *There are No Rules*, and I can't recommend both books highly enough. He wrote:

66 *It's essential [...] for a creative company to have a point of view and a philosophical foundation for their work."*[12]

And a point of view is an essential part of design. Like the best art, the best design must stand for something. We should ask ourselves: What does my work, or my company, stand for? What are our principles? We must stand behind our work because we believe in it, not because our point of view has evolved through iteration, been validated by testing or driven by research.

David Ogilvy, whom the New York Times once called "The Father of Advertising," was fanatical about George Gallup's research work and the company Gallup founded in 1935 after leaving the Young and Rubicam advertising agency where he'd been director of research. Ogilvy wrote in his book *Ogilvy On Advertising*:

66 *For 35 years I have continued in the [research] course charted by Gallup collecting factors the way other men collect pictures and postage stamps. If you choose to ignore these factors, good luck to you. A blind pig can sometimes find truffles, but it helps to know that they are found in oak forests."*[13]

---

12 http://www.hegartyonadvertising.com/assets/pdf/hegarty-extract.pdf (PDF, 695KB)
13 http://www.ogilvy.com/About/Our-History/David-Ogilvy-Books.aspx

I disagree with Ogilvy. I believe that research should *inform* creative decisions, not direct them, and that no amount of research is a substitute for a good idea. At least not on its own. I guess that by disagreeing, I'm simply proving Ogilvy correct when he wrote in his book that *"Creative people are stubbornly allergic to research."*

I worry, though, that as an industry we've become too heavily focused on conversations about research-driven, data-led design and subsequent implementation issues including performance and responsiveness. Perhaps this is because our industry's press writes more about apps than it does about websites. Just as our press needs to find a better balance, so do we. I'm happy that Cennydd and I agree. In a follow-up to our letters, Cennydd wrote:

> 66 *As with any discussion about beliefs, the danger lies in the extremes. It's possible to become so invested in a data-only or idea-only approach that you become blind to the value of fitting your approach to the context."*[14]

That's true: we should temper our use of data with hunches and vice versa, because, as Cennydd went on:

> 66 *Product design that's driven entirely by data is horrible. It leads us down a familiar path: the 41 shades of blue, the death by 1000 cuts, the button whose only purpose is to make a metric arc upward. It's soul-destroying for a designer."*

We should acknowledge that data-informed design "reduces risk, and encourages confidence and accountability." But at the same time we must understand that the creative process is, by definition, unpredictable and so we should embrace risk because we may never know what direction an idea will take us.

---

14 http://www.cennydd.com/blog/ideas-andor-data

Process And Predictability

I'd like you to cast your mind back to advertising ideas that have stayed with you. If you're a British beer drinker, you might remember BBH's The Cream of Manchester campaign for Boddingtons Brewery in the 1990s. In 1997, Boddingtons' sales peaked, largely attributed to its clever advertising.

If you have more exotic tastes, you might recall Saatchi & Saatchi's campaign for Castlemaine XXXX. The XXXX brand was first introduced way back in 1924, and the campaign taught thirsty Brits that Castlemaine is a town in the state of Victoria and XXXX refers to a tradition of using Xs to indicate the strength of a beer. Saatchi made the beer a household name in the 1980s with a campaign that featured the tagline, "Australians wouldn't give a XXXX for anything else."

BBH's 'The Cream of Manchester' campaign helped Boddingtons Brewery boost sales in 1997.

Foster's Lager is owned by a South African brewing group and the brand is licensed in Europe by the Dutch company Heineken International. Still, Fosters is stereotypically the "amber nectar" in the UK and "Australian for beer" pretty much everywhere else; except Australia, where they sell very little beer to thirsty Australians.

Personally, I'm more of a tea drinker, and I bet you can guess that I drink PG Tips. "Tips" was added to the brand name in 1955, to emphasize that PG used only the freshest parts of the tea plant, but it wasn't until 1956 that Peter Sellers provided the voice for the first chimpanzee commercial.

Where do you think the idea for that first commercial came from? Did it come from asking a focus group? Did Brooke Bond conduct consumer research?

The idea for a campaign that lasted three decades came when a copyrighter at Davidson Pearce Berry and Spottiswoode, stuck for an idea for a new commercial, went for a walk around Regent's Park, including London Zoo, where he saw chimpanzees dressed in human clothes having a tea party to entertain visitors.

I bet that if you'd asked a group of 1950s tea drinkers to personify tea, they would've suggested a beautiful Indian woman picking those tips before they told you about Ada the chimpanzee tea lady, played in the advert by Choppers, who said, "Cooey Mister Shifter!" No market research, no listening to consumers, no work on personas could stimulate an idea of the magnitude of the PG Tips chimps.

THE BUILDING BLOCKS OF CREATIVITY

The web has meant that anyone with an idea can communicate it. You no longer have to spend big money on advertising in print media or on TV; and what mattered in the 1950s, in the early days of television advertising, matters today on the web.

It's the idea.

An amazing, brilliant, crazy, delightful, entertaining, fantastic, gigantic, hilarious, inspiring — I don't think I can make it all the way to Z — idea.

An idea can inspire, encourage, engage, make people think, and change their perceptions.

An idea that demands attention — not for its own self-gratification, not for exploitation, not for shock value — but attention to what it stands for.

As John Hegarty, the creative force behind Boddingtons' The Cream of Manchester campaign, wrote in *Hegarty on Advertising: Turning Intelligence Into Magic*:

> 66 *Ideas are the building blocks of creativity. Whatever you create, from writing to filmmaking to painting to composing, you start with an idea. Without one you have nothing."*

Dominated By Process

When I imagine a website designed to sell me my favorite tea, I expect it to be well designed, technically proficient and easy to use. I expect to be able to find what I'm looking for quickly and for information to be well presented. When I'm buying a packet of PG Tips, I expect the process to be quick and the experience to be smooth.

The aspects of user experience and usability that focus on ensuring a product or a service works well are important, but that's not enough for me. There's no magic in simply making something easy to use.

Where do chimpanzees fit into the process?

While some of us revel in creating that's chaotic, impulsive and unpredictable, others identify patterns and create systems because they crave predictability. We regularly hear the word "process" in relation to designing for the web, and recently our conversations about responsive design have been dominated by process.

One process that has been spoken about regularly over the past year — largely as a result of designers experimenting with different approaches to responsive web design — has been designing the elements of a web page or application outside the context of layout to create a form of style guide. Not a guide that's used to document design principles after work has been completed, but a working tool that contains not only common elements (typographic styles, button designs, the visual appearance of form elements), but also consists of common patterns that will be used across a website or application's design. These may include layout patterns for components such as form elements, modules, or navigation.

In my studio we often refer to this approach as building a toolkit, and the approach to creating one is something I described in early 2012 in my "Designing Atoms and Elements" chapter in Smashing Book #3, *Redesign the Web*. I wrote:

> 66 *Whereas the **layout's** arrangement of components will undoubtedly be different across screen sizes, the **design** of those same components will almost certainly transcend (damn, I hate that word) layout."*[15]

I gave this combination of typography, color and texture in the absence of layout a name, and I called it "atmosphere."

Atmosphere describes the feelings that are evoked by color, texture and typography. You might already think of atmosphere in different terms. You might call it "feel," "mood" or even "visual identity." In whatever way you describe it, the atmosphere of a design doesn't depend on layout. It's independent of arrangement and visual placement. It will be seen or felt at every screen size and on every device.

Trent Walton summed this up extremely well in his article "Content Choreography"[16]:

> 66 *Web designers will have to look beyond the layout in front of them to envision how its elements will reflow & lockup at various widths while maintaining form & hierarchy."*

INTOXICATED BY PROCESSES

Separating components from layout can help everyone focus on their designs while setting no expectations of how the components will be arranged across responsive viewport sizes — but I worry that we're becoming intoxicated by processes like this, and that we're losing sight of what we're ultimately making.

---

15 http://stuffandnonsense.co.uk/blog/about/an-extract-from-designing-atoms-and-elements
16 http://trentwalton.com/2011/07/14/content-choreography/

Design system thinking also includes using pattern libraries as design tools rather than as post-design documentation. Several examples, including those from the BBC, MailChimp and Starbucks are widely cited.

One design system that's become synonymous with responsive web design is Brad Frost's atomic design. He describes it as "a methodology used to construct web design systems."[17] This methodology even has a tool, Pattern Lab, to "create atomic design systems."

Brad first wrote about atomic design in 2013 when he said:

> ❝ Lately I've been more interested in what our interfaces are comprised of and how we can construct design systems in a more methodical way."

He went on to describe how his atomic design system comprised of atoms, molecules, organisms, templates and pages.

- Atoms are the basic building blocks of HTML, elements including buttons, form inputs and labels.
- Molecules are groups of elements that function together. For example, a label, input and button that combine to make a search form.
- Organisms are groups of molecules joined together to form part of an interface.
- Templates are mostly organisms combined to form page-level objects.
- Pages are essential for testing the effectiveness of the design system.

The result of atomic design should be:

> ❝ [...]a clear methodology for crafting design systems. [...]Because of this, we can create systems that promote consistency and scalability[...] And by assembling rather than deconstructing, we're crafting a system right out of the gate instead of cherry picking patterns after the fact."[18]

---

17 http://patternlab.io/about.html
18 http://bradfrost.com/blog/post/atomic-web-design/

Brad's inspiration for atomic design was chemistry's periodic table of elements. Although I can't think of anything less creatively stimulating, I can imagine someone who's driven to make the creative process predictable finding comfort in the atomic design process.

Not everyone has been convinced by abstracting design the atomic design way, though. In December 2013, Mark Boulton outlined his concerns:

> 66 *Conformity and efficiency have a price. And that price is design. That price is a feeling of humanity. Of something that's been created from scratch. What I described is not a design process. It's* **manufacturing**. *It's a cupcake machine churning out identical cakes with different icing. But they all taste the same."*[19]

I think it's important to remember that creativity can never be — almost by definition *should* never be — as predictable as manufacturing. We can't and we shouldn't attempt to rationalize creativity by turning it into a process.

PEOPLE WITH IDEAS ARE NEVER SERIOUS

Creativity is often chaotic and unpredictable. Go for a walk and you may get an idea. Take a shower and you might get another. Ideas come when you least expect them.

Enjoy yourself, laugh and above all have fun.
David Ogilvy wrote in his book *Ogilvy on Advertising*:

> 66 *Make it fun to work at your agency. When people aren't having any fun they seldom produce good advertising."*

"A serious-minded person has few ideas", wrote the French author Paul Valéry. "People with ideas are never serious."[20]

---

19 http://markboulton.co.uk/journal/design-abstraction-escalation
20 "Un homme sérieux a peu d'idées; un homme à idées n'est jamais sérieux."
    Paul Valéry, *Mauvaises pensées et autres* (1941)

Get away from your computer, notebook or sketchbook and get inspiration from the world around you. Look at the world you know from a different perspective every day. Take a different route to work, take a bus instead of driving your car, or maybe don't show up at all and spend the day at the cinema or at the zoo watching chimpanzees.

Ideas come when we least expect them and that makes what we do so exciting. I can imagine some of you are wondering how, if creativity is so chaotic, can it work within a disciplined business framework?

We see other people answering this question by formalizing their process into a workflow. You will probably have seen this if you've bought or worked in creative services. Former head of design at Google and Yahoo, Irene Au outlined: user research; followed by interaction and product design; visual design; then prototyping and developing. Skills required for this process include: formative and summative research; qualitative and quantitative data collection and analysis; psychology, anthropology and human–computer interaction. Deliverables might comprise wireframes, prototypes, functional specifications and flowcharts.[21]

Where is the space in her workflow for creating work that is anything more than the "adornment" she describes when she wrote so dismissively:

> ❝ *They [visual designers] understand that visual adornment is meant to support the experience, and not **be** the experience."*

Her assessment of creativity shocks me. In her article, she wrote about the question of whether to hire a visual designer:

> ❝❝*[...]hire a visual designer on a freelance basis who can create the look and feel of the site, deliver a style guide, and work with your front end engineering team to build the visual assets (e.g. grid, typography, color palette, icons, button styles, etc) into a front end library that then makes it easy for developers to create UI that is consistent."*

---

21 https://medium.com/@ireneau/understanding-ux-skills-21ad9c22f0bf

Is it any wonder why Au and others have such a low opinion of how designers work when we are busy promoting processes like atomic design?

A process is a tried and tested method we've used to do something we've done before. But what's the point of following a formula? A formula will lead to a predictable and ordinary result — and who wants to make something ordinary? I hope you don't.

How much chaos and unpredictability you accept will depend on you and the people you work with. It's a question I often struggle to answer as someone who runs a creative business. I know that the answer lies somewhere on a curve between chaos and process. I also know how vital it is to find the right balance, so that your creativity isn't limited in any way by the parts of a process that you adopt.

That work begins before we've even started to create. It starts by working with others to ensure that we have a platform for creativity. It starts with a creative brief.

A PLATFORM FOR CREATIVITY

My company works mostly in client services. We work with small and medium-sized businesses and sometimes with larger organizations. I know that not everyone likes dealing with clients, but we like the variety of people we work with and the challenges that they bring us.

Our work's mostly rewarding, frequently challenging and it's sometimes frustrating. We've found that one of the best ways to eliminate that occasional frustration is to start a project and a client relationship in ways which emphasize creativity.

We try to ensure that everyone understands that the most effective solution to a problem will probably be something that no one has yet thought of; that prior work, often in the form of specifications, personas, user stories or wireframes, should inform and not dictate that solution; that approaching a project in this way will encourage a process that's respectful to everyone, be creatively fruitful and, above all, successful.

HOW MUCH FOR A WEBSITE?

I think every designer has their own "how much for a website" email story. We joke about these inquiries but they don't just demonstrate a potential client's misunderstanding of the commissioning process. They present us with an opportunity to do what we should do best, to communicate well and build trust while we develop relationships.

If you're part of a design team, think back to an inquiry you received recently. How specific was what you were sent? Was it embarrassingly vague, fastidiously complex, or somewhere on a spectrum in between?

Some inquiries are little more than an attempt to start a conversation: a "Hey, we'd like to talk to you about a project." Some offer more insight, and others provide requirements that are so detailed that they verge on becoming specifications, complete with personas, user stories or wireframes.

While professionals have experience in starting new projects, a prospective client may have little or no experience of commissioning design work. It's common among inexperienced people to want us to direct the process. This vagueness allows us to set the direction and tone for a conversation and use that opportunity to hear a client explain their business and learn how our work can help them. It's during these early conversations that we can begin to build relationships.

When we handle early interactions well, we earn the opportunity to help shape a client's brief which will ultimately lead to a more creatively flexible project.

Not every client offers an invitation to talk. Instead, some offer insight and outline specific goals that coincidentally often follow the order of questions they've found on agencies' request for proposal forms. Agencies routinely ask prospective clients to complete a request for proposal form, so clients have learned to format their information in a similar way.

It's important to remember that a request for a proposal isn't the same as a creative brief, even though the two are regularly conflated.

Mike Monteiro is the founder of Mule Design and the author of *Design Is a Job*[22]. In his book he shared his agency's screener questions. They start with

---

22 http://abookapart.com/products/design-is-a-job

questions like, "What's the primary business and structure of your organization?" before moving on to ask about motives and goals, and how the client rates the importance of strategy, design, engineering, writing and, finally, cost. This helps Mule Design to quickly understand a client's priorities. Do they value cost over design? How will they measure success?

Earlier, I mentioned the importance of confidence and the Mule Design team communicate theirs through their screener questions. Their final question is one that most of us think, but too few ask:

"How many people are you talking to and when do you expect to be making a decision?"

Most importantly of all, Mule Design doesn't ask questions that demand a client suggests a solution, because it's those solutions we are ultimately paid to create.

IT DOESN'T FIT THE BRIEF

It's common for clients to provide detailed requirement documents that verge on functional specifications. These sometimes include site maps, wireframes and detailed descriptions of a site's content structure and functionality. This documentation may be useful in the future, but we need to ask why they are sending it to us now. Do they think that we'll be able to estimate a price more easily? Watch out for this, as designers often make the mistake of discussing price before a client has agreed in principle to hire them.

Have you ever worked under a brief that was designed to be a checklist, intended to judge creative work, rather than as a platform for it? A brief shouldn't be prescriptive; nor should it contain solutions, as no designer likes to see their job attempted before they've started.

A prescriptive brief is often a client's attempt to add predictability to a creative process that should embrace the unexpected. In the worst cases it provides a framework under which work that doesn't conform to predetermined expectations can be rejected, simply by saying, "It doesn't fit the brief."

SOLVING PROBLEMS, NOT DEFINING THEM

People who crave predictability often see creative work as akin to anarchy, and a seemingly risky process with an undetermined outcome can be a daunting prospect. The way some people attempt to compensate is by solving problems instead of defining them.

Receiving a brief that includes answers instead of questions should serve as a warning as it usually indicates that a person is nervous about hiring, or is unfamiliar with working with designers and so is trying to stay in control by circumventing the design process.

It can tell us that the client already has an idea of the work they want to see. More worrying is that work is probably something they've seen somewhere else. Nowhere is this better demonstrated than in a brief that contains a "Sites we like" section. These are the creative equivalent of the slick haircut photographs you'll find on barbershop walls.

Never acknowledge even the existence of that prior work. If a client mentions it, politely remind them that they're hiring you to design a solution to their problem, not copy another designer's solution to someone else's. The truth is that no one can predict where a solution will come from. Nor can we predict what it form it will take. What we can know is that it will probably not conform to predetermined assumptions and we must help clients understand that.

It's natural for clients to want to avoid risk. After all, who wakes up thinking, "I want to have a risky day?" Even gamblers part with their money with the expectation that their bet is sound. So how can we explain the importance of an unrestricted creative process without frightening clients with talk of risk? Replace the word "risky" with something else. I replace it with "inspiring."

STRIKE UP A CONVERSATION

If you receive a prescriptive brief you should use it to foster discussions that develop trust and build relationships.

It's in some people's nature to want to define what a designer makes even before we start work. Why would someone want to control the design process this way? It's possible that they're simply not used to hiring designers, that they're unfamiliar with both the commissioning and the creative processes. So they try to shape them both into something that feels familiar. We need to resist this as much as we can, by explaining to a client that inspiring solutions only come from unpredictable sources.

When a brief dictates design specifics, use it as an opportunity to speak to the person who wrote it. And I do mean speak — don't email, just pick up the phone. Introduce yourself and ask questions about why a client is presenting solutions so early.

This approach will help both of you, and it will also help differentiate you from the 29 other agencies the client wrote to. As Mike Monteiro wrote in *Design Is a Job*:

> 66 *Make friends with the person who wrote it. Strike up a conversation with them and get as much detail as you can."*

We should never take a brief at face value and ought to question it, challenge it, interrogate every part of it. If that sounds familiar, it should, as it takes us back to Cennydd Bowles' "Letter to a Junior Designer" when he wrote:

> 66 *Ideas aren't to be trusted. They need to be wrung dry, ripped apart."*

Simply replace the word "ideas" with "creative briefs" or "requests for proposals."

A brief should help define a strategy to be followed not just in the next piece of work, but in the months and years following. The strategy is as much for the client to follow as their design partners.

When we receive a brief, it's our responsibility to question not only what has been written, but why. It doesn't mean being awkward, simply that we're already thinking about a problem. As Mike Monteiro wrote in his article "These 8 Tricks to Selecting a Design Partner Will Amaze You":

> ❝ *Your designer's goal should be your success, not your happiness. So don't work with anyone who just automatically bends to all of your whims and wishes.*"[23]

Asking why not only helps clients and designers to understand what's at stake, it also sparks conversations that will inevitably lead to opportunities. It's the most important question we can ask when presented with a brief.

A FINE LINE BETWEEN CONTROL AND CHAOS

A client may be the best in their chosen field. They might be an expert in making their product or delivering their service, but that doesn't necessarily make them the best qualified to write a brief. That's where designers should step in — not to write the brief for them, but to work on it as a joint venture.

Writing a brief often walks a fine line between control and chaos, and it's the designer's role to help achieve that balance. If designers want to avoid being presented with a brief that lacks strategy and contains predefined solutions, we shouldn't allow a client to write it in isolation. Instead, we should make it clear that before we can help them implement a strategy, we must first help them define it.

It's essential that a brief should have a clear, singular voice that states a single, simple purpose. Ideally, it should be written by just one person, someone who has the power to accept what may become an unpredictable design process that in turn might lead to unconventional work, but that's not always possible.

What can designers do when there's not a single person who can take responsibility? We should work with a client to help them develop that singular voice, a voice with the clarity to communicate their goals in the most concise way.

Before we ask a client to think about what we're going to make, we should encourage them to think about their business. After all, they know it better than we do. We should start by listening and understanding their business goals. We need to aim to see things from a client's perspective as we're ultimately working for them and no one else. This is not the time to talk about a user's goals, but the

---

23 https://medium.com/@monteiro/these-8-tricks-to-selecting-a-design-partner-will-amaze-you-84f40d290296

goals of the business, be they to communicate better or to sell more. This focus on a business's needs rather than a customer's could be seen as conflicting with the goals of user experience.

To be most effective, we shouldn't conduct these conversations via a written brief. The best way for designers to start building a relationship with clients is to sit and talk with them face-to-face. As well as helping to earn their trust, these conversations also establish us as organized and serious about what we do.

When we understand what a client is aiming to achieve, we can help them reduce the brief to a set of clear goals understood by everyone who will contribute during the project and long after it.

A brief should outline a client's goals, which might include:

- We need a website for our company/organization or campaign.
- I want to sell more of my product than my competitors.
- We need a website that performs well on every size and type of screen.

Every brief should express business goals like these. It should describe challenges, explain opportunities and even talk about dreams. A brief's most important role is to inspire people to do inspiring creative work. To achieve this the brief must be a friend to creative thinking, not its enemy. It should act as a platform for creative thinking, not a set of chains to drag it down. Above all it should inspire and never limit creativity. It must respect the creative process while at the same time communicate the problems a client is trying to solve.

Buying Creativity

If we accept that a brief should come after an agency has been hired, how can a client without a brief choose an agency to work with?

If your last received inquiry, request for proposal, or brief was anything like the one sent to me, it included a question about the likely cost of a project. But the purpose shouldn't be to ask about price but to invite potential design partners to discuss a project.

Perhaps there's a misconception about what commissioning design means. It's not like buying a product; it's buying creativity, expertise and knowledge. More than that, it's entering into a relationship.

How can a client decide on a designer to work with? In the 1960s, David Ogilvy offered advice on exactly that in his book *Ogilvy On Advertising*. In it, he wrote:

"*Sir or Madam*"

(He was formal like that.)

> 66 *If you have decided to hire a new agency, permit me to suggest a simple way to go about it. Don't delegate the selection to a committee of pettifoggers. They usually get it wrong. Do it yourself.*"

(If you're interested, a pettifogger is an inferior legal practitioner who deals with petty cases or employs dubious practices. I'm sure I've met at least one.)

> 66 *Start by leafing through some magazines. Tear out the advertisements you envy, and find out which agencies did them. Watch television for three evenings, make a list of commercials you envy, and find out which agencies did them.*"

(This was the Sixties, after all, but today clients can apply that general principle to websites.)

> 66 *You now have a list of agencies. Find out which are working for your competitors and thus are unavailable to you. By this time you have a short list.*"

(And this is where his advice hits home.)

> 66 *Meet the head of each agency and his [or her, of course. This was the Sixties, remember] Creative Director. Make sure the chemistry between you is good. Happy marriages fructify, unhappy ones don't. Ask to see each agency's six best print ads and six best television commercials. Pick the agency whose campaigns interest you most.*"

That advice may be fifty years old, but it's still relevant because it respects the process and creative people by basing hiring decisions on personalities and past performance, not on how well someone is judged to have passed any challenges set by a request for proposal.

Common Ground In Creative Teams

David Ogilvy was a strong advocate of long copy — sometimes very long — and he wrote ads that contained more words than you'll find in many of today's pocket-guide-style books about web design. Ogilvy wrote in his own *Ogilvy On Advertising* book:

> 66 *All my experience says that for many great products, long copy sells more than short."*

He cited one successful advertisement for Merrill Lynch in the New York Times that ran to 6,450 words. His Ogilvy and Mather agency made an ad for US Trust that contained 4,500 words. Another for World Wildlife Fund: 3,232 words. Ogilvy wrote:

> 66 *Advertisements with long copy convey the impression that you have something important to say, whether people read the copy or not."*

This runs counter to what many people would expect, particularly on websites, but Ogilvy was clearly from a school of advertising that believed that "the more facts you tell, the more you sell."[24] We might flinch at the thought of reading thousands of words in an advertisement today.

IT'S UGLY BUT IT GETS YOU THERE

Things changed in the late 1950s with Doyle Dane Bernbach's widely cited "Think Small" and "Lemon" ads for Volkswagen of America, art-directed by Helmut Krone.

---

24 http://www.ogilvy.com/About/Our-History/David-Ogilvy-Books.aspx

Here's the body copy from "Think Small" written by Julian Koenig. Count how many selling points there are:

"Think small.

Our little car isn't so much of a novelty any more.

A couple of dozen college kids don't try to squeeze inside it.

The guy at the gas station doesn't ask where the gas goes.

Nobody even stares at our shape.

In fact, some people who drive our little flivver don't think 32 miles to the gallon is going great guns.

Or using five pints of oil instead of five quarts.

Or never needing anti-freeze.

Or racking up 40,000 miles on a set of tires.

That's because once you get used to some of our economies, you don't even think about them any more.

Except when you squeeze into a small parking spot. Or renew your small insurance. Or pay a small repair bill. Or trade in your old VW for a new one. Think it over."

Doyle Dane Bernbach's iconic work for Volkswagen of America is widely thought to have changed the advertising industry.

139 words, eight selling points, not including probably the most important fact that the VW is free of college kids. Having had a kid at college, I can tell you how important that is.

From "Think Small" and "Lemon" onwards, the Volkswagen of America ads were consistent in their format: a large space for a photograph of the car, and a smaller one for everything else: tagline, body copy and logo. The car didn't always fill the space but was mostly shot against a plain background.

In 1969 they ran "It's ugly but it gets you there." That tagline, a photo of the Apollo 11 lunar module and a VW logo. I love 1962's "And if you run out of gas, it's easy to push." The cleverness of that tagline and the body copy that ran under it:

> 66 *It's a little surprising that VW owners don't run out of gas more often. A figure like 32 miles to the gallon can make you a little hazy about when you last filled up."*

And more classic taglines:

"It makes your house look bigger."
"The only water a Volkswagen needs is the water you wash it with."
"After we paint the car we paint the paint."

WE'RE №2, SO WE TRY HARDER

Bill Bernbach is not only credited with changing the style of advertising with DDB's work for Volkswagen of America; he's also credited with changing the way that copywriters and art directors worked on ads.

Before Bernbach, copywriters and art directors worked separately. Copywriters wrote the copy for an ad and sent it to an art director, who worked in another department, to add visuals. If this were Mad Men, that would mean Peggy Olson and Stan Rizzo work not just in separate offices but on different floors.

Bernbach had a theory: if art directors and copywriters worked together in a creative team, they would produce better advertising. He was proved right: out of these creative pairings, his agency produced some of the most iconic work of that period including not just Volkswagen of America, but also the classic "We're Nº2, So We Try Harder" campaign for Avis rental cars.

Throughout the decades that followed Bernbach, creative teams of art directors and copywriters remained at the center of advertising. But a copywriter's role changed and while imaginative headlines remained important, long copy became unfashionable and the emphasis in advertising shifted more towards the visual and away from long passages of written copy. Copywriting focused on reduction and writing a tagline meant using as few words as possible.

MAKE COPYWRITING A PRIORITY

Today I think that copywriting matters more than it has at any time since Ogilvy's era. On the web we need copy that's effective from 140 characters in a tweet, through a Facebook message, to an email newsletter and up to long-form website content.

Designers need to either write copy themselves or work very closely with a copywriter throughout all stages of a project. Clients should also make copywriting a priority and make provision for it, not only within their budgets but from the beginning of any project. Copy should never be an afterthought, something to add to predesigned page templates, because thinking about words is a catalyst for new ideas and can help develop better strategies.

Designers must take greater responsibility for copy, too. For years we've complained about waiting for clients to provide us with content. Then we complained some more about the quality of what we eventually received. Why are we surprised by a lack of quality and by a client's lack of writing skills? After all, a client may know their business inside-out or their product better than anyone, but that doesn't necessarily give them the skills to write. Why do we expect someone who works in finance, manufacturing, or services to be good at writing advertising copy, for the web or anywhere else?

Communicating through written copy is as creative a task as creating color palettes, designing with type and working with layout. At my agency, we think of copy as being at the center of everything we design. We spend an increasing amount of time editing existing and writing original copy for our clients.

THINKING STRATEGICALLY

Working with people to write copy helps us develop deeper relationships with our clients than when we work on design alone. We get to know our clients better and their businesses in much more detail. That's why we know more today about Drupal development, health and safety inspections, and pension planning than we did a year ago.

Copywriting is now as integral to our business as creative design and accomplished technical development. Of course, copywriting means more than being creative with words. When we write, we're thinking strategically. We're balancing a user's goals with those of our client, so in many ways a copywriter is as much a strategist as anyone who works in user experience.

We consider how headlines define a content's hierarchy and create structure within body copy, just as information architecture would. We think about how those same headings can be used to convey the meaning of each section of content, making a page easier to scan and understand without the user needing to read every word. For us, this is as much part of a user experience design process as devising personas and making wireframes.

All this makes me wonder whether "copywriter" is now an outdated term. But what can we replace it with to better explain the work that goes along with writing words? "Creative writer"? Probably not, because what writing isn't creative? What about "writer"? That's simple and it gets straight to the point.

CREATIVE DIRECTION, ART DIRECTION AND DESIGN

An art director's role has also changed as new media and technologies have emerged. Just as it did when the advertising industry moved from print-based work to embrace television, we've seen a similar change demanded by the web and everything that's associated with it.

One of the biggest issues facing art direction on the web is that so few people understand what it is and how it differs from design. Ask a web designer what they think of when they hear the words "art direction" and many will mention the trend for individually designed articles and blog entries made popular by Jason Santa Maria, Trent Walton and Gregory Wood.

There are overlaps between creative direction, art direction and design, so it shouldn't come as much of a surprise when people use those terms interchangeably.

Of course designers can, and sometimes do, art-direct and art directors can design, but the role of designer is different from the role of art director. Art directors provide a concept and designers provide ideas and expertise to implement that concept.

Art director and designer at Philadelphia-based design studio SuperFriendly, Dan Mall does a great job of explaining the difference between art direction and design. He wrote:

> 66 *Art Direction [is] the visceral resonance of how a piece of work feels. In other words, what you feel in your gut when you look at a website, app, or any piece of design work."*[25]

Whereas he explained good design being "measured in precision."

> 66 *Design is the **technical execution** of that connection. Do these colors match? Is the line-length comfortable for long periods of reading? Is this photo in focus? Does the typographic hierarchy work? Is this composition balanced?"*[26]

FIXATED WITH PROBLEM-SOLVING

I studied fine art and not graphic design in any form. I'm largely self-taught, so I've always been slightly uncomfortable describing myself as a designer. I almost feel that it's disrespectful to people who can legitimately call themselves "designers."

These days, we employ designers who are far more technically accomplished than I am, so my role has developed into one where I'm more regularly working on the atmosphere in a project and not on its look.

---

25 http://danielmall.com/articles/on-creative-direction/
26 http://alistapart.com/article/art-direction-and-design

I'm more often concerned with how our work conveys our clients' messages than I am with the implementation details of that work.

I know that many people treat "look" and "feel" as synonyms and use them interchangeably. Yet the two are distinct attributes. We need the skills of a designer when we create a look, but the feel requires the skills of an art director who can ensure that those messages aren't lost through design.

Phil Coffman is an art director at digital strategy agency *Springbox*. He said:

> ❝ *Design is about problem-solving, whether you are a designer or an art director. The two roles differ in that the designer is more concerned with execution, while the art director is concerned with the strategy behind that execution."*[27]

On the web we've become so fixated with problem-solving and execution that our work has lost the creative soul I spoke of at the start of this chapter. Soul that embodies individuality, personality, originality and opinion. Soul that connects people with ideas. Soul that makes an idea memorable. Soul that makes what we do matter.

As Dan Mall explained:

> ❝❝ *Art direction brings clarity and definition to our work; it helps our work convey a specific message to a particular group of people. Art direction combines art and design to evoke a cultural and emotional reaction. [...] Without art direction, we're left with dry, sterile experiences that are easily forgotten."*

Even though we seem obsessed by designing experiences, much of the work I see on the web today is exactly as Dan describes, dry and sterile. I partly blame lack of art direction for its lack of soul.

---

27 http://alistapart.com/article/art-direction-and-design

DECORATING INSTEAD OF COMMUNICATING

Irene Au's list of UX skills includes only:

- User research
- Interaction and product design
- Visual design
- Prototyper
- Web developer
- Front end developer

Where is anything approaching the role of art director in her list of UX talent?

Why is art direction on the web so rare? Jeffrey Zeldman himself comes from a New York advertising background, and in 2003 Zeldman wrote:

> 66 *On the web, art direction is rare, partly because much of the work is about guiding users rather than telegraphing concepts, but also because few design schools teach art direction."[28]*

He went on:

> 66 *Talented stylists continually enrich the world's visual vocabulary. The bad news is, we are decorating instead of communicating."*

Stylists. Decorating. Just like the "visual adornment" Irene Au described 11 years later. I think art director and designer Stephen Hay summed up the importance of art direction for us when he wrote:

> 66 *Good design is pretty, but good design based on a solid concept will help make your sites much more effective and memorable, especially when compared to the competition."[29]*

---

28 http://www.zeldman.com/daily/0403b.shtml#ma0103
29 http://alistapart.com/article/artdirweb

A Varied Pool Of Talent

Many of the agencies I deal with today still favor the types of creative teams that were first established in the late 1950s. Advertising itself has changed since those two-person copywriter and art director teams were first formed. The web is a significantly more complex medium to work in than print, so we need a variety of people with an even wider variety of skills on our teams today.

When we're building a team we may need to include an art director, writer, developer, UX specialist, and any number of diverse skills to deliver great work. There may be less of a requirement for a traditional copywriter/art director pairing today, but there is a requirement to bring people with different skills together so they can collaborate in the ways art directors and copywriters did in the past.

Of course, no single working structure will suit every organization or even every project. What matters is that project leaders can draw from a varied pool of talent for each account or individual project.

It used to be the case that agencies could make great ads — ads we've remembered for decades — with just a copywriter and an art director. If we want work that will be as memorable today we need them, too, but we also need information and UX specialists, technologists and others working together. This is a significant change for many agencies who still structure their businesses along departmental lines.

Dave Bedwood is a creative partner at London-based Lean Mean Fighting Machine and he wrote:

> 66 *There can be no doubt that the creative team 'mix' has to evolve. [...] This means we need creatives of all kinds of skill sets working together. [...] Unfortunately[...] the digital world has not[...] understood the difference between them, a designer, a programmer or creative technologist."*[30]

30 http://creativesocialblog.com/advertising/the-death-of-art-directorcopywriter-teams

In a creative organization we need people to be familiar with one another's work so they feel comfortable enough to share ideas and, sometimes, to take risks. Proximity matters, as does uniting teams of diverse skills together so they can sit near one another in one creative space and not be isolated in separate departments. That space is vital to the creative process, as is a working process that genuinely supports and promotes creative ideas.

Giving Our Work The Creative Soul It Deserves

Much of what's changed since I began working on the web has been for the better. In many ways we've made a better web and I'm proud of what we've achieved. In other ways I'm dissatisfied because for everything we've gained, we're losing something else and that something is soul.

Still, I'm hopeful that all is not lost and that we can make work that's memorable if we focus as much on creativity as we do on implementation; if we amplify conversations about ideas as much as we do those on process; if we create processes that promote creative ideas from the very beginning; if we remember the importance of art direction; if we make spaces for people with diverse skills to work together, in creative teams.

If we remember all these things, we'll give back to our work what it, we and the work itself deserve: its creative soul. Improvement is a matter of steady, ongoing iteration.

ABOUT THE AUTHOR

Andrew is an art director and web designer at the UK website design studio *Stuff and Nonsense*. There he designs websites and applications for clients from around the world. Based in north Wales, Andrew's also the author of two web design books, *Transcending CSS* and *Hardboiled Web Design* and is well known for his presentations and over ten years of contributions to the web design industry.